T0288616

Making
A Bridge Too Far

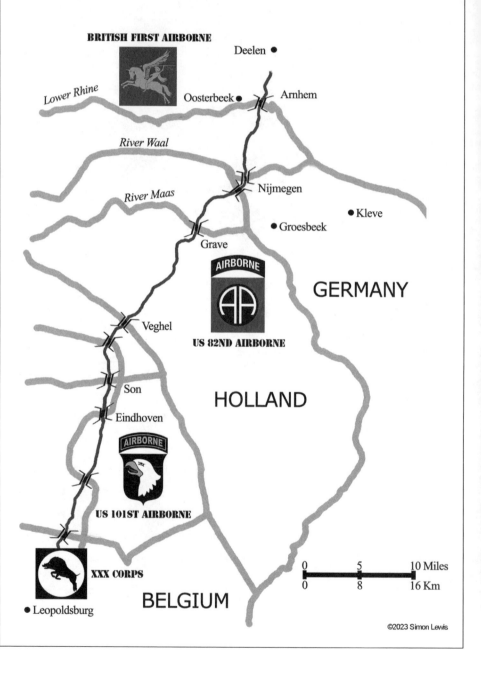

OPERATION MARKET GARDEN
September 1944

BRITISH FIRST AIRBORNE

Deelen

Lower Rhine

Oosterbeek • Arnhem

River Waal

Nijmegen

River Maas

• Kleve

• Groesbeek

Grave

AIRBORNE

GERMANY

Veghel

US 82ND AIRBORNE

HOLLAND

Son

Eindhoven

AIRBORNE

US 101ST AIRBORNE

XXX CORPS

BELGIUM

• Leopoldsburg

| 0 | 5 | 10 Miles |
| 0 | 8 | 16 Km |

©2023 Simon Lewis

Making
A Bridge Too Far

Simon Lewis

GoodKnight Books
Pittsburgh, Pennsylvania

GoodKnight Books

© 2024 by Simon Lewis

Published by GoodKnight Books, an imprint of Paladin Communications, Pittsburgh, Pennsylvania.

ISBN 978-1-7352738-9-1

Library of Congress Control Number: 2023950875

Printed in the United States of America.

To Claire and Sam

Contents

Preface

Just south of the noise and roar of London lies a charming seven-teenth-century mansion house in the Palladian style. Surrounded by a rolling estate with lush gardens and a world-famous championship golf course, it is called Moor Park.

During the 1970s I would stay with my grandparents for a week during the summer holidays. My grandfather was a keen golfer and a member of the prestigious club. On each Sunday of my visit, he along with my grandmother and me, all dressed in our best, would troop up to the mansion clubhouse for a pre-lunchtime drink. While the grown-ups talked, I would wander off around the plush building with its impressive murals of cherubs and angels up high on the ceiling. Outside, at the foot of one of the imposing entrance columns, sat a small plaque bearing an insignia of a blue-winged Pegasus ridden by the Greek warrior Bellerophon wielding a spear, set against a maroon background. Next to it were the words commemorating the "occupa-tion of this clubhouse by the headquarters, the First British Airborne Corps from February 1944 to October 1945." Not mentioned was that it had been the birthplace of the dramatic events over three weeks in September 1944.

Despite a hazy four-decade-old memory, I'm sure I first noted the plaque during the summer of 1977. In late June that year I was at boarding school, and during term-times we were allowed two Exeats, or weekend passes to non-Latin scholars. During one, my father picked me up and drove us to the nearest cinema some 20 miles away. I was given a treat—*A Bridge Too Far*. It made a huge impression on my 11-year-old mind. On the following morning I woke up early and hastily constructed my own Arnhem bridge out of some wooden toy roadblocks. To defend it amid a motley assemblage of buildings was a group of green plastic HO-OO Airfix British Commandos. To dislodge them, accompanied by my whistling sound effects, I deployed an assortment of model Airfix German tanks. Almost half a century later, the smell of the cordite from that impromptu game still lingers in my memory.

While many of my contemporaries were excited about the Bay City Rollers, Evel Knievel, and the skateboard craze, my passion was history—and its spectacular reconstruction on film. I recall the excitement of reading about *A Bridge Too Far* in a free preview magazine. Without my knowing it, research for this book had already begun. I still remember one bit of trivia: in the filming of the first scene with American troops (probably with James Caan as Sergeant Dohun), the U.S. army expert, Colonel Frank Gregg, pointed out that officers and NCOs had simple white markings on the backs of their helmets. The article explained how a crew member suggested using strips of white gaffer tape used by the camera team, to save the day.

My love of history and cinema has continued, albeit on often parallel lines. Making a career in TV production as an editor, director, and video journalist, I also achieved one ambition and directed a feature film, *Jackals*, in 2011. While my interests in the movies are truly eclectic (inspiration for future books), the historical epics of the '50s and '60s have a special place in my heart. Indeed, six months before seeing *Bridge*, I saw the TV premiere of *Waterloo* (1970). This extraordinary spectacular caught my imagination and never left. It formed the subject of my first book in 2021.[1] The central point I argued in that book—and will in this—is that a filmmaker or dramatist must obey the tenets of drama before the facts of history.

This is at odds with historians of all stripes who often bemoan, "Why can't they just stick to the facts?" For the same reasons book adaptations are routinely altered, the tight structure of most screenplays, with a max of three hours, demands simplicity and erudition. It is a truism to say that not a single dramatist from Homer through Shakespeare and beyond ever began penning a historical tale and said: "How can I tell this as accurately as possible?" Instead, all have said and will continue to say: "How can I fashion these facts as dramatically as possible?" Once one accepts this, it's time to enjoy a book, play, or movie and judge it as drama—not history. That said, most talented writers try to honour the spirit of the history as far as narrative demands allow. One such was William Goldman with his script for *Bridge*. His work is a textbook example of how to distil a vast historical canvas with a multitude of incidents and characters into an easily understandable but also deeply moving piece. As we will see, his screenplay was often in the front line of criticism.

Bridge has its detractors. First, critics shoot down the inaccuracies, but as this book will show, many changes were deliberate by telescoping and amalgamating elements of Cornelius Ryan's source book. Some are less excusable, but one must remember that movies like this cost such eye-watering sums of money that compromises are inevitable. This brings up the other contentious issue—the use of stars. I hope to show how such charismatic talent, immediately identifiable, works to the film's benefit.

And what of the film's virtues? Primarily, it is the extraordinary realism. Except for a handful of optical effects, everything on the screen was done not just for real but also full-size. Much of the book will look at how these visual marvels were created.

The predominantly British crew was a team of exceptionally skilled individuals at the top of their game. Most are legendary within the industry but little known to the general public. While the stars receive their due respect, I make no apologies for giving equal weight to the unsung heroes who collectively have contributed to a host of other much-loved and highly regarded films. (This narrative will make occasional pauses to profile certain individuals; the choice is arbitrary and personal with omission implying no disrespect.)

Behind the superstar talent and the visual splendour was director Richard Attenborough's brilliant experiment. Running like a seam of silver, 50 young actors became believable soldiers. Like instruments in an orchestra, they were not intended to be identified individually but instead to create a rich texture of believability. Their collective contribution forms the heart of the movie. You will meet some of them and see why this experience in the hot summer of 1976 has continued to resonate in their lives.

This is a story of cooperation. What you will not find in these pages is tittle-tattle, gossip, and clashes of ego. Inevitably, filming long hours in arduous situations frayed tempers and personalities, but almost none of these spats have survived the passage of time. What remains is a tale of extraordinary hard work and dedication by a group of supreme professionals, all coalescing under the inspired leadership of Sir Richard Attenborough.

When this film was conceived and filmed in 1976, it seemed unthinkable that full-scale warfare would ever scourge Europe again. The film bears Attenborough's unmistakable liberal and compassionate values, which imbue every frame with a heartfelt anti-war message.

For me, these sentiments morphed into a different hue the very day I signed the contract for this book: 24 February 2022. Russia's illegal and brutal invasion of Ukraine marked a dark historical turning point. I, like millions of others, was shocked and revolted by this action. At first, I felt reluctant to write anything about war. But if people can be mobilised to fight, a group amassing together in pursuance of art (albeit with some commerce) surely is a positive act of human endeavour. And that's what this book desires to celebrate.

And the film's superlatives?

Often, writers of movie books cannot resist inflating their beloved subject as the greatest, the most iconic, or whatever, but these subjective terms simply make eye-catching cover blurbs. To define the greatest war film is perhaps much harder than for any other genre: the subject is too vast and complex. It's worth remembering that movies have grown up alongside bloody, state-sponsored, industrial slaughter. Cinema has tried to adapt and reflect a reality that is often beyond human understanding. Only by the end of the twentieth century was the medium able to show the visceral nature of combat. Does that make the previous, more refined works of less value?

Let's take a sniper's eye view at the genre up till 1977.

The First World War yielded few cinematic gems as the medium was still finding its feet. Arguably, Lewis Milestone's *All Quiet on the Western Front* (1930) was the original war masterpiece of the sound era. It contained some harrowing combat footage before the censor's scissors adjudicated with good taste. Its strong anti-war theme was in tune with the times, although warmongering Nazi Germany disagreed—and banned it. Ten years later, films were pro-war as the major powers recognised the enormous emotional reach of cinema. Thus, outpoured hundreds of exhortations to fight. *Sahara* (1943) and *The Way Ahead* (1944) are excellent examples, both stressing the need for a collective effort and the will to win.

In British cinema, post-war grieving was soon replaced by celebratory tales of pluck and derring-do, perhaps the most notable being 1955's *The Dam Busters*. This decade-long cottage industry helped to form a potent myth that pervades British society to this day. Hollywood, at the same time, dealt instead with the more recent Korean War and a perceived threat from communism. This all changed in the 1960s when the war film became a spectacle in living colour and CinemaScope.

There are two main strands to the portrayal of war on film. One is the fictional action adventure, kicked off with the Oscar-winning *Bridge on the River Kwai* (1957) and followed by *The Guns of Navarone* (1961), described, to quote Quentin Tarantino, as the original "guys on a mission movie." This would prove to be an immensely popular strain, even borrowing from the then-current James Bond phenomenon with *Operation Crossbow* (1966) and *Where Eagles Dare* (1968).

The other strand, and more pertinent to this book, is the rarest: the historical war epic. Leslie Norman's *Dunkirk* (1958) was one of British cinema's few homegrown epics, an impressive reconstruction of a defeat that spawned a national myth of survival, Operation Dynamo. Despite a limited budget, the Ealing production did an admirable job of conveying the scope and scale of the "miracle," as over 350,000 men were lifted from the bombed beaches by an armada of ships. With the turn of the decade, Hollywood felt it was time to recreate the glories of the recent past.

Darryl F. Zanuck's recreation of D-Day for Cornelius Ryan's *The Longest Day* (1962) remains an outstanding achievement. The production was decked with nearly 50 stars, and several directors filmed their respective nations' contributions. British Ken Annakin's four-minute single-take helicopter shot of the storming of a German-held casino is still jaw-dropping. American Andrew Marton expertly handled the Omaha Beach sequence, upon which rested the fate of the operation, while Bernhard Wicki imbues the German defenders with a rarely seen humanity. The ultimately uplifting story of an Allied victory proved an enormous success and swelled the studio coffers.

Is Paris Burning? (1966) was a less-successful French (but American-backed) account of the recapture of the city in August 1944. Ken Annakin was a last-minute replacement to direct *Battle of the Bulge* (1965), a hugely spectacular if inaccurate epic of a pivotal encounter. Hampered by copyright issues corralled by a rival company, the script had to fictionalise all the characters, and it heavily telescoped events, which outraged ex-president and wartime commander Dwight D. Eisenhower. Despite its limitations, *Battle of the Bulge* remains a splendid piece of entertainment for the giant 70-mm Cinerama screen, helped by liberal use of the Spanish army.

These films that attempted to show the scale of their subjects were complex and expensive. Certainly, the biggest and worst was the

Russian seven-hour *Liberation* (1970), which told a highly partisan account of the Eastern Front. Despite outstanding action using a division of the Soviet army, the heavy propaganda and leaden direction doomed it as entertainment. Back in the West, the decade bowed out with two worthy attempts to encompass huge historical events: *Battle of Britain* (1969) and *Tora! Tora! Tora!* (1970).

The bloody Vietnam War in Southeast Asia blunted the thirst for these movies. The genre seemed to be consigned to history. The early 1970s would see a paucity of war films, and the few made, *Operation Daybreak* (1975), *The Eagle Has Landed* (1976) and *Midway* (1976), were not crowd-pleasers. To buck this trend, a maverick producer came out of retirement to stake much of his personal fortune on the biggest film of his career. Hell or high water, Joseph E. Levine had a promise to keep and hoped to lure back the public with a war epic to top them all.

So far, we have considered only combat stories. Many films of note relate the civilian experience from the Blitz to the Holocaust. *Schindler's List* (1993), *Two Women* (1961), and Elem Klimov's harrowing *Come and See* (1984) surely show the true horror of conflict.

Where does that leave *A Bridge Too Far*? I contend it is a great war movie and will go further to suggest it is top of the class of all the sprawling historical war epics. It conveys the facts and the history with painstaking economy and fastidious fidelity to authenticity, almost without parallel.

The film's poignant legacy is how it has been adopted by the Dutch people. Despite the terrible privations Montgomery's bold plan engendered, the Dutch continue to honour the sacrifice every September. The movie, which was filmed entirely in their country, helped to not only boost the economy but also tell the world about the fearful cost and importance of Operation Market Garden.

It is impossible to tell this movie story without describing the history of the battle. As the film is essentially an adaptation of a book, I have chosen to consider Cornelius Ryan's original as the bible. While subsequent works have challenged elements of Ryan's early 1970s research, screenwriter William Goldman would not have been privy to them. So, I have resisted more recent accounts.

As for the film's production in 1976, I chose a detailed article written 10 years later by Colonel John Waddy, the film's historical advisor, as the bedrock of facts. When you meet this consummate soldier later, it will be obvious why he can be trusted implicitly as a source. This book makes copious use of cast and crew recollections, but after almost half a century, memories can be hazy. Scenes often are filmed out of order and even spread over months; for the sake of this narrative, I have conflated some reminiscences. Where there were contradictions, I trusted surviving production paperwork, Waddy, or my own assessment. Considering the hundreds of people involved in this movie, of which only a relative handful are given a voice, I do not describe this book as definitive. Instead, I have striven to give a flavour of the effort the cast and crew expended during a hot summer in Holland in 1976.

Introduction
Market Garden 1944

On 5 September 1944, three months after the Allies stormed the Normandy beaches on D-Day, the Germans were in headlong retreat in what was later dubbed Mad Tuesday. Field Marshal Bernard Law Montgomery's British and Canadian army had taken Brussels and was poised to drive north into Holland. Far to the south, Patton's American Third Army was charging full pelt through France and knocking on Germany's back door. The Allies scented victory, and all dreamed of being home for Christmas.

The supreme commander, Dwight D. Eisenhower, suffered a dilemma. He didn't have enough supplies, which had to be manhandled from the Normandy coast, for both advances. Montgomery presented a daring plan that, he was convinced, would win the war. Operation Market Garden involved dropping three divisions of airborne troops to seize a series of bridges in Holland. The paratroopers would lay an "airborne carpet" for the British Second Army, led by XXX Corps, to punch through 64 miles to Arnhem's bridge across the Rhine. Once taken, Arnhem's position on the river would allow the Allies to pivot into the German industrial heartland of the Ruhr.

Given the go-ahead, Montgomery allowed his subordinate, General Frederick Browning, head of the First Airborne Corps, just seven days to plan "Market" at his Moor Park HQ. Dapper and sophisticated, this Old Etonian and former Olympic athlete was a popular leader.

During the First World War, while serving with the elite Grenadier Guards, he had won the DSO and the Croix de Guerre amid the hell of the Western Front. To lead the British First Airborne Division, a fresh unit untested in combat, he appointed his friend Major General Roy Urquhart, an experienced and adept infantry officer, but who had never commanded parachute troops. Urquhart was well-served by battle-scarred airborne officers, including the highly capable Colonel John Frost.

Ordered to take bridges around Nijmegen was the U.S. 82nd "All-American" Airborne led by the youthful Brigadier General James "Jumpin' Jim" Gavin. Promoted as divisional commander at age 37, he was the youngest U.S. general since the Civil War. Gavin always jumped with his men, and his unit had already been bloodied in the chaotic drop on the eve of D-Day. The same was true of the other American unit, the U.S. 101st "Screaming Eagles" led by Major General Maxwell D. Taylor, who had orders to take and hold the bridges around Eindhoven and be the first to be relieved by British XXX Corps.

Although the PAN (Dutch Resistance) reported that the headlong retreat had now stilled, Browning believed the Germans were unlikely to offer much opposition. To stem the rout, Hitler had appointed the elderly Field Marshal General Gerd von Rundstedt as overall commander in the west. It was a wise choice. The veteran general quickly and pragmatically organised his forces by regrouping disparate units into flexible battle groups. Their whereabouts were almost unknown to Allied intelligence, who knew only that General Bittrich's crack Waffen-SS II Panzer Corps had been withdrawn to Arnhem. This unit, with only a few serviceable tanks, had been tracked all the way back from Normandy, where it had been severely mauled. Entrusted with the defence of Holland was Field Marshal Otto Model, who had chosen the Tafelberg Hotel as his HQ together with the nearby Hartenstein Hotel, both in Oosterbeek—directly on the route of the British First Airborne's proposed advance to Arnhem bridge.

On the morning of 17 September 1944, scores of airfields dotted across southern England shook to the roar of hundreds of transport planes, including the versatile C-47 Dakota. Tens of thousands of men packed into what became a vast 90-mile air armada flying towards Holland. Eventually, after the planes fanned into three giant columns, thousands of parachutes drifted down to earth, and hundreds of gliders landed on the bright Sunday afternoon. Almost everywhere, the men landed with little opposition. The Germans had been taken completely by surprise.

On the Belgian–Dutch border, 350 artillery pieces pounded the enemy front line. Then at 2:10 p.m., tanks of the Irish Guards, led by Colonel J.O.E. Vandeleur rolled forward for "Garden." They were part of the Guards Armoured Division, spearhead of XXX Corps, which totalled over 100,000 men and 20,000 vehicles. Lieutenant General Brian Horrocks commanded. Known as "Jorrocks," he had proved a popular commander but was now showing the strain after months of fighting since Normandy.

Within hours, the U.S. 82nd had taken the Grave bridge and pressed forward towards Nijmegen. Unfortunately, the first hiccup occurred when the U.S. 101's objective at Son was mined before the bridge could be seized. Despite light German resistance, XXX Corps managed only seven miles before darkness fell. What was happening at Arnhem? Browning, who had travelled with the U.S. 82nd, had received no information.

With drop zones eight miles west of Arnhem, Urquhart's British had landed unopposed. But almost immediately, things unravelled. Many of the radios worked only intermittently, severely hampering communication. The crucial strike force of Colonel Freddy Gough's jeep squadron had been badly shot up—there would be no lightning strike to the bridge. As the various detachments hoofed it along the cobbled road, they were at first mobbed by ecstatic locals before being pinned down by German fire. It took only a handful of motivated Waffen-SS soldiers to site machine guns at strategic positions and blunt the advance. All except one battalion.

Hugging the Rhine was Colonel Frost's Second Parachute Battalion, who, discovering the railway bridge blown, pressed on to the main road crossing of the Rhine. Finding the north end of the Arnhem Road bridge unguarded, Frost immediately dispersed his men to various houses on each side of the roadway. In the fading light, an attempt to take the south end failed. An exploding ammunition dump caused the bridge superstructure to burn brightly over a city now aflame.

The Germans, who had been caught on the back foot, quickly reorganised, helped by a stroke of fortune. Two gliders belonging to Browning's HQ were lost during the drop, and on one someone had brought along a complete set of plans for the entire operation. This found its way to the Germans. Hitler, far away in his East Prussian lair, was incensed by the attack and directed vast resources to Holland. Also, the Luftwaffe that had been cleared from the Normandy skies still had some fight left and entered the fray. Within hours, Bittrich's badly mauled Panzer Corps was reequipped and ready for the fight. Bittrich ordered *SS-Brigadeführer* Heinz Harmel and his *SS-Kampfgruppe "Frundsberg"* to concentrate around Nijmegen while *SS-Obersturmbannführer* Walter Harzer's *SS-Kampfgruppe "Hohenstaufen"* battled it out in Arnhem.

Over the next few days, the two American divisions, the 82nd and 101st, fought hard to consolidate their captured bridges. For 36 hours, XXX Corps waited at Son while engineers threw a Bailey bridge across the canal. At Arnhem, a spirited attack by *Haupsturmführer* Viktor Gräbner's lightly armoured SS Recce unit of Harmel's *"Frundsberg"* was repulsed, allowing Frost's men to maintain their foothold. The rest of the division was now firmly on the defensive—all attempts to push to the bridge had been cut off. Instead, Urquhart's forces were grouped in the Arnhem suburb of Oosterbeek, dug in and fighting back. The Paras (and their glider-borne infantry comrades), who had earned their proud nickname, the Red Devils, in the North African campaign, were living up to their reputation with dogged resistance.[2]

Inexplicably, their top commanders were nowhere to be seen. Frustrated by the intermittent radio communication, Urquhart went forward to investigate what was happening. He and a brigade commander, Lathbury, found themselves cut off and were forced to hole up in an attic room at Zwarteweg 14 in Arnhem. He would be away from his HQ for 36 hours.

Lack of command and control permeated the entire operation. The patchy radios meant that Browning's HQ in Holland was almost redundant. His London HQ at Moor Park, where he should have been, resembled a ghost town, so no one coordinated the vast resources. Poor communication with the RAF resulted in supplies and reinforcements failing to be deployed correctly. This was not helped by the dire losses of transport planes at the hands of a rejuvenated Luftwaffe and lethal flak anti-aircraft fire.

At Arnhem on 18 and 19 September, more drops brought in reinforcements, but these men received a warm reception as the Germans had infiltrated many of the landing zones. Crucially, the Polish brigade that was planned to land south of the bridge was delayed for days by bad weather.

While the Guards Armoured brigade clattered over the Son Bailey bridge and on to the U.S. 82nd, its commander, Jim Gavin, had a dilemma. On his right lay the Groesbeek Heights along the German border, which if seized by the enemy would seriously compromise his flank. Simultaneously, Gavin needed to seize the vital road and rail bridges at Nijmegen. He had scant men to do both, and so chose to seize the heights. Meanwhile, small detachments were street fighting through the once beautiful city of Nijmegen.

By 19 September, despite fierce German resistance, XXX Corps's vanguard had reached Nijmegen and pushed up to the banks of the Waal River—just nine miles from Arnhem. A plan was hatched for a daring night crossing to take both bridges at Nijmegen. This would be coordinated with a heavy thrust of British tanks. But the required boats for infantry to cross the river were far back down what had now been dubbed the Devil's Highway. Although the U.S. 101st had been relieved, the Germans made continuous forays to cut the route. These American paratroopers would continue to defend the area for many weeks to come. Dodging shot and shell and a nightmarish traffic jam, a column of trucks laden with boats threaded its way north.

At 3 p.m., two companies of the U.S. 82nd 504 Regiment piled into 23 plywood boats and struck across the Waal. The Germans had dug in, supported by heavy artillery. Given suppressing fire from XXX Corps, which pounded the far bank and laid down a smoke screen, the impromptu armada rowed into a maelstrom. Despite appalling casualties, the men of the 504 stormed the German defences and, reinforced by a second wave, fanned out to take both the railway and road bridges. General Harmel was itching to blow the bridge. Ignoring orders from Bittrich, he had instructed his engineers to prime the structures with explosives. As British tanks debouched from the town to roll onto the causeway, the Germans blew their explosives—but the wires had been cut by the Dutch resistance. With both bridges taken, Gavin watched with dismay as Horrocks' tanks stood idle, despite a promise to press on. Horrocks justified his inaction by the fact that the infantry were still heavily involved in street fighting.

Unbeknownst to allied commanders, the prize was already a chimera. After four days of the bitterest fighting, Frost's men, now commanded by Freddie Gough after the colonel was wounded, were compelled to stop fighting. Arnhem had fallen to the Germans. In Oosterbeek, First Airborne had created a defensive pocket and were resisting with extraordinary tenacity—five Victoria Crosses would be won in separate engagements. By now, Urquhart had escaped confinement and returned to his HQ at the Hartenstein Hotel. His command was in dire straits. All their landing zones had been overrun, so the RAF unwittingly dropped much-needed supplies to the enemy. First Airborne's wounded, in the thousands, were taking respite in any nook and cranny. Ordinary houses became makeshift hospitals, their owners, such as Kate ter Horst, serving as impromptu nurses. The St. Elizabeth Hospital in Arnhem overflowed with wounded but, as it formed part of the defence, was in the line of fire.

The Waffen-SS had a fearsome and bloody reputation on the Eastern Front, but this battle would see a rare moment of humanity. A daily truce of one hour was negotiated to allow for the wounded of both sides to be taken to the rear while hasty graves were dug for the fallen. And then the carnage would begin again, with neither side prepared to lose. Having finally arrived, Sosabowski's Polish Parachute Brigade, who were concentrated around Driel, south of the Rhine, made various valiant attempts to reinforce Urquhart's dwindling command in Oosterbeek. It was obvious to all that Arnhem was lost.

Under cover of pouring rain, the remnants of the First Airborne staged an exemplary withdrawal on the night of 25 September. The badly wounded and medical staff volunteered to man the perimeter to fool the Germans. Barely 2,000 men of the original 10,000 made it across the fast-flowing Rhine that night. While the recriminations and arguments would begin, Arnhem hadn't finished with tragedy.

The Dutch living under German occupation suffered appalling privations during the following brutal winter, with many dying of starvation and cold. It was little comfort to hear that Montgomery considered the operation "90 percent successful," prompting Prince Bernhard of the Netherlands to conclude, "My country can ill afford another Montgomery success."[3]

The merits and failings of Operation Market Garden have been endlessly debated. While this is primarily a film book, it is worth some discussion about the battle. What seems extraordinary is the sheer dash and ambition of the operation: an enormous achievement planned and executed in seven days.

The American divisions carried out their orders with tenacity, ingenuity, and courage. The crossing of the Waal is unquestionably one of the most courageous feats in military history and deserves to be celebrated. Whether Horrocks should have ploughed ahead to Arnhem without his infantry is a moot point. The prized bridge had by then fallen. And what of First Airborne? They faced hell. The choice of drop zones so far from Arnhem was a crucial flaw. The failure to drop the Poles in the first few days south of the bridge meant Frost's hold was always tenuous at best. On the other side, the Germans fought an admirable battle. Their military doctrine had always put great emphasis on vigorous counterattack, and at Arnhem they proved it. This was helped by the speed of reinforcements from the Fatherland and other parts of Holland, so quickly and in force.

Retired Dutch Major General Mart de Kruif, who commanded part of the International Security Assistance Force (ISAF) in Afghanistan in 2008, overall considered that "the defeat was not due to the Germans but to Montgomery's ego in his competition with Patton, the desire to deploy the airborne troops, inaccurate planning, and the far too slow advance of XXX Corps."[4]

The plan was bold, and it could have succeeded. Should it have been prosecuted? The brutal winter of 1944 caused immense suffering to the Dutch people. The sobering fact of war is that battles must be fought with the utmost prejudice to win. It is a tragedy that so many have to die. The enormous and profound emotional connection the Dutch have to Montgomery's great war-winning gamble showed they understood the almost unbearable sacrifice required from not just them but also the sons of three other nations, all prepared to end the war by Christmas—and bring the boys back home.

1

Theirs Is the Glory

It was the smell that got him. The sickly, almost sweet stench of death and decay. It hung around the ruins, lingering like a malevolent spirit to remind everyone that war was never far away. He could close his eyes and momentarily forget, but that noxious odour could not be so easily assuaged. At least he had his pipe, as he puffed on the tobacco, which escaped in a cloud from his mouth. Thankfully, the smoke from the pungent tobacco in his pipe, gritted between his teeth, helped to soothe his nostrils.

Known as Penny, Cyril Pennington-Richards was a tall, gangly fellow in his mid-30s with a thick, bushy beard giving him a Bohemian air, or what would soon be described as beatnik. Crouching amid the debris with his cap turned back to front, he looked quite different from the other men around him. They were all dressed in green and khaki camouflage, many with helmets, some with maroon berets with the silver badge of Pegasus. While none had Penny's impressive facial hair, all wore three-day-old stubble, their faces covered in grease and mud. They were prone or huddled, each behind a mound of rubble, each aiming rifles or machine guns towards the shattered roadway beyond. They were waiting; bubbles of chit-chat alternated with titters of laughter. It was relaxed and good-natured, no doubt born of long stretches of boredom awaiting action to begin. Penny noted how nothing fazed these tough men. Once when a burial party was re-interring its grim subject, a voice chirped up: "Cor, there's old Ginger. He'd make a lovely stew, wouldn't he!"

Penny carefully repositioned his legs amid the rubble. None of them could be certain what lurked beneath their feet. Before they had taken up positions here, six glum-looking German prisoners armed with metal detectors had gingerly scanned the entire area. They had been doing it for days, each time unearthing at least one unexploded shell beneath the shattered town.

Penny shuddered at the memory of a little Dutch girl a few days before. She had approached him amid a group of soldiers and held out her hand with a grenade complete with its rusted pin. The others' reflexes were better than his, as the tough bastards dived into a ditch. The girl, unmoving, stood with her hand still outstretched with its lethal discovery. "All right, love," said a shaken sergeant major, as he pulled himself out of the ooze. "Give it to me, darling," he said as he carefully took the grenade. "That's it, there we are. Now, run away, dear." Then, he promptly pulled the pin, threw it and all ducked as it exploded.

Penny's reverie was interrupted as his arm was knocked. Next to him sat a gruff-looking man, his face creased with concentration. With greying hair, he was older than all the other men. He winced as he looked first at his watch and then at the ugly sky above. It was September, and the dampness of autumn was giving way to the chill of winter. Time was of the essence. The older man muttered in a clipped voice with the slight trace of a brusque Northern Irish accent: "Where the hell is that tank?"

Down the street could be heard the clanking and groaning of a metallic beast, punctuated now and then by throaty exhaust emissions. This was a 50-tonne Panther tank, armed with a 75-mm gun—part of Germany's mighty Panzer fist. It lumbered forward, intent with extreme prejudice.

A grim smile illuminated the gruff man's face. He turned to wave at a figure a few yards away. A series of semaphore signals followed as everyone poised to leap into action. The soldiers gripped their weapons, and each took careful aim. So did Penny, as he huddled his eye against the viewfinder of a lightweight Vinten H newsreel camera. He punched a switch, and the mechanism whirred as film threaded through. "Speed," he said. The gruff man cupped his hands to his mouth and shouted: "Action!"[5]

It had been Leonard Castleton Knight's idea. He was head of the newsreel company Gaumont British News, and in early 1945 with war still raging, Knight suggested a film about Arnhem to the Rank Organisation. It would be a unique venture in which veterans would return to the scene of the terrible battle. For £3 per day, these men would replay their own actions for a movie. The chosen director was a veteran of the disastrous 1915 Gallipoli campaign, a tough and bluff Northern Irishman, fastidious and openly gay, Brian Desmond Hurst. He enlisted a young novelist, Louis Golding, to pen a script that would copiously use the veterans' own memories. A protégé of Hurst was Terence Young, who later directed the first Bond films. He'd been a tank commander with XXX Corps during Market Garden and helped to beef up the script. Penny would serve as cameraman. A committed documentarian, Penny had filmed the Blitz sequence for Humphrey Jennings' *Fires Were Started* (1941) amid the real bombing. Later he would gravitate to features and photograph Hurst's most celebrated film, an adaptation of *Scrooge* (1951) with Alastair Sim.

With a small crew, Hurst and Penny filmed amid the ruins of Oosterbeek still littered with unexploded ordnance, some of it used as special effects. Six German prisoners were press-ganged to mine sweep areas before filming. War veteran Hurst once ventured into a dangerous area, telling the crew: "There's no need to risk the unit. Penny and I will go and choose the setup." As Penny later recalled, "He walked in front and I put my feet where his feet were—no messing, you know!"

Two German Panther tanks, one a survivor of the battle, became film props. The entire landscape showed the scars of war: burnt vehicles full of bullet holes, parachutes hanging limply from trees—and the dead. The Graves Registration Unit was still busy re-interring bodies and identifying remains of thousands of corpses. While filming in the ruined Hartenstein Hotel, one veteran remembered making a hasty grave in the cellar during the battle a year earlier. "I hope they dug up that Gerry buried under the coke," Penny heard him say. "But they hadn't," said Penny. "And so, we put a lot of disinfectant down, we got a whiff of corpse and a whiff of disinfectant. But they were really tough, those parachutists."[6]

The arcane filmmaking process amused the soldiers. "To us," recalled Gunner Robert J. Christie, "the production crew seemed to operate on a very casual basis . . . major decisions seemed to emerge casually. Trivial points could be the subject of prolonged argument, often heated." While Penny was described as "the soul of patience—calm and imperturbable," Hurst, bearing his heavy responsibility, could be "unpredictable in mood," recalled Christie.[7]

All took the venture seriously. "There was nobody who appeared in the film, officer or soldier, who had not fought at Arnhem," Hurst commented in the film's publicity. "I selected the men carefully. It was great working with these soldiers because they were accustomed to discipline. The results were superb!" Several senior officers, including Freddy Gough, reprised their roles, joined by the civilian Kate ter Horst, dubbed the Angel of Arnhem, and two war-correspondents, Stanley Maxted and Alan Wood.

A year later, in September 1946, *Theirs Is the Glory* premiered to almost universal acclaim. While the authentic soldiers have a stiffness and awkwardness in their performances, the film (seamlessly intercut with real combat footage) oozes with a blunt reality and an air of unimpeachable honesty. The *Monthly Film Bulletin* commented at the time, "The result is a film with authentic documentary in atmosphere but which depends much on the remembered tension of those Arnhem days for its drama. There are moments of outstanding pictorial incisiveness, but the poetry comes less from the cinematic virtues than from emotion recalled plus the commentaries of Alan Wood and Stanley Maxted . . . who are mainly responsible for making the heroism articulate."[8]

Although it enjoyed phenomenal success despite a war-weary audience, the film has largely dropped from public consciousness. In 2016 it was given a DVD release, while authors David Truesdale and Allan Esler-Smith produced a superb book, *Theirs Is the Glory: Arnhem, Hurst and Conflict on Film*, which gives this unique movie the recognition it deserves. Hurst, who would make several more war movies, recognized its importance. "The film is my favourite because of the wonderful experience of working with soldiers, and because it is a true documentary reconstruction of the event. I say without modesty, it is one of the best war films ever made."[9]

Theirs Is the Glory would be screened in early 1976 at Twickenham Studios to an eager audience of 50 young men. Almost all wore their hair long, and many were clad in flared trousers, some wearing cowboy boots. They watched their forebears up on the screen from 30 years before, short-cut hair and full military bearing—and incredibly brave. They, and the film, would form the spiritual wellspring for their own endeavour.

2
Ryan's Final Battle

While popular fiction usually dominates bestseller lists, nonfiction brings up the rear, often with celebrity kiss-and-tells or cookbooks. One writer bucked this trend with three landmark classics that sold millions of copies about key events in World War II.

Cornelius John Ryan was born in Dublin, Ireland, on 5 June 1920. Barely a year old, he was thrust into violence when his country erupted into open hostility against the ruling British Empire. Pursued by British troops, a group of IRA men retreating through the Ryans' backyard deployed Cornelius' baby carriage as a shield to aid their escape. Echoing the famous Odessa Steps sequence in Eisenstein's masterpiece, *Battleship Potemkin* (1925), Ryan later wrote: "The carriage kept rolling back across the lawn and backed down a flight of steps where the baby was left hanging upside down, screaming his lungs out." This would not be the last time Cornelius courted death.

His Anglophile father was adamant that the young man's future lay across the Irish Sea in the heart of his country's late occupiers. The London of 1939 must have been an exciting and challenging place for an ambitious youth determined to make his mark. When Germany invaded Poland that September, Britain declared war and history's most destructive conflict began.

As an Irish national, Cornelius Ryan was exempt from British military conscription but keen to get involved with his adopted country's fight. For years, he had continued to hone his writing skills. In late 1941 he became a reporter, joining London's prestigious newspaper, *The Daily Telegraph*. One of his first assignments took him away from the conflict and back to his neutral-declared homeland. His sources suggested a dramatic increase in German personnel at their Dublin embassy having been secretly landed by submarine and plane. When his "scoop" splashed across the paper, the Irish Garda arrested Ryan, who was apparently roughed up in prison before being unceremoniously ejected from his native land. For now, his Irishness proved to be an advantage and opened an exciting new chapter in his life.

In 1943, as American forces began forming up in Britain, Ryan was summoned to the cloistered office of Lord Camrose, the *Telegraph's* owner. "You being Irish and all that," he said, "I wonder . . . would you mind covering the Americans?" So Ryan, age 23, became by default a war correspondent assigned to the U.S. Army Air Forces based out of fields in East Anglia, flying into a hailstorm of flak, fatigue, fighters, and fear. Air force statistics suggested 11 missions as the average life expectancy of a bomber crew, and Ryan would fly 14 in a single year. On two occasions, his planes were peppered with lethal splinters of red-hot shrapnel, which luckily didn't cause any casualties.

The sixth of June 1944 saw the largest combined military operation up to that time—D-Day—and Ryan, one day past his birthday, operated in the thick of it. That morning, he had hitched a ride aboard a bomber attacking the imposing coastal defences. Flak hit the plane, which only just made it back to base in East Anglia. Undaunted in his desire to witness history, Ryan made his way down to the coast and jumped aboard a British motor torpedo boat, which cruised off the smoke-shrouded beaches.

In early August 1944 Ryan was accredited to the newly activated U.S. Third Army under the command of the controversial George S. Patton as his force broke out of Saint-Lô and made a ferocious dash along the southern German flank deep into France. For the young war correspondent, it must have been an exhilarating if frightening time. He witnessed the battles at the Mortain Gap, Coutances, and Avranches. During one of these bloody encounters, Ryan and his unit stumbled into a minefield. He recalled the strange sense of calmness when so close to the prospect of death. "Neither do I recall any sense of courage. I think my reaction was mechanical." They all managed to get through it unscathed. "Luck would appear to play a rather enormous factor in life."[10]

Ryan would end the war in the Far East for the surrender of Japan in September 1945. He reported on the bungled arrest and attempted suicide of Japan's top commander, General Tojo. Ryan teamed up with fellow correspondent Frank Kelley to write what would be his first book, *Star-Spangled Mikado*,[11] a breezy and irreverent portrait of the American occupation under General MacArthur.

In 1949 Ryan was at the dawn of television, producing the topical news show *Newsweek*. By age 30 the Irish born journalist had made the United States his new home while never forgetting his roots: "To be Irish is to be a little mad to begin with. Otherwise, our whole mystique would crumble." In 1950 this was cemented by his becoming a naturalised U.S. citizen, and perhaps more personally significant, by his marriage to Kathryn Morgan, the editor of *House and Garden* magazine and later an author.

Much of the 1950s would see Cornelius Ryan producing more than 50 articles for *Collier's* weekly magazine. His pièce de résistance, which the magazine devoted an entire 130-page issue to, was a special edition called "Preview of the War We Do Not Want—An Imaginary Account of Russia's Defeat and Occupation, 1952–60." For the project, code-named Operation Eggnog, Ryan enlisted 20 of America's leading journalists and commentators, including Edward R. Murrow, Arthur Koestler, Philip Wylie, Marguerite Higgins, and Walter Winchell, to present a hypothetical feel-good scenario in which a Third World War is won against Russia, with the extensive use of nuclear weapons. It proved to be a hit, with nearly four million copies sold, and helped double *Collier's* sale of advertising.

Ryan received a Benjamin Franklin Magazine Award for his article "Five Desperate Hours in Cabin 56" about the sinking of the SS *Andrea Doria* in 1956. Critics praised Ryan's storytelling skills, particularly in a husband's anguished account of losing his wife as water poured into their cabin. The woman was one of the 46 people who drowned. This along with several other articles were published in an anthology with the byline "Prize-winning True Stories of the Supreme Moment—When Men Suddenly Face Death . . . In these and other stories, Cornelius Ryan, ace journalist, has caught the essence of that split-second that may be a man's last."

As Ryan honed his distinctive style, some of his contemporaries, such as Tom Wolfe, Gay Talese, and Norman Mailer, were seeking to elevate nonfiction as a literary form, Truman Capote's 1965 *In Cold Blood* being the most famous. Dubbing the loose movement New Journalism, Wolfe argued that achieving the desired "novelistic effect" required dogged skills of acute watching and listening.

Michael Shapiro, a professor at the Columbia Journalism School, believed New Journalism had often allowed itself to be swallowed in "stylistic flourishes and one-liners and the witty turn of phrase," and that it had forgotten what was the bedrock of nonfiction. "To achieve what Talese and Thompson had accomplished meant performing the very act that Norman Mailer, whose best work was arguably his nonfiction, had dismissed as 'chores': reporting."

Shapiro's 2010 article, "The Reporter Whom Time Forgot," sought to elevate Cornelius Ryan's reputation, as Shapiro felt Ryan had been unfairly overshadowed by New Journalism's proponents. Shapiro suggested Ryan's solid, painstaking research coupled with an almost novelistic approach marked his mature style: "There is nothing, it turns out, like a densely reported story propelled by the palpable sense of a reporter chasing his story."[12]

🐎   🐎   🐎

It was a return to the Normandy beaches in 1949 that would set Ryan on a new and dynamic trajectory. He felt that despite an outpouring of publications about D-Day, the intimate human side of the fateful day had been largely ignored. Devouring official documents, books, and articles, he endeavoured to contact as many participants as possible. He placed notices in multiple media outlets in America and Europe, asking: "June 6th, 1944, Were You There?" He resolved to tell the complete story from all sides, including that of the defeated Germans. With war memories still fresh—and bitter—this would be no simple matter. In an era before the internet, communication took time and money, and it would consume him for nearly a decade.

In 1957 Ryan was in difficult financial straits. Determined to turn his vast amount of research into a book, he made a deal with the widely considered unhip magazine, *Reader's Digest*. It would be the start of a mutually beneficial relationship. *Reader's Digest* provided him with assistants, translators, and offices in New York, Ottawa, London, Paris, and Bonn. The accumulated cost would be $150,000. In return, the magazine would serialise Ryan's story before Simon & Schuster released the hardcover.

To organise his mass of material before the age of personal computers proved a formidable task. First, the research and interview notes would be typed onto index cards, all arranged in chronological order by 55-minute time periods. Particularly for the fighting zones, there could be more than one card per person. These were called "travellers," which would be woven throughout the narrative.

Doug McCabe, now retired, was the curator of the Ryan papers at Ohio University and explained how Ryan formed this vast amount of material into a coherent structure. "This was certainly more than simply writing bridges between notable events. As good writers do, Ryan had to decide how to open the story, how to move it along, and just when it had to end. He had to apply his best writer's craft to know what key to run with, whether to bring in counter themes, and when to build to crescendo . . . This approach, combined with his prior musical training and work in theatre, explains 'the Ryan style.'"[13]

Published in 1959, *The Longest Day* was a sensation, selling more than 35 million copies in America alone and many editions in more than 30 languages.

Surprisingly, it wasn't Hollywood who swooped the movie rights, but Belgian film producer Raoul Lévy. In 1960 he paid Ryan $100,000 for the rights and a further $35,000 to write the screenplay, even though he had never written one before. But Lévy, who had attached British director Richard Anderson of *The Dam Busters* fame, struggled to raise enough finance for the epic.

For 30 years, Darryl F. Zanuck had run the major Hollywood studio 20th Century Fox, but by the mid-1950s he sat in self-exile as an unsuccessful independent producer in France. Still smarting that he had missed the war, Zanuck saw an opportunity to get back into the big-movie league. He paid Lévy $175,000 for the movie option and set his friend Elmo Williams on the task of producing the film. Ryan, still on board, packed up the family and went to Paris to write the screenplay.

The relationship between writer and producers didn't begin well, as Elmo Williams noted, "It was hate at first sight." Conflict grew from Zanuck's desire to sprinkle Ryan's meticulous authenticity with a liberal dose of Hollywood licence (the ageing mogul's then-girlfriend, Irina Demick, was cast as a glamorous French Resistance fighter). Ryan described Zanuck as "... one of the last of the great vulgarians."[14] Relations didn't improve when the producers brought in additional writers, albeit all high-profile literary talents, to beef up their respective nationalities. While their collective contributions were relatively minor, Ryan successfully appealed to the Writers Guild for sole on-screen credit as screenwriter, with the four others credited for "additional scenes." Despite his reservations, the film was an enormous success, garnering two Oscars and bringing Ryan's work to an even bigger audience.

So, what kind of man was Cornelius Ryan? His daughter, Victoria, born in 1960, recalls: "He was the guy you always wanted to invite to your parties. He had wonderful stories where everybody's listening, and then there would be a roar of laughter. He was just a lovely, gregarious guy."[15]

For his next book, Ryan elected to retell the enormous canvas of the final collapse of Hitler's Reich in 1945. This project would illustrate the tensions and reality of the Cold War. While he interviewed more than 500 Americans and Germans, only 35 Russian voices were heard. Had he lived to see the end of the USSR, Ryan may have sought some of those stilled voices for a new edition. While less known than his other two books, *The Last Battle* is a fine piece of work. There were plans for MGM to film it in the late 1960s, with Ryan again writing the screenplay, but the project withered.

On 23 July 1970, 50-year-old Cornelius Ryan was diagnosed with prostate cancer. Arriving home from hospital that evening, he tried to put his thoughts in order via a Dictaphone. He was concerned at not only the impact his illness would have on his family, but the fear that he could not finish his latest book, *A Bridge Too Far*. "I haven't even reached the halfway mark in my histories I am writing. If I have to get cancer, why can't it show later, say 20 years from now?"[16]

His daughter, Victoria, who was then just 10, remembers the uncertainty that descended on family life. "They never told me and Geoff (her brother) for a long time about his diagnosis. And we both knew as you could hear him on the phone having doctor's appointments. It was a little off-putting that they hadn't shared it with us, but I think that was their way of protecting us."

While he battled for his life, he faced the financial squeeze of mounting medical bills. To receive the rest of his fee, he needed to submit a completed manuscript. But as his cancer took hold, progress was slow. From August 1970 to the end of May 1973, he had written only half, about 300 pages. "I am three years late with it and the publishers are screaming," he wrote to a friend. "The advances have been spent and we are trying to keep our heads above water with the hope that the book will be finished within the next four to six weeks."[17]

Instead, much of his time was devoted to accumulating information about his cancer treatment. He was concerned that, despite the doctor's urging, chemotherapy would dull his mind and, therefore, his writing. "I think a lot of his focus during the four years was basically to stay alive to get it done," Victoria explained. "He forced himself every day to go to his office and write. There were enormous maps all over with little different coloured pin heads in them, indicating who was where, etc., and they had three-by-five cards laid all over the place, saying certain characters and where they were."

More than 1,200 people contributed interviews, of which only 400 were quoted. Ryan enforced a strict discipline with his material, ignoring hearsay, rumour, or third-party accounts, and only including a statement or quote that could be backed up with documentary evidence or corroborated by an eyewitness. All of this was cross-referenced in his card system. In his vast list of acknowledgments, he drew attention to Prince Bernhard, husband of the Queen of the Netherlands, who had proved invaluable in locating many Dutch sources. The family would sometimes go *en masse* to Europe for these marathon research sessions, as Victoria recalled. "I remember meeting Kate ter Horst, and she was just such a divine lady. These people trusted him. They told him their stories, and so he never forgot about them. He kind of welcomed them into his life."

Meanwhile, the battle against his cancer continued as Victoria, a medical professional before she retired, explained: "They irradiated him with seeds of radiation. And the theory at the time was that, it would kill the cancerous cells, and then it would keep on working as new cells became dysplastic and changed from normal cells to cancer cells." Despite constant, debilitating hospital stints, he kept his spirits high. On one occasion, he joked with the nurses that "... with all that radiation [that] was coming off of him, for a small fee, he would offer any woman who wanted to be sterilised to sit on his lap for a while. He was just so funny."

But there was a flip side to his treatment, namely an acute social misunderstanding of the disease. "In the '70s it kind of exploded, this insidious entity, the big C. But there was not all that much research going on. There were some of my father's friends who wanted him to eat off different plateware, as perhaps they might get it too."

Victoria, then a teenager, coped as best she could, but noted the strain on her mother, Kathryn. "She got very thin. But unfortunately, I was more intrigued by my own life. It's something that's always in your mind, but somehow you think your parents are always gonna pull through it. And so sometimes just being busy keeps you from thinking about it."

Over five months, despite the pain of his advancing cancer, Ryan found a new lease on life that propelled him through the final 350 pages. His wife offered not only pastoral care, but also edited the material and "watched for my dangling participles." Thanks to the marital writing team, the manuscript was completed in October 1973. Ryan noted how the disease had influenced what he deemed his finest work. "I had the opportunity of looking into the darkness of the abyss, and I gained a greater insight into the emotions of my subjects than I ever had before."

At more than 600 pages, *A Bridge Too Far* is his longest book and possibly his best. The author considered Operation Market Garden the most "significant" action after D-Day in the Western Theatre. Yet, he noted, that while Arnhem had been celebrated and copiously written about in Britain as a second Dunkirk, in America it was virtually unknown. He felt the American actions, particularly the Waal crossing, deserved to be told, not out of nationalistic zeal for his adopted country, but as a universal celebration of courage. Over seven years, he had striven to "unscramble some of the riddles" and present the "first complete version"[18] of the ground–airborne battle, giving equal, non-partisan weight to all, soldiers and civilians alike.

He had finished in the nick of time, as Victoria explained: "He had a thing called lymphoma angiogram done to see if the cancer had spread into the lymph nodes. It had moved. So eventually it wound up in his bones, and he ended up with pneumonia. And that's the way cancer is."

Published in September 1974, the book was greeted with almost universal praise and stayed on the bestseller chart for many weeks in both America and Western Europe. Ryan, despite his failing health, hurled himself into a punishing publicity tour. Victoria was at college at the time: "I remember one morning in my college room, turning on the TV and he was on the *Today* show with Jane Pauley—it was delightful."

Despite the extraordinary success of his books, serious critical appreciation eluded Ryan. "There's probably little chance that I may be cited for a Pulitzer because so many of these bastards sit on the board," he wrote to a friend, "but it would be nice to get one, anyway."[19] The 1975 prize in History went to the distinguished scholar, Dumas Malone, a director of the Harvard University Press, for his 27-year magnum opus: *Jefferson and His Time, Volumes 1–5*.

With his wife, Ryan made a series of whistle-stop promotional trips to Europe. He had packed his screenwriter hat too. Independent producer, Joseph E. Levine had bought the film rights for $350,000, and discussions were underway on the practical problems to be solved: where would the movie be shot? One day, a strikingly attractive tall, blonde, 24-year-old Reineke Kramer-Pirk, who worked in the Arnhem tourist office, was told to expect important guests. "Levine had been in Arnhem before," said Kramer-Pirk, "and saw that there were huge modern buildings by the bridge. So, Arnhem was no-go, but Ryan wanted to convince himself. I showed him and his wife, Kathryn, around the bridge, and he agreed it was not suitable. Then we went to a sleepy Dutch town on the Ijssel River. And that was the location to be—Deventer became Hollywood!"[20] Reineke could not imagine that this encounter would lead two years later to her becoming assistant to the film's director.

The punishing international promotional tour wiped out Ryan.

The cancer returned. He was rushed into hospital on 22 October 1974, and with his wife by his bedside, he died a month later. On his tombstone, inscribed beneath his name was just one word: *Reporter*.

A Bridge Too Far was not Cornelius Ryan's last book. His daughter recalled her father's daily ritual—and the secret that was discovered only after his death: "Early in the morning, unbeknownst to Mom, he would go down to the enormous office; it was a separate building from the house. He had these audiocassettes, and he talked about what was going on with his cancer and how he felt about it. My mother found these cassettes after he died. She did not know that he was keeping them. And then unbeknownst to him, she was keeping her paper diaries." This would eventually form the powerful and emotional memoir, *A Private Battle*, which Kathryn put together, intercutting both her and Cornelius's private hopes and fears. In 1980 the book was dramatised for TV and starred Jack Warden and Anne Jackson as the Ryans.

While the epic subjects of Ryan's great trilogy have continued to be mined by other authors, few can deliver his extraordinary emotional punch, which sits upon a bedrock of ironclad authenticity. Few would disagree with his daughter's summary of the Ryan style. "I am amazed at how he could take, let's just say, 10 people, at the same moment in time at 10 different places, and talk about what each one of them was doing, and what they experienced, and what the temperature of the community was, and how he could organise all that so things are happening simultaneously. He was so acclaimed for his fact gathering and basically telling stories of the little people who are caught up in the tragedy of the war."

With the movie rights in his pocket, a retired 70-year-old film producer was about to make the most expensive film of his career, and with his own money too.

3
"Forget That B Picture of Yours"
Levine and Attenborough

"He is the epitome of a Hollywood mogul: short, Jewish, a deep rasping voice, occasionally cantankerous, often benign."[21]

Joseph Edward Levine was born in the slums of Boston in 1905. He was the youngest of six children of a Russian–Jewish immigrant tailor who died very young. Joe would later say that he didn't have "one happy day" growing up. This was not helped by the endemic antisemitism on the streets. "When they had a pogrom in Poland, we'd have one on Billerica Street the next week[22] ... Being Jewish ... is like being black."[23] By force of circumstances, he was a grafter from an early age, determined to support his family. "My mother always called me the *brategiber*—the bread giver."[24]

After leaving school at 14, partnering with his two brothers in a basement dress shop, he hit the road as a salesman, learning the art of flimflam. Buying into the Cafe Wonderbar in Boston, he met Rosalie Harrison, a singer with the famous Rudy Vallee band. Their subsequent marriage would last for 49 years. The formidable Rosalie insisted her dynamic husband sell the cafe and find a new avenue for his restless drive.

In 1938 he entered the movie business, purchasing the Lincoln Theater in Boston. There he ran a diet of B Westerns and exploitation films, such as *How to Undress in Front of Your Husband*, and became a successful, if small-time, independent East Coast exhibitor who accumulated another six venues. His showmanship skills were instantly apparent. During the war, he ran a no-holds-barred propaganda film, *Ravaged Earth*, exploiting its rabid anti-Japanese tone with an expensive marketing campaign summed up by the slogan "Jap Rats Stop at Nothing – See This. It Will Make You Fighting Mad."

Post-war, he recognised a gap in the market. European films had traditionally been shunned by Hollywood, but Levine believed there was an appetite for the exciting material emerging from the shattered continent. He pounced on documentary-style Italian neo-realist films like Roberto Rossellini's *Rome, Open City* (1945), *Paisà* (1946), and Vittorio De Sica's *Bicycle Thieves* (1948), and tapped into an enthusiastic discerning audience. He found a winning business balance between these art movies and low-brow, trashy drive-in fare.

Levine formed his own production company, Embassy Pictures, and put an extraordinary taste for risk taking on display. In 1956 he paid $12,000 for the U.S. rights to a Japanese science fiction thriller called *Godzilla*, then invested a colossal $400,000 promoting it with mass print and TV advertising. His gamble paid off, achieving $1 million in rentals. Upping the ante with the Euro epic, *Attila* (1954), his $700,000 investment returned $2 million.

In 1958 on a visit to Rome, Levine discovered another treasure chest. When major Hollywood productions like *Quo Vadis* and *Ben Hur* had been shot in Italy, it had sparked a spate of very cheap Ancient World movies, dubbed "peplums." One peplum called *Le Fatiche di Ercole* caught Levine's eye. Pietro Francisci directed, and wooden-but-muscular American bodybuilder Steve Reeves starred along with Yugoslavian beauty Sylva Koscina. "The picture broke down when we were showing it," said Levine, "but there was something about it that made me realise there was a potential fortune."[25]

He bought the U.S. distribution rights for $120,000 and retitled it simply *Hercules*. The move would be a game changer for both Embassy Pictures and the industry. Levine spent another $120,000 on dubbing and improved sound effects. He then topped this with a cool $1 million on promotion in a massive publicity blitz launched three weeks before the film's release. At the time, such exploitation was unknown as was the wide release in 600 cinemas simultaneously, staying true to the advertising slogan: "Where Ever You Are, You Are Never Far From HERCULES!" Levine's supreme effort bagged $4.7 million, making it one of the top earners that year. Next, he picked up a lurid British effort, *Jack the Ripper* (1958) and rolled the dice again. He famously displayed $1 million in cash for exhibitors as a taster of success. "It cost me $3,000 to borrow, but I got $100,000 worth of publicity out of it," said Levine. "It even made the papers in Australia!"[26] This time, however, the gamble didn't pay off. "It dropped dead in every theater, in spite of a mammoth campaign," he explained, "because the public didn't want to see it. They smelled it out even before the reviews."[27]

The 1960s saw Levine's Embassy Pictures become the most powerful independent production company in the American film industry. In 1963 he signed an extraordinary $30 million deal with Paramount Pictures to produce his own films, which they would finance with Embassy taking a cut of the profits. A canny investment of $900,000 bought Levine the rights to three Harold Robbins books, including *The Carpetbaggers*. The 1964 film grossed $40 million against a $3 million budget. The following year, he produced the splendid *Zulu* (1964), although his involvement was primarily the deal; he left the coalface production work to its star, Stanley Baker. The epic battle story had been a pet project of the Welsh actor, and around this time another actor with a dream movie knocked on Joseph E. Levine's door.

Richard Attenborough wandered into one of Levine's ad hoc offices at the plush Claridge's hotel in London. Levine's enormous suite buzzed with activity as executives and their lawyers huddled in groups discussing deals. "Between the long-distant phone calls, like some cruising dreadnought, Joe glided from group to group, dropping pertinent observations into their deliberations as he passed," remembered Attenborough. "Almost without stopping, his first words to me were: 'Why the hell do you want to make a film about Gandhi?'"[28]

On 11 April 1983 at the Dorothy Chandler Pavilion, Los Angeles, Richard Attenborough, a bulldog-built man with receding grey hair flowing back around his temples and wearing a pair of large glasses, strode up to the podium at the 55th Academy Awards ceremony. Moments before, U.S. television comedienne Carol Burnett had just read out the winner of Best Picture.

Gandhi.

Attenborough accepted the statue and paused, gently stroking it. The road from Claridge's to this moment had taken almost 20 years, with many twists to bring to the screen a depiction of arguably the most extraordinary figure of his age. "Gandhi simply asked that we examine the criteria of the manner of which we solve our problems," said Attenborough to an enrapt audience, "that surely, in the twentieth century, we human beings searching for our human dignity could find other ways of ultimately solving our problems than blowing the other man's head off ... I believe he had something to say to all of us, everywhere in the world . . . and you honour his plea to all of us—to live in peace."[29]

This sentiment was at the heart of Attenborough's world view. Fame and fortune would occasionally produce verbiage and pomposity in Sir Richard, but with a natural ebullience and charm, he liked to put all at their ease: "Call me Dickie."[30]

Born on 29 August 1923, he was the eldest of three, his father, Frederick Levi Attenborough, a principal of University College, Leicester, and his mother, Mary, a suffragette with a strong social conscience. She was, he said, "eternally poised in action like a hummingbird." During the Spanish Civil War, she cared for 50 refugee children and encouraged her own brood to work free for charities. The family adopted two German Jewish refugee girls who had fled Nazi persecution. Her death while journeying to a marriage guidance council, which she had founded, was for Dickie "a void which can never be filled."[31]

Dickie, unlike his more intellectual brother, the esteemed naturalist David Attenborough, was not university material and had his heart set on a different path. "It was Granny who really supported his ambition to be an actor," recalled Dickie's son, Michael, "because Grandpa was desperately opposed to it: his firstborn son to not want to go to university when he was such an academic was quite bizarre to him. To put it rather crudely, if Grandpa was the intellect, Granny was the heart, and Grandpa in lots of ways probably was closer to David. And Granny was closer to Dad. If I'd been around, I would have gone to Grandpa and said, 'I think you should stop arguing with Richard, because he's unquestionably the most obstinate man in the world, and you're never going to dissuade him.' When Dad set his heart on something, he did it. He was a very determined man."[32]

During the blitz of 1941, his mother took Dickie for an audition at the Royal Academy of Dramatic Art in central London. Then 17, the young man so impressed the examiners that they awarded him the Leverhulme Scholarship at the princely sum of £2.50 per week.

Call-up to the RAF interrupted his studies. Rising to sergeant, Dickie saw active service as an air-gunner cameraman flying missions over occupied Europe. Sitting in the tail of a Lancaster bomber—"that was my position: arse end-Charlie," said Dickie—he filmed targets before and after they had been bombed. "I'm ashamed to admit it now, but I didn't look down at the burning buildings and empathise with the dead and dying . . . The only thing that scared the bejeezus out of me was the airsickness."[33]

Despite his proven courage, his first significant part on film was as a coward in Noël Coward's *In Which We Serve* (1942). His baby-faced looks often found him playing either weak innocents or psychopaths. "I had this round, ridiculous, cherubic face,"[34] he lamented. Dickie embarked on a crash diet to acquire pinched and nasty looks for his role as Pinkie in the adaptation of *Brighton Rock* (1948). He achieved a mesmerising portrait of menace and darkness and, considering his own personal liberal outlook and sunny disposition, demonstrated his skill as an actor.

Dickie's lighter side found an outlet on stage in 1952 in what would become the world's longest-running theatrical show, Agatha Christie's *The Mousetrap*. Dickie and his wife, Sheila Sim, were in the original cast, and cannily, they took a 10 percent profit participation in the production. "It proved to be the wisest business decision I've ever made,"[35] Dickie said later, although a short-lived restaurant venture coupled with the decades-long effort to keep his Gandhi project afloat dissipated much of it. Despite being forced by the COVID-19 pandemic in 2020 to close for more than a year, the show continues to be one of London's top tourist attractions.

In the early '60s, tired of being typecast, Dickie put his acting career on hold and teamed up with director Bryan Forbes as partners in Beaver Films. "It wasn't that he didn't like acting; he loved acting. He was just sick of playing the same sort of roles," commented his son, Michael Attenborough. With Dickie wearing the producer's hat and Forbes directing, the pair made a string of superb chamber pieces, *Whistle Down the Wind* (1961), *The L-Shaped Room* (1962), and arguably their best, *Séance on a Wet Afternoon* (1964), which also featured Dickie (persuaded to act once more) portraying a beautifully understated would-be kidnapper in a pitch-perfect story that explores an unfulfilled marriage. By contrast, his performance as the "anachronistic strict" Regimental Sergeant Major Lauderdale in *Guns at Batasi* (1965) won him a BAFTA and reenergised his acting career. "Suddenly he was playing in a different class," said Michael. "That led to a whole series of roles which broke the mould of his typecasting playing somebody 25 years younger."[36]

It was inevitable that Dickie would become a director, but he wisely followed David Lean's advice, "God's sake, *don't* until you find something you're prepared to give your life for, and you know if you don't direct it, you'll die."[37] But Lean now became his rival. The great director had long cherished filming the life of Gandhi and would continue to do so well into the 1970s.

That day in Claridge's, Levine in a dressing-gown and his minions listened enrapt as Dickie spent half an hour describing the life of the Mahatma. At the end of the performance, Levine leant forward and said, "We've got a deal." Asked what he wanted, Dickie replied boldly, $3.5 million. "Make it 5,"[38] exclaimed Levine. Despite the producer's largesse, *Gandhi* did not happen, in part due to the death that year of India's Prime Minister Nehru, who had been a supporter of the project. Other problems included the fact that Gandhi had been a divisive figure in India (he had been assassinated by a disgruntled Hindu) and a byzantine Indian bureaucracy that mired the permissions Dickie would need.

Meanwhile, Dickie had been noticed by Hollywood and followed up a leading part in John Sturges' *The Great Escape* (1963) with a role in Robert Wise's epic *The Sand Pebbles* (1965), in which he and Steve McQueen played buddies aboard a U.S. gunboat in war-torn China. Dickie gave a heart-warming performance as a sailor embroiled in a doomed relationship with a local girl. He then shook a leg, illustrating skill as a dancer and singer in *Doctor Dolittle* (1968), playing a circus owner alongside the bizarre animal dubbed pushmi-pullyu.

In 1969, following David Lean's advice, Dickie embarked on his debut film as director after charming $5 million from Paramount's chief Charles G. Bluhdorn, with a tour de force solo cabaret of the entire prospective film, complete with songs, story, and dances. *Oh! What A Lovely War* was a satirical and caustic look at the madness of World War I. Dickie called in many favours from friends to deploy a star-studded cast that included Maggie Smith, Dirk Bogarde, John Gielgud, Laurence Olivier, Jack Hawkins, Vanessa Redgrave, and Ralph Richardson. John Mills played General Haig, presented as an unfeeling automaton who sent men to their deaths, flippantly emphasised by the use of cricket scoreboards. The action, harking back to its theatrical roots, revolves around Brighton's Victorian West Pier, before stepping out into the mud and filth of the trenches. Dickie uses all the power of cinema for the last image: a helicopter shot starts on a handful of white crosses in a field before pulling back to see a vast collection of another 16,000 hammered into the rolling South Downs. No modern CGI could compete with the sheer visceral impact of so many markers of death, all painstakingly planted for real. The shot remains both breathtaking and intensely moving.

In the early '70s, Dickie began his second film holding the megaphone, *Young Winston* (1972), an ambitious retelling of Winston Churchill's formative years. Written and produced by the American, Carl Foreman, *Young Winston* is a hagiographic work that rarely presents its hero in a lesser light. Honoured to have been approached by the ailing Churchill to dramatise his book, *My Early Life*, it took Foreman, producer of *The Guns of Navarone* (1961), a decade to achieve it. The wartime leader, who would die in 1965 without seeing the film, quipped he had opened the Second Front (D-Day) in less time than it took to get the film into production, to which Foreman responded, "But you had more money, sir."

The film boasts several splendid action sequences that show Dickie's almost Lean-esque ability to stage epic spectacle. For the battle of Omdurman, staged in Morocco, the colourful Dervish army is quickly dispatched in a staccato montage of crashing British artillery—the romance of war meets industrial slaughter. This is followed by the very last charge of British cavalry in history. Simon Ward as young Churchill joins the fray amid the thunder of horses as he rides into a ravine of Dervishes. A would-be assailant is frame-frozen in mid sword strike. Later, riding in an armoured train on a routine mission, Churchill is caught in an ambush, well staged in Wales, standing in for South Africa.

Overall, *Young Winston* proved a fine achievement and firmly established Dickie's style of expansive storytelling. Despite positive reviews, it was a box-office disappointment, and ominously Hollywood labelled him an accomplished, if uncommercial, filmmaker. Nevertheless, in January 1974 Dickie announced that his next film would be *Gandhi*.

"Joseph E. Levine Presents," meanwhile, became a moniker of success. After a run of hits with *The Graduate* (1967), *The Producers* (1967), and *The Lion in Winter* (1968), Levine took his foot off the accelerator and sold Embassy to Avco for $40 million, staying on as its chief executive officer. He would later consider this decision a "horrible mistake which made me rich."[39] After several disappointing films, he resigned in 1974. With a hefty payoff, Levine, now in his late 60s, finally retired with wife Rosalie. Taking his 100-foot yacht for a spin on Long Island Sound near his Greenwich home in Connecticut, legend has it that on his first day off, he crashed into the dock wall, then grumbled to Rosalie that he wasn't enjoying his life.

While Cornelius Ryan lay dying in hospital, Levine came to visit his friend. The writer "struck a fist out towards the sky and half yelled at heaven" that he was going to finish his "goddamned thing. And you're going to make a movie out of it." Levine would honour his friend's wish. He snapped up the film rights to *A Bridge Too Far* and resolved to get back into the game. "Most people in my business thought I was a nut," Levine said. "It was too foolhardy, much too expensive, and, they predicted, impossible to bring off."[40]

War films were out of favour. To compound things, even during its glory days, British-themed war stories rarely did well at the all-important North American box office. At the time, this usually made up half of any film's haul. But the international slice could tip the balance. Unsurprisingly, the Pearl Harbor reconstruction *Tora! Tora! Tora!* and *Battle of Britain* did exceptional business in Japan and the UK, respectively, which nicely compensated for their more sluggish American returns.

To produce *A Bridge Too Far*, Levine turned to United Artists, which had been formed in 1919 by a quartet of superstar names, including Charlie Chaplin. In making a home for creatives, it differed from the other Hollywood majors. Principally, it had no facilities, so did not charge the dreaded elastic "overheads." Instead, UA financed and released independent productions on a profit-sharing basis. Over the years, many major figures, including Walter Mirisch, Stanley Kramer, Blake Edwards, and Cubby Broccoli with his Bond franchise, enjoyed what one UA executive described as "benign neglect."[41]

A huge war movie with a depressing ending was a perilous venture for any studio. Despite Levine's pedigree, there was serious doubt he could pull off such an enormous project. To prove his determination, he invested $5 million of his own money. By keeping ownership, he used a concept known as "pre-sales," which involved selling distribution rights to various territories and using this money for his budget—before the film existed. It was and is still a popular if hazardous method of film finance. The key was the package: top stars, elite director, and a story with wide international appeal. United Artists would pay the lion's share for the North American and European distribution rights ($12 million)—provided Levine could get the "package."[42] He was up to the challenge. "I've always been a gambler. Second, I'm not exactly on my first time around."[43]

To direct, Levine believed he needed a British talent—and if he used an 85 percent UK crew, he could take advantage of the country's lucrative tax breaks, known as the Eady Levy. This had encouraged many American-backed films to the UK as so-called runaway productions throughout the 1960s.

In February 1975 Dickie, while in California in final negotiations with Warner Bros. for *Gandhi*, received an invitation to Levine's palatial suite at a Beverley Hills hotel. "Look what I've got!" said the veteran producer, brandishing a large paperback version of *A Bridge Too Far*. "Forget that B picture of yours. This is the big one!"

It had been more than 10 years since the pair had first met. Although Dickie had yet to score a commercial success, Levine was convinced Dickie was a worthy talent, appreciating his "orderly mind,"[44] and Joe admired Dickie's pair of directed films and graciously attributed their poor box office to lacklustre marketing—a subject about which he was an expert.

Although he was "totally bowled over," by the offer to direct *A Bridge Too Far*, Dickie balked at the proposed scale. "I expressed the feeling to Joe that it was unbelievably complex. He said, 'It's the greatest movie that everybody will ever see.' And on he went and raved about the subject. And I did read it. I wondered whether it was shootable." But Dickie still held out to ink the *Gandhi* contract.

Like an ardent lover, Levine called Dickie repeatedly to see what progress he was making. "The fifth call came on a day on which we had hit another financial snag on *Gandhi*. Joe said, 'Are you going to do *Bridge* for me now?' I agreed."[45] To reel in Dickie, he offered a $250,000 salary, 10 percent of the net profits, and guaranteed (again) he would finance *Gandhi*. Dickie was seduced by the "extraordinary brigand's"[46] charm offensive.

"The offer was typical of Joe," said Dickie. "If he felt instinctively that somebody was right for a particular project, convention or cowardice would never deter him."[47] The two would forge a strong partnership built on mutual trust and respect. "[Joe] is first and foremost a man of massive loyalties," Dickie considered. "If he is fond of someone, there is almost nothing he will not do for them." Conversely, the director was very aware that, "if you cross him or he feels you have betrayed his friendship—God help you."[48]

On 12 June 1975, the world's press gathered at the swanky Les Ambassadeurs Club in London's exclusive Mayfair district. Levine, with Dickie by his side, announced *A Bridge Too Far*. It would be his 49th movie and by far the most ambitious with a projected budget of $15 million. "This picture will be 75 percent British," he said, "with just a few ugly Americans and a few Poles to make Polish jokes about."[49]

With the unadulterated images of war in Southeast Asia regularly beamed into people's homes, what, Dickie was asked, would be his approach? "The days of false heroics have long since gone," he explained. "Television removed that by putting Vietnam on our screen evening after evening: the population now has a fair idea of what war is like. No. I'll go back for a start to the footage made by the RAF Film Unit, in which I served for a time. Those cameramen caught the moment in every sense of the phrase—there was no way of staging it a second time. We will be trying to seize the moment."[50]

For reasons that have never been clear, Levine announced that the film would open in exactly two years on 15 June 1977. By striking a line in the sand, he was showing his commitment and determination. Now the starting gun had been fired, the next job was to find a writer capable of distilling Cornelius Ryan's 650-page tome into three hours of movie entertainment.

4
"But Which *Story?"*
Goldman and the Raid

"Always in Hollywood, no one wants to hear this, but everything depends on the screenplay."[51] So said William Goldman, probably the most influential screenwriter in Hollywood history. He would write 33 produced screenplays, doctor scores of others, and win two Academy Awards. Not only did he change the form of his craft; he also was an accomplished novelist and a perceptive commentator on the movie business.

His bestselling 1982 book, *Adventures in the Screen Trade*, a caustic but also compassionate summary of over two decades of writing for the movies, is perhaps best summed up by his observation: "Nobody knows anything (in Hollywood)."[52]

On the one hand, he was a consummate industry player who took no shit from anyone. But his apparent brash and bristly persona[53] hid a deeply passionate, self-deprecating, brutally honest, vulnerable, and humorous individual. This smorgasbord of traits gave him an almost Dickensian understanding of human nature, which he poured onto the page. Over his career, he rolled with many knocks, caught between the Hollywood unholy trinity of stars, money, and ego. But he would single out *A Bridge Too Far* as his "best experience," and "the most unusual"[54] he had been involved in to date.

Goldman was born in 1931 to Jewish parents in Chicago.[55] He suffered a traumatic home life after his alcoholic father committed suicide, and his mother struggled with deafness. As an escape, young William holed up in the movies, especially devouring Westerns. His early writing efforts found few advocates. "Do you know what it's like to want to be a writer and get the worst grades in the class?" he asked. "It's terrible."

After achieving his master's degree from Columbia in 1956, he became a copywriter at an ad agency. Frustration led him to pen his first novel, *The Temple of Gold*, in just three weeks. "I am basically a novelist, and I fell into screenplay writing rather by misinterpretation."[56]

He got a break, of sorts, when actor Cliff Robertson hired him to do a script adaptation for Daniel Keyes' *Flowers for Algernon*. Knowing nothing about the craft, he raided an all-night bookstore in Times Square at 2 a.m. and bought their only screenwriting book. It would help him naught, as he was duly fired.[57] But his time on the set taught him valuable lessons about the stark realities of making movies. Undeterred, he busied himself with a spec script in his favourite genre—the Western.

It was his screenplay for *Butch Cassidy and the Sundance Kid* (1969) that earned an Oscar and elevated him into a major industry player. Directed by George Roy Hill and starring Robert Redford and Paul Newman, it revitalised the tired Western genre with energy, humour, and romance. It was also daringly simple in construction. Almost a quarter of the movie is given over to a chase, as an unidentifiable posse hunt the two outlaws, with little dialogue apart from Butch Cassidy's repeated, "Who are those guys?" This boldness coupled with Goldman's knack for pithy dialogue established his renowned style.

He continued in this whimsical manner with *The Great Waldo Pepper* (1975), with Redford as a barn-storming airman caught up in a hazardous Hollywood war movie. With Redford again, he tackled the controversial Watergate conspiracy in *All the President's Men* (1976). This true tale of two journalists who broke the White House coverup story brilliantly wove historical strands with some choice fictionalisation. His effort would bring him his second Academy Award.

For any aspiring screenwriter (including the present author), Goldman is The Guru. While a plethora of how-to books would appear from the 1980s onwards, very few were written by coalface practitioners. Perhaps his best single advice to all wannabes is to come into a scene as late as possible, and then "get the hell out." Goldman's guidance was always tempered by the stark realities of a multimillion-dollar business, for instance, giving the star the best lines, etc. In *Adventures in the Screen Trade*, he mentions some compromises star talent foisted on his work.

Conversely, Goldman told an affecting story of the world's greatest actor, Lord Laurence Olivier, who was having problems saying one of his lines while working on *Marathon Man* (1976). "'Bill,' said Olivier, 'could I suggest an alteration?'" Goldman was more than happy to oblige. "Olivier," said Goldman, "calling me 'Bill.' Asking me would I mind. That's high cotton."

Signing on for *Bridge* in the summer of 1975, Goldman immediately regretted his decision when he met Dickie: "We had a bad meeting in England in which he got the impression, I think, that I didn't want to do it . . . and that I didn't want him to do it." Then, sitting down with Cornelius Ryan's immense incident-packed book, Goldman was stumped: "But *which* story?"[58]

He knew what he *didn't* want to write. "If it had been a standard WW2 story where John Wayne drags the poor but cuddly Americans to victory up the hill, I would have not done it. Because I hate those movies."

While he grappled with finding the structure, he was acutely aware that Levine was already spending millions gearing up for production. "I've never felt such pressure," Goldman admitted later. "They had to start building before they had anything [from me]. And if the script had stunk, and they hated it—it was too late."[59]

Despite their awkward first meeting, he and Dickie soon struck up a strong rapport. "He is by far the finest, most decent human being I've met in the picture business,"[60] said Goldman of Attenborough.

Dickie was equally impressed by his collaborator, saying, "He was very shy, a man of few words, really, until you got to know him. He is an avid sports fan, and one of the most knowledgeable wine connoisseurs I have ever met. Bill taught me a great deal about the disciplines of screenwriting."[61]

The pair shared a few intensive weeks where they would meet in the evening to discuss progress and ideas. Both read the extensive, mainly British memoirs of the battle, and Goldman noted a peculiar form of national masochism. "They take their battles very seriously. And they love disasters. So, the most famous World War II battle was Dunkirk, which was a gigantic disaster for them. And Arnhem was the second largest."[62] He began to realise the potential minefield he was walking into. There were just so many dramatic incidents, including several that merited Victoria Crosses. "Surely," he reasoned, "I needed those five."[63]

An absolute was that his screenplay could not run longer than 180 pages—or three hours. It was a duration he was unfamiliar with, as "climaxes could not come at the same intervals as in something of more normal length." It would be his childhood love of Westerns that gave Goldman the spine of the story and inspired one of the film's most memorable moments. In essence, he used the classic Western idiom of a cavalry-to-the-rescue motif. The plot hinges on the drive for Arnhem bridge over the Rhine, with the script touching base with all the major historical beats. With the exception of a fictional Dutch family, nothing was purely invented. Instead, Goldman telescoped, swapped, and simplified the record.

He had noted that despite the violence, none of the principal figures in Ryan's book died. Not good for an anti-movie, he thought. He addressed this by making minor roles "instantly sympathetic—so I could have someone to kill." Not everyone would agree with his choices, but he was constrained not only by the running time, but also by the need to give a fair crack at all the warring nations. He strove to reflect that Arnhem was "the last battle in which any of the notions of human decency applied. But it was a disaster for the Allies. There were so many screw-ups by everybody."

There are three components to a screenplay—and the audience only experiences two: the structure and the dialogue. The third is the action. This describes what is happening; it needs to be terse and evocative. It should never tell the director how to shoot a scene but must contain enough information to help the producer set the budget by indicating what logistics might be required. Goldman wrote as if he were an audience member seeing it for the first time. A great example is how he introduced "Mad Tuesday" as the Germans retreat from Holland.

> *EXT. A DUTCH ROAD (RETREAT) - DAWN. As the noise we've been hearing takes a quantum jump in volume, and this is it folks, the first giant shot of the film . . . this road is ALIVE, it's packed, jammed, clogged, with every kind of vehicle imaginable . . . Because what we see is a panic like no one's ever looked at before: German soldiers pumping bicycles, but not just ordinary ones, these are loaded down, laden, giant suitcases draped over the handlebars. And trucks stuffed with more soldiers . . . everywhere, smoke and dust, dust and smoke . . .*

When Goldman delivered his first draft in November 1975, Dickie was literally moved to tears. "I was bowled over with joy." He was in awe of Goldman's command of the material, using index cards detailing each episode. "And he then sat back at his desk and said, 'Oh, my gosh, yes, I'd better get the Poles in now . . .' If he tried to do it in his own head, he'd never got through it. The result was that it was a highly complex script, but a brilliantly assessed and attuned one, with an enormous clarity and integrity." As an actor, Dickie also appreciated the "economy of dialogue. Bill had that wonderful gift of making the actors totally at ease in speaking the lines."

Because of the time constraints, Goldman could not fully research British idioms and military terminology. Dickie assured him that a battalion of veterans would read and correct his "Americanisms." It would become a brickbat for the New Yorker as he later rubbed shoulders with the famed veterans of Arnhem.

🐦   🐦   🐦

While Goldman hammered away on his typewriter redrafting, Levine set to work finalising his "package" with the glamour of stars.

Ever since the waning of the studio system with its contract actors, thanks to canny agents, stars' salaries had ballooned. Elizabeth Taylor had been the first to bust the $1 million mark for *Cleopatra* (1963) and with husband Richard Burton had negotiated over $2.5 million for *Boom!* (1969). Not only had their salary consumed most of the production budget, the film had been a resounding failure. To offset some of the risk, producers increasingly lured stars with profit percentages, with varied results depending on box-office success. (Alec Guinness famously became a multimillionaire with a 2.5 percent stake in the megahit *Star Wars*.)

Levine knew he needed stars—lots of them. "Joe decided that he would get this wonderful phalanx of huge star American names," Dickie said.[64] But profit sharing could be in danger of echoing his unscrupulous fictional counterpart, Max Bialystock in *The Producers*. He had no choice but to pay upfront, and Hollywood could smell his money.

In January 1976 Levine and Dickie went to Hollywood for a busy week, in what Goldman dubbed "The Raid." For 12 roles, Levine offered several stars $250,000 a week each, but the wary agents insisted on pay-or-play guarantees. Whether or not the film was made, the old-time producer would be personally liable. "I never screamed louder in my life," Levine railed. "I'd never given into a guarantee before. I swore I never would."[65] With a few exceptions, they got whom they wanted. The ones who got away included Charles Bronson for Polish commander, Sosabowski, and a lady for whom Arnhem had a special significance—Audrey Hepburn.

Hepburn's mother was a Dutch Nazi sympathiser who had even shaken Hitler's hand. Her father was British and working for the Nazis when the 10-year-old girl left boarding school in England to join her mother in Arnhem just as war broke out. Her mother soon lost her idealism after a close relative was executed by the German occupiers. Audrey, her already lithe figure not helped by rationing, dreamed of being a ballerina and attended a dance school next to Arnhem bridge. By September 1944 the family had moved to the village of Velp, adjacent to Arnhem, and it was there they watched the battle unfold.

"Audrey was 15 and working for the Dutch Resistance during Market Garden," said Robert Matzen, author of *Dutch Girl: Audrey Hepburn and World War II*. "She volunteered at the Velp hospital and cared for wounded civilians and soldiers. Velp was a staging ground for the Panzer Divisions, and so she was right there. Plus, she had family in both Oosterbeek and Arnhem—her aunt lived at the end of the Arnhem bridge and died during the battle."

When the British Airborne withdrew, the girl and her mother, aunt, and grandfather, along with their countrymen, suffered through the appalling Hunger Winter, when 20,000 Dutch died of famine.

Audrey Hepburn, with her luminous talent and a figure graced in stylish Givenchy, never forgot those dark years. A huge international star of the 1950s and '60s with *Funny Face* (1956) and *Breakfast at Tiffany's* (1961), she had largely withdrawn from the screen by the '70s, partly to concentrate on her family and later to focus on her passionate work with UNICEF. Levine believed she would add not only class but authenticity to the role of Kate ter Horst. His offer forced Hepburn to read Ryan's book. "I was destroyed,"[66] she reacted. Some years before, she had also rejected the role of Anne Frank as too raw.

The biggest goal for Levine was to bag one of the two top male box-office stars—Steve McQueen or Robert Redford. Dickie and McQueen had become firm friends while making *The Sand Pebbles*, but in the early 1970s the star had stepped back from the limelight and enjoyed his wealth and high-octane motor racing hobbies. Despite turning up to the Tuesday meeting "prompt, courteous, terrific," much to Dickie's disappointment McQueen passed. Hopes were now pinned on the Friday Redford meeting. But the star, who was also the producer of *All the President's Men*, was distracted by post-production work and asked for the weekend to mull it over.

Born in 1936 in California, Joseph Robert Redford, Jr., had a challenging upbringing. He survived a childhood bout of polio, but his mother's death when he was still a teenager caused the young man to veer off the rails. He described her death as the first great hurt in his life. Despite winning a baseball scholarship to the University of Colorado, he began drinking heavily and was even caught stealing beer and was duly kicked out. He drifted across America picking up odd jobs, often hard graft, including a spell in the California oil fields. Eventually, he saved enough to travel to Europe, where in Italy and Paris he lived the bohemian life as a painter.

Returning home, he studied film at the American Academy of Dramatic Arts in New York. It was here that he transformed himself. His obvious good looks drew comment, and the suggestion that his talent lay in front of the camera took hold.

Staying in New York, he quickly found work not only on stage but in the burgeoning TV industry. Starring in Neil Simon's *Barefoot in the Park* on Broadway soon brought him to the attention of Hollywood. His rise to stardom was rapid. He starred alongside Natalie Wood in *Inside Daisy Clover* (1965) in a risky career move (at the time) as a bisexual character. It paid off, bringing him a Golden Globe for the Best New Star.

But it was thanks to Paul Newman, who had pressured the studio to hire him, that Redford became a superstar with *Butch Cassidy and the Sundance Kid*. He was then on a near continuous roll, topped with another pairing with Newman for the crime caper *The Sting* (1973) which proved to be his biggest hit. Success brought power, allowing him to produce some of his movies, often with political themes, including *The Candidate* (1972) and *All the President's Men*.

As Levine successfully got his noteworthy scalps during that week, McQueen reconsidered. Despite the last remaining part having been formally offered to Redford, McQueen's people pushed their man—insanely so. For $3 million, he would appear as long as he could work back-to-back with another film for another three big ones. Then there were his people—$50,000 for them. Oh, and the house in Palm Springs—McQueen wanted $475,000, and on it went. Then the phone rang. Redford, for a cool $2 million for four weeks work, was in, and an ecstatic Levine and Dickie were on the next plane home. For a total of $9 million, they had booked 12 marquee names. On 12 February 1976, Levine proudly announced his "package" to the press.

Two days before, Dickie, along with his wife, Sheila, and their three children, had trooped off to Buckingham Palace. As Dickie's name was called, he stepped solemnly along the red carpet and knelt before Queen Elizabeth, who tapped his shoulders with a sword and said, "Arise Sir Richard Attenborough." He had been recommended for a knighthood by Prime Minister Harold Wilson, and it had been announced in the Queen's New Year's Honours list. It was a mark of his enormous contribution in many walks of British public life. Thrilled by the honour, the knight still insisted on being called "Dickie."

While he eschewed a movie mogul's traditional accoutrement of a fat cigar (being a lifelong nonsmoker), Levine used a cane. For the handle, he had ordered an exquisite miniature of Arnhem bridge made in gold. One day, during the fevered pre-production with negotiations stalling over the question of bridges, Goldman met Levine in the street. The producer appeared troubled as he walked, gripping his cane. The writer wondered why he would heap so much grief and stress on himself—when he didn't need to. "And he whirled on me and took his cane and pointed it dead between the eyes and his voice got very loud. He said: 'I'm 70 years old and I want to do this thing.'"[67]

5
"It's All a Question of Bridges"
Preparations

Operation Market Garden had taken just seven days from planning to battle; the film reconstruction would take almost a year before cameras could turn over. Once the ink had dried on the contract, Levine ceded essentially all control to Dickie, who would produce the show through his own company.

The key figure—and unsung hero of this gigantic project—was Eric Rattray as production supervisor, considered "the major brains of the whole operation." The 43-year-old Rattray had progressed through the British film industry as an assistant director, notably for Stanley Kubrick's *Dr. Strangelove* (1964) and then as production manager on Billy Wilder's *The Private Life of Sherlock Holmes* (1970) and another Conan Doyle yarn, *The Adventure of Sherlock Holmes' Smarter Brother* (1975). Following *Bridge*, he would produce, amongst others, *Memphis Belle* (1990).

Working directly under him was Terence Clegg, another Kubrick veteran who had toiled under the taskmaster on *Barry Lyndon* (1975). For *Bridge* he served as the production manager. "My job as PM was to run the organisation in Holland on a day-to-day basis, find the workspaces, get the permits and permissions, control and service the workforce, recruit local labour and extras, and deal with the flood of paperwork necessary to keep the local and national politics on our side. I was assisted in this by an English-speaking member of the council

46

named Cornelius Van Eijk."[68]

The other leading figure was associate producer John Palmer, an old-school gentleman well-versed in managing epics (notably David Lean's lauded 1960s trio) and considered a "dedicated organiser,"[69] as Clegg recalled him fondly. "Dear old John Palmer was near the end of his career and gave us the benefit of his vast experience. His military connections were impeccable."[70] He would assemble the army vehicles and a fleet of planes, plus negotiate with various NATO armies.

Joe Levine enlisted his son, Richard, as his representative, a young man of little practical film experience but who attempted to walk in his father's very large shoes. Off the record, few paid Richard more than lip service, with staff hiding when they heard he was coming into the production office. It appears he was politely tolerated out of respect for Joe.

But all agreed that it was Eric Rattray who held everything together.[71]

During the summer of 1975, the production team, hiding or not, had their hands full. Many things had to happen all at the same time, with the most important single decision being where to film the project. Levine and Ryan had talked about a potential film while the writer was alive—Ryan had visited rebuilt Arnhem and recognised its unsuitability.

While Holland had bridges, it was not geared up for a major Hollywood production. Marshal Tito's Yugoslavia in Central Europe seemed more suitable as cinema had been a passion of the Communist dictator, and he had invested heavily in a homegrown industry. Avala Film's Filmski Grad studios in Belgrade had for a time become a popular base for large-scale movies looking to shave costs, such as the comic war film *Kelly's Heroes* (1970), which had used Tito's military to make one of the best, if hilariously anachronistic, World War II films of the decade. But these had paled compared to Tito's own dream project, *Battle of Neretva* (1969), a truly epic reconstruction of his own desperate battle against attacking German and Italian armies in 1943. It was the destruction of a bridge over the Neretva that proved pivotal in turning the tide. Tito agreed to its replacement being blow up again for the cameras in 1968. It appeared Yugoslavia was awash with bridges, although its rocky, barren landscape proved a world away from the flat, open Dutch countryside. But by 1975, hampered by a crumbling economy, the once impressive movie facilities had fallen into disarray.

There was no option other than Holland.

The producers homed in on the sleepy city of Deventer, with a population of 65,000, as the centre for the film. Barely touched by the ravages of the twentieth century, it also boasted a bridge almost identical to the famed Arnhem original 25 miles to the south. Situated on the east bank of the river Ijssel, Deventer received city status in A.D. 934, making it one of the oldest in the Netherlands. For the next half a millennium, it flourished thanks to a harbour that could take large ships bringing in dried haddock and cod from Norway. Although Deventer had been an early adopter of the printing press, the lowering of the Ijssel River and the century-long Dutch Revolt (1566–1648) against Spanish rule saw the city's fortunes decline.

By the nineteenth century, the city had become a hub for industry, boasting a foundry for heavy manufacturing and textile production as well as two cigar companies and the world-famous Deventer honey cake (*Bussink Deventer Koek*). The city largely escaped World War II, although its railway bridge was targeted in several Allied raids that killed scores of Dutch civilians. In the final stages of the war, the Germans prevented the local fire brigade from tackling a burning retirement home in favour of a factory. The death in the flames of more than 20 of the elderly residents was considered a war crime.

Deventer, with its twin-towered St. Nicholas Church, offered a charming pre-twentieth century snapshot of a picturesque, quintessentially Dutch city. Fortunately for the filmmakers if not the town, the economic downturn of the 1970s had led to many factories closing resulting in high unemployment. Also, tucked away unwanted and unloved was a district called *Noorderbergkwartier*, its dilapidated and crumbling buildings resembling a mini-Stalingrad—or Arnhem.

Joe Levine's interest in the community as a base must have been a welcome boost. But to secure his location and clinch the deal would require all his charm and *chutzpah*. Equally, Deventer was determined to extract a good deal from Hollywood. A local TV crew captured one of the sit-down conferences during which an official stated that the bridge was owned by the state and not the city. He asked Levine, clad in his usual dark glasses, "to address this meeting to see the problems and wishes." Levine replied in a slow, almost-growl, "It should be made here because this is where it happened. It shouldn't be made anywhere else." With his mix of flattery and flimflam, Levine was in his element making the deal.

Determined not to be steamrollered, the municipality of Deventer enlisted a lawyer, Herman Ribbink. "You had to crack hard nuts, but that's always the case with these kinds of cases," said Ribbink. "The English [*sic*] thought they could get everything at a bargain price, that was their commitment. At first, we were impressed by their professional approach. But we immediately hinted at what they could expect from us. They had to deposit two tons [*sic*] as a bank guarantee for accidents, and they had to insure themselves against anything and everything."[72]

Early in the morning of 20 September 1975, cub reporter Nolly Speyers sat alone in the *Deventer Dagblad* newsroom when the phone rang with news that the city fathers were going to give a press conference. She asked why. *The New York Times* had just broken the story that the Dutch government had given permission for *Een Brug te Ver* to be made in "a sleepy Dutch town on the Ijssel river." For the next two years, Speyers became the unofficial *Bridge* correspondent, covering the filming almost every day on set.

While the film unit would bring in a great deal of cash, it would also inflict day-to-day nuisance for the city. Not only would areas need to be cordoned off, thus forcing the locals to follow sometimes lengthy diversions, they also would lose their prime highway. The bridge would be closed for some weeks and a ferry service laid on to allow the flow of traffic across the river.

According to the publicity department, a plebiscite about whether to allow the bridge to be closed was put to the 65,000 citizens, and 90 percent voted yes. Journalist Iain Johnstone, who would write a book about the production, spoke to several locals who assured him the approval vote was pure fiction. Diligently, Johnstone returned to the publicity office to confront them that the story of local support was "hyperbole." They doubled down and insisted that there had been a vote, and "there the matter rests,"[73] concluded Johnstone.

Mostly Deventer played the consummate host for Hollywood, but as familiarity breeds contempt, the relationship would eventually sour.

On 13 October 1975, three Englishmen, one greying around the gills, and a fourth much older, gruff Irishman arrived in quiet Deventer. Curious locals would have scratched their heads, wondering what they were doing as the men wandered around the town's arched Wilhelmina Bridge. In between snapping copious amounts of photographs, they would take turns with a trundle wheel, periodically shouting out numbers in arcane-sounding "yards/feet/inches." That evening, amid pitchers of beer, the four poured over diagrams and faded photographs as they discussed their efforts that day. If any local had asked them, they may have given a dull cover story about road resurfacing or the truth—introducing themselves as on a recce, or recon, for the film company.

It would be the job of these four to turn the peaceful bridge into a war zone and design several period buildings that could be systematically destroyed. "This bridge over the River Ijssel was of similar design, a 'coat hanger' type construction, although slightly shorter and not quite so wide—you might say it was a 90 percent scale model of the Arnhem Bridge,"[74] said Alan Tomkins, the youngest of the group. He was an art director who had already worked with Stanley Kubrick and David Lean. In fact, all four were veterans of work with Britain's finest director, and none more so than the eldest, construction manager Peter Dukelow. This tough, hard-living and hard-drinking, no-nonsense Irishman from County Wexford ran his team on military lines. He had built the immense bridge on the River Kwai amid the Ceylonese jungle. Using hundreds of trees, Dukelow's team had battled extreme heat and venomous snakes, even recruiting elephants to complete the job. Dukelow's structure had to be sturdy enough to take a train, albeit for a few seconds, before the entire span was blown up.

For *A Bridge Too Far*, Dukelow's set constructions would be designed by the other three, led by production designer Terence ("Terry") Marsh. Marsh had started as a draughtsman at Pinewood Studios in the early '50s and learnt his trade under the brilliant production designer, John Box, perhaps best known for his work on Lean epics. The fourth member was another art director, Stuart Craig, who was a Marsh protégé. "Terry had already just crossed the threshold into big-time production design," said Craig. "And he came from the stable of extremely prestigious movies, David Lean['s] being the best of them."[75]

Broadly, a movie production designer dictates the overall visual style or look of the film in close discussion with the director. The art director works more with the crew to ensure that the production designer's vision is manifested. Marsh had served as assistant production designer for *A Man for All Seasons* (1966) and *Oliver!* (1968) before moving up to the top job on his own for *Scrooge* (1970), which required an imaginative reconstruction of Dickensian London. He would design two historical dramas, *Mary, Queen of Scots* (1971) and *The Abdication* (1974) before getting to work on *Bridge*.

Having finished measuring the Deventer bridge and with a construction start date arranged just after Christmas, Marsh and his team had to get their building designs ready in time. They set up in an empty High Street shop next to Twickenham Film Studios, where Tomkins quipped, "Who said filmmaking is glamorous?" Their first job was to construct a large-scale model of the bridge and surrounding area, which included an unsightly 1960s apartment tower block. "Half the houses were built for real so that we could shoot inside on all levels. We also included the block of modern flats into the model to show the camera angles that wouldn't work."[76]

Bridge would be an important career moment for both Craig and Tomkins, who would both become successful production designers. Tomkins would design the ruined war-torn towns for both *Saving Private Ryan* (1998) and the TV series *Band of Brothers*. One advantage, if also a potential pitfall, of making a historical film is the usual wealth of information to hand. "Attenborough employed a special researcher for months before people like me and Terry Marsh's art department started," Craig explained. "The Second World War is extremely well documented, so there was never any shortage of research."

The key figure in this research was an Arnhem veteran, who would live to be 100 years old. Tall and lean, with a taut face and sandy hair, Colonel John L. Waddy was the epitome of the British officer class and well suited to serve as the film's chief technical adviser. In 1944 at age 24, Waddy parachuted into the Arnhem battle, which had already tilted towards disaster. "I was a major commanding a company in the 156 Parachute Battalion," said Waddy. "And we came in on the second day just north of Oosterbeek. We ran into a very strong line of enemy armour. I got wounded in that battle in the woods, and virtually in the space of two or three hours, the battalion was destroyed."[77]

A career soldier, Waddy had served in India with the Somerset Light Infantry. Keen for more adventure, he joined the fledging parachute battalion. He got more than he bargained for when he was seriously injured jumping from a plane, ending up in a coma for three days. In 1943 he joined the war in the Middle East and Italy, where the 156 Battalion helped capture the port of Taranto.

He jumped into Arnhem as part of Brigadier John "Shan" Hackett's 4th Parachute Brigade, and after being wounded in the groin, he was tended in the Tafelberg Hotel in Oosterbeek. While recuperating in relative safety, he was hit again by two mortar-round shell fragments, which damaged his foot and scarred his face and shoulder. Captured, he spent six weeks in a hospital, narrowly avoiding amputation, and saw out the conflict in Stalag VII-A.

Post-war, Waddy stayed in the army, serving in hot spots like Palestine and Malaya. He would later become the first Colonel SAS and expanded the Cold War role of the Special Air Service. In 1970 he witnessed the Vietnam War during a stint as defence advisor at the British Embassy in Saigon before joining Westland Helicopters, based in Taunton, in 1974. The company gave him six months' leave to work on the film, and his enlistment was considered a perfect choice by all veterans, which illustrates the high regard and respect he had earned during a formidable career.

The eight days he had spent in the cauldron of Oosterbeek would stay with him for the rest of his life. He lost not only many of his comrades but also his brother Peter who, after successfully disabling a German tank with a grenade, was killed; it would be months before Waddy found out the news of his sibling. Waddy would be a prominent presence at the yearly commemoration events at Oosterbeek, where veterans dutifully gathered to remember the dead. He was an authority on the entire campaign and would eventually host battlefield tours. The veteran cared passionately about the truth of what happened and about the need to honour the memory of the fallen.

Many books had been written about Arnhem, almost all about the British end of the battle. Waddy recognised that Ryan's original book, in which he makes several brief appearances, had "used a wider canvas to give the whole picture from both sides with the developments which led up to the operation." Despite, he said, its "journalistic approach," it gave an "excellent account" of the strategic overviews of all the warring sides. He lamented the writer's untimely death as Ryan would have been "a strong influence . . . as regards the integrity of the story in the script."

Goldman's script often became Waddy's battleground. Commenting 10 years after production when the dust had settled, Waddy considered that, "on the whole, it's fairly accurate but obviously . . . some liberties have been taken with history. Some of these are minor and excusable, such as amalgamating several characters and incidents." He took issue with some historical elements that had "been enlarged or altered merely to give a specific actor a better part in keeping with his image." He finally conceded that it was not "a documentary—it is a dramatic portrayal of an event in history."[78]

Speaking just a few years before his death in 2020, he looked back fondly on his flirtation with Hollywood. "We had many of the discussions mainly to try to see that the scenes are being filmed authentically, as possible . . . Sometimes on location if I said, 'No, it's simply wrong,' he [Dickie] would put his hands over his ears and say, 'I can't hear you!' But quite a lot of the times he would accept it, and we came to a compromise which is always the best solution."[79] Waddy's contribution to the film cannot be overestimated; his forceful and forthright personality helped to steer the screen story along the narrow-rutted road of accuracy within the drama.

With the infrastructure now in place, the next problem to solve was to find the scores of vehicles, from tanks to jeeps, to depict mechanised world war. Luckily, associate producer John Palmer was more than up to the task and often enlivened production conferences with tales of working as David Lean's production manager on *Lawrence of Arabia* and *Doctor Zhivago*. Managing the day-to-day headaches and imponderables of these epics had made him the ideal choice to oversee the colossal job of assembling the air armada for *Battle of Britain* in 1968. Journalist Leonard Mosley, who wrote a book about the film, described Palmer as "a nut-brown, cheerful, bustling little man with a penchant for blazers with brass buttons."[80]

In August 1975 Palmer approached the specialist military history magazine *After the Battle*. The editor, Winston Ramsey, recommended that Dutch historian Jan Voskuil, considered a leading authority on the Arnhem battle with his own extensive archive, be appointed historical adviser to the film. For the mechanised army that Palmer sought, they were directed closer to home.

Charlie Mann was an engineer with a passion for collecting vintage military vehicles. In 1975 he had opened the Lamanva Military Vehicle Museum three miles from Falmouth in Cornwall. Mann would provide over 100 vehicles for the film, including half-tracks, trucks, motorcycles, and even a Bedford OY NAAFI tea van. A few additional machines were supplied by the 1939/45 Group and Bapty and Co. As the film's military vehicle advisor, Mann was very proud of his contribution and subsequently displayed several props in his museum, like the replica Horsa glider fuselage, which visitors could walk through. A few years later, he modified three replica Mercedes trucks on lengthened 6x6 GMC chassis for one of the best chase scenes in movie history: Indiana Jones in hot pursuit of a Nazi truck in *Raiders of the Lost Ark* (1982). Sadly, Mann's death in the late 1980s saw the museum's collection sold off, making such a large concentration of vehicles impossible for another film production.

What Mann could not provide was the armoured fist of XXX Corps that had spearheaded the race to the bridges. Palmer enlisted ex-Tank Regiment Major John Larminie to scour Europe for as many running Sherman tanks and a plethora of spare parts and engines as he could find. The M4 Sherman had been the Allied armoured backbone. Cheap to produce, it was agile and fast but hopelessly outgunned by the German Tigers and Panthers. The more formidable Cromwell and Churchill tanks formed a large part of XXX Corps force, but few had survived the war. The Sherman, which had been constantly modified, was still fighting on battlefields, notably the Six-Day War in 1967.

Eventually, Larminie corralled nine useable Shermans to be overhauled in a workshop in the village of Twello, near to Deventer. The Dutch Army supplied one, which was transformed into the weightier Sherman Firefly. Also, a 'Dozer Sherman was given a plastic turret and featured clearing the blocked "Devil's Highway." Two towable hulks would see use farther back from the camera. Five Shermans were found in next-door Belgium, with two being former gate guardians at military bases, Ecole de Troupes and Blindees at Arion, and another dug out of a cabbage patch behind the Royal Army Museum in Brussels. Finally, two post-war models with 76-mm guns rounded out the force. In the workshop, they were machined up and transformed into their authentic look with additional metal and plastic adornments before being painted and given the correct decals. Personnel on leave from the Tank Regiment's depot at Bovington and the British Army on the Rhine in Germany served as crew.

These nine veritable old busters, supplemented by moulded plastic upper superstructures on Land Rover chassis, would take the brunt of the movie action and needed constant repairs and loving care. Each one had its own low loader to ferry it to the location. For some scenes, more than 100 of Mann's vintage machines, many going by their own steam, would thread through the narrow roads of Holland and resembled a travelling circus stretching for miles.

Germany's final defeat in 1945 owed greatly to the almost total destruction of its military matériel, leaving little available for the film. Bittrich's Panzer division had taken a terrible thrashing in Normandy and was a pale shadow of itself at Arnhem. So, while the might of the Nazi war machine did not need to be depicted, some sense of the formidable German Panzer would be required. "It was a challenge, but it was a logistical one," Stuart Craig explained. "Could you convert a modern Dutch tank to look like a German Panzer tank? And indeed, that's what we did. They're actually modern Dutch tanks with some souped superstructure put on by us." A Dutch Army Leopard I bore a passing resemblance to a German Tiger, and thanks to some extra metal plates along the sides and fibreglass additions to the turret, it passed muster.

By early 1976 Peter Dukelow's construction team of more than 100 men was busy with the three biggest tasks: constructing eight three-dimensional sets upon the carpark surrounding Deventer's bridge, converting a gutted country house into the Hartenstein Hotel, and in Bronkhorst village, recreating Kate ter Horst's rectory and a two-dimensional church. Also, Dukelow constructed a large water tank to film closeups of the storming of the Waal River.

To echo General Browning's line, *"It's all a question of bridges,"* two more would be needed. One was at Grave, east of Eindhoven, which the U.S. 101st successfully took with barely a shot fired. The other was over a central Dutch highway, both road and river, at Nijmegen. This would prove to be the most difficult and time-limited effort in the entire production. The bridges were fully functioning and would require complex negotiations to temporarily close them.

Ensuring the locations that would be dotted around Holland was the role of Norton "Nifty" Knatchbull as location manager. Knatchbull came with a high pedigree if a lack of experience, which cut little ice with Terence Clegg: "He was not my choice—Richard Attenborough begged me to take him—but he turned out to be a quick learner and served us very well. Our major 'coup' on that film was arranging for the bridge at Nijmegen to be closed three Sunday mornings. This is a bit like stopping the M1 for three hours on a Bank Holiday!" Knatchbull, who was often seen speeding around the Dutch countryside in his red sports car, had a secret. "When his heritage was leaked to the crew, he suffered a great deal of chivvying, such as 'How's your aunty?' The Queen was his godmother."[81] Following his father's death in 2005, Knatchbull became Baron Brabourne and later, following his mother's death, the 3rd Earl Mountbatten of Burma.

Still not finished with bridges, Dukelow had to add a replica of the Son bridge to his list. This needed to look convincing when mined by explosives. It was this destruction that fatally halted XXX Corps' advance until a Bailey bridge could be rustled up. The film would need to depict one of these engineering marvels too, but luckily a NATO exercise would conjure one up for the cameras.

In downtown Deventer, a disused cheese factory served as a workshop. Seventy carpenters, painters, riggers, and plasterers began building six full-sized Horsa gliders. Another factory in town, Twentrac, was used as a studio facility. Inside it were constructed a variety of small sets, including interiors of a Dakota and a Horsa, plus Urquhart's attic, Frost's barrack room, etc. In Twello an immense wardrobe unit occupied another empty factory. Its extensive floors were stacked with endless racks of uniforms and civilian items, all managed by Anthony Mendleson, well-known as a designer of mediaeval costumes in films like *The Long Ships* (1964). The minute differences between regiments in all the armies had to be scrupulously followed, and Mendleson and his assistants took meticulous pains to ensure absolute accuracy. The research had been painstaking, as for such recent history unforgiving veterans would quickly spot mistakes. As generals often had the clout to ignore the regulation mode of dress, Airborne Corps Commander General "Boy" Browning had designed his own jacket, which was based around a Great War RFC-style one. The wardrobe unit borrowed the original from the Airborne Museum at Aldershot and copied it exactly to Dirk Bogarde's measurements.

Some sequences would involve more than 1,000 extras. Those involving civilians would present immense logistical challenges to get all changed into costumes and—with women—to dress their hair in '40s style. All would need to be fed before filing onto buses to the location—and the entire process reversed at the end of the day. The production line at Twello often would start around midnight and not finish until after sundown the following day.

Watching the day-to-day logistics of film production, the ex-military man Colonel Waddy noticed how similar the two were. "Periodic schedules were issued, weekly schedules and then daily orders or 'The Unit Call' as it was termed, which were issued during the late afternoon for the next day's shooting."[82]

This coordination was the work of one of the most crucial, if unsung, roles in film production. The first assistant director must wear many hats, all at the same time: regimental sergeant major, diplomat, nursemaid, and sometimes fall guy. This role is the link between the director's creativity and the producer's pocket. It is not uncommon when a production is in trouble to fire the "First" as a useful, if often unfair, scapegoat. Traditionally seen as the "company" man, the first assistant director bears immense pressures and responsibilities. The very best know how to balance all the different demands to keep a production on track. At the time, a small select group of British Firsts were considered the best in the world.

One of those was David Tomblin.

"He was a bear of a man," remembered the actor John Morton. "Big men—gaffers and grips—worked for him and did so with the greatest of affection. Broad and full were his shoulders, carried high, pushed tight against the neck. With his barrel chest, he squeezed his words through the back of his throat and nostrils, as is the manner of those suburban London lads; that communicates controlled authority, experienced professionalism." Morton, who played the U.S. 82nd padre in the Waal crossing, considered him a friend over subsequent films. "I characterised him as a great who orchestrated symphonies out of chaos. I'm going as far as to say that David Tomblin was the greatest first assistant ever."

The 44-year-old Tomblin had been born just down the road from Elstree Studios in Borehamwood. There, as a teenager, he would begin his tentative steps before being interrupted by a National Service stint in the Royal Marines. This background gave Tomblin what those in the forces call military bearing. He commanded complete respect and not only enjoyed good working relationships with his crew but also navigated the rulebook with union reps and ensured safety when dealing with potentially hazardous stunts and special effects. Rising through the burgeoning TV series of the 1950s, *Hawkeye and the Last of the Mohicans* and *William Tell*, he broke into A features on Robert Wise's masterful ghost story, *The Haunting* (1963). The tortuous year-long shoot in Ireland on Kubrick's *Barry Lyndon* would have crushed a lesser man; the production saw several key personnel, including production designer Ken Adam, walk off citing the director's perfection-ism. Tomblin would work on many of the big American productions shooting in the UK during the next few decades, including all three Indiana Jones films. He would garner a place in the *Guinness World Records* for controlling the largest number of extras in a film.

Morton later worked with him on *The Empire Strikes Back* in 1980 (he played Dak, Luke Skywalker's back-seater in the Battle of Hoth). "Dave gave back. An unaffected man, he was absolutely secure in him-self and who he was. Taking from his career the understanding that great filmmaking is a collaborative art, he had a bottom-up view of how one got things done. Often, I witnessed how he maintained mo-rale on the set by ensuring that all hands appreciated how everyone contributes, right down to the tea lady. Not that he suffered fools—far from it—but Dave took the attitude that if you did your job without complaint, with the right attention and professionalism, he wanted you on his team. And moreover, he would look after you."[83]

Tomblin was also a skilled director in his own right. He worked on several high-end TV series made in the UK with the influx of Amer-ican money keen to tap into the zeitgeist of the "Swinging Sixties." These included *The Avengers* and *Danger Man*, and another acknowl-edged cult classic, *The Prisoner*. He formed a professional partner-ship named Everyman Films Ltd. with actor Patrick McGoohan. As co-creator of the series, he regularly changed hats as producer, director, and writer over the 17 episodes, which were filmed at Portmeirion, Wales. The often-innovative filming and complicated special effects the series required added to his experience portfolio, which paid divi-dends on later big-budget films.

Working with the First are the Second and the Third. Steve Lan-ning was Tomblin's right-hand man on *Bridge*, and his responsibilities as the Second were many and varied. "The second assistant was the oil that kept the engine running," explained Lanning. "He's the gap between David on the floor and the office. I did all the call sheets based on conversations with David. It's all logistics. You have to work out how long it takes to get from A to B? How long does it take to get them ready? Who travels with who? Who has a longer make-up? How many crowd? What time does the crowd need to be there? Do you feed them? Etc."

At 27, Lanning, who had started off as a runner, was a key member of a select team. "*Bridge* was big on every scale. We didn't have a lot of ADs. In the end it was Dave, Peter Waller, myself, and Roy Button, and we had another third assistant for a little while [Geoffrey Ryan, son of Cornelius]. But we were a very lean and mean. Then, we were the A-Team."[84]

Roy Button was one of the Thirds. He also had started as a runner at MGM in Borehamwood in 1969. "You had to fight your way through to get an ACTT ticket to get into the union, and then I became a Third. So I did Third, Second, First, production manager, location manager, producer, executive producer and then ended up running Warner Bros. for 29 years. But *ABTF* was really special. My day involved everything from planning, scheduling, location finding, crowd dressing, crowd rehearsing, issuing weapons, getting planes to fly over. A massive amount of prep, which was fantastic. I just lapped it up."

To photograph the film, Dickie chose from a small and select group of British cinematographers who were respected worldwide. Geoffrey Unsworth had entered the industry with Gaumont-British at Denham soon after the introduction of sound as the proverbial tea boy in 1932. Six years later, he joined the UK operation of the then technical marvel Technicolor. He learnt his trade by assisting the brilliant young cinematographer Jack Cardiff. Encouraged by maverick director Michael Powell, Cardiff perhaps did more than any other cinematographer to push the boundaries of the complex three-strip colour process in a series of masterpieces starting with *The Life and Death of Colonel Blimp* (1943). In the 1950s Unsworth rose to become a cameraman for the Rank Organisation on films such as *A Town Like Alice* (1956) and *Hell Drivers* (1957).

A quiet, diffident man, Unsworth hit the high note of his career in the 1970s with *Cabaret* (1972), *Alice's Adventures in Wonderland* (1973), *Murder on the Orient Express* (1974), and *Bridge*, before going on to *Superman: The Movie* (1978) and *Tess* (1979). "He was old school," recalled Roy Button. "He started at Denham. In those very early days, it was so regimented in the studio. The cameraman chose the dress—if you are on location, you can either wear normal stuff, or shorts. The cameraman would tell you what to wear! Peter Mac was the guiding light with Geoff."[85]

Twenty years Unsworth's junior, Peter MacDonald, was by his own admission a "bit rough around the edges," with a short temper. "I'm almost totally uneducated, as most people were in those days. At 15, I'd left school, and my uncle wanted me to be an apprentice printer; that was the last thing in the world I wanted to be—as I couldn't spell!" Nevertheless, he landed a job in Fleet Street "working with miserable arsed-holed Australians." He saw an advert for a clapper boy in a film studio ramping up to make commercials for the new ITV channel. During the job interview, MacDonald later admitted, "I lied totally about my love of film. I didn't even have a box brownie!" He got the job, and it proved to be a revelation. "To me it was like magic. It sounds silly, but as I walked through the doors of that studio, all the lights were on and I saw the camera crew. I thought, *this is it*—I loved it."

He soon moved to the Walton studios, which were busy making popular TV series like *Robin Hood*, *Lancelot*, and *The Buccaneer*. Many of these were written by Americans using false names, having been blacklisted by the McCarthy witch hunts. "The first bit of really good luck was I got a call to work on the *Titanic* film, *A Night to Remember*, at Pinewood Studios for night work," said MacDonald. "Geoffrey Unsworth was the DP, and Johnny Alcock was his camera assistant. And I became their clapper boy."

When their employer, Rank, shed hundreds of jobs, the team went freelance and MacDonald would work under Unsworth, whom he considered a father figure, for the next three decades.

But not everyone appreciated Unsworth's talent. "You know what the director wants, and you try to make it all moody and dark, and then the producer doesn't like it," said MacDonald. In 1964, a vast set had been constructed of Canterbury Cathedral for *Becket*, produced by Hal. B Wallis, who had produced *Casablanca* (1942) and several Elvis Presley musicals in a lengthy career of accomplishment. "And Wallis said: 'I paid 30 fucking thousand dollars. I want to see it, Unsworth. Do it again—lighter!' because Geoff had made it look so beautiful with candlelight. And this guy wanted a bright musical look to it. So, you've got to get that balance. You have to make the money happy—or you leave the film, but also try to keep your own integrity, which Geoff did wonderfully."

Although still a clapper boy, "I knew I wanted to be a camera operator," said MacDonald. "I'd watched very carefully the setups. I would try to anticipate what lenses were needed." His break came in 1967 on the Shirley MacLaine comedy *The Bliss of Mrs. Blossom*, which also featured Dickie. Needing a second camera operator, Unsworth and director Joseph McGrath both thought MacDonald would be an ideal choice. Given a zoom lens, he received orders to follow Shirley MacLaine, "very tough, bright lady—loved her," in closeup walking around the set. Next day, when viewing rushes, the star stood up and said: "Who the fuck shot that?" MacDonald vividly recalled his dread. "I sat thinking, *this is the end of my career.* 'I had no idea you were shooting it,' she said. When I asked if it was okay, she said I was a sniper. It gave me great confidence." When camera assistant John Alcott left the team for Kubrick's *2001*, MacDonald became a full-time operator. "It changed my life and allowed me into the elite."[86]

Steve Lanning worked with the pair on several films. "Peter Mac was a force of nature. He was without doubt the best camera operator in the business. And he had a relationship with Geoffrey Unsworth that was unique. Geoffrey let him shape the shot, and Peter knew what would work for Geoffrey's lighting. In the American system, then and now, the cameraman picks the setup and the operator points where the cameraman wants him to. All the great cameramen of England had great operators."[87] (Traditionally, in Britain, the cameraman was known as lighting cameraman, to better distinguish the role. The grander American term director of photography, or DP, has since become the universal designation.)

After several films, including the underrated British epic *Cromwell* (1970), the pair would earn one of nine Oscars given to *Cabaret* in 1972. Set in Germany in the 1930s, Bob Fosse's film starring Liza Minnelli is not just a brilliant musical but a terrific portrait of a society falling into the abyss. While MacDonald and Fosse designed the shots, Unsworth created the heavy diffusion look. "There were always two filters in front of a lens, [of] which Geoff was a master," said Peter MacDonald. "Some cameramen's nerves went when they were asked to do that type of thing, but Geoff knew how far he could push things." The film's producers were less enamoured by the look and decided to seize the offending box of filters. "We'd been warned by the German production secretary what they're up to. So, we were five minutes ahead of time. John Campbell, my assistant, got a separate box and filled it full of crap. At last, they came and demanded we hand over the box. We did, and Geoff went ashen, and I said to him, 'Don't worry, we have the real box.' So, the following day at rushes, the producer is sitting there next to Bob Fosse. And he said this is 10 times better without those fucking filters. They never knew that we still carried on using them. It also showed Geoff's courage as they threatened to sack him. *Cabaret* had a filter on every shot. In my opinion, it's one of the most beautifully photographed films ever. It's the trademark of Geoff's 1970s films; that use of diffusion was very distinctive."

For many of the crew, *Bridge* was a career-changing assignment. Little did one young man in particular know he would discuss his love life with one of Hollywood's top stars. Zelda Barron was already a respected continuity lady and later a director. Her son Steve planned to follow her into the fickle and competitive industry, but despite her contacts, there would be no leg up for Steve Barron. If the lad wanted a job, he would have to find his own way: "It was 1971, I left school at 15, and I got a tea boy job, at 12 pounds a week, with Samuelson's camera hire firm company in Cricklewood, London. That job was all about cleaning lenses and cameras and getting them ready for big productions."

In preparation for an upcoming shoot in Rome, Unsworth and MacDonald went to Samuelson's to choose the kit to hire. "We had a meeting with Sydney Samuelson in his office, and it overlooks the floor where all the equipment was. We're talking, and outside the window I can see this young boy running backwards and forwards with equipment on his back loading trucks. And I said to Sidney that he never stops running, and he said, 'Oh, he's always like that.'"[88]

"I spent most of the week running and getting the lenses to show them," recalled Barron, who was then 18. "When they left on the Friday, I remember Peter saying to me, 'Can you get a union ticket?'" To progress in the film/TV industry, this would allow you to get other jobs, and was highly prized. "He said to see if I could by April. I didn't know what he was talking about."[89]

MacDonald: "So I got Steve aside, and I said, 'If I offered you a clapper boy job, would you take it?' He said: 'What?' He was, like, knocked out."[90]

Barron went home to tell his mother and ask what he should do. "Pray that he keeps living!" she exclaimed. "That'd be the greatest break of your life."[91]

MacDonald: "Sure enough, we came back from Rome and employed Steve and Eamonn O'Keeffe as our two clapper boys."[92]

In early April 1976 Falmouth Harbour, which had been one of the many launching points for D-Day, once again shook to the rumble of tank tracks. Charlie Mann had arrived with 103 vintage vehicles from his museum at Lamanva. It was Falmouth dock master Captain Jim Skelley's job to oversee the laborious operation of loading the movie's entire motorised cast safely onto Sea Link's *Cambridge Ferry*, ready for the choppy voyage to Zeebrugge. Meanwhile, another boat loaded with a lethal cargo of 12 tonnes of ammunition, explosives, and pyro-technics left the ICI factory in Scotland for Holland.

Finally, all the months of planning were over, but success lay in the lap of the gods. While movies can go over budget for several reasons, not least star temperaments, often the primary culprit is the elements. While Hollywood held its place as the movie-making capital in the world for several reasons, prime among them was almost continual sunshine. Conversely, the unpredictable weather of Northern Europe has often caused producers many a headache. In 1960 the first attempt to make *Cleopatra* at London's Pinewood Studios was largely scup-pered by the drizzly grey skies that hung ominously over the immense sets of Ancient Rome and Alexandria.[93] In 1968 John Palmer and the *Battle of Britain* crew found the dismal British weather grounding their air fleet for weeks, driving the budget into nightmarish levels.[94] *A Bridge Too Far* could not absorb many delays—Levine's premiere date was carved in stone. Thankfully, freak conditions were to lend a helping hand.

The European summer of 1976 would be one of the century's hot-test. It was caused by a large high-pressure area that moved in mid-May and didn't shift until the end of August. The British Met Office considered the continuous 16-week dry spell the longest since 1727. Most of Western Europe was bathed in an average of 14 hours of sunshine per day. The heat, which would lead to drought conditions, was rarely less than 32°C (89.6°F). While the heat led to a 20 percent increase in what were euphemistically dubbed "excess deaths," it also saw a dramatic increase of ladybirds, 23 billion of them. Ever since, that balmy summer has been used as a meteorological benchmark.

By April 1976, almost everything was ready to go. Set construc-tion was on schedule to be ready for the cameras at the month's end. Joe Levine was rolling the dice on his biggest gamble, with a budget that was edging towards $25 million and likely to rise higher. Wearing his thick black glasses, he was affable and relaxed. "Joe was absolutely in awe of what was going on," recalled Roy Button. "He couldn't believe how many people it needed."[95]

Steve Lanning recalled Levine shaking his head at the daily food bill. "One of Levine's complaints was why he's feeding so many people," said Lanning. "So, add the unit, which was probably 150, and construction was 150. And I think it's the only thing that pissed him off. It's quite funny, he didn't mind spending 25 million on everything else. But he hated spending on 300 breakfasts!"[96]

The production was a popular subject for local Dutch TV, and prior to filming, one reporter asked Dickie if ". . . this film project will be fairly expensive?" Dickie, looking relaxed and still with the trace of a once youthful cherubic face, laughed heartily, "That's one of the nicest understatements."[97]

Stuart Craig, who worked with Dickie several times, was unequivocal about Attenborough's qualities as a filmmaker. "Quite untypical of British directors, I think Richard Attenborough always had a sense of scale and was never intimidated by size and spectacle. And that was one of his great qualities, and I don't think he had to learn it. He just inherently had it. I'm sure he had his private worries and panics. But he was always more than man enough to take on the scale of that."[98]

6

"The Party's On"
Filming Begins

Monday, 26 April 1976, was a bright, clear spring morning. As the sun rose, heralding a warm day, the narrow streets of old Deventer stepped back in time to 1944. This first day of production for *A Bridge Too Far* proved an appropriately busy logistical one. A local man picked up his black-and-white video camera and filmed almost 30 minutes of behind-the-scenes action that day.[99]

To the uninitiated spectators, the scene looked like chaos with ragged lines of German troops and civilians in rumpled '40s clothing interspersed with men and women clad in T-shirts and long hair, amid an assortment of trucks and vans, surrounded by tall batteries of lights and miles of snaking cables. Shrill amplified commands from megaphones echoed around the cobbled square, followed by disparate groups quickly coalescing into prearranged positions. Watching all this activity were a grinning Joe Levine and his wife, Rosalie, perched on two canvas chairs. Levine, who boasted he had never looked through a camera viewfinder for over 40 years, was enjoying his new toy. But the glacial pace of filmmaking soon prompted him to retreat to New York to sate his craving for wheeling and dealing. Shortly after nine o'clock, a single word rapped out: "Action!"

The location was 48 Rijkmanstraat, a three-storey house in a narrow side street next to a cobbled square, just a few hundred yards from the Wilhelmina bridge. Three days had been scheduled to film several scenes of a fictional Dutch family watching what they hoped would be the end of their war. Goldman constructed an Arnhem family unit that would stand in for the Dutch population. The central character is a teenager described by Goldman as *"kid with glasses."* In a sad indictment of war, the boy enthusiastically embraces the struggle. *"I was 12 when they got here,"* he exclaims.

Born in 1961, the "kid," Erik van 't Wout of Haarlem, was a rising star thanks to the children's TV series *Q & Q*, whose story involved two children taking it upon themselves to track down criminals when neither their parents nor the police believe them. The first series aired on *Katholieke Radio Omroep* (KRO) in 1974, and two years later a shortened version released in Dutch cinemas followed. In the 1980s, van 't Wout would go behind the cameras in a variety of technical roles before establishing himself as a TV director. Still working in 2022, he has directed episodes of many Dutch TV series, including *Baantjer*, *Spangen*, and *Dokter Deen*.

The father, played by Siem Vroom, is the local Resistance leader, and his wife was played by Marlies van Alcmaer. Both were well-known faces on Dutch TV. Vroom had won Holland's top acting award, the Louis d'Or, in 1974 and again in 1985, tragically the same year he died at just 54. Alcmaer would go on to star in the popular *Dallas*-style Dutch series, *Westenwind*, between 1999 and 2003.

These Resistance characters allowed viewers to see the heartbreak—and courage—of the Dutch people hopeful that the German retreat is permanent. When Marlies van Alcmaer as the mother asks, *"Then the war is over?"* Siem Vroom's face brims with an ecstatic smile before he defines the sound in the street: *"Panic."*

The day depicted, 5 September 1944, would go down in Dutch history as *Dolle Dinsdag* or "Mad Tuesday." The German army that had fought for months to hold the Allies in Normandy was now streaming back in disorder. This day was the high-water mark of the German army's rout. While the battered formations retreated to the Fatherland, they were joined by collaborators terrified of reprisals. The film depicts this in a suitably epic dishevelled, chaotic column traipsing along both sides of a canal.

The first day's filming would depict the moment the German's retreat faltered, watched by Erik van 't Wout's "kid" sitting in the top-floor window of 48 Rijkmanstraat. Peter MacDonald's camera-operating talent is evident in this sequence. The scene begins with a cafe waitress (Josephine Peeper) appearing carrying beers. In one move, the camera follows her, handing the drinks to a group of rowdy locals. They are watched by an envious German soldier, who has paused his retreat. The camera then continues to track before the lens zooms up towards the open window where the kid is watching. "I always mixed the zoom in with camera moves," MacDonald explained. "So, you have a left-to-right move when you slowly go from a 24 to 50 to 75 mm married into the move. I'd have one extra assistant who only did the zoom. They did not do silly moves; they understood how to make it flow. You could always move the camera on the dolly, the crane, or handheld, but the zoom was an extra dimension that I grabbed with both hands. I loved it." The gratuitous crash zoom shots, which had been a mainstay of 1960s cinematography had become passé by the mid-'70s, and MacDonald's subtle use of it has since become the norm.

Van 't Wout vividly recalls his first taste of multimillion-dollar filmmaking. "Earlier at breakfast, I had looked at the call sheet, and I wondered why there would be 200 extras on the set for that scene. Somehow it didn't dawn on me that the activity of all those extras down there on the street had anything to do with our small scene on the third floor." Although the camera is inside the room, simple trickery shows that the boy is watching the German troops below. The windowpane with the black shutter behind is angled to catch the reflection of the activity in the square. "I thought they were practising some other scene. Anyway, I made some mistakes, and we had to redo the shot. After a while, I noticed the lights on our little set upstairs were suddenly switched off, and the crew one by one left the set. Suddenly, there was Sir Richard. He sat down and started some small-talk conversation with me: 'How's school?' and 'Tell me about that TV series you are doing this year.' It was very pleasant, and Sir Richard was very charming. So, I relaxed somewhat, and all of a sudden, the crew was back on the set, and the lights were switched on. Immediately, the camera was rolling, and we did another take in which I finally didn't mess up. Later, I realised that those extras had to go back to their first positions every time we needed an extra take up there on the set. Thank God, I didn't know that during the shoot. It would have made me a lot more nervous."[100]

This being one of many days requiring extras, it was the job of Paul Kamphuis to recruit and organise them. "I was allowed to make a call for extras on TV's *Ted de Braak*, and on the following days I received thousands of applications with mail bags full. We were mainly looking for young men who could pass for soldiers. But there was also a need for the elderly, children, babies, and even the disabled. We had 3,200 people in the card catalogue at the end."[101] They were very well paid for their trouble: 68 guilders for 10 hours of work, and a tenner every hour after that.

Many of them that day were issued weapons. Assistant director Steve Lanning recalled the strictly enforced rules regarding firearms. "Every day, you would have 500 people picked out, dressed, and then shipped to the location. They were issued a gun, which they had to sign for (even though some weren't functional). And that process was reversed at the end of filming. So, the days were colossal."[102]

"Even before dawn, restless sleepers woke and lights came on behind shuttered windows."[103] These opening lines in Ryan's book also formed the first page of Goldman's screenplay. He described the effect of the German retreat on the Dutch family's darkened room *"as if somehow, some giant was jiggling the place,"* causing chandeliers to shake. The first image seen in the film is a backlit blind, which immediately sets the tone for a very different war movie.

Filmed on day two, the shot typifies the director of photography

Geoffrey Unsworth's artistry and visual approach. "The Art Department had bought these window blinds of the type you pull down. I had them made in the natural biscuit colour because we shall be treating the film, in the early stages, with not exactly sepia, but a very desaturated colour effect. The lighting is very subdued, and it looks like it's just coming through these shaded windows. It has a very interesting character."

Unsworth's old friend Herb Lightman considered the DP "a delightful bloke to know." Lightman was the widely respected editor of the trade journal *American Cinematographer*. He had been invited to Holland to cover the filming for an in-depth article in the April 1977 edition. He described Unsworth as "the quintessential gentleman cinematographer and blessed with a sly and dry sense of humour . . . one of the acknowledged great artists of the camera." During the long pre-production, Unsworth had spent his time in Holland's many museums. He was drawn to the Dutch Golden Age paintings of the seventeenth century, its notable figures including Rembrandt, Vermeer, and Steen. The Calvinist Dutch largely ignored the then-prevalent religious themes and instead focused on everyday life, with a degree of naturalism that echoes much later documentary photography. Unsworth considered that "they had a wonderful knowledge of light and shade." The cameraman was particularly drawn to a prolific if lesser-known landscape artist of the era. "I'm very fond of the work of a Dutch painter named Jan van Goyen, and I've followed him for years. He has really captured the quality of this light. I think he has it right down to a T."

While the shoot would be blessed with unseasonably good, sunny weather, this light posed a challenge for Unsworth, best represented by an early shot of Resistance leader Siem Vroom talking with the kid in their dingy attic. As he smiles proudly at his son in closeup, behind his shoulder, the fateful bridge is visible through a rear window. Both are perfectly exposed. Most audience members would never register this as any kind of feat, but to any photographer, these extremes in light levels are immediately obvious. To achieve this kind of image effortlessly required great skill from Unsworth. "I've had to go along with a daylight balance—building up the interior light to balance with the exterior light. Sometimes this has been difficult to do, because our interior shooting has seemed to coincide with the days when the light outside was very hot."[104]

Siem Vroom's warm and fatherly smile in this early scene contrasts with an extraordinary piece of acting much later as war engulfs the fictional family.

Goldman's use of the kid is inspired. His seeming innocence allows him to go cycling out of Arnhem and through the leafy suburb of Oosterbeek. When stopped outside the Hartenstein Hotel by a German MP (Hartmut Becker), the teenager's whining wish to see his girlfriend down the road convinces the guard to allow the boy to pass. An adult character, even perhaps an attractive woman, may have aroused suspicions. In his screenplay, Goldman humanised all the warring parties and made the German MP, perhaps not much older than the kid, empathetic. Next, the kid rides across the heath and is surprised by a Spitfire on a recce mission.

For the scene, renowned British aerobatic and display pilot Neil Williams flies Spitfire F Mk IX (MH434). Dickie was keen to make it as real for young Erik as he could. "Sir Richard took great care that this shot was not rehearsed. "When I was there with the bicycle, I had no idea what we were going to do. Only the most necessary instructions were given to me (you start here—and on 'Action,' you go there).

"So, when the cameras were rolling, and I heard 'Action,' I just started to ride," said Erik van 't Wout. "Then I heard a sound, becoming louder and louder. And the Spitfire flew right over me, really low. My reaction was completely natural and truthful to the situation: it scared the hell out of me. I believe that shot was done in one take (with multiple cameras)."[105] It was a poignant scene to shoot for Peter MacDonald, who photographed it with a very long lens. "Watching the Spitfire below the level of the road come up from behind like a helicopter would now—it was just amazing flying. They were just saying *We're coming*, which must have given people a lot of hope and faith that they will be saved."

The flat landscape of the Netherlands, which leant itself to the wide anamorphic Panavision frame, inspired Geoffrey Unsworth's cinematography. "I think there is probably more sky in Holland than anywhere else in the world . . . there is this fantastic light, which may be related in some way to the amount of water there is about the country. Everything is desaturated: you don't get harsh colours. Nothing sticks out in vivid colour; it's all very subdued. There's a natural diffusion. This is what I've based the look of the film on. In fact, I've added to it a little more by using certain fog filters."[106]

The Dutch Resistance family appears much later in the film in one of its most harrowing and moving scenes. The battle for Arnhem bridge is almost lost, and civilians are creating makeshift barricades out of corpses. Alan Tomkins, a member of the Art Department, designed the human roadblock for the sequence. On first reading the script's description, he found it "totally unbelievable."

A HUMAN ROADBLOCK THE DUTCH are building. It is made up of anything that can be piled in the street, including, even, the bodies of dead Dutch civilians. It's six feet high and it blocks the street the armored car is soon to try to pass. All kinds of Dutch are doing this, ignoring the firing, scurrying across, building the roadblock.

Dickie, at pains to be truthful, assured Arnhem veteran Kate ter Horst, that they had restaged "virtually the terms that you have described it, rather than those which appeared in the script. Coincidentally, on the day that we were shooting this particular scene, the burgomaster of Deventer was watching our work, and he remarked that he was involved in an incident almost identical to that which we were portraying."[107]

"They actually did that," Tomkins noted. "So, for me, it was very upsetting and I think the way it was portrayed in the film was very moving."[108] Of particular note in this scene is Siem Vroom's heartrending performance on seeing his son's lifeless body. The look of unimaginable grief is hard to watch. It contrasts with his warm fatherly pride beaming across his face in the earlier attic scene. Siem Vroom's role as a Resistance father is small, but thanks to his skill and some highly articulate direction from Dickie, Vroom encapsulates the utter horror of this and every other war. MacDonald's camera runs on tracks across the bloody human shield and zooms into the faceless tank, which spits out cold, brutal death. The shot is beautiful, if ghastly, and starkly shows the mercilessness of war.[109]

Filming scenes in Deventer inevitably brought back unpleasant memories for the older generation. Steve Lanning, whose job it was to marshal extras, observed the effect of particular uniforms. "The Dutch of a certain age group could not bear seeing Germans in uniform on their streets. We were always getting complaints like 'Do you have to film here?'" Stuntman Vic Armstrong also noticed the emotion when he and his team went to a local cafe. "I noticed a little old man staring at us with mounting fury. I then realised we were all dressed as SS officers, and it was obviously invoking terrible memories. If he'd had a gun, he'd have shot us all. That also made us think about what the local Dutch people must have gone through."[110] This antipathy also led to a problem in finding suitable-looking Aryan soldiers—a headache for Lanning. "We were always trying to find decent faces and haircuts for the older German soldiers. Because it was a very specific look, and not a lot of Dutch of that age wanted to get into German uniform."

Successfully recruiting one Dutch local to play a general had a most unfortunate outcome. "We had an important scene with German High Command, and I took a lot of time picking people," said Lanning. "And one came in. He was perfect, but mouthy. He did two days' filming, and on the third day, he didn't arrive. It turned out on the second day he was talking about how wonderful it was to be wearing the uniform of the Third Reich again, and it was published in the local Deventer newspaper, and the guy disappeared that day, and wasn't seen ever again. And I remember talking with locals and they said he's in the river."[111]

This story is confirmed by Jane Hershey, an American film student who had landed a summer holiday job in the film's publicity office. "A small part in the script called for an actor who looked the very image of a Gestapo officer. The casting division thought that it would be a nice touch to offer the part (which involved no speaking) to one of the locals in Deventer. An appropriate face was found, and the man had no objections to playing the part of a Nazi. All went well with the scene, but later, one of the British gossip papers interviewed this Dutchman who had to wear his enemy's clothes. It turned out the man was a Dutch Nazi who confessed quite freely that he still thought Hitler was OK, and that he enjoyed his little role." An embarrassed Miriam Brickman, the film's casting chief, admitted, "You can't check everyone; he seemed right for the part."[112] A local Dutch newspaper identified the man with the headline, "Ex SS Man C.G. Mulder Lets the Past Live in a Film Role," next to a photo of a benign-looking old man with a full head of grey hair.

The scenes in which the mysterious C.G. Mulder had appeared revolved around the appointment of a new German commander. The collapse of the Western Front had forced the Führer to reappoint Field Marshal General Gerd von Rundstedt, a gifted strategist with little time for Hitler and his regime. He was played by the distinguished German actor Wolfgang Preiss. Von Rundstedt's entrance to the impressive town hall in Zutphen, while maybe not a cliché, represented a war movie trope. Played over a stirring martial theme, the grand entrance of the German High Command often involves a cavalcade of cars covered in pennants led by motorcyclists, which leads to a succession of resounding thumping metalled footsteps, interspersed with heel clicks, and *Sieg Heil* salutes. The trope was effortlessly and no less effectively transposed to space, with the arrival of Darth Vadar and the Empire in the *Star Wars* movies.

Despite being a septuagenarian, the field marshal seized his new job with energy and drive. Preiss perfectly encapsulates the outward confidence but also pragmatism of a soldier who has no belief in victory but who will do his level best. For the audience to understand the German army's woes, Goldman gave the job of describing the pitiful condition of the forces to a subordinate, who pointedly cuts in to say, *"Morale—non-existent,"* as von Rundstedt arrives in his new office. The commander notices how upbeat his officers are, confident that he will bring victory. *"I am still young,"* the elderly soldier jokes. Preiss undercuts the joviality with a steely resolve *"to turn this rabble into an army."*

The 66-year-old Preiss was born in Nuremberg, the son of a well-known actor. With greasepaint in his blood, he studied theatre sciences alternately with dance training combined with philosophy. Making his stage debut in 1932 in Munich just as Hitler came to power, he quickly established himself, appearing in many theatres in Germany during the decade. When war came, he received an exemption from military service and made his film debut with *The Great Love/Die grosse Liebe* (1942) starring Zarah Leander, the Third Reich's top box-office draw. After the war, Preiss returned briefly to the theatre, but soon found his melodious voice in high demand dubbing foreign films into German.

In 1954, his career would take a new direction and make him one of the most recognisable of European character actors for the next three decades. He was cast as the heroic Claus von Stauffenberg, in Falk Harnack's dramatisation of *The Plot to Assassinate Hitler*. His performance earned wide praise, cemented with the 1956 Federal Film Award. An aristocratic air of command, undercut with charm and sensitivity, made him ideal for casting as sympathetic German officer characters. There are few war films of the 1960s in which he didn't appear and always in nuanced performances. Notable ones include *The Longest Day*, *The Cardinal* (1963), *The Train* (1964), *Von Ryan's Express* (1965), *Is Paris Burning?*, and he played the Desert Fox with a touch of class in *Raid on Rommel* (1971).

Unlike most Allied commanders except for Patton, the Germans dressed their officers in colourful and impressive uniforms edged with scarlet and gilt. It seems, despite the pre-eminence of Preiss as a European actor, he was not recognised by some on *Bridge* with resulting embarrassment. Steve Lanning directed actors to the costume department upon their arrival on the set. "The wardrobe guy, Johnny Hilling, was very basic. Whether they were an actor or crowd person, he treated them the same way. It was, you know: Get over there, drop your trousers . . . And one day he was waiting for Wolfgang Preiss. And then I got a phone call from John Hilling, saying this guy is nothing like you told me. And it turned out that the chauffeur had said to Jonny: 'I have Mister Preiss in the car.' And John told the guy to drop his trousers and insisted on getting him into the uniform."[113] According to third assistant director Roy Button: "He was the East German agricultural minister! Wouldn't you think he would have said something? He's got in a car driven all the way to Deventer, got fitted as a Nazi general, before he tells us! So, we apologised profusely and sent him back to Amsterdam."[114] Lanning added, "But because it's John Hilling, no one said anything because he's dressing 1,000 people a day."

Without a doubt, Hilling's busiest day was one Sunday, where the people of Deventer celebrated the arrival of the Allies.[115] The town doubled for Eindhoven, the first major centre to be liberated by XXX Corps. Unfortunately, the euphoria of the locals hampered the drive to Arnhem.

"It was the only time we had a big civilian crowd," recalled Steve Lanning. "When you gear up for soldiers, it's easy. As long as they're in the correct uniform with the correct gun, they're gonna look right. We had about a crowd of 1,200, who had to mix and celebrate. We put together something like 25–30 hair and make-up people. It was the biggest hair and make-up job I've ever done in my life. Because normally you don't dress crowds. And if you do, it's the first 20, and the rest you let them alone. But we never knew where the filming was gonna be."

Dickie had originally conceived the scene to be encompassed in one continuous crane shot, presumably taking in the immense crowd, before swooping down to find Elliott Gould as Colonel Stout fighting through the crowd towards Michael Caine, as J.O.E. Vandeleur in his tank. Peter MacDonald persuaded the director it would be more effective to use a variety of angles, including up-close-and-personal hand-held shots. "And I argued with him saying, 'Well, that's a nice shot, but there's no immediacy there; you're not in amongst it.' And that was what's wonderful about Attenborough, because he trusted us. Many people's ego wouldn't even allow them to go there. But Dickie was kind of big enough to say, 'That's a better idea, we'll go for that.'" But the change of plan required summoning many more crew members to man the multi-camera set. "We had about five irate camera crews who had been phoned up Sunday morning at about eight o'clock, and most of them weren't feeling too good after Saturday night out!"

Noteworthy about this sequence is the attention to detail with the female costumes. A bugbear for this author with many war films of the 1950s and '60s is while the uniforms are often correct, women are invariably dressed in the height of post-war fashion. Perhaps only in the 1970s was there a serious attempt to be authentic. Certainly, in *Bridge*, the women are all made up with the shoulder-length hair cut, a fashion popularised by Hollywood pin-ups Betty Grable and Lana Turner. Also, the simple dresses reflect the period and four years of austerity under German occupation. This fastidiousness became important, as cameras would cover the scene from all angles.

"It's why that one scene was pretty unique," explained Lanning. "There's a gigantic amount of happy people celebrating. You can only go close on them because they're in the right costume, hair, and make-up."[116] Peter MacDonald swung a lightweight Arriflex onto his shoulder and got amongst the jubilant throng. "I think it has a great feel to it. It's the immediacy of a wide-angle lens in amongst the crowd that makes you feel you are there, and free."[117]

That Sunday would be the only time the good people of Deventer would feature *en masse* on camera. But despite some minor disruptions, the city enjoyed a welcome boom with Joe Levine's cash—as much as $5 million injected into the local economy. Ranging from the direct fees paid to the town, both municipal and private, for hire or rent of locations and facilities such as fire appliances, police and ambulance services for the 150-strong unit strewn across hotels, lodging rooms, suburban houses, and caravan parks.

While Phil Hobbs' catering copiously fed the unit, the long, hot summer caused many parched throats after a long days' filming. The sale of cold beer at the many bars and restaurants went through the roof thanks to the generous per diem. The influx of so many thirsty Brits quickly persuaded local hostelries to get the UK's standard pint tankards in place of the usual Continental, mug-size glasses.

A local taxi firm, Ritmans, was virtually taken over for the run to Schiphol Airport in Amsterdam, ferrying actors great and small in a fleet of Mercedes. A regular dash involved the all-important exposed film to be flown to Technicolor's lab near London for processing, and the printed rushes returned for viewing the following day.

7

"You Wouldn't Really Have Killed Me, Would You?"
James Caan

On Wednesday, 28 April 1976, the first of the 14 big stars stepped up for his scenes. James Caan was cast as veteran Staff Sergeant Charles Dohun of the U.S. 101st Airborne, 502 Regiment. Caan was one of the anti-hero actors who broke through in the cynical 1970s, described as an "unreconstructed action hero both onscreen and off."[118] He said he chose his roles carefully, and with the stream of tough guys he portrayed, it's easy, if unfair, to conflate the two personas.

Born in the Bronx in 1940 to German Jewish immigrants, Caan and his siblings grew up amid the rough streets of Queens, New York, where he learned to look after himself from a young age and projected a don't-mess-with-me facade. He was known as "Killer Caan" by the tender age of 11, and his right hand sported a home-made gang tattoo. "It wasn't tough as such, but it could be scary getting your ass kicked out into the schoolyard with 100 other kids and learning how to win and lose. It's the stuff of life."

But he masked his intelligence and academic ability at passing exams with quick-fire wisecracks that would break up his classroom audience. "My neighbourhood was not conducive to the arts. But one thing I knew is that I wasn't going to be a butcher, and that's what was waiting for me at the end of the road."[119] At 16, rather than join his father's meat distribution business, Caan earned enough credits to graduate to Michigan State University. His passion as a freshman

81

was football, although it seems his energy was not matched by his talent. Sixteen years later, Duffy Daugherty, Michigan State's coach, told Caan, now a major a star, "I ought to get 10 percent of your career . . . because I told you to quit playing football."[120]

Enrolling at New York's Hofstra University led to the burgeoning of a new passion. "I always had the desire to act in me, but I wouldn't allow it to surface consciously until the time was right." A classmate was Francis Ford Coppola, who would play a pivotal part in the actor's career a few years later. Inspired by Brando—"anyone of my generation who doesn't tell you Brando was the man, they're lying"—Caan enrolled at New York City's Neighborhood Playhouse and was tutored by the highly respected Sanford Meisner.

With his income supplemented by pool winnings and Friday night poker sessions, small parts on the stage and theatre soon followed. In 1966 he co-starred with John Wayne and Robert Mitchum in Howard Hawks' *El Dorado*, but his big break would come five years later in the ABC-TV movie of the week, *Brian's Song*, playing doomed Chicago Bear Brian Piccolo, for which Caan earned an Emmy Award. At about that time, old college mate Coppola cast him as the incendiary Sonny in *The Godfather*. Surprisingly, Caan originally was slated for the role of Michael before good sense prevailed and Al Pacino stepped in. Caan's powerhouse performance as Sonny Corleone has often been seen as a reflection of the actor himself, something he strongly denied, although Caan's eldest son, Scott was adamant: "Basically, that was my dad up there. You know, he's got a temper, and he thinks he's Italian."[121] His Academy Award nomination for Best Supporting Actor marked the beginning of a decade as a major star.[122]

He had a singular approach to prepping his lines. "People laugh when I tell them that I read a script once and I'm through."[123] For *Bridge*, Goldman gave his *"terrific looking, leathery and hard"* Dohun character few lines and instead required Caan to embody a hard-bitten veteran who, for all his nonchalance, cares.

Caan, although he didn't play opposite any other stars, seems to have ruffled some feathers with the crew. "James Caan was a bit of a tartar at times," recalled Peter MacDonald. "He often came a bit late, after having a night out on the drink." Off the set, Caan was a practicing martial artist with a particular love of rodeo, an enthusiasm camera assistant Steve Barron felt he took too far. "There was a bit of a weird vibe from James Caan because I remember him practicing lassoing. And he kept lassoing the prop guy, who didn't feel like he wanted to be lassoed. But James kept on and on. I don't know whether that was all just great fun, or he just felt a bit mean."[124]

The Dohun sequence is the film's only completely self-contained section. Goldman very effectively telescopes this small vignette of war from Ryan's book. Dohun, in reality, was "almost dumb" with worry at the prospect of the upcoming battle. This he shared with his captain, 22-year-old Le Grand Johnson, who had dropped into Normandy during the chaotic landings before D-Day and now was resigned to his fate. Ryan picks up their story as the U.S. 101st are valiantly fighting oft-repeated German attempts to cut "Hell's Highway." During the ferocious fighting, Johnson was wounded in the arm, but on the way to the rear received a wound to his head. Arriving at the dressing station, the unconscious officer was dumped in the "dead pile." But convinced his commander was still alive, Dohun elected to drive him and four other casualties to another aid post near Son Bridge.

The film echoes this, and hints at the ferocious battle fought by the Americans, with Dohun looking for the stricken captain (called Glass). A grizzled sergeant (Peter Gordon), combat fatigue etched over his face, says he's dead. *"I didn't ask how he was, just where he is,"* says Caan's Dohun. The location was in Forestry Commission land and featured the pretty Sprengenberg Castle in the background. It was production designer Stuart Craig's job to recreate the shelled wood where Dohun goes in search of his captain. "It was a woodland landscape which was already decimated for tree management. And we could dig shallow holes, and wrap tree stumps with explosive, and make shattered ends, and so on."[125] The set also featured an all-important atmospheric for a war movie—and a particular favourite tool of Unsworth. "Geoffrey loved using smoke to defuse," recalled Peter MacDonald. "Like most good cameramen, he would love things to be either backlit or three-quarters backlit. So, you get that magic look." The distinctive defused look of the film was augmented by the use of fog filters on the lens. It was estimated over 10,000 old rubber tyres were burned during the course of the film. "It would be totally illegal now," commented Macdonald. "We burned tyres all over Holland. I mean, it's a wonder Holland isn't a totally black country now."

The highlight of the Dohun sequence was the Jeep chase. In just a sentence, Ryan described how Dohun hid in the woods and waited for a German patrol to move before continuing. Goldman, in contrast, gives us an action-movie sequence with added suspense: full-throttle action as Dohun careers through the German hornet's nest, dodging trees, bullets, and tanks.

Several stuntmen led by Vic Armstrong and Alf Joint donned German uniforms to jump out of the way of the charging jeep, while Dicky Beer doubled as a lifeless Captain Glass and Romo Gorrara for Dohun. To achieve the speed and drama, the camera crew used a small Citroën car, renowned for its smooth suspension. Peter MacDonald found it an exhilarating experience. "You could just go through shit chasing it. This is before Steadicam, so you had to improvise." But filming at speed with a telephoto required all of MacDonald's skill. "When you're operating with a 1000-mm lens, you got to be very brave and go with it. You kind of obey an instinct. I was very lucky because it came quite naturally. Unlike other things in my life, I was never ever really nervous operating, as I loved it so much. It was always so exciting because you put 1000 mm on the Jeep with this guy going through the woods, a head and shoulders with all the trees going through foreground, and explosions in the background—it's really tremendous. I just love that feeling it gives of speed."

For closeups of Caan driving the jeep, MacDonald had to be strapped to the bonnet. "Funnily enough, I was never ever scared when

James Caan was driving. Although he was a wild man, he was a very good driver." For some point-of-view shots, Caan was replaced by stunt double Romo Gorrara, much to Peter MacDonald's discomfort. "It was only when I had the stunt guys drive that I got quite a few bruises and got thrown off the jeep a couple of times. You had to have the speed; it couldn't be leisurely. I remember saying to the stuntman, when I was shooting behind him: 'We're very close to that tree.' He said, 'What tree?' And I went, 'The tree we almost smashed into!' It was a bruising experience, but a good one."[126]

Escaping the Germans, Dohun arrives at a field hospital. The set, built on farmland near Averlose Houtweg, comprised a series of tents and duckboards designed by Terry Marsh to be filmed from any angle. "You just didn't do the bare necessity. You actually see the Jeep arrive, you see the wounded captain taken and the scene setting. The establishing shot is rich, detailed, authentic, muddy, and urgent. It's good stuff."[127]

The *"Tough Colonel"* was played by Canadian Arthur Hill, who had recently worked with Caan on *The Killer Elite* (1975). In 1963 Hill established his name on Broadway with a Tony Award for Best Dramatic Actor for his portrayal of George in the original Broadway production of *Who's Afraid of Virginia Woolf?* He had several supporting parts in *Harper* (1966), Richard Lester's *Petulia* (1968), and *The Chairman* (1969), and played the lead in Robert Wise's *The Andromeda Strain* (1971). But it was on the small screen that the taciturn Hill would best be remembered, most notably starring in *Owen Marshall, Counselor at Law* for three seasons between 1971–74.

When the tough colonel doctor refuses to even examine the wounded officer, Dohun pulls a gun—and insists. Goldman lifts almost verbatim the tense original conversation from the book but omits the detail that Dohun continued to train his .45 on the doctor during the operation. It was this confrontation that first attracted Caan to the role when he met Dickie during the LA casting raid: "He offered me the choice of several roles. I chose the sergeant chiefly for that one scene."[128] The sequence, which took three days to film, ends with Glass on the road to recovery, *"with one hell of a headache,"* and Dohun facing a court martial. He is put under arrest for just 10 seconds, and then released. The colonel's final thought is to ask whether Dohun would have actually shot him. Caan bows out of the film with a quizzical look.

Goldman bristled that many critics considered this section mere Hollywood "horse shit." In Ryan's account, Dohun's 10-second arrest was one minute at the hands of his commanding officer instead. And in a footnote, Ryan referenced his correspondence with the reticent Dohun, who said he couldn't answer whether he would have shot the doctor. Goldman telescopes all this. It's a perfect example of great dramatisation, which while not strictly following the letter, stays faithful to the spirit.

To allow for delays caused by rain, all movie shoots usually plan a contingency indoor scene. Every day for 10 days of James Caan's stint, "weather cover: INT.101 Dakota" was listed on the call sheets. Thanks to the bucolic summer of '76 there were no rain clouds, and so this tiny scene was pushed back to the very last hours of the star's schedule. A mock-up of a Dakota interior sitting on rockers to simulate flying is the setting for a brief shot of Caan, in full paratrooper garb, sitting patiently and stoically with eight other soldiers on their way to Holland. He has one line when a soldier asks him about what Goldman describes as *"the sound now that is reminiscent of rain on the wings,"* to which the laconic Dohan replies, *"Flak."* It only required four takes before Dickie called it a wrap and bid Caan a safe journey home.

It was the responsibility of young camera assistant Steve Barron to extract the exposed film from the camera magazine and put it into a light-tight can to send to the lab. All must be done in complete darkness. It was a Saturday, and he, like all the crew, was keen to get back to Deventer for a night out. Rather than finish his job at the location, to save time he elected to do the tricky canning on the road. "They'd built me a little darkroom inside the camera truck, and I had quite a lot of rolls of film to unload. I was also dying to get back to have a full Saturday night. So, I was unloading a 400-foot magazine in there, when suddenly, because we went over cobblestones, the top of the darkroom door opened. Just as I opened the magazine, a shaft of light came onto the film. It was one of those horrific moments when you're a clapper loader. I quickly slammed it shut. I was absolutely petrified. As soon as I got back to the hotel, I rang up Peter MacDonald."[129]

"You could say that he shouldn't be doing it on the move," said MacDonald, "but when he arrived, he'd aged about 20 years!" Mac-Donald, who had given the young man his break, appreciated the lad's honesty. "[He] could have said nothing. And no one would have known. It could have been fogged on a flight to England or in the lab. He explained he'd thrown himself on top of the film as the light came behind him."[130]

MacDonald asked Barron how tightly wound the film was, as this would prevent the light from penetrating. Barron recalled: "How long did the light land on it? I said, 'Well, for me it felt like forever, but it was probably just seconds.' And he said if it was tightly wound, it had a better chance."[131]

MacDonald reassured his protégé, "You're probably going to get away with this. But I said the most important thing is that you've been honest, because he thought he would be immediately sacked." Telling Barron to stay in his room, MacDonald had to phone Dickie and warn him it would be Tuesday before they got the lab report. "I said he'd better have a word with Caan that we needed to reshoot, and he wouldn't. I said, 'If it's screwed up, what are you going to do if James is back in America?'"[132]

Meanwhile, young Steve was sweating in his room and recalled, "The phone rang and it was Richard Attenborough. I had rarely talked to him. I'd given him cups of tea, and he always said thank you sweetly. Anyway, he's like: 'Steve, I don't want you to worry, darling. I'm going to get Jimmy back from Schiphol Airport.' So, I'm, 'Oh no! I've cost all this money, because they're gonna have to reshoot it.'"[133]

From here the two stories divide with MacDonald saying, "I went up to James Caan myself. I told him there's a problem. Well, he said that it would be silly to leave; he was totally understanding."[134] Barron recalls MacDonald phoning and saying that Caan had left on the flight. "He wasn't on the flight, but he was on the way to."

Whatever the exact truth, Caan had gone, with Barron not enjoying his weekend. "I was on tenterhooks. Finally, I hear from the cutting room that despite some mild edge fogging on the film, they could save it by blowing up the picture."[135] MacDonald, who would go on to be a cameraman on Steve Barron's early films, thought it was a salutary lesson for the young man. "I think it was a very good thing for him to experience. I'm sure once he started being a director on his own shows, if a young kid messed up, he'd be very calm with them. Mind you, Steve is always very calm, but it was a terrifying thing to happen."[136]

With Caan's departure, 13 more top names would arrive that Levine hoped would give the film the box-office clout it needed. The international media, eager for gossip, were convinced there would be ego and rivalries that would generate inches of copy. Years later, Dickie was pressed on whether he had any difficulties with his marquee toppers. Only one, he said, and would not be drawn as to the name.[137]

8
"There's a Lot of Money on That Lawn"
The Famous Fourteen Part 1

"What really scared me," Dickie confessed at the time, "was the logistics of the film. If they went wrong, I was in trouble." But his biggest headache was not any of the myriad of huge action sequences but getting four men into a room. "The schedule was for 23 weeks and in the middle of that I had a frightening 6-week period when some of the stars were finishing their roles, others were in the middle of theirs, and others were just about to start. Some, like Sean Connery, Dirk Bogarde, Ryan O'Neal, and Gene Hackman, all had to meet on one particular day. If we'd have lost that day for whatever reason, it would have been absolute chaos."[138]

Steve Lanning said, "The most important thing on *Bridge* was the coming and going of the stars. That's what conditioned the schedule. We had blocks we had to do. We did James Caan first. It was a block, and then another block, and occasionally, a couple of the lead actors mixed. But the Americans were the ones who would come and go. It was interesting."

William Goldman defined a movie star "as someone who opens." In the very early days of cinema, the identities of the ghost-like silver shadows flickering on the makeshift screen in a smoke-filled nickelodeon were unknown. It didn't take long for the industry to realise the lure of a star; millions of people would clamour to see Charlie Chaplin,

Mary Pickford, and Douglas Fairbanks (founding members of United Artists). The stars, often from very humble beginnings, had been elevated into superior beings, illusionary projections of what we all aspire to—or desire. A century later, star power continues unabated despite the inevitable scandals that remind us they are but human after all. A millennium earlier, all powerful Roman emperors would be reminded, "Remember thou art mortal." But even the most megalomaniacal tyrant could have walked through a Roman street blissfully ignored, unlike the modern celebrity for whom privacy has been sacrificed in a Faustian pact.

Post-war, as the film industry contracted with the rise of TV, stars became one of the few perceived guarantees of success. This often led to many being miscast or shoehorned into unsuitable roles, sometimes with surprising results—the Duke himself, John Wayne as the Mongol warlord Genghis Khan in *The Conqueror* (1955), is one of the most bonkers! So desperate have producers been to enlist a bankable name that salaries have spiralled exponentially. The rise of New Hollywood in the late 1960s, with counter-culture films such as *Easy Rider* (1969), signalled a brief move away from star-heavy, big-budget behemoths to more intimate fare. It was this new direction that prompted Joe Levine to comment, "This business has done a circle many times. Now it's come and done it completely around. And now the public wants stars . . . they're a great part of the glamour of our business."[139]

In *Adventures in the Screen Trade*, Goldman paints a stark and unflattering portrait of star behaviour. "Add one-third for the shit," being an oft-heard grumble about the added costs a major star incurs, with the largest percentage caused by the "shit" behaviour. "Some stars do misbehave, in infinite ways, but always for the same reason: They do it because they can . . ."[140] The screenwriter suggested this was because of a basic fear—insecurity.

To make his point, he listed the top 10 stars from 1971–81, according to the Quigley Poll of American cinema owners, with John Wayne heading the list at the start of the decade, Clint Eastwood in second place, Steve McQueen in fourth, and Sean Connery in ninth. By 1976 Robert Redford topped the list and Eastwood was in fourth; Connery was gone from the list, but Ryan O'Neal's 12-year-old-daughter, Tatum, placed eighth. Five years later, only Eastwood was still on the list rubbing shoulders with newcomers such as Harrison Ford and Bo Derek—but no Redford, Connery, or even young Tatum. Goldman's point couldn't be clearer: "Stardom just doesn't last."

For all those attached to *Bridge*, there was safety in numbers. "I like sharing the glory," commented Ryan O'Neal, cast as General Gavin. "It means you're not responsible for carrying the movie. I feel very little pressure on this set."[141] Perhaps this and the prestige of the project, plus an enormous respect for Dickie, led to a harmonious atmosphere. This is borne out by assistant director, Roy Button: "I've never found a top-end actor to be much problem, so long as you accord them the respect with someone like that. It's the actors who are halfway there that sometimes become a problem. There wasn't one person who was any trouble. They were all an absolute joy."[142]

In 1976 the "fourteen" were all "openers" in their own right, almost all having fronted several major films apiece. What is remarkable is that nearly a half century on, most still resonate. While then-box-office draw Robert Redford's polling position dipped after a few misfires in the early 1980s, his successful switch to directing and kick-starting the hugely influential Sundance Film Festival has secured his reputation. Arguably, it is Anthony Hopkins who has gravitated to the top as the greatest screen actor of his day. His casting in the film represented a watershed in life, both personally and professionally.

A commercial movie needs the oxygen of publicity, and for *Bridge*, with its immense budget, it was vital. So, the comings and goings of big names were huge attractions for the international press.

Jane Hershey, a young American woman living in London studying at film school, had wangled a summer job on the film. She had spent the princely sum of $75 in phone bills trying to track down

Joe Levine. Impressed at her persistence, he offered her a position in the publicity department in Holland. Hershey kept a diary, which she eventually published as an article for *American Film* in July 1977. Wanting to show she was an industry insider, she cast an astute and critical eye towards the production, but sometimes betrayed her blasé when in the orbit of star magnetism.

June 22, as she landed at Schiphol Airport: "A crisp Scottish voice breaks through my airport stupor. 'Have you seen my golf clubs come down yet?' Sean Connery plays a mean game of golf. An eight handicap. He is tanned, healthy, and intriguingly bald." Picked up by a chauffeur-driven Mercedes, she noted sardonically that this is one reason for the film's huge budget. She was taken to the "Postiljon Motel which stands behind a clump of hearty Dutch weeds on the outskirts of Deventer—my home for the next six weeks."

June 28: "Today is Sean Connery's press conference in Amsterdam. Now I find out what publicity is really all about. It's about sheltering people from themselves and others. But it's also about selling the film before the film is ready to be marketed. Excitement, but not too much too soon."[143]

Despite Connery's fame as 007, not everyone was aware of his polling position in the movies. "I'm not a great cinemagoer. So, I'm afraid these names don't mean quite the same things to me as they do to other people," commented 75-year-old Roy Urquhart, former commander of the British First Airborne and the real-life character the world's most famous secret agent was engaged to play. When Connery was announced, there was a great deal of excitement in the Urquhart household, with both his wife and daughter thrilled by the news. "Well, he'll do!" they exclaimed after a trip to the movies to see him in *The Man Who Would Be King* (1975), which co-starred Michael Caine.

Engaged as a technical advisor with John Waddy, Urquhart spent many weeks on location. He had expressed reservations over Goldman's original script draft. "I didn't care for it in some places at all, because I'm being disrespectful in this manner, but it was obviously written by an American. And we've got to accept the fact there's a great difference in the way we express ourselves." Goldman was aware of his script's shortcomings and knew it would pass through the hands of the eagle-eyed veterans.

Connery bore a strong likeness to the general, with not only their shared Scottish heritage, but also physical gait. "I think it's a remarkable resemblance in some ways, especially from the back,"[144] the general considered approvingly.

For Connery, the onetime Glasgow milkman and bodybuilder, *Bridge* represented another attempt to escape the long shadow of a certain secret agent. Sean Connery's breakout role has been so oft discussed, there is little need to do so here. After five outings as 007, he jumped and tried to reinvent himself. Despite some fine films like *The Molly Maguires* (1970), which was an undeserved flop, Connery relented and took out the licence to kill once more in *Diamonds Are Forever* (1971). In 1975 he played an ageing Robin Hood opposite ex-Arnhem resident Audrey Hepburn as Maid Marian in Richard Lester's moving and elegiac *Robin and Marian* (1976). Despite excellent reviews, the Scotsman was still seen as Bond although cameraman Peter MacDonald liked to remind him of an early work in his career—for Disney. "He'd made *Darby O'Gill and the Little People*. I used to tease him about that!" They worked together several times, and MacDonald found the actor a consummate professional, but still with traces of a very deprived childhood. "Sean smelled bullshit a mile away. I mean, if you just do your job as hard as you can, no bullshit. Great. But if he sees there's someone giving out crap, he will have a go at them. He's probably the tightest, meanest man financially you're ever gonna meet in your life. And I remember on *Zardoz* in Ireland, the crew had a snooker championship in some little dump near Bray (Ardmore Studios). Sean comes in wearing a three-piece suit, gold chain, gold shades. I mean, to intimidate. So, the winner gets 300 pounds, which was quite a lot of money then. But Sean played so hard to win—he cheated! Luke Quigley, who was the grip, a lovely Irishman with a glass eye, was a great snooker player. Sean would squeeze the chalk to do whatever he could to put Luke off. Normally, whoever wins buys everyone a drink. Sean won, pocketed the money, and disappeared. Even then, he was on a million dollars a film."[145] During his career, the actor supported several charities in Scotland. He donated his entire salary for *Diamonds Are Forever*—more than $1 million—to one that he had co-founded.

Despite appearing in a minor role in *The Longest Day* playing a lowly British soldier as a bit of comic relief, he twice turned down *Bridge*, considering it glorified war. He said, "I really felt it was too disturbing to resurrect what took place, all those tragic deaths." But following Dickie's impassioned pleading, Connery eventually agreed, believing the film could help to educate a younger audience. "If it's going to be an anti-war film with a terrific explanation, I'm glad now that I did it."[146] After starting work in Holland, echoes of that Irish snooker room surfaced when he realised his $250,000 a week was half of Robert Redford's fee. It was rumoured the Scotsman threatened a one-man strike, which led to a few tense days before his fee was adjusted in a compromise.

Despite his foibles and perhaps deserved perception of his talent, there was no doubting Connery's raw power and presence onscreen. Dickie felt that out of all his "fourteen," Connery had the most challenging role. Dickie focused in on the distinctly un-Bond-like situation where Urquhart is cut off impotently from his command. For much of a day, he is forced to sweat it out in a suburban airless loft with a German tank outside the front door. "He was in a situation where he couldn't lose his dignity and could never for one moment allow himself to be seen lacking in courage or responsibility. It's a part that's very difficult to play and get the balance right. I think it's Sean's best performance."[147]

The flow of marquee talent kept Jane Hershey and the publicity team very busy. Halfway through July, with the production in full swing, the inexplicable happened. "I am suddenly without a department,"[148] Hershey wrote abruptly in her diary on the 21st. Levine had returned from New York and ordered his publicity chief, Gordon Arnell, to fire his personal assistant. She was a highly respected English journalist who was popular with the unit. Arnell, who was required to do the deed within the week, flatly refused. "In that case," Levine demanded, "you'll both have to go."

The reason for the dismissal was not clear, but Levine refused to budge even though the episode caused immense ructions. Film critic and journalist Iain Johnstone, who had been hired by his friend Arnell to cover the production for an eventual documentary and book (with editorial independence), was unable to discover the reason. He noted that Dickie was in tears, and the atmosphere in the production office was like "ice," with "cabals discussing the methods open to them to repair the seemingly unfair act."[149] The unit threatened to go on strike until Arnell persuaded them otherwise. Levine attempted to calm things down by offering an extra 50 pounds a week across the board. Hershey watched nervously as Levine strode into the near-deserted publicity office, "catching me with a puzzled look on my face: 'Oh, good, you're still here. Don't worry, there will be another department here in the morning. Met any cute guys?'" She had noticed the septuagenarian had a little twinkle in his eye when they had first met. "He gives me a fatherly squeeze and walks over to talk with Attenborough. As I look over my shoulder, I catch him winking at me. Seventy-one?"[150]

Whatever Levine's reasons, it left a bitter aftertaste. Production manager Terence Clegg does not remember this event but suggested that "instant firing is an American habit rife with old-time producers who love to show their power. Gordon Arnell had no clout, and Attenborough was not about to support him as Joe had promised to deliver *Gandhi*."[151]

True to his word, Levine got the vital publicity machine up and running with a coup. He landed the services of one of the best PR gurus in the business, who ran the top New York agency, Pickwick, with

Robert Redford as a leading client. "By the next morning, Lois Smith arrives and gets things moving again," recalled Hershey. "With Smith is her super-active son, Luke, age nine. 'Is Tatum O'Neal coming? I wanna beat her up!'" A week later, the young lad would get his wish—he was not the only one.

🐝   🐝   🐝

July 27 was the crucial day that Dickie had most worried about. Thankfully, he was able to breathe a sigh of relief. "We're loaded with stars today," Jane Hershey noted, "or as Sir Dickie said to a reporter, 'There's a lot of money on that lawn.'" He had his vital names assembled.

The location was the Huize De Voorst, a beautiful, gleaming white seventeenth-century mansion built in 1695 (and now a boutique hotel) 10 miles south of Deventer. Its driveway is formed around a circular lawn with a gilded sculpture of revolving planets: it was a perfect backdrop for scores of photographers keen to snap Levine's bevy of talent on display: Dirk Bogarde, Gene Hackman, Edward Fox, and Sean Connery. Jane Hershey was busy that day ensuring each member of the press had their piece of the money. "Ryan O'Neal, I find awkward, like an oversized teenager at his first adult party. His uniform is more dashing than many of the others, but he still looks ill at ease. Yells Hackman to O'Neal. 'You haven't even read the book. You don't even know who you're playing!'"

It was a 12-year-old girl who upstaged them all. "Tatum O'Neal is looking for four-leaf clovers on the wet grass." With her was her dad's girlfriend, Melanie Griffith, then an up-and-coming actress with a famous mother, Tippi Hedren. "The two girls show off their many-carat ruby friendship rings, clutching and cuddling like two women in a Claude Chabrol spectacular. Ryan wants me to dress up Tatum in soldier's gear, so that he can have a parting shot at a cover for *Time* magazine. But Tatum is removed from the premises before I get underway—it seems that she 'borrowed' and subsequently wrecked a boat that belonged to the mansion's caretaker. One of the crew said, 'You should have been there at the hotel when she wanted passkeys to everyone's rooms.'"[152] It is not known if young Luke Smith got his wish to beat up the blossoming star on the cusp of her teens.

Later, her dad inadvertently caused a production mishap when he made a surreptitious request to the catering team. "Ryan O'Neal was dying to have some space cake," production assistant Reineke Kramer recalled. "Our cooks had to make them for him. Unfortunately, quite a lot of extras also had a piece of cake."[153] Chuck, one of the lighting sparks, was heard to cry out that he was "dying." Kramer had to take the walking wounded to the hospital.

O'Neal, a former amateur boxer, began his acting career in 1960, and his rise was meteoric, if ultimately fleeting. Just four years later, he landed the plum role of heartthrob Rodney Harrington on the popular TV soap opera *Peyton Place*, a spinoff of the 1957 movie. His all-American handsome looks made him an ideal choice for the doomed onscreen romance with Ali MacGraw in *Love Story* (1970). The sentimental story proved to be a much-needed tonic for American audiences bombarded by images of the brutal Vietnam War, and it propelled him into superstardom. Teaming up with his eight-year-old daughter for Bogdanovich's *Paper Moon* (1973), he enjoyed a few years in the limelight before his star trajectory stuttered during the 1980s. Without doubt, his career high was starring in Kubrick's *Barry Lyndon*. Surrounded by a stellar cast of character actors, including Hardy Krüger, Barry is a cypher, a weak man of little substance, but O'Neal's performance is nuanced and makes us care about this Everyman: a victim of circumstance and fate and his own flaws. Kubrick's notoriously grinding perfectionism appeared to have hollowed out his superbly understated performance to the master's exacting standards. Although the film was an expensive flop on its release, time has bestowed greatness upon it, and it is now recognised as one of the director's finest works. O'Neal noted that Kubrick was a taskmaster who always sought to explore the intention of a scene, while Dickie was more exacting with the nuance and intonation of lines. "From Richard, I get wonderful enthusiasm and encouragement as he's an actor. There's a rapport. He differs from Stanley . . . some would say a slave driver, although not to me . . . I've never worked so hard in my life. They all have their own magic tricks."

The actor didn't meet his real-life counterpart, the U.S. 82nd Airborne commander, General Jumpin' Jim Gavin, until almost the end of his five-week block, so he'd had to fashion his performance from scraps of info. "I heard they called him "Slim" Jim, so I lost five pounds," O'Neal joked. When the film came out, his youthful looks were criticised for "Hollywoodizing" the general. In 1944 Gavin was only a year older at 37 and possessed similar all-American good looks. He jumped with his men into battle, sharing their dangers and privations. "He was a kind of romantic figure to them," O'Neal considered, "and they were very proud to have him as their leader . . . The idea of taking care of thousands of men frightens me. I can barely take care of Tatum."

The film's action is augured by O'Neal's Gavin stumbling across a German sentry in a forest. Before he can fire, a shot rings out, killing the soldier. It is a straight lift from Ryan's book, where Gavin's trusted Dutch liaison officer, Captain "Harry" Bestebreurtje, seeing the tiny gap between the German's helmet and his gun, fired and "took the top of his head off," Gavin recalled gleefully, ". . . very exciting."[154]

Surveying the press feeding frenzy on the lawn that day with a certain aplomb was Dirk Bogarde, immaculately dressed as General "Boy" Browning. Jane Hershey noted how he "blends into the elegant landscape of the seventeenth-century garden in which we're camped. He smokes continually but discreetly, as if not to encourage others in his bad habit. He waxes happily over the mention of Alain Resnais' *Providence* in which he plays John Gielgud's son. Otherwise, he prefers to be by himself."[155]

Dickie, who had a holiday bolthole near Bogarde's home in Provence, had been keen to enlist him. The actor, who saw himself as a leading figure of European art cinema, was privately condescending about appearing in an epic. "It is not a great part," he said, writing to a relative about his casting as Browning. "Rather, a prick. I think . . . however, it's loot, and it's going to be a massive picture on the lines of *The Longest Day*, and all that sort of thing." Renovating his beautiful sprawling French property, where he lived with his partner, Tony Forwood, was ongoing, with repairing a long, dilapidated wall being a major project for the couple. He refused Levine's original offer of $80,000, but a renewed one of $100,000—for 12 days' work over three weeks convinced him to take the role. "If they want me to play and pay, I'll do so happily! Can't afford to be proud now, dear!"[156] While it paid for his wall, he would come to regret his decision to play the "prick."

Although he had never met him, Bogarde had history—literally—with Browning. During the war, he had been a very junior member of the general's staff. Arriving in Holland for the film, the actor had passed over Arnhem bridge, which he had last seen as an unobtainable smoke-shrouded prize during the battle some 32 years before. It was an unsettling experience: "It wasn't pleasant, any of it. And particularly the evacuation at Oosterbeek . . . it seems even odder that I'm back here, in familiar territory. I don't know if I like it."[157]

In the film, he would cross swords with a lowly intelligence officer over reconnaissance photographs. During the war, it had been Bogarde's job to assess combat photographs and in some cases recommend more bombing missions to complete a target's destruction. "I was responsible at the age of 23 for a lot of deaths," he said later.

Without doubt, his most harrowing experience was at Belsen concentration camp, which he visited as a young lieutenant with the Queens Royal Regiment, shortly after its liberation in April 1945. He didn't speak publicly about it until 1986, when he was interviewed by Russell Harty for Yorkshire TV. "I mean nothing could be worse than that the gates were open and I was looking at Dante's Inferno. I still haven't seen anything this dreadful and never will. And a girl came up who spoke English. She had no top on, and a pair of men's pyjamas, and no hair, but I knew she was a girl because her breasts were empty. And we talked, and she was so excited and thrilled, and all around us there were mountains of dead people, and they were slushy and slimy, so when you walked through them, you tried not to."[158]

Interviewed during the filming of *Bridge* about his attitude to war, his words have the weary tone of a witness to Dante's inferno. "War is going to happen. It always will. And unfortunately, I think youth seems to need it. It releases some violence or some inherent thing in the human spirit which has to be contained by violence. I don't think it'll ever change, and I think peace would be totally unhealthy."[159]

On that day the scenes that Dickie was desperate to get in the can revolved around the planning of the daring operation. They were set at Moor Park Golf Club (illustrated by two extras with a golf caddy glimpsed through the window) in England, which was General Browning's HQ for Operation Market Garden. Filmed in one of the Huize De Voorst's ornate rooms, the scene shows the key commanders coming together for the crucial briefing.

Not helping Dickie's stress that day, two of them were late arriving, as assistant director Roy Button recalled. "So, there's mega-stars in the room, and two of the Americans were like an hour late because they came from Amsterdam. They were late—and you don't keep Sean and Dickie waiting. Sean was lovely, but he's got no patience about anything. As they walked in the room, you could cut the atmosphere with a knife. The first person to speak was Sean: 'Typical! Americans late! Just like in the last war—now let's get on with it.' Everybody just cracked up, and it broke the moment."[160]

"So long as people are professional," Sean Connery commented, "it's got nothing to do with their star status. Incompetence is the only thing I abhor."[161]

As Browning explains the plan, the scene is primarily exposition, which for the movie audience has to be extremely brief, yet clear. A sense of urgency, perhaps foolhardy, is already baked in when he announces, *"And we go next Sunday."* The other commanders are stunned, with O'Neal's Gavin, driving the incredulity home with, *"Seven days!"*

But it is the foreboding voiced by Gene Hackman's Polish commander, Sosabowski, that supplies the drama and tension. He is unhappy about the operation, *"I am thrilled that your great Montgomery has devised this plan. I promise I will be properly ecstatic if it works,"* he says half-heartedly, much to Browning's chagrin. The Pole's unease will only continue through subsequent scenes.

Stanisław Sosabowski, like his fellow countrymen who had escaped to Britain after the fall of Poland, was an experienced and tough veteran. He had fought in the First World War as part of the Austro-Hungarian army in Italy. Staunchly patriotic for the newly formed Polish Republic, he held a variety of military posts before being appointed to command the prestigious 21st "Children of Warsaw" Infantry Regiment based in the capital. The German invasion in September 1939 saw his unit defend Warsaw, which held out for two weeks of relentless assaults. Sosabowski launched a series of counterattacks, which, although ultimately futile, drew praise from General Juliusz Rómmel, who awarded the 21st Infantry Regiment with the *Virtuti Militari* medal.

After a brief spell as a POW, Sosabowski escaped and joined the Resistance in Warsaw before being smuggled out to France. Here, he attempted to rally a brigade of Poles to fight alongside the French, but following the German blitzkrieg, evacuated 6,000 Poles to Britain. Excited by the possibilities of Airborne operations taking the fight back into his conquered homeland, he formed the 1st Polish Para, which had the unofficial motto: the shortest way (*najkrótszą drogą*).

At 49 years old, he successfully completed the arduous training. He was considered a strict yet just commander but having little patience with opposition either below or above him. Inevitably, he would clash with some major figures, notably Montgomery, who would unfairly pin the Arnhem disaster on his shoulders. Sosabowski and his men covered themselves in glory during the battle despite suffering almost 40 percent casualties. After the war, he became a factory worker in London, and few at his funeral knew his illustrious career as a Polish patriot and war hero. "He [Sosabowski] was a bright guy," Hackman considered. "He wasn't necessarily a hero-type who wanted to jump just to get into action . . . He was a seasoned soldier and even though I guess his ambition was to liberate Warsaw, he was smart enough to know that there was a time and place for it."

Gene Hackman's performance in *Bridge* is perhaps not his finest hour. While he presents a plausible picture of a gruff commander at odds with his superiors, his Polish accent just doesn't convince. Ironically, he had gone to great lengths to get it right: "Most of my research for the film had to do with the accent, which was somewhat difficult for me, having been brought up in the Midwest in the States where we kind of slur about with our words. The Polish accent is one of pronouncing each syllable, but it's fun trying it."[162] It is a shame it does not quite work, as the actor in almost every other role displayed a raw energy and total believability.

Born in 1930, he had a troubled childhood and was brought up by his grandmother. Considered a shy boy, he found inspiration at the movies. "I was so captured by the action guys. Jimmy Cagney was my favourite. I could see he had tremendous timing and vitality."[163] Following a four-year spell in the U.S. Marines, in which he admitted he was not a good soldier, because he "couldn't take the discipline,"[164] he followed his dream to act. He joined the Pasadena Playhouse in California, where he and peer Dustin Hoffman were considered to have such little talent their classmates voted them "The Least Likely to Succeed."[165] Proving nothing succeeds like rejection, Hackman moved to New York City where he, Hoffman, and Robert Duvall shared an apartment as they attempted to carve out careers. "It was more psychological warfare, because I wasn't going to let those fuckers get me down . . . There is a part of you that relishes the struggle . . . You lie to people, you cheat, you do whatever it takes to get an audition." It worked. Although he was 37, through his friendship with Warren Beatty, he was cast in *Bonnie and Clyde* (1967), earning him an Academy Award nomination as Best Supporting Actor.

His breakout role was as "Popeye" Doyle in *The French Connection* (1971). William Friedkin's terrific direction, rarely shooting more than a single take for a scene, meant the action and energy are all upon the screen. You totally believe Popeye Doyle's determination to get his man through a series of high-octane chases. His hard work brought him an Oscar for Best Actor and firmly established him as one of Hollywood's leading star character actors.

With success came a reputation for being difficult, at least with weak directors, but his raw energy and his will to succeed—"it's a narcotic"[166]—were the keys to his talent. He considered that actors are always competitive. "But I think that's good. If somebody is really good in a scene and then . . . you want to come up with it too. You want to have your moment."[167] Hackman shared a brief scene with a British actor who, he admitted, acted him off the screen. Denholm Elliott played an RAF squadron leader who patiently tries to explain to the Polish general why his "drop" cannot go ahead. The delay in landing Sosabowski's Poles would prove to be a decisive factor in the battle. The film shows the general's mounting irritation as he listens to the RAF man's description of fog: *"I don't wish to bother you with a good deal of meteorological mumbo-jumbo, but the fact is, you see, whether or not we like it, fog moves."* Exasperated at listening to the mumbo-jumbo as to why they cannot fly, the general makes clear his frustration, *"I feel an overwhelming urge to play 'Castrate the Weatherman' . . . It's an old Polish game, you know."* The filmed version omitted this lurid line.

During a filming break, the American star stepped over to assistant director Steve Lanning and asked: "Where did he come from? He took me apart!" Elliott had adopted the beloved RAF accoutrement prop—a pipe—and it had thrown Hackman. "It took me out of the scene," he grumbled. Lanning, who worked again with Elliott in South Africa on *Zulu Dawn* (1979), said of his scene-stealing performances, "I think he was one of those actors that would sort of kill it." Hackman was thunderstruck by this—to him at least—little-known actor and kept repeating, "He took me apart! Who is that guy?"

Elliott was an extraordinarily talented character actor, mainly on the British stage and TV. He had starred in the infamous *Scent of Mystery* (1960), cinema's only foray into Smell-O-Vision. In it, he delivers a quirky performance that is briefly upstaged by Diana Dors, resplendent in all her natural glory, before he makes a zip wire fall with an umbrella into the arms of superstar Elizabeth Taylor (the producer was her stepson, Michael Todd Jr.).[168]

Dirk Bogarde described the pleasure playing with such top-level talent. "It's very exciting, because you're actually working with thoroughbreds. And any race is more exciting if you've got the best horse." Ryan O'Neal was in awe of Bogarde. "I love to watch Dirk. He's an acting lesson for me. In each take, he found something new."[169] Bogarde was pleasantly surprised by the younger American: "Very nice, clever, bright, and not at all *Peyton Place*."

Recognising that Gene Hackman's acting style and approach was different, Bogarde was equally impressed: "very Methody but nice and respectful." The Method, which encouraged actors to inhabit their roles, had been a popular hothouse for talents like Marlon Brando and Rod Steiger. Bogarde respected Sean Connery's no-nonsense approach to his craft: "I like him a great deal."[170]

Amid those star heavyweights was an actor who held his own. Paul Maxwell played Maxwell D. Taylor, commander of the U.S. 101st "Screaming Eagles." He was one of several Canadian actors who had made the UK their home in the 1950s. The introduction of Independent Television often called for transatlantic characters for the plethora of new shows, and he would prove a popular face on TV. His most famous role, albeit to British audiences, was as Steve Tanner, the ex-GI lover of Elsie Tanner, played by Pat Phoenix, in the world's longest running TV soap opera, *Coronation Street* (which still tops the TV ratings over 60 years later).[171]

Maxwell does succeed in conveying the aura of a commander, but it's not always the case when a lesser-known actor is called upon to play a charismatic leader. Even with very talented performers, there is something that does not sell a commanding presence to an audience. Looking again at John Wayne in *The Conqueror*, what can be said for his casting is that his larger-than-life personality suggests this is a man who could unite the Mongol tribes and conquer the world—almost! Dickie was convinced that his "fourteen" could display that charisma to enhance his project.

Citing the wartime leaders Montgomery and Eisenhower, Dickie explained that "their persona is such that they are superstars." He then listed Browning, Gavin, Urquhart, and Maxwell Taylor as exemplary leaders that could inspire and command respect. "Tens of thousands of men followed them into battle unhesitatingly. They were huge men with massive personalities." To convey these qualities onscreen required the "star" magnetism that would allow audiences to immediately reorient themselves with the numerous concurrent storylines. "Within 30 seconds of them arriving on the screen, that presence has to be felt—bang!—on the audience," he said, slapping his fist hard into his palm. The only way to get that effect is to use stars, the biggest we could get."[172]

No one encapsulates this charisma better than Edward Fox as General Horrocks. He is the epitome of the upper-class British commander, full of bonhomie, charm, and innate leadership ability. Fox is introduced riding in a jeep with an impressive crane shot in Deventer's town square, known as The Brink. He is whisked into closeup, and before climbing out of his jeep, he thanks his driver—Waddy—a reference to the film's chief technical advisor. (A running in-joke throughout the film was to give the names of crew members to incidental characters.)

Fox had shot to fame just two years previously for his riveting performance as the mysterious but tenacious would-be assassin in *Day of the Jackal* (1974), one of the cinema's greatest thrillers. While Fox had many years of experience, the pressure of a starring role proved too much on the first day of *Jackal*'s production. The director, Fred Zinnemann, immediately understood Fox was nervous, and after putting him at ease, gently coaxed the actor over three days of filming. It did the trick. Fox found not only his confidence, but also the cold heart of The Jackal. Before then, he had played Julie Christie's would-be beau in *The Go-Between* (1971). Covered in disfiguring make-up, he creates a picture of an honest man, perhaps aware that he doesn't have the spark that will ignite her passion. It is a subtle and moving performance which does Fox proud.

Despite his "plummy drawl and pukka background" (educated at Harrow) Edward Charles Morrice Fox is not of the British aristocracy but the son of theatrical agent Robin Fox and actress Angela Muriel Darita Worthington, both with ancestors comprising inventors, dramatists, and stockbrokers. Fox is part of a respected theatrical dynasty. His brother James has carved out a successful career and had co-starred with Bogarde in *The Servant* (1963). His daughter Emilia is a leading actor of her generation.

Despite his pedigree, Fox was not Dickie's first choice for Horrocks—Attenborough originally offered it to the then-007, Roger Moore, who was forced to decline because of a scheduling conflict with *The Spy Who Loved Me* (1977). When the Bond shoot was delayed, Moore became available, but General Horrocks, it was said, vetoed the casting. This seems doubtful. According to Horrocks, a ridiculous story had appeared in a British newspaper suggesting that he would play himself. "Can you think of me, an old man, bobbing about?" he exclaimed to his highly amused wife. Later, he asked two actor friends who should play him; both agreed unanimously—Edward Fox.

The general, who had seen *Jackal*, approved. Perhaps Fox's innate military bearing also appealed to the old war horse. Despite his theatrical upbringing, the young Edward had intended to be an officer in the elite Coldstream Guards. But during his training, he found "I was insubordinate and stubborn and perfectly beastly. A rather disorderly person." To fulfil his two-year National Service, he transferred to a regular regiment instead, "and I had a very good time."[173] Knowing which way to dress with his Sam Browne officer's belt endeared him to the old general who was a household name in the UK, thanks to a popular series of TV documentaries he presented about the war (this may have prompted the baseless newspaper story). It's easy to see how charismatic and popular Horrocks must have been as he led his men into the din of battle.[174]

Looking back at his hundred-plus roles, including The Jackal, Fox had a special affinity for one role in particular. "I enjoyed all of the films, but *A Bridge Too Far* is the one I enjoyed the most because of the character, Lieutenant General Brian Horrocks. Brian was alive then, and I knew him well—we were friends until his death. He was a very particular type of general, and it was important that I play the role correctly.[175]

"I visited General Horrocks once before I started the film, had a day with him, which was the greatest help to me, and a great pleasure too, wonderful . . . I never wanted to imitate him, but the spirit of the man was essential, really. So, to try and catch hold of something of that, as near as one could, and to portray it in a performance, was very necessary."[176]

The essence of leadership is often defined as going in four directions: upwards to your superiors, horizontally to your peers, downwards to your subordinates, and inwards to yourself. Fox captures this beautifully in what must be the standout acting moment in the film. The setting is an operations meeting for XXX Corps and filled with extras. It was filmed in Deventer's creaking old Luxor cinema. Dressed in an informal sweater, Fox as Horrocks beams with a childlike grin as he bounds up to the stage amid the raucous applause of his officers. Wielding a cane against the gigantic map, he begins to describe Operation Market Garden. It's not only a masterpiece of screenwriting but also an extraordinary performance.

His opening salvo is a brilliant example of how to get your audience in the palm of your hand: *"This is a story you'll tell your grandchildren—and mightily bored they'll be."*

"That's Horrocks' line," William Goldman explained. "When you come across something like that, you've got to use it. That's gold for a screenwriter." The page-and-a-half speech brilliantly encapsulates the plan, not just for the officers, but for the movie audience. It brings to mind George C. Scott's opening five-minute speech in *Patton* (1970). His is brash, lurid, bombastic, right-between-the-eyes—utterly American and completely mesmerising. Horrocks' speech, by contrast, is quintessentially British: humorous, understated, more of an invitation than an exhortation. Both superbly capture their respective cultures, and both are magnificent examples of inspirational leadership.

In subsequent interviews, Goldman cited the speech as his way of crystallising the story. His stroke of genius was to boil it down to a "cavalry-to-the-rescue" plot, and he memorably added this metaphor to Horrocks' speech. Curiously, this must have been a later addition. The original shooting script has Horrocks wrapping it up with the line: *"Gentlemen: I'm not telling you it will be the easiest party we've ever attended…"*

What led to the superb addition is not known, but it is inspired: *"Gentlemen: I'm not telling you it will be the easiest party we've ever attended, but I still wouldn't miss it for the world. I like to think of this as one of those American Western films—the paratroops, lacking substantial equipment, always short of food—these are the besieged homesteaders. The Germans, naturally, they're the bad guys. And XXX Corps? We, my friends, are the cavalry on the way to the rescue . . ."*

Speaking a quarter of a century later, Goldman wondered whether his metaphor still worked with modern audiences. "Back before the beginning of time, Hollywood used to make a lot of Westerns. So, all those terminologies were common parlance for everybody that went to a movie in those days. But an 18-year-old kid who goes to all the bloodbath movies won't get it. That whole speech is absolutely archaic today. And so, all those standards of heroism have gone."

Goldman, who seemed to enjoy being a curmudgeon in later life, liked these grand, sweeping statements. While it's true, the direct reference may be hazy to a new audience, perhaps the Western's mythology (born in the mid-nineteenth century) has embedded itself so deeply into the DNA of pop culture, that it would still resonate.

Another Edward Fox scene that at first glance looks quite simple has him driving Michael Caine as his subordinate Vandeleur along the column of waiting tanks. He intersperses his last-minute instructions, emphasising *"for God's sake keep your tanks on the move"* with jokes to the various tank commanders: *"Hallo, Bob—hope that's not my funeral they're going to . . ."* The timing is flawless. Seemingly done in one take, the scene was split into three separate positions with the vehicles and soldiers rearranged along the stretch of road.[177] The bonhomie with subordinates is a masterclass of leadership. Horrocks is about to order these men to their potential deaths, and they will go willingly for a popular commander who has earned their respect and affection.

A few years later, Fox would play another general when Dickie cast him in *Gandhi* as General Reginald Dyer, who ordered the unprovoked Amritsar massacre in 1919. It would form the halfway point of the film and was dramatic, moving, and deeply unsettling. Fox's Dyer is the opposite of Horrocks and shows both his innate skill as an actor, but also Dickie's subtle direction. Dyer is a fool but a dangerous one. During the subsequent court of inquiry, he is asked what provision was put in place for the wounded. He replies flatly without a tinge of irony that provision was available upon request. The judge then asks how a wounded child is meant to seek support. The general cannot answer. Has the penny dropped, or is he unable to compute the question? Dyer's blinkered bluster and stupidity are deeply etched on Fox's face. It is a brief part but utterly convincing, if chilling, and a fine performance.

Fox was appointed an Officer of the Order of the British Empire for his services to Drama in the 2003 New Year Honours. He continues to act: "I've been a working actor for 60 years, and I've had long periods when I've been out of work for months, but this is normal. There are actors who seem to work all the time, but I don't think you can be any good . . . You'll be bad quite a lot of the time anyway, but I think when you take something on, you've got to be able to say to yourself, which I hope I have, that I think this is something worth doing and that I can bring something to it that's going to be of use."[178]

🐝   🐝   🐝

When Michael Caine as Colonel J.O.E. Vandeleur, commander of the Irish Guards, leads the XXX Corps breakout in his staff car, Dickie played a trick. As the scene progressed, one of the passing tanks was to burst into flames as if hit by German artillery—the goal was to have Caine look suitably surprised, but keep in character with a commanding coolness. Setting up action as a surprise is an oft-used technique by directors, as long as it is safe and unlikely to terrify the actor. Dickie got just the right response. It's unlikely that the director knew his trick tapped into a very raw emotion in the cockney actor.

"The closest I got to death and the incident that still haunts my dreams from time to time," Caine wrote in his memoirs, "was a night-time observation patrol in no-man's-land." In 1951, Caine served for eight months with The Royal Fusiliers along the contested 38th parallel in Korea. One night, he and two others were on a mission to grab a prisoner from the opposing Chinese lines. They picked their way up the hill when they "suddenly caught the whiff of garlic." This was the signature smell of the Chinese soldiers—very nearby. In the nick of time, Caine's unit threw themselves to the ground just as a patrol emerged from the long grass. "I lay there absolutely terrified, my hand on the trigger of my gun. With the enemy circling so close. We could hear them talking. I was conscious of a growing fury. I was going to die before I'd even had a chance to live ... I decided I had nothing to lose. If I was going to die, then I was going to take a lot of Chinese with me." But first, they decided to answer the call of nature. Then, suitably relieved, the three hurled themselves recklessly into the darkness. With bullets whistling around them, they found themselves running towards the enemy lines. This proved to be a lucky strategy as their pursuers lost interest. Feeling it safe, the sweat-soaked Brits doubled back to their own lines. "Somehow, we got back in one piece, but it was a close-run thing." While he said the incident didn't cause him sweat-drenched nightmares, he did acknowledge, "It does come back to me at moments of difficulty when someone is looking to attack me."[179]

Caine rarely discussed his combat experiences, but this clearly left a mark. Caine didn't mention whether Dickie's trick had any primal impact on him, and he probably expected such a sleight of hand. Caine shot to fame in *Zulu* and quickly consolidated his fame with *Alfie* (1965), and then three Harry Palmer espionage movies.

Born Maurice Micklewhite, he was the first generation of British actors that didn't gentrify themselves for the genteel homegrown industry. "My whole career has been being rather guided by the fact that I never went to an academy in as much as I never had voice lessons. I never ever played the classical roles as opposed to all the other English actors. I was forever kind of forced into a kind of working-class background by my own voice."[180] To play Vandeleur, he softened his vowels to echo Lieutenant Bromhead in *Zulu*. Sometimes overlooked is that Caine had played a number of military types and always with a swagger and quiet authority. Just prior to *Bridge*, he played a crack German paratrooper in *The Eagle Has Landed*, which had echoes of his seventeenth-century German mercenary in *The Last Valley* (1971).

The star-packed filming block was rounded off with the soulful scene atop the *Grote Kerkhof* church in Deventer. With Nijmegen taken and XXX Corps barely a mile from Arnhem, the generals realise it is not enough. As Bogarde, Caine, Fox, Hackman, and O'Neal stood surveying the Dutch landscape, special effects supervisor John Richardson had been busy setting off plumes of smoke in the background to suggest the bloody battleground. Goldman, who accompanied Dickie on a recce, found the lofty location a challenge. "It was a small staircase. It was tiny; there were no windows. I remember panicking and crawling down on my butt like a little baby down all those stairs and then getting to the bottom of the church. I don't know if it was a panic attack. I can still remember myself running out of the church, and I wouldn't allow myself to stop for a long way."

Goldman was on set almost every day. "He was like a child in the best way," recalled Stuart Craig. "He was just absolutely overwhelmed and fascinated and loving every second, such was his enthusiasm for the project and his commitment to it. Everything that was manifesting his written script, I'm not overstating it, was a first for him." Peter MacDonald considered he "was a proper filmmaker. He wasn't just a writer; he understood what was needed to make the film. As the shooting crew, you know what you want to shoot. But it also helps if the writer also suggested the same type of coverage."

In the scene, MacDonald's camera tilts from MPs clustered around Jeeps up the church tower to see the generals grouped around the spire. They were all doubles, including stuntman Vic Armstrong. The cut to the stars on the top was filmed later the same day atop an enormous grain silo over 50 metres high in a derelict factory elsewhere in Deventer.[181] A small replica set of the church balustrade was constructed, which allowed for a variety of camera angles with a backdrop of the Dutch countryside.

The filmed scene differs ever so slightly from the script. In the script, while all agree that Urquhart and his command must withdraw, each commander mutters his reasons for the failure. Gavin blames himself for not taking Nijmegen quick enough; Horrocks admits he did not move faster with his tanks; Vandeleur blames the narrow road, although he knows he and his men did their very best; Browning laments that none of this was in Monty's plan.

The filmed scene is subtler, its terse and abrupt nature underscoring the admission of defeat. Gavin states simply: *"It was Nijmegen."* Is he blaming himself, his men, or others? Horrocks: *"No, it was after Nijmegen."* Fox's dejected performance suggests Horrocks carries the burden of failure himself. As they all leave, it is left to Sosabowski, who has been the voice of Cassandra from the beginning, to boil it down to an eternal anti-war message, *"It doesn't matter what it was. When men decided let's play war games . . . everybody dies."*

9
"We've Got to Get This Right, Boys!"
The A.P.A. Part 1

As charismatic as those 14 marquee names were, the soul of *A Bridge Too Far* belongs to the combined talents of 50 young actors, mostly at the start of their careers.

"It was a brotherhood of man," recalled David English. "You go through life, and suddenly you get a collection of people, like the Dirty Dozen or whatever, and you can take on the world. We were all together in the hottest summer in Holland in 100 years, dressed in those army outfits and running down the road throwing grenades—adrenaline pumping. It was fantastic."[182]

While few of their faces registered individually onscreen, collectively they convincingly portrayed fighting soldiers. In war movies of the '50s and '60s, most of the cast and crew would have had military experience. But with the end of British National Service in 1963 and the changing attitudes towards war that developed through the decade, almost all young men in 1976 were thorough long-haired civvies. Dickie, very early in pre-production, recognised that many war epics had been tripped up by employing often bored and uncommitted extras to thicken out the background. "I was so conscious of documentary impact. I knew that it would be idiotic to have a group of guys who had to use rifles looking like they're drinking a cup of tea."[183]

While professional soldiers may have solved the problem, this was precluded by theatrical union rules. His genius solution was to recruit actors and train them to pass as warriors. It proved to be an inspired concept and would be *de rigueur* for almost all war movies made since. Perhaps only a director who cared passionately for performance would have conceived it. "Dickie could have gone entirely for extras," actor Edward Seckerson recalled. "But he wanted intelligence and some kind of ability to transform ourselves into the real thing, or as near as dammit."

At the end of filming in October 1976, some of this select group of actors clubbed together and paid for a back-page spread in the *Stage*.

The A.P.A. back from 'Bridge.' "Attenborough's Private Army" has now demobilised and is ready for further action at home and abroad. Our thanks to "A Bridge Too Far" Producer, Joseph E. Levine, Director, Richard Attenborough, and Casting Director, Miriam Brickman, for a battle well fought.

While it was a calling card, it also showed the enormous pride this bunch of young actors had in a unique thespian assignment. "We all paid into it, about 50 quid a head," said Edward Seckerson, "and I actually got a job from it. Everybody who worked on that movie thought they would never be out of work again. You get lulled into a false sense of security when you're earning that kind of money. We were pretty well paid."[184]

In early 1976 the call went out for hundreds of young male actors. Many applied and were whittled down to a short long list of 300, and then invited to a dance centre in Wembley. One of the youngest, barely 21, was Sebastian Abineri. "I was working in Lindsay Anderson's company, the Lyric Theatre." One day, Sebastian was killing time in London's venerable bookshop, Foyles, and came across a copy of Ryan's book. "So, I grabbed it because I love military history and sat down in Valoti's in Soho and read a large chunk of it. I looked at the back cover, and it said shortly to be made into a major film. So, I've got to get into this!" Returning to the theatre for the evening performance, he collared Miriam Brickman, who'd cast him in the play, "Oh, Miriam, I don't suppose you know who's casting it, do you? And she said, 'I am!' Fantastic!" She agreed to ask if Abineri could be released from his contract. She came back and said, "Yes, Lindsay thinks you'd make a wonderful paratrooper."[185]

Jack McKenzie was an actor with a background as both an ex-policeman and ex-Royal Marine. "My old Pop was a tough old ex-Royal Scot. And he knew that I, aged 15, was going to go down the wrong path, and he gave me a railway ticket to Deal in Kent—the Royal Marines barracks!' I went in as a boy, came out as a girl!" After service as a Marine, McKenzie joined the police in Edinburgh before being bitten by the acting bug. Keen to break into the film industry, he had landed a job at the distribution company Cinema International Corporation at 139 Piccadilly. Hearing of the casting call, he resolved to go straight to the horse's mouth—the producer. "You never leave an actor in a room with a telephone. I had 20 lines to play with. And I rang his office, Avco Embassy in New York. And the woman said, 'I'm terribly sorry, sir, but Mr. Levine is not in these offices at this moment. Can I give you his home number?' So, I rang his number!"[186] McKenzie then rang the producer and got a curt reply that Miriam Brickman was casting it, before the phone banging down. Luckily, Brickman was more forthcoming and immediately saw Jack's military background as an asset. Some months later, Jack's *chutzpah* would boomerang back to him.

Tim Morand was born of English and French parentage—"trendy, bohemian artists"—and had been brought up with tales about his heroic father's wartime experiences. The war had split up the family, and while young Tim and his mother stayed in Portugal, his father joined the Free French army. He saw action at Narvik and later as a liaison officer with the American army. He landed on the bullet-ridden Omaha Beach on D-Day before slugging his way across Europe to war's end. "He was a bit of a legend to me," said Morand. "I didn't really meet him till I was 11. He was great."

After appearing in several TV series, Morand landed a part in *Barry Lyndon*. He was excited to be in a major movie for one of the world's top directors. He spent six months filming in Ireland and even got to ride in a cavalry charge with Ryan O'Neal. Unfortunately, all his hard work was for naught, as all his scenes ended up on the cutting room floor. Hitting a fallow period, he was driving delivery vans to make ends meet.

So, the welcome call from his agent that he was on Brickman's list gave him a spring in his step as he entered the Wembley dance academy for the audition day. "Up the stairs, open the door, and about 100 actors fell out. It was like a cattle market. So, I literally had to edge my way in. As the crowd thinned out, this voice said, 'Oi! Tim, over 'ere.'" It was assistant director Dave Tomblin, who had also worked on *Barry Lyndon*. Tomblin put in a good word for the actor, and Morand made the coveted final list. "I was very honoured."[187]

For one hopeful, acting was just the latest in an already star-packed career that would eventually play second fiddle to a sporting passion. Cricket was in David English's blood from an early age. "I joined the Lord's ground staff when I was 17, but my passion was born at the age of four. My father used to bowl to me in our local Hendon Park, with three stumps chalked up on an Air Raid Shelter."

In 1963, following his Lord's job, he played for Middlesex Seconds team. The need for a paying day job led to a stint on the *London Evening News* in 1966. Five years later, a new career beckoned when he was made head of press and publicity for Decca Records and rubbing shoulders with the likes of the Rolling Stones and Tom Jones. Two years later, the music impresario Robert Stigwood invited him for an interview. "I've heard all about you. You're the one. We're going to start a record label." With Stigwood, RSO Records was born, and English would manage Eric Clapton and the Bee Gees, overseeing iconic albums such as *Saturday Night Fever*.

In 1976 he wanted to try acting and had a particular talent to offer Dickie. At the audition when English's time came, Dickie, after glancing at his notes, said, "David, darling, now you are a cricketer." English replied, "That's right, Sir Richard, let me be the grenade thrower."[188]

Happy with the reply, Dickie took note. English was in.

It didn't go quite to plan for others. Sebastian Abineri felt confident with Lindsay Anderson's endorsement. "I thought I was going to do a speech." Instead, the hopefuls were all lined up and inspected by Dickie as if on a military parade ground. As he paced up and down, eyeing each man, he would either offer a thank you or say, "We'll see you in Twickenham," ready for training. "And he went: 'Thanks very much for coming.' And I thought, *Oh, no.*" When Abineri returned to the Lyric with his tail between his legs, Lindsay Anderson was surprised by his protégé's news. A few days later, Abineri received a phone call from his agent to say he was in, "I can only assume that Lindsay had a word with Miriam and she got me in, which doesn't happen very often. But when it does, it's very welcome."[189]

Unlike almost all in the hall, Christopher Good had been offered a named part. Tall, with a cut-glass aristocratic accent, he almost embodied the cross section as the middle of his two siblings, one a vicar and the other a soldier. Acting had always been his passion. As an eight-year-old, he would cycle to Stratford theatre to watch the greats like Olivier and Gielgud. "They had an orange box that I stood on, because I wasn't tall enough, at the back of the stalls. And I saw lots of really extraordinary actors then."

Despite attending Cirencester's Agricultural College, Good jumped ship and went to the Central School of Drama in London. "I was slightly older than them. I always played the older parts in the end of term shows. And that was very galling. But when I left drama school, I was playing 18-year-olds. It was as if my youth started when I left drama school."

His most prominent theatre role was in the first post-war revival of R. C. Sherriff's searing World War I play, *Journey's End*. Good played the cub Lieutenant Raleigh, a thinly veiled portrait of the playwright's war experience. "I met Sherriff in rehearsal in London. He talked about the war, and that was very poignant because it was a totally different generation. My grandfather never talked about it." He didn't discover if this performance as a soldier on stage led to being recommended by Miriam Brickman. The two would later become close friends, and Good visited her in hospital as she lay dying from cancer.

On that day in 1976, Good jostled amid a throng of actors. "It just kind of knocked me for six. It was very funny, as it wasn't really a casting session." A few days later, he was called for a one-to-one at Dickie's office. "I remember it had the most wonderful porcelain. It was hardly a chat. I don't flatter myself, but I think he wanted to see me out of that vast mass of people just to see whether I would match up with Tony Hopkins."[190] He was cast as the umbrella-wielding Major Carlyle, playing opposite Anthony Hopkins' Colonel Frost.

Not all had to attend the cattle-market casting session. Edward Seckerson had known Dickie for a long time, thanks to the director's lifelong friendship with Seckerson's aunt. In 1972 Seckerson had secured a tiny part as a footman in *Young Winston*. "It was a distance shot when Anne Bancroft as Lady Churchill comes home with Winston after being beaten at school. And I literally had one line: 'Welcome home, my lady.' Except that Dickie said: 'No, Edward dear, you must bear in mind why she's come home.' So, there was all that method stuff going on during the two days of shooting it. I was in the moment, and that's what always mattered to Dickie. I didn't audition (for *Bridge*) because when Miriam Brickman mentioned me to Dickie, he said, 'Oh, I know Edward, so yeah, we'll have him on board.'"[191]

A few weeks later, the short-listed 100 assembled at the dreary wastes of Twickenham Studios, just north of London. Dickie, flanked by Dave Tomblin and Miriam Brickman, "raised his hand to calm the hubbub," remembered Abineri, and then detailed the stellar cast and enormous budget arrayed to tell the Arnhem story. Then, with the 100 still waiting to hear who would make the final 50, Dickie explained that there would be two waves of actors. The very first name read out was Sebastian Abineri. "I had to restrain myself from punching the air with my fist," the actor recalled later, perhaps just as well as he was wearing slippery high-heeled leather cowboy boots.

They were then shown *Theirs Is the Glory*, and as the lights came up over the hushed audience, Dickie, with tears in his eyes, said, "We've got to get this right, boys! For those men who fought so bravely and sacrificed so much." He urged them to do their research and to "think 1940s."[192] Crucially this would have meant many chopping their fashionably long '70s locks. They were engaged with a minimum of six weeks at £125 a week plus £50 expenses, considered a good wage.

Once the selection was complete, the plan had been to give them weapons training and up their physical fitness at the Parachute Regiment Depot at Aldershot. Instead, they were given their marching orders to assemble in Deventer at the end of April. Abineri recalls the flight over from England being "absolutely terrifying as I'd never flown before. I'd have made a very good paratrooper because, given half a chance, I would have jumped out the fucking thing."[193] The Edinburgh ex-copper, McKenzie, felt a fish out of water as he arrived in Holland. "We arrived at Schiphol. Nobody knew anyone. I didn't know anybody in the theatre. I was a detective, for God's sake. I knew nothing about acting—still don't!"[194]

They were driven by coach to their home for the next few months, a former orphanage dubbed "The Old Folks' Home," which sprawled along the Bagijnenstraat in Deventer. An ex-Desert Rat, Jack Dearlove, "a cadaverous figure" who bore a startling resemblance to the rat mascot of the famous 7th Armoured Division, was given the unenviable task of looking after this wayward bunch of men "of varying sexuality who were raring to get off the leash," and dealing with "things like outbreaks of crabs and all the ghastliness that goes on."[195]

While on the journey, Dearlove suggested the disparate group of strangers buddy up and bag their sleeping quarters. There were some options, as Edward Seckerson recalled, "Now this is interesting, because it shows how human beings bond with each other. There were certain people one could see from the word go are going to be the rebellious ones and the heavy drinkers. I sussed out among my fellow actors who might be a good person to share a room with."[196]

Arriving at the "imposing and grim-looking building," Abineri felt it looked the part as a military barracks with "lino floors and rows of beds, each with a sleeping bag and pillow."[197] He duly found a bed in one dormitory filled with the "rebellious ones." Meanwhile, Seckerson and his small band "found ourselves a room with five beds near the showers and bagged it."[198]

There was no time to unpack as Dearlove ordered them all back onto the coach for their first dose of military training—and the sounds of battle. As they got off the coach at nearby Bussloo, ready to get their uniforms, they were greeted by the sight of black-clad German Waffen-SS with their chilling death-head insignia. These turned out to be a bunch of Dutch extras. Suddenly, there was a very loud bang and a chorus of swearing. Rushing towards a cloud of smoke, the group saw a Sherman tank engulfed in flames. Mechanics immediately jumped off amid a chorus of swearing. It appears the precarious fuel system had exploded, and "the whole thing brewed up. That was our Welcome to Holland first day there."[199]

Filing through to pick up their uniforms and kit, they came face-to-face with the formidable Colonel John L. Waddy, who besides being chief historical advisor had been tasked with whipping these "Max Factors" into passable soldiers. At first sight of this new regiment, he was less than impressed: "I was understandably shocked at seeing this bunch of actors portraying men of my regiment. But the few ex-soldiers and marines could at once be spotted by their soldierly bearing."[200] Apart from ex-Marine Jack McKenzie, these included Shaun Curry, ex-battalion sergeant major in the Coldstream Guards; Mark Sheridan, ex-Royal Norfolks; Dan Long, ex-The Buffs, "who had a superbly honed physique";[201] and ex-Para, Mark York. Two stuntmen, Dougie Robinson and Paul Weston, joined ex-sergeant Bill Aylmore, who would be the film's armourer. All worked to transform these raw recruits to pass muster for Colonel Waddy.

The next day at 5 a.m., in what would become a daily ritual, they were awakened by Jack Dearlove. "He would come and rattle the lockers with a metal thing to wake us up. There would be curses galore around the room," remembered Edward Seckerson. "One chap in my room, Richard Ommanney, very tall and cool, would stand in front of a mirror sometimes, and say: 'Christ, you look a c**t, you really do. Look at the state of you!' And so being woken up with rattling at five in the morning was not pleasant."[202] For others, the late-night partying didn't help, as Sebastian Abineri would discover. Being the youngest at 21, he considered himself fit, having worked on a farm, and threw himself into the first day's training of a run round a lake. As the groggy recruits formed up, Abineri thought, "I'm going to try to win this." While some pretended to faint halfway around, he edged towards the front, which was led by the tall Christopher Good. Ahead was a hill, and Abineri was confident that he could take him. He made it to the crest before plunging downhill with a forward roll. Not having done his helmet up properly meant it was banging up and down. "And then this bloke ran up with a parachute regiment tie on, and said: 'Put your helmet on properly, go back and do it again!' It was Colonel Waddy. So, I put it on properly, did a forward roll, by which time about 15 blokes had passed me."[203]

Military training centres around the repetitious ritual of drill, all designed to install a sense of cohesion and unthinking obedience. "I taught the guys drill," said ex-Marine Jack McKenzie, "and it was a simple thing of getting into that mindset of a soldier. And they actually loved it. Marching them up and down, presenting and sloping arms, just to familiarise themselves with the handling of weapons."[204] Trained actors, like Tim Morand, found their drama school training came in handy. "We learned the square bashing and arms drill like a dance routine."[205]

Not all, though, enjoyed the training regimen. "I bonded with a chap called Tony McHale, who wrote *East Enders* for a long time," recalled Seckerson. "We both absolutely loathed physical training, particularly in 90-degree heat." Christopher Good was convinced if anyone was going to throw in the towel, it would be Seckerson. "Edward was very funny. I thought he's going to quit. I mean, he couldn't run to save his life!" In the end, all would stay the course. "I was exhausted at the end of it," Good recalled, "but it had a purpose for me. Because I was working towards understanding about the character who would have been quite fit."[206]

One day was given over to weapons training with the film's armourer, Bill Aylmore. They learnt to handle and dismantle the large array of weapons, including the British Bren, Sten, and Lee Enfield .303 rifle, the American M1 Garand, and the German Schmeisser and MG 40s. Perhaps the most important lesson was devoted to the firing of blanks, which were made of wood and could cause damage in close proximity. To graphically illustrate the point, Aylmore hung up a dead rabbit and, using a Bren gun, fired at it at close range. "He stood about ten yards, quite a distance back," remembered Tim Morand, "and he shot at the hare, and the whole thing disintegrated to show us how dangerous what we were doing was."[207] For Seckerson, it starkly brought the brutal reality of the Arnhem battle to life. "It was upsetting for some of us. I remember feeling quite depressed, because I could identify with the age and emotions of the soldiers in the real situation; how vulnerable they must have felt. The reality was at hand, as we were actually handling weapons. It had quite a profound effect on me. I remember thinking the numbers of casualties were appalling, and the age groups were so small. I think this is why Dickie wanted our fresh faces."[208]

By the time the basic training was completed three weeks later, Jack McKenzie was impressed by these actors-cum-soldiers. "When the guys were relaxing, they didn't just go and have a fag; they were cleaning their weapons. Out came the oil bottle, and I thought, that's what soldiers do. Everybody made sure all their rifles and machine guns all worked. I thought it was quite an interesting touch."[209]

To mark the end of basic training, there was a passing out parade where Dickie inspected his troops. "We all marched. It was terrific," recalled McKenzie, "and they looked great when you consider the average squaddie takes weeks to learn all that stuff. And these guys were actors, and they marched up to the location in ranks of three, came to a halt, did a left turn, and faced Richard Attenborough. And somebody said, 'No, the Paras don't come through till next month.' And he had to be convinced that they were actually actors. That's how good they looked."[210]

Dickie could see his experiment was going to pay huge dividends. "I knew that if there was a piece of action: of getting up from behind that wall, and crossing that road, and dodging down behind wherever they were going—they just knew how to do it because they were comfortable and confident as they were trained. But the expertise of those guys brushed off on the reality and the truth of what we were doing, and the preparedness of making sacrifice the tone of the day."[211]

By Dickie's side was Colonel Waddy, who was amazed at the transformation. "They started to look and act the part, and much of the credit for this must go to the actors themselves who soon became known as the A.P.A.—Attenborough's Private Army. Their morale and standard of performance were an example to the whole unit."[212]

Many people take credit for the name. Stephen Churchett, an actor and later TV screenwriter for *Miss Marple* and *Inspector Morse*, was the one who claimed it. "I think I'm responsible for that name . . . as they had to tap out all our 40 names on a call sheet. Then I said if we officially call ourselves Attenborough's Private Army, it would go a lot faster. With that, the A.P.A. became official. The mail just addressed to A.P.A. also arrived without any problems."[213]

10
"You Get the Prize..."
Deventer Bridge Part 1

The film's biggest star was the Wilhelminabrug at Deventer, which had been inaugurated as the Ijssel Bridge in 1939. Still under construction when war broke out, in 1944 as the battle raged at Arnhem, Allied air forces tried unsuccessfully to destroy it. The retreating Germans the following year added a few more knocks. Three years later, fully restored and bearing her name, it was reopened by Queen Wilhelmina.

The script required the bridge to be the epicentre of carnage as Frost's small force waged a bitter battle against immense odds. The production would require the complete closure for two weeks, with some additional days. A ferry across the Oder River was organised to maintain vehicle traffic, and a half-hour window for the bridge's cycle lane was dubbed the "five o'clock rush." The film company leased the area immediately around the structure for five months.

What is extraordinary is the serendipity that graced the production. The company had found not only a bridge that closely matched Arnhem's, but also a large carpark around the base surrounded by period buildings. To top it all, the south side again resembled Arnhem in comprising open fields complete with that most quintessential of Dutch objects—a windmill. Goldman presented his principal character with a splendid description in his screenplay:

It's the first time we've seen it all and here's the thing: it's lovely.
The arches are soaring and graceful. The river is several hundred

yards wide, and the approaches to the bridge make it a considerable structure. But despite its size, it's really a pretty thing. Painted a rust colour that is, even in this dim light, wonderful looking.

But a large fly in the ointment was a brutalist 1960s tower apartment block overlooking the bridge. It had been a frustrating obstacle for the designers and later the camera team. Dickie, standing next to the art department's impressive model of the bridge area, explained the issue to a visiting local TV crew. "We are shooting the film, as you probably know, in Panavision, which is this sort of proportion (he signed a rectangle with his hands) so that obviously everything has to be designed and conceived in order to accommodate that proportion. And that is one of the problems," he said as he tapped the offending apartment building represented in painted grey wood. One of the A.P.A., Stephen Churchett, recalls a tall tale, probably apocryphal, that circulated around the set. "The story was that Joe Levine actually offered to cut off the top four stories, and Deventer quite rightly said, 'No. You will have to find a way of shooting around it.'"[214]

It would be in the carpark, at a cost of £70,000, that would see the most extensive efforts by the art department. Using surviving photographs, Terry Marsh and his team reconstructed the buildings that Frost's men had so gallantly defended. Five structures, some with detailed interiors, spanning both sides of the north ramp, were constructed by Peter Dukelow and his construction team. The structures needed to be robust and durable to allow the effects team to blast the hell out of them, and still be safe enough for the cast and crew.

On Tuesday, 11 May 1976, filming began for a series of shots showing Anthony Hopkins as Frost leading his men through the deserted streets of Arnhem towards the bridge. It is the first sighting of the A.P.A. in battle formation as the detachment covers its tentative advance for snipers, "and they go from corner to corner approaching the bridge." Ex-Marine, Jack McKenzie, was one of them: "It's all very quiet except just a patter of feet on the cobbles, and that's quite a remarkable shot as soldiers prepare themselves for an assault." One shot in a backstreet includes a nice touch of a couple of civilian extras peering over a rickety balcony at the edge of frame. Strangely, the Resistance family was not called upon to appear. The call sheet details 35 members of A.P.A. to play the paratroopers, with a handful of named characters: Christopher Good as Carlyle, Paul Copley as Frost's batman Wicks, Ian Liston as Whitney, Ben Cross as Recce Trooper, and Edward Seckerson as British Padre.

"I was actually very disappointed to be cast as the padre, because I thought what the hell have I been going through all this military training for, if all I need to do is comfort people!" exclaimed Seckerson. Jack McKenzie, as he recalled his military years, understood Seckerson's disappointment. "As John Waddy said, they had this bloody padre at Arnhem, and everybody avoided him like the plague. Edward's kind of lovable, but when he came out with a clerical collar nobody spoke to him, because he was a priest!"[215] Seckerson complained to fellow A.P.A. Sean Mathias, "I said, 'After we've been through this stuff, I don't feel that I'm a part of it anymore.' And he said, 'Come on, what are you upset about? You've got a named part.'"

Every member of the A.P.A. would appreciate the sense of brotherhood. "There was that wonderful camaraderie and supportive spirit at all times," said Seckerson, "and it outweighed all the monkeying around and bullshit." Once he had been talked around, he enjoyed the added benefit that being named meant more money. "Every day we filmed as our character, we got featured fees on top of our wages."[216]

The principal set next to the bridge rampart, which would become Frost's HQ, was the home of an elderly lady and her middle-aged son. They appear on the first evening of the battle as Frost and his men arrive at the bridge unopposed. In a splendidly written scene, Hopkins as Frost yanks on the doorbell and, while he waits, notices the countryside and then the "twigs/leaves" camouflage they are all wearing. He suggests to Major Carlyle (Christopher Good) that camouflage helmets won't be much use in the town. When the owner finally opens the door, Frost's polite, if abrupt, request to requisition the house is a nicely judged piece of writing: part genial—part ruthless. *"Look here, I'm extremely sorry, but I'm afraid we're going to have to occupy your house,"* and without waiting for the owner, a "bachelor" played by Hans Croiset, to respond, Frost beckons his men inside. The home of the civilians, and possibly their lives, seem doomed to destruction.

Inside, as the soldiers hastily convert the quaint home into a military fortress, the extraordinary detail the art department has tendered to their set is obvious. It has the air of a Victorian museum that is in keeping with the "old lady," played by Mary Smithuysen, who is rooted in a more genteel past. As the civilians retreat into one room and close the door, the film cuts to the rooftop door opening. Frost steps out and the camera pans to show his panoramic view of the bridge. Hopkins as Frost makes a bolt-upright military stand to attention as he raises his binoculars. His action adds a nice character touch that not only suggests the born warrior but also conveys a respect for the enormous job before him. And in the process, he masks that most human frailty—fear. The film boasts many of these brief moments that deserve to be noted and applauded.

Led by Major Carlyle, a small detachment attempts to storm the south side of the bridge. This was the first action sequence to be filmed on the structure. Christopher Good, brandishing an umbrella, plays his character with suitable eccentricity. Carlyle is closely based on one of the most colourful personalities of the battle—Digby Tatham-Warter, who did indeed carry an umbrella. Commanding A company, 2 Para, Tatham-Warter was considered by Frost to be "a Prince Rupert of a man; he would have been a great cavalry commander on the King's side in the war with the Roundheads." Standing over six feet, Tatham-Warter possessed nerves of steel, no doubt helped by tiger hunting during his pre-war India posting. Described as an exemplary leader, he had a weakness with alcohol, often leading to drunken fistfights in the officers' mess. Yet the following morning, he would be impeccably turned out—oblivious to the previous night's shenanigans. Arnhem would be his first battle, and at one point he asked his commander how it compared to tussles that Frost had seen before. Frost, in his airy matter-of-fact manner, replied that it was hard to say as some things were worse but others weren't—they still had food and water, but were low on ammunition.

As the bitter battle continued, Tatham-Warter, wearing his maroon beret and sometimes a borrowed bowler hat but always carrying his umbrella, was often seen walking nonchalantly around the defences despite heavy mortar fire, and he led several bayonet charges. At one point, he stopped a German armoured car by shoving the umbrella through the observational slit and poking the driver in the eye. During an intense firefight, he noticed the battalion chaplain, Father Egan (probably the basis for Seckerson's padre), was pinned down but assured him, "Don't worry about the bullets, I've got an umbrella," before escorting him to relative safety. Later, a fellow officer jokingly scoffed at his faithful prop, "That thing won't do you any good," to which Tatham-Warter replied, "Oh my goodness, Pat, but what if it rains?"[217] Tatham-Warter was later injured by shrapnel, and after the fall of the bridge was taken to the shell-shattered St. Elizabeth Hospital. Escaping, albeit into German-held territory, he remained at large thanks to the bravery of Dutch civilians. Gathering many other Airborne fugitives behind German lines, Tatham-Warter helped to plan and execute Operation Pegasus. With the aid of the Dutch Resistance, 150 men made a daring escape across the Rhine to the Allied front line. For his extraordinary conduct both during and after Arnhem, Digby Tatham-Warter was awarded the Distinguished Service Order, and he died in 1993.

By strange coincidence, Christopher Good's schoolmaster, Frank Florrie, had been a close friend of Tatham-Warter. "I rang up Frank, and asked him what he [Tatham-Warter] was like, and Florrie just said he was very brave—very tough. But Dickie said my character was an amalgam of people, which embodied that eccentricity that you find in situations of survival."[218]

Historically, the assault led by Tatham-Warter on the bridge's south side was also supported by flamethrowers stationed across the street from Frost's men. Goldman split the action into two halves. Given 12 members of the A.P.A., including Sebastian Abineri, Colonel Waddy organised the action. Using a blackboard and pointer, he divided the men into three units for the attack. The retired officer clearly relished planning another combat mission as he smacked his pointer at a chalk mark: ". . . the fucking Krauts are at the other end of the bridge." Someone chirped up that these men (the Germans) were "now our allies." To which Waddy replied tartly, "They may be our allies . . . but they're still fucking Krauts!" Abineri recalls this got a belly laugh, "and rather set the tone for the rest of the shoot."[219]

On Sunday, 16 May, with the bridged closed, Waddy's rehearsed pillbox attack was filmed. The call sheet specified that the wardrobe department supply arm/knee pads to protect vulnerable body parts when tumbling onto concrete. The scene starts with Christopher Good's Carlyle making good use of his umbrella, as he directs the advance like an orchestra conductor. Good recalled his creative process: "I thought, this is terribly important to understand the person, how strong he was, and what was he showing to the enemy. Walking on the tarmac, I suddenly got a feeling of how he might appear. I remember my father with his shooting stick under his arm. All these things were going through my mind because I was the character. I think Dickie must have seen in me what he wanted. And so, I had to trust that."[220]

Helped by the hump in the bridge, their furtive movement is hidden and promises complete surprise. Unfortunately, a machine gunner in a pillbox next to the bridge opens up, and the attack is repulsed.

Stationed in the mock-up pillbox was Bill Aylmore, the armourer, firing blanks from a belt-fed MG42 Spandau machine gun. Sebastian Abineri's section had to move along the main road, and although it was preplanned make-believe, Abineri wanted to treat it for real. His description of the attack in his entertaining memoir, *The Boys from the*

Bridge, is worthy of any combat account. "We started to move rapidly towards the pillbox. After about 10 seconds, the MG42 opened fire on us with the sound like a malevolent sheet tearing, such was the rate of fire. I hurled myself down by the kerb and crawled forward; I got to within 10 feet of the pillbox and jumped up and leapt over the rail on to the western cycle track to find myself staring straight down the barrel of the MG42 as it opened fire. I could feel the hot air from the barrel and the splinters of wood hitting me as the shredder in the barrel ground up the wooden bullets going through it . . . I was well and truly 'brown bread' as Bill, the armourer, who was operating the MG42, took great pleasure in telling me later!"[221]

Christopher Good, who led the charge with his umbrella, remembered how his mental preparation was soon swamped in the adrenalin rush. "After Dickie said, 'Put your umbrella out for the signal to go forward,' my instinct took over. I became just this guy, rather than me actually thinking about it. Once it started, you're in the moment."

With the scene over, Good and the others, slightly out of breath, trotted back across the bridge, where a crowd of onlookers had gathered to watch the action. "When I went back, there were these two little boys on the side of the bridge, and I said, 'Are you okay?' Some Dutch man came up and said, 'That's exactly what happened. This guy [Tatham-Warter] came and talked to us two small boys. Which was an extraordinary thing.'"[222]

While the visual action was authentically presented, the soundtrack is devoid of the Red Devils' famous war cry: "Wahai Mohammed." This had been first used by the paratroopers in the rugged hills of North Africa in 1942. It was copied from the local Arabs who used it to kick off communication with one another. At Arnhem the war cry took on a special and urgent meaning instantly determining friend from foe as the Germans found it unpronounceable. It's not known why the cry never made it through the sound dubbing process. Abineri remembers his fellow A.P.A.s shouting it out during this first sequence. "We screamed 'Wahai Mohammed' during the attack on the pillbox, but it was drowned out by the general din, after which I went slightly deaf for a couple of hours."[223] A professional sound recordist like Simon Kaye would have almost certainly recorded the shouting separately as wild track, which would be offered up as one of the multiple tracks for final balancing. The decision to hear it would then have been Dickie's and that of sound mixer Gerry Humphreys at Twickenham Studios. Perhaps the most probable reason for muting it was one of confusion.

The assault is quickly dispersed by the unseen machine gun stationed in a pillbox beside the bridge, and Frost then orders its destruction. Two soldiers, Private Dodds and Corporal Davies, are ordered to the job using a flamethrower. These two were played by Anthony Milner and Alun Armstrong. The latter is a familiar face on British TV, where his roughly hewn features have seen him cast in "the full spectrum of characters from the grotesque to musicals . . . I always play very colourful characters, often a bit crazy, despotic, psychotic."[224]

Perhaps cast for their unmistakably rough-and-ready British look, the pair are introduced sitting inside a Dakota during the drop. Seen in a tracking shot that incidentally includes Sebastian Abineri dealing with a toothache is the head of a chicken on Davies' lap. While these characters are fictional, the bird is not. Myrtle—the parachick, a reddish-brown pet chicken—belonged to Lieutenant "Pat" Glover of the 4th Parachute Brigade. Strapped to his body, Glover's special pet had made six training jumps that earned her parachute wings, which were fastened to an elastic band around her neck. She was so adept that Glover could free her at 300 feet, and with "a frenzied flutter of wings and raucous squawking,"[225] Myrtle gracefully floated down to earth, where she would wait patiently for Glover to land and collect her. Arnhem was Myrtle's first combat jump, which the pair managed without a scratch. As the battle became fiercer, the officer would regularly exchange Myrtle, in her satchel, with his batman for safe keeping. Sadly, this valiant bird came a cropper.

Goldman's script has Dodds jokingly offering a 10-shilling note in exchange for Myrtle, *"in case the bleeding grub runs short."* Davies, who is supposed to be Welsh, replies: *"Put your fucking money away, boyo, and I'll try and forget I heard that. This lady is the only qualified parachick in the whole British Army, and we both intend to come out of this one with our wings on—don't we, Myrtle, my lovely?"* In the film, there is no conversation in the Dakota scene, so it's not clear if this dialogue was even filmed. While Myrtle can be glimpsed clasped to Davies during the forced-march sequence and again in the foreground as Frost waits for the house owner to open the door, she then disappears. In the night scene as Dodds and Davies gingerly approach the pillbox, Goldman's script had a bit of interplay about the parachick where Dodds apologises, *"We was only joking about Myrtle."* Davies replies he knew they didn't mean it, and with a twinkle pats the flamethrower, adding *"I'd make sure you roasted before she did."* This was replaced with Dodds warning Davies to be *"sure to hit that slit first time."* Why poor Myrtle was written out is unclear, but in line with the adage "never work with children or animals," Myrtle may have been considered a production issue too far!

Unfortunately, Davies doesn't hit the slit, and his flames ignite an ammunition dump next to it. As Goldman described in the script, *"The burning shed explodes like Krakatoa, and there are tracer bullets shooting all hell around like fireworks . . ."*

The night sequence would require three evenings to complete as Davies, minus Myrtle, manhandles a flamethrower against the pillbox. FX supervisor John Richardson faced three major effects challenges. First, he needed to build a real flamethrower that could not only spurt a sufficient flame but also be handled by an actor. "We actually found a rather old flamethrower that was correct for the period from Bapty's, the gunsmith. We stripped it down and rebuilt it in a safer way. We could get the flames to go about 75 feet. We did lots of testing with it, setting fire to the field at the back of our workshop with great glee."

Second, wooden huts that housed ammunition would need to explode with tremendous force and spectacle. Third, the already battle-scarred Wilhelmina bridge would need to be set alight to simulate the paint igniting through the exploding ammunition. "We laid in 55 charges, and we had charges to blow up the hut sending debris in the air," said Richardson, "fireballs, flares, you name it, we had it in there."[226] The enormous noise generated made one key crew member wince. "I don't like noise and bangs, but it was a pretty good display actually,"[227] recalled Geoffrey Unsworth, the director of photography, who was in the thick of battle noise for six months.

The bridge on fire would prove to be the most complex and lengthy effect to accomplish. "It was predominantly propane gas," recalled Richardson, "all piped up through special burners. We ran it through fireproof fabric tubes so that it disburses the gas out."[228] The various takes offered the locals a colourful night-time illumination, with Unsworth facing the challenge of exposing the film correctly. "Actually, I didn't need too much source light, because the effect was all coming from the explosions. The smoke silhouetted the bridge."[229] This had been the first image to capture Dickie's imagination a year earlier as he read the Ryan book: "The Bridge Caught Fire," he had scribbled in his notes. Seeing his initial excitement finally made manifest by Richardson's team at 1:30 a.m. "was very exciting and I wanted to weep a little,"[230] Dickie admitted.

"The initial explosion was terrifying," recalled Unsworth. "Sheets of flame and the ammunition shooting off into the night sky. It was really a horrifying spectacle. I'm sure the townspeople must have thought it was the end of their bridge."[231] John Richardson is at pains to explain that the structure suffered no damage:[232] "We clad the bridge with asbestos attached with galvanized wire, which was a hell of a job, and then we had to position gas burners on it, to try and make it look as though the paint was burning. We had to do all that without chipping the paint. That was the funny bit, but we managed to do it without burning the paint as well."[233]

The flaming bridge is one of the film's memorable moments with Frost's hunting horn, described by Goldman as *sounding 'Gone away' . . . the sound is haunting, cutting through the night,"* and prompts the watching German General Bittrich, played by Maximilian Schell, to shake his head. He *"half smiles"* with admiration, saying, *"Fools' courage."*

🦋 🦋 🦋

At first light on Monday, 18 September 1944, Captain Gräbner, commander of *SS-Kampfgruppe Hohenstaufen*'s crack reconnaissance battle group, led 20 lightly armoured vehicles to dislodge Frost's men.

GRÄBNER'S CHARGE. It is a wild act, the half-tracks and armoured cars roaring up the approach onto the bridge itself, then roaring across the part of the bridge that spans the river down into FROST's positions on the other approach—all the guns firing full out and the drivers doing an incredible job because the bridge is full of debris from the explosion of the previous night.

For the production team, a lot rode on Gräbner's charge sequence. For Levine, this first epic action sequence to be shot would set the pace and quality for the rest of the shoot. But barely a month into production Joe was keenly aware he needed more money and intended it to wow potential backers.

With only limited time available on the bridge, most of the preparation had been done elsewhere. First, Michael White had produced a series of storyboards, a method Dickie found extremely helpful. White would stay attached for the whole shoot and would often sketch new ideas as the production developed. Cameraman Peter MacDonald was closely involved in this pre-planning. "Sometimes storyboards are a total waste of time. But I think in this case, it was really necessary. We storyboarded the entire film; often me and David Tomblin used to work them out with Michael on a Sunday. We contributed by suggesting compositions, and then showed Dickie the rough idea. And he could say, maybe not this, or that, and then Michael would go and do it properly." From these storyboards, hours were spent using Airfix model tanks on a scaled-down miniature. Then the stunt drivers in the various armoured cars, half-tracks, and *Kübelwagens*, in what came to be known as Charlie Mann's Squadron, rehearsed on a marked-out area of the factory at Twello.

For the first shot as the column arrives on the bridge, MacDonald, who had been watching the final rehearsal through his extreme telephoto 800-mm lens that flattens perspective, had a flash of inspiration. "I saw something that's quite interesting: the bridge dipped down the other side. So, you had an empty frame, and then you saw this little aerial waggling up, then followed by the armoured cars." The foreshortening effect exacerbated by the heat haze was immediately obvious to his cameraman's eye. Said MacDonald: "It was one of my favourite shots in the film. The good thing about Dickie was, if you had an idea like that, he would back you, even if it wasn't storyboarded and suddenly you saw it on the day. It might take two or three takes to do because it's quite a difficult shot. If you thought it was worth it, he would back you to the hilt."[234]

While Geoffrey Unsworth decided on the correct exposure and the use of lights and filters on a given shot, he left MacDonald to choose the lens and composition. This being his first film shoot, actor Christopher Good was impressed by how the pair strove to involve the actors in the dark arts of cinema. "Geoffrey was quiet and was very concentrated on the job. But once he got it how it should look, he relaxed, and you could talk to him. But Peter was much more available. He'd explain when the camera comes towards you, just turn your head this way, then we'll get a much better shot, things like that. That generosity of taking time with you, making you feel comfortable with what they were doing. For a novice like me, it was enormously helpful."[235]

Hired to document the production as *The Arnhem Report* was film critic Iain Johnstone, who had made several documentaries on stars including Clint Eastwood and John Wayne as well as producing *The Frost Interview* and the BBC's Watergate coverage. Johnstone would later front the BBC's popular *Film '82* programme during regular presenter Barry Norman's sojourn from the show.

With Gordon Arnell, Levine's head of publicity, serving as producer, Johnstone and cameraman Martin Bell had unfettered access to the entire production. Bell's 16-mm camera, supplemented by sound recordist Keith Desmond with another camera, got superb coverage of the action sequences.

At the beginning of *Report*, Bell's camera catches Levine, complete with German officer's peaked cap, grinning like a schoolboy as he strikes up conversation with a group of extras on the bridge. Dickie politely suggests that being Dutch, the extras have no idea what he is saying. "Joe reminded me of a mafia hitman," Peter MacDonald recalled fondly. "I loved the man, but you really wouldn't want to cross him. He was a great character, but he never knew my name. I was always 'eyes.' And it was like, 'Hey, eyes, will it be okay?' I said, 'It's going to be fucking great, Joe.' And he'd say, 'It better be, it's costing me money.'"[236]

The Arnhem Report also showcases the imposing figure of First AD (assistant director) David Tomblin, whose measured, laconic, cockney tones exuded quiet control and authority. Perhaps a hint at the stressful burden he carried was his incessant rolling of 'ciggies' from a tin of Dutch shag tobacco. His right-hand man was Second AD Steve Lanning, who worked with Tomblin on many films. What set this select group of Brits apart from their American counterparts was their coolness and even temper. "David was not a shouter," recalled Lanning. "On *The Omen*, with Dick Donner directing, the American producer felt we weren't noisy enough! He wanted Dave Tomblin to have a megaphone. So, David spent a day loud-hailing into both Dick Donner's and the producer's ear, to the point where they asked him to put it away. That was the difference between the American AD, who would shout and be the only voice you heard. If you did it properly, you didn't need to shout. If you do, it means that there's no control. I was very fortunate to grow up with him as an assistant director. We were the first choice for quite a long time."[237]

With the bridge in the background, *Report*'s cameraman Martin Bell had a ringside seat for Gräbner's attack. David Tomblin calls out, "Turn over." The camera team answers: "Speed. 105. Take one." In the foreground, on the Frost house veranda next to the Panavision camera team is Dickie with his hand on Anthony Hopkins' shoulder. He tells Tomblin that he'll give the command for Charlie Mann's growling German half-tracks at the far end of the bridge to move. Tomblin then asks, "Do you want a pause before they come in?" Dickie replies calmly, "You can go straight away, dear." Via the PA, Tomblin instructs his assistant on the bridge to "bring them ahead" before shouting: "ACTION! GO!" Then Dickie, with a tap on Hopkins' shoulder, ushers him forward, "Action—Tony." [238]

As the German half-tracks come thundering across the bridge, there is a hail of gunfire amid multiple explosions. On the veranda next to Hopkins, an A.P.A. member rapid-fires his Bren gun. He finishes a magazine and immediately changes it. But the new mag doesn't fit properly. Like a trained soldier, rather than force it, he calmly reaches down for another clip, changes it, and continues to fire. "It's called the first IA, or Immediate Action." Jack McKenzie, ex-Marine and A.P.A. member, explained. "The first IA changing magazine is cock gun, take off mag, new mag, cock gunfire. So, they did it automatically. Our chaps had been trained to do that without thinking about it." [239]

The *Report*'s film editor, David Elliot, cuts together many takes from multiple angles to create the impression of one sequence for the documentary. In a series of brief shots, we see Johnny Richardson's effects control table being played like a piano as close-by vehicles slip and slide, engulfed in plumes of smoke and flame. One capsizes and careers to barely feet from the camera crew. Peter MacDonald noted that with each subsequent take, concentration could ebb and danger threaten. "A few times, I had to give the camera crews a big bollocking," he recalled, "when some of the younger ones after one take thought it's safe to be closer to the action than they should be. Just because it went right once does not mean it's gonna go right twice. Everyone is so much on the ball on take one, often people get overconfident. People have been hurt and even killed going to take two or three when it wasn't necessary." [240]

This sequence would have been covered by several cameras, all at a safe distance. In the final film, there are some hair-raising closeups of grinding metal as the half-tracks careen into each other. "We had several lightweight *Kübelwagens*," explained John Richardson. "The tanks would either just bat them out of the way or drive straight over them, crushing them down to a sardine can size."[241] To achieve these close shots, cameraman MacDonald dared not risk the expensive Panavision cameras—or indeed, an operator. "We had these little tiny clockwork Bell & Howell Eyemo cameras, with a chunky Panavision lens on it—the lens is bigger than the camera!" said MacDonald. "You could put that camera under a tank, and if it got hit—it wasn't a problem. It was almost indestructible." Originally used as combat cameras, one person was very familiar was them. Dickie had used one while squeezed in the tail of a Lancaster bomber during the war for capturing the destruction wrought by the bomb run. "I'd film them crouched on my knees in the cramped turret space, then struggle with my frozen fingers to reload the Eyemo in time for the next run."[242]

For the movie, MacDonald had the Eyemo's clockwork mechanism replaced with a motor. "I worked with Desmond Davis (later a DP), who was a service cameraman during the war, and he told me that once he was filming Montgomery inspecting troops. Desmond would wind up the camera to film Monty coming down the line talking to the men. But when he heard the camera stop, he just walked away. Monty just wasn't interested in what the private wanted to say."[243]

The intense action, with explosions, shooting, smoke, and flames, is quickly ended by the curt order "Cut!" Tomblin's quiet authority is visible in *Report* as the take ends. Using a PA, he calls out, "Hold it," only to be upstaged by Dickie's louder and impassioned, "Hoooold it!" Once all stilled, Tomblin addresses the priorities. "Let's see if everyone's all right." Next, he orders up the fire engine to deal with the flames, but stresses, "Don't panic, just take it up there, slowly and quietly . . ." and then again waits for conformation that nobody's hurt.[244]

Peter MacDonald forged a strong rapport with Tomblin over several major films: "I was always a bit hot-headed. I would fly off the handle, and he would just grab hold of the scruff of my neck. He was much stronger than me and just picked me off the ground and pulled me back to where I should be. And he said, 'That's not the way to handle this or that. This is the way we're going to handle it.' David was pretty much a one-off. I think then there were about two or three ADs that really would make a difference. You had to become the director's baton in their back pocket. I always wish that the ADs were more appreciated. He, like me, loved doing what he did. I guess it sounds a bit corny. We both came from fairly humble backgrounds. The film industry allowed us to become a superstar in some respects. It gave you a job that had enormous responsibilities and often a lot of respect."[245]

Actor Christopher Good also noted Tomblin's calmness and good nature. "I remember him getting more exasperated than angry if people weren't moving too fast. David was a lovely guy. When you'd finished for the day, he would always say, 'Chris, thanks.' I think that was the nature of that particular man."[246]

While Tomblin would be busy readying all the logistical requirements for a scene, it allowed Dickie to concentrate on the actors. *Report* also shows glimpses of Dickie's precise direction. During the attack, one paratrooper fires prematurely out of fear and Colonel Frost reprimands him. Before they go for another take, Dickie suggests a tweak to Anthony Hopkins' delivery of the line. "Tony dear, may I make two suggestions? One, that 'hold your fire' should be more of an instruction than a reprimand." While suggestion number two is sadly lost to time, it's clear how easily understandable and concise Dickie's direction is for an actor.

Later, with the bridge strewn with crashed vehicles, Fred Williams as *"exceptionally handsome blonde"* SS-Hauptsturmführer Gräbner takes some last-minute direction. Dickie, complete with tweed hat, converses calmly with Williams, perched high in his vehicle. Having changed his mind about his previous instruction, he asks the actor to "assume a moment's hesitancy from the driver," as he faces the burning pileup and then asks what the German word for forward would be. Williams, whose real name was Friedrich Wilhelm Löcherer, suggests, "*Weiter!*" Dickie asks if he'd be happy to use that word. "Weiter! Weiter! Weiter!" Williams replies enthusiastically. Content with the suggestion, Dickie requests, "Just make it twice Fred, will you?"[247] Colonel Waddy noted, "SS-Hauptsturmführer Gräbner with his SS Reconnaissance Battalion must have thundered across Deventer Bridge more than a dozen times, and he himself suffered his fiery death at least six times over."

Major-General John Frost, surveying the recreation of his own heroic stand on the Deventer bridge that day, turned to Colonel Waddy and remarked, "It was better than the real thing!"[248] Frost was reticent to express more than politeness and genial affability to questions about those grim days in 1944. *Report*'s Iain Johnstone tried to probe him, questioning if watching the filming was painful. The veteran soldier echoed the same response he had given to Digby Tatham-Warter during the battle, that one forgot the worst and only remembered the good things, but conceded "There's a wonderful sense of achievement and glory."[249]

John Dutton Frost, hero of the stand at the bridge, had been born in 1912 in Poona, India, into a military family. His sister Diana noted his tactical skills at a young age: "John used to take my toys as prisoners with his tin soldiers. We had a big playroom, which we all shared. And we each had a section of it. But he had a tactical advantage because he had a model railway which went right around the room. I had a peaceful little farm set in my area, and he would send his soldiers on the model railway to raid my animals."[250]

In 1932 Frost was commissioned as a second lieutenant into the Cameronians (Scottish Rifles) and saw service in Palestine in what was later dubbed The Great Palestinian Revolt (1936–39). When the world war came, he was attracted to the new concept of airborne soldiers and eagerly joined the Parachute Regiment in 1941.

With years to go before Allied forces could land in occupied Europe, it was left to elite commando and parachute units to make hit-and-run attacks. On 27 February 1942, Frost led one of the most celebrated, Operation Biting, a raid to grab the German Würzburg radar equipment from a villa at Bruneval on the Normandy coast. Frost and his 120 men landed by parachute on the frozen winter landscape. As they prepared for the assault, one NCO, Jimmy Sharp, was amused to see his commander "having a pee in a field. But seeing his example being so cool in occupied territory, a lot of us did the same, and made little holes in the snow. It got a wee bit hectic after that."[251] After a sharp firefight against stiff opposition, they achieved all their objectives at a cost of twelve casualties and six captured. Later, his unit was picked up by Royal Navy vessels from the beach below the villa. Churchill applauded the raid and invited Frost and his officers to his War Cabinet, where he was awarded the Military Cross.

Following Montgomery's victory at El Alamein, Frost and his paratroopers attacked German airfields in Tunisia. In one firefight, his detachment found itself heavily outnumbered and had to fight back to Allied lines. Despite dogged resistance, the unit lost 16 officers and 250 men. Years later, the German commander, Colonel Rudolph Witzig, met Frost and complimented him and his men as worthy opponents. "The men fought so fiercely that we gave them the name 'The Red Devils.' You gave us much trouble, but you fought as fairly as you fought well. You were in the same situation with your troops as I was with mine, always where the battle was fiercest. Now, 34 years later, we are enemies no more, and I'm glad we are friends."[252]

After some action in Italy, Frost and the rest of First Airborne Division were withdrawn to England, given a new commander—Major General Roy Urquhart—and would not see action again until September 1944.

Frost, with a taut leathery face, sleepy eyes, and a bushy moustache, was at pains not to cast himself as a hero. But to others, he was the quintessential leader who earned the respect of every man in the battalion, succinctly summed up by one speaking for all: "He didn't mince his words and seemed to inject confidence in everyone, even if you didn't like what he said. We would have followed him anywhere."[253]

In a quiet moment on set, away from press and cameras, Frost opened up candidly to 21-year-old Sebastian Abineri. "I was standing talking to General Frost," said Abineri, "and he said, 'I was furious when I got to the bridge at Arnhem, because it was just like this.'" He pointed out the remarkable resemblance of Deventer's topology to Arnhem, with its green fields stretching out from the south end of both bridges. Abineri remembered, "He said, 'They could have dropped us there, all six battalions.'" Clearly, the general had spent the intervening years running through the what-ifs. "He said there were Dutch Resistance in the town who were ready to grab the bridge. They were ex-Dutch Army and had hidden weapons all over Arnhem. They were ready to go. If they'd only got the order from our intelligence people." Abineri remembered the old soldier looked at him, nodded sadly, before saying, "It was a cock-up."[254] It would be a later sequence on the bridge that would cause the stoic general to get very upset and take issue with William Goldman's script.

Meanwhile, film editor Antony Gibbs cut the hours of material shot for the bridge attack down to an exciting three minutes. With this, Joe Levine intended to wow would-be backers. According to Goldman, he succeeded in raising the remaining finance. "We had a cutting room and everybody was invited to come look at whatever we had," said Goldman. "Because he [Joe] was convinced the quality was so high, people in various countries bid for it. We were $4 million in the black before we opened in America."[255]

Levine was ecstatic and felt vindicated with his choice of Dickie to helm his epic. "All the credit belongs to you," Levine proclaimed. "This of course does not preclude me from screaming at you, but I will scream a little softer."[256] Dickie said later: "Joe displayed great generosity to me. He paid me very well, gave me 10 percent of the net profits and, halfway through the schedule, having seen the first assembly of six weeks' work, increased my salary. He never once interfered with my decisions in relation to the shooting of the film or to its editing. Equally, he kept a meticulous eye on the production affairs."[257]

11
"There's More Power in Stillness"
Anthony Hopkins

"Tequila was my best friend because I hallucinate on it, and I started getting quasi-religious visions: I saw Jesus walking on Malibu beach, and the stones around were talking to me, and I talked to the beach. I looked at the stars and I went right through the Milky Way and back. I drank because I didn't like people, I drank because I didn't like crowds. I was a lonely man, and I kidded myself that I was a loner."[258]

🐦   🐦   🐦

The Anthony Hopkins who arrived in Holland to play Colonel Frost was a transformed man. Barely six months before, he was in a very dark place with his life spiralling out of control. At Christmas 1975, having bid his wife farewell back to England, the actor took a road trip in search of the mind-bending concoction, peyote. On Christmas Eve, he ended up in "a crummy hotel" in Phoenix, Arizona, propping up the bar. "They had an old-fashioned jukebox," said Hopkins. "I kept playing Neil Sedaka's 'Solitaire' ('There was a man, A lonely man, Who lost his love, Through his indifference . . .') over and over again, and I remember these two big guys sitting on the bar stools. One said, 'You gonna change the tune?' I said, 'Don't you like it?' 'Yeah, but not 15 times!' I went up to my room and I felt the despair and loneliness. I decided I was going to become a country-western singer. I wrote on a piece of paper: *I found myself in Phoenix, Arizona.* I thought that'd be good. Kris Kristofferson will sing that. I put the piece of paper on top of the cupboard and so nobody would find it. Probably still there. I think I was sending a message to myself." A few days later, on 29 December 1975, Hopkins admitted to himself that he was an alcoholic and attended his first Alcoholics Anonymous meeting and began the long road back to sobriety.

Born in 1937 in Port Talbot on the Welsh coast, Hopkins always considered himself different, and it was this sense of being an outsider that created his demons. "Ever since I was a little kid, I felt like I was on an offshore island with a pair of high-powered binoculars looking at the mainland. I felt there's something wrong with me."

Shunning the overtly masculine world of South Wales rugby playing, Hopkins found a new, exciting world in the local YMCA drama class. "I felt comfortable for the first time [when] they put me on the stage." It was something that lit the touch paper inside the offbeat teenager who perhaps as a mask and defence was, in his words, "a very good mimic and impersonator, and a compulsive joke teller. I wasn't being me; I was being all these different people. And I guess that's why I came into the acting profession."[259]

In 1960 after a stint of National Service studying at RADA (Royal Academy of Dramatic Art) and a spell in rep, Hopkins joined the English National Theatre under the "big-cheese guy Laurence Olivier."[260] Asked to do an audition, the young man did *Othello*, which the thespian knight was then appearing in. "He said that I had damn nerve to do it, but it was the devil in me. I admire him. He has figured a lot in my life. I've stolen unashamedly from him."[261]

Olivier saw great promise in the actor, but suggested he tone down one of his then-current mannerisms. "I used to be very fidgety. I thought I can't be acting if I wasn't moving. But it was Olivier who advised me to keep still; there's more power in stillness. And I think when you watch people like Spencer Tracy or Brando, their greatest power comes out of stillness, especially onscreen."

Picked to understudy the star, Hopkins had to fill the master's boots one night when Olivier was struck with appendicitis during the production of Strindberg's *The Dance of Death*. The veteran, renowned for his generosity to younger actors, praised the "exceptional promise" of his protégé, who "walked away with the part of Edgar, like a cat with a mouse between its teeth."[262]

Hopkins was keen to break into films. Peter O'Toole recommended the Welshman for *The Lion in Winter*. Filmed in 1968, this Levine-produced medieval royalty Christmas-from-hell story saw Hopkins hold his own as a repressed Richard the Lionheart, one of the sons caught in the power play between Peter O'Toole's Henry II and his wife, played by the much older Katharine Hepburn. Hopkins followed with what he considered his favourite role, Pierre Bezukhov, in the exhaustive BBC TV dramatisation of *War and Peace* in 1972, and was awarded the British Academy Television Award for Best Actor.

His professional relationship with Dickie would prove to be one of the most enduring of his career. Their partnership began with *Young Winston*, where he was cast in the small role as David Lloyd George. This dynamic and charismatic Welsh politician, who was renowned as a great orator and womaniser in almost equal measure, steered Britain through the dark days of the Great War. Hopkins, in just a few minutes of screen time, does a superb job to suggest these qualities with his eyes alight with fire and passion.[263] Almost immediately, he was considered one of the most talented actors of his generation. This, admitted the actor, led to a hugely inflated ego that vied with an almost childlike need for applause and affirmation. "I was addicted to approval—people's applause. I think one of the biggest killers is ego. And when it's the negative side of perfectionism, when one starts playing God, I really was self-destructive."[264]

Despite receiving recognition for his burgeoning talent, he fuelled these demons with a growing reliance on alcohol. Looking back at his dark days, he believed drink was a helpful prop. "I'm not going to be puritanical and say I hate booze. I love booze. And it did great things for me in the early years. It gave me a kind of confidence. But it also gave me a lot of fuel for my rage. I drank to quell the anger, but of course it made me more and more angry. I mean, I could empty an entire room. I'd go to a party and insult everyone."

Hopkins was on the cusp of stardom, but his demons held him back. "I was a menace to work with. I heard somebody say to the cameraman once, 'We'd better get him before lunch because he's just fooling around.' Because I wasn't fit for anything and yet the director said to me, 'Why are you doing this, Tony? Don't you know you're so talented? It's such a shame as you're gonna kill yourself.'"

🦋   🦋   🦋

Bridge was one of his first jobs after besting his demons. He threw himself into the part of Colonel Frost with gusto but was determined to avoid a caricatured impersonation. "What was unnerving was to play the fellow because I knew that he knew that we weren't as accurate as we should." Christopher Good noted how Hopkins would perfectly mimic the almost impossibly upper-class haughty tone of General Frost but chose not to adopt it on camera. Watching Frost closely, Hopkins sensed that he and the soldier shared a common gift: "You had to be a bit of an actor yourself when you are in command of these men. He's incredible, and I admire him very much. I'd like to meet him again under different circumstances. I think it must have been a little upsetting for him to be back there and to see a bunch of Hollywood people, you know, recreating a battle."[265]

Once he takes on a role, Hopkins prepares with extraordinary care and attention to detail, routinely reading the script hundreds of times. "All life is magical. Because we are the instruments, and all problems are technical. Stanislavsky called it 'the plane of inspiration' that takes off on the runway. The runway is the technique, the getting on with it, the pain will take off. And I think if it's used well and there's a lot of positive out of all the anguish and the pain and discomfort."[266]

Becoming the erstwhile commander of the A.P.A., he clearly felt a responsibility to the young actors who looked upon him as a role model. "Anthony Hopkins was the greatest actors' friend," remembered

David English. "He was one of us. He's obviously a very wonderful actor, but he never took himself very seriously."[267]

Stephen Churchett: "Tony Hopkins became like one of the lads and would make sure that we were looked after. On those very hot days, he had a trailer and we didn't, but he had us in and made some ice water or whatever. He was terrific."[268]

"I really admired Hopkins, he was a lovely man to work with," Edward Seckerson recalled. "He cared passionately about all the guys, particularly those who are drinking heavily, and would not waste any opportunity to lecture us on the evils of it. He said, 'You know, you are literally in the gutter until you make that decision: I have got to do something about this. It's got to be a revelation moment, sometimes it never happens.' But he said, 'In my case, I realised that I couldn't go on the way I was.'"[269]

Hopkins, speaking in 1978, was able to extemporise his journey that he would have explained to the A.P.A. "My drinking and my smoking were really a symptom of a kind of psychological, spiritual disorder. And that all I had to do was shift back in line with whatever it is that runs this universe, because I'm convinced that I don't run it anymore, as I always thought I did. And I don't need to do those things anymore."[270]

Hopkins endeared himself to the company by pulling star rank. He noted that the A.P.A. were having to travel to and from the wardrobe department, which was some distance from their digs. "And this was adding about 45 minutes, an hour to our daily schedule," recalled Edward Seckerson. "One of our group said, 'Why don't we take the uniforms home?' Tony was very instrumental in making that happen. He said, 'Look, this is absurd, these guys are going to be on set in this heat all day. We don't want to prolong the day.' He was great like that. None of the other stars of the film got involved in the same way that he did." Hopkins also used his leverage to provide extra mod cons for his erstwhile command: a brand-new dishwasher, a table-tennis table, and—less popular—a battered, out-of-tune piano, which tended to host a new Beethoven, fuelled by several pints, at 3 a.m.

The A.P.A. recall him as being very generous with both his time and talent. Seckerson remembered a fine example in one scene in which he featured, albeit fleetingly. During the later battle around the bridge, Frost is summoned up to the roof of his battered HQ. Frost has to thread his way through the throng of wounded and exhausted men up the stairs. During the rehearsals, he insisted on acknowledging the men individually on his way. "Tony, being the kind of man he was, identified them, and what relationship he had to them. Dickie was ready to shoot and he said, 'Tony, dear, can we move on?' And Tony was saying, 'No, I need to establish what I'm going to say as I go past—Morning, Padre, or whatever.' It's that matter-of-factness, that you're there in the heat of this situation and it's business as usual. That was the feeling that Hopkins wanted to get in his relationship with his unit. And so, there's that little moment he created. And Dickie got quite impatient on that day but had to yield to his star's wishes. I really admired Hopkins."[271]

While the script gives little indication of the warm friendship between Frost and his eccentric second-in-command, Major Carlyle, Christopher Good built a great rapport with Hopkins, which is echoed in their performances. "We laughed a lot together. He was the most brilliant mimic, doing people like Olivier, Anthony Quayle, Orson Welles. I just felt very relaxed with him. And I think that was the clue to our (onscreen) relationship that he embraced the eccentricity of this guy. He also invited me several times to supper with him and his wife; it just was such a lovely thing to do to bond with him." It was Good's first film role and he appreciated Hopkins' experienced advice. "I was helped by it. There was one scene in which he said, 'If you come a little faster upstairs,' things like that tiny detail, which of course an experienced guy like him would know about. He was very accepting of me."[272]

At the end of the day, Hopkins would join the unit in the Rijnhotel bar in Arnhem, which overlooked the Rhine. "Of course, he wasn't allowed to drink," Peter MacDonald recalled. "But he would sit in the bar at night sometimes with his wife and put money on the counter so all the crew could have a drink, which after you've been out for 12 hours running around in dust and smoke, one thing you crave, before even a shower, is a nice ice-cold Dutch beer. And he'd just sit there having a lemonade."[273]

Dickie's follow-up was *Magic* (1978), written by William Goldman and produced by Levine. The story of a ventriloquist and his dummy has always proved fertile dramatic ground, and *Magic* proved to be one of the best. Despite reservations in some quarters, Dickie knew who he wanted to play the title role of Corky. It would prove one of Hopkins best performances and would firmly place him as a star who could "open."

Hopkins, speaking during the press junket for *Magic*, was able to look back with pleasure and pride at how he had pulled his life together. "It's been an interesting journey. The last couple of years have been the best of my life. Maybe it's come with success or better work. And people used to tell me, you're a good actor, why quarrel with it? Well, I could never accept that on a deep level, and now I've accepted gratefully."[274]

12
"Is He Nuts? Run!"
Deventer Bridge Part 2

For several weeks in May and June, Deventer's proud Wilhelmina bridge was a war-torn mess. Littered around charred and wrecked German vehicles were smatterings of debris and shards of burnt and blasted timber. Throughout the long, hot days, black oily smoke from burning tyres drifted over the sweating unit and the legion of curious sightseers. To the chagrin of some locals, this smoke also covered much of the town, blighting the usually immaculate Dutch houses. By now, the chatter of machine guns and explosions was a familiar sound to the inhabitants, but on one day it all went eerily quiet.[275]

Through the drifting smoke, a solitary figure picked his way through the debris-strewn bridge. Young Dutch actor Lex van Delden, dressed in a German uniform, clasped a stick with a crumpled white flag. Reaching his mark, he shouted: *"My general says, there is no point in anymore fighting . . ."*

After several bitter days of fighting on the bridge, General Bittrich called on Frost to surrender. It was a moment that had caused immense trouble behind the scenes and had forced a script rewrite.

William Goldman had originally written a conventional dramatic moment where the two warring commanders meet in the middle of the blooded bridge: *"EXT. ARNHEM BRIDGE - DAY. The sun is going down. BITTRICH waits on the bridge."*

It echoes many similar moments in westerns and war films: the

150

protagonist and antagonist confront one another so they can each see the white of the eyes.

"*BITTRICH, watching as FROST stops, a good distance away. They face each other and after a long moment,*" Bittrich, via his translator Matthias, suggests, "*There is no point in continuing this fighting.*" Frost agrees, and Matthias says they are willing "*to discuss a surrender.*"

Goldman has Frost considering the offer in "*a long, long pause,*" with Bittrich waiting. Then, to the consternation of the German translator, Frost replies: "*We haven't proper facilities to take you all prisoner, sorry . . . I'd like to, but I can't accept your surrender; was there anything else?*"

While echoing rather more eloquently General McAuliffe's defiant "Nuts" at Bastogne during the Battle of the Bulge, the lines were taken directly from Ryan's book but not spoken by Frost. Goldman had merely shifted them. "I was just making a 'moment,'" the writer explained later. "I was trying to build up the star, which is what you do. It's pointless to give a terrific moment to a secondary character. And I had no idea that it would have upset the general, no idea at all."

Goldman was on his way back to New York when he got a call from the distressed General Frost asking to meet for dinner in London. After a few minutes of polite pleasantries, Frost came straight to the point: "'You've got to change that scene.' And I saw this horrible look of fear on his face. And I said, 'What scene?'" It was the surrender request. "He said, 'People will think I'm making too much of myself because I did not say that line.' And he was so upset, and I thought, *oh my god*, as I revered him." Sitting opposite a real, unequivocal hero, Goldman felt conflicted because he believed the lines underscored the stubborn courage of an inspiring leader. But like almost all veterans, regardless of their exploits, Frost considered he was a professional doing his job, just like his men—no more or less.

Similar lines had been said and in the same context. Bittrich had charged a British POW with the unenviable job of persuading his countrymen to surrender. He went to Frost; whose reply was short and blunt: "Tell them to go to hell!" Later, a German carrying "a not-very-white hanky tied to a rifle," approached Captain Mackay (in the film called Lieutenant Cornish and played by Keith Drinkel), who commanded the Royal Engineers in the schoolhouse on the other side of the bridge causeway. According to Ryan, Mackay assumed they wanted to surrender to him, but with only two rooms, he thought it would be "a bit cramped." He then told the German: "Get the hell out of here. We're taking no prisoners."[276] Iain Johnstone interviewed Mackay for *Report*, and the old soldier, with an officer's hat jauntily askew on his head, recounted very lurid descriptions of the battle. One wonders whether he added some spin to his surrender tale. Goldman merely strung the various utterances into a single, coherent line that draws to mind the legendary retort by Napoleon's Old Guard at Waterloo, "The Guard dies—it does not surrender!"[277]

Goldman was happy to find a compromise. "I remember saying to him, would you mind being present when it was spoken? He thought for a moment, and he thought that would be okay. I thought, *what are you doing this for?* I had caused discomfort to a man who was, for me, a great hero. After that dinner, I thought, I'll never get involved again with people who are alive."[278]

The eventual scene is a big improvement on the scripted original. Frost is summoned to the roof by Major Carlyle. They look down to see a solitary German soldier with a white flag. He says his general requests they surrender. Hopkins then delivers Frost's original blunt response—to go to hell—leaving the "moment" to Christopher Good's Carlyle. It is an inspired decision; a typically barmy thing for the eccentric officer with the umbrella to say. It is in character and underscores the dogged courage with that strangest of beasts—British humour.

Interviewed for *Report*, Frost was very keen to stress that the battle, despite its ferocity, did not involve hate. "We found that the Germans fought with great chivalry. And I hope that's depicted in this film. They were extremely meticulous about not shooting our wounded. Our stretcher bearers were always given a clear run, whether they had wounded with them or not." He was standing near one of the damaged sets beside the Deventer bridge that depicted his defence perimeter. During the battle, only one of his occupied houses escaped the flames, partly thanks to vigorous firefighting. Once the water supply was cut by the Germans, the house, which now contained 200 wounded, was about to be consumed. A medic "asked his permission to request a quick truce with the Germans. And this they rapidly did, and the Germans came in themselves and took quite a lot of risks to get us out. In fact, the building collapsed as the last chap was brought out."[279]

The script contained another scene that Frost may have objected to as "making too much" of himself. After the failure of Gräbner's raid, the Germans send over the heavy stuff in the form of a Tiger tank that crushes through the wrecked vehicles on the bridge and then rumbles menacingly towards Frost's men. The only defence is the PIAT, a handheld anti-tank gun, which fired a high-explosive round. Goldman describes: *"A SOLDIER beside him aims a PIAT gun at it and fires."* The projectile misses, and the Tiger fires again, knocking out the soldier, *"but FROST is braced, ready, and he's got the PIAT gun to his shoulder as CARLYLE slips in a projectile, and FROST fires … the PIAT round explodes harmlessly on the road behind it."*

In the film, Frost calls out *"Bring up the PIAT!"* and does what any commander would do—leaves the shooting to his men. Onscreen, it was the armourer, ex-army Bill Aylmore, who fired a dummy projectile (it is visible thanks to the slow velocity) and deliberately missed the moving tank before landing in one of the wrecked half-tracks. Each time, at that precise moment, John Richardson fired a suitably messy explosion. "During all the various takes, he (Aylmore) was able to put the bomb exactly to coincide with the special effects explosion,"[280] remembered Colonel Waddy with an approving professional eye.

Hopkins' Frost, unlike Robert Redford taking Nijmegen bridge, does nothing "heroic" in conventional cinematic terms, reflecting Frost's influence, and it is for the better. Frost's heroism onscreen is primarily his inspired leadership: giving concise orders and maintaining coolness under fire. Hopkins' insistence on name-checking his men that Edward Seckerson noted epitomises the essence of Frost, who is every inch the hero onscreen.

Frost spent a lot of time on set with Waddy at his side. Usually, he made small observations, and one of them has become legendary.

"We had arguments with John," Dickie recalled with a wry smile. "One marvellous one: Tony Hopkins is meant to be moving from one building to another. And Tony set off slightly crouching down as he ran across the road."[281]

Hopkins said, "I had to run across the street amid gunfire. And I did it as fast as I could, because I know that I would in that situation run as fast as I could, being a coward."[282]

Dickie added, "As we were still shooting the scene, suddenly Johnny was—'No! Stop!'"[283]

The exchange that followed became Hopkins' most oft-repeated anecdote from the filming: "He said, 'You ran too fast.' I said, 'What do you mean I ran too fast?' He said, 'Well, I didn't run as fast as that under gunfire. I tried to show the Germans contempt for their machine-gun fire.' So, you had to be a bit of an actor yourself when you are in command."[284]

Despite Goldman's adoration of Frost, he was bemused: "Well, you can't do that, because if you have Tony Hopkins walking across the street, the audience is going to say: 'Is he nuts? Run!'"[285]

It was a tough call for Dickie. Should he completely take Frost's point and risk ridicule, or find a compromise? "I just cut the sequence, got everybody back, reloaded the explosions. And Tony still crouched that bit." Dickie was always aware of the dilemma of trying to honour the courage, whilst making a believable movie. "But those guys actually did it. We have to capture the selflessness, the bravery. If we fail to capture that, and if we belittle that, we will defile the ultimate sacrifice made by a number of men who actually took part in the thing."[286]

Even as an old man, Frost's contempt for danger was still evident. One day, a Doberman Pinscher dog guarding the armoury trucks escaped its leash. The general had been passing by when the dog began to menace him. Watching the standoff was Sebastian Abineri, who affixed his bayonet to his rifle, ready to intervene. "Instead of running away as most men would have done, Frost seemed to swell in size and advance on the snarling animal. An element of doubt seemed to cross the dog's eyes and as Frost advanced towards it, he retreated from his imposing figure, put his tail between his legs . . . quivering with fear."[287]

Colonel Waddy, a young lieutenant during the battle, was determined to make the film as accurate as possible. Inevitably, there were clashes with the demands of cinema. Peter MacDonald recalled one scene that involved snipers embedding themselves as undetectably as possible. "Colonel Waddy was a nice man but lacking in humour. We'd lined up a very complicated shot with all the German snipers on the other side of the bridge. I went off to shoot something, and when I came back, I looked up, and said to David Tomblin: 'Where are all the snipers?' Colonel Waddy had hidden every sniper, so we couldn't see them, but I guess logically, that's probably what snipers do. I said this is a film, and all we see with all these different windows are puffs of smoke coming out, like someone burning their frying pan, so I had to persuade the colonel to change it."

MacDonald recognised that being too cinematic could also have its problems. "You always go over the top. You always add a bit more and a bit more." Having read Ryan's book, MacDonald used to call out Dickie ". . . if he might be tempted to change things a bit—filmmakily [*sic*], especially make the Americans more of the heroes than they were. I was very tough with him: 'No, Dickie, because in the book that doesn't happen.' He'd say, 'Stop it, you mustn't tell me that. I'm the director, Peter.' I said, 'Yeah, that's why I'm keeping an eye on you!'"

The film was blessed with a phalanx of veteran experts led by Waddy, including Frost, Urquhart, Horrocks, J.O.E. Vandeleur, and Gavin—all highly decorated commanders resplendent with pips and medals. But with the story's top-down point of view, MacDonald felt the ordinary Tommy and GI were underrepresented. "I said to Dickie, 'You know, war is not fought by officers. Like films are not made by directors! Which upset him a little bit! I said, we should get a private, someone low down."[288]

One morning, Sebastian Abineri was surprised to hear a Vickers machine gun "reeling off rounds at a terrific rate." With no filming going on, he knew Bill Aylmore "jealously guarded" his .303 bulleted blanks. Walking over to the armoury truck, he saw an old boy sitting on the ground firing the heavy Vickers. The man had an eyepatch and two metal claws for hands, which were clasped around the handle trigger, "his one eye glinting in a steely sort of way." After finishing firing with a satisfied grin, he turned to Abineri, and said in a rich Geordie accent, "That's the *furst* time *ahv* fired a *Vickah's* since I had *mah* hands blown off!"[289]

This was Andrew "Andy" Milbourne, one of the "low downs"— and an extraordinarily brave one. In 1938 with the war drums sounding across Europe, Milbourne, then just 15, left his job as an apprentice tackle maker and enlisted into the Royal Northumberland Fusiliers. In 1943 he joined the First Parachute Battalion and saw action in Italy.

At Arnhem, he fought as part of a machine gun platoon with the heavy Vickers. During the height of the battle around the Oosterbeek church, he was stationed to cover a vital crossroads heavily contested by German fire. He suffered horrific injuries when a German shell exploded directly in front of him, damaging his arms and killing two of his comrades. He recalled a voice saying, "Lord, he's copped it." His friend Terry "Taffy" Brace, a medic, came to his aid and constantly reassured him, "It's just a scratch, Andy,"[290] as he manhandled him to the dressing station.

Severely injured, he was later captured in the ter Horst house in Oosterbeek. The German doctors had to amputate his hands, and he also lost an eye.

After the war, Milbourne, a married father of one child, refused to be restricted by his war wounds. He worked in a coal pit in Ashington, Northumberland, using his fitted steel claws to pull on the pulleys and chains in the haulage house. "Naturally, I'd be a liar to say that I wouldn't rather have my hands," Milbourne confessed to Iain Johnstone. "The main thing that you've got to try and remember is that you've got to accept this." At the time of the film, he was the manager of Newcastle's war pensions office, dealing with many veterans, including those involved in the "Troubles" in Northern Ireland. "I'm the last of the Mohicans. I have seen some dreadful cases. You see, these things are still going on to this day—terrible. Wasn't it the great Bard, Robbie (Burns) once said, 'Man's inhumanity to man will cause countless thousands to mourn.'[291] It'll go on as long as there are people in the land, and they'll blame God."[292] Milbourne worked in the Ministry of Pensions until he retired, and then wrote two books on his experiences, *A Lease of Life* and *The Hovering Eagles*. Milbourne summed up his life with, "If, as a young soldier, I could have seen, in all its reality, the bloody streets of Arnhem and me sitting here in my steel hooks, I would have held my head high and, like a good soldier, marched forward."[293] Andrew "Andy" Milbourne died in 2009.

Unlike Milbourne, his friend Taffy Brace was depicted in the film by the thickset actor David Auker. During a scene around the Hartenstein Hotel, *"the giant medic"* Brace tends one of the wounded and hefts him onto his back before trudging to the aid point. Meanwhile, the wounded soldier complains, pleading for morphine. Brace replies, *"Morphine's only for people who are really hurt."* During the battle, Brace's irrepressibility and good humour were severely tested as vital medical supplies became scarce. "The only thing I could do for most of them was to take off their smocks and cover their faces,"[294] Brace recalled. "It was fantastic to see people who were willing to give everything, the last drop of blood, the last drop of water, their last crumb of bread. There was this fantastic comradeship."[295]

Jane Hershey, the young American who had secured a summer job with the publicity team, described the pair's irrepressibility in her journal: "Milbourne is semi-bionic. Proud of it, too. These men have no guilt about the war. In fact, they behave like two young boys playing soldier, or two old footballers remembering old cup matches. Brace talks with pride about how he stripped down his first German prison-er. And Milbourne insists that we pose him for stills behind a Vickers gun, the kind he was operating when his hands were shot off."[296]

Strangely, the film credits do not list as advisors the colourful and brave Brace and Milbourne. But Peter MacDonald felt they brought a unique insight into the ordinary soldier. "This Welshman 'Taffy' Brace came to join us in a wheelchair. And he was fantastic, because he was saying exactly what they did, what they felt, and so he was really in-spirational. And I said to him, 'Just whisper in my ear. Don't shout out loud. If you see something that we're doing is not what you would have done, etc., then we'll see what to change—but we are making a film.'"

The "surrender" scene at the bridge—in which the German soldier under flag of truce is told by Carlyle that the Tommies would like to accept the German surrender but lack facilities to do so—ends with the soldier trudging back to a stern-looking Bittrich in his staff car. To finally eliminate the Red Devils' tenuous hold on the bridge, Bittrich orders gravely: *"Flatten Arnhem."*

A brutal sequence follows as German Tiger tanks blast what was left of the set in a spectacular battle scene. Stuart Craig was amazed by the tolerance of the Deventer locals as his art department created the look of war devastation amid the historic district of their town. "It's a mark of the enthusiasm and generosity of the Dutch in their atti-tude to this project that they let us go in there with big earthmoving equipment, JCBs," said Craig. "And we could dig bomb craters, shell craters, and deposit mounds of rubble, and it truly looks like Dresden or Cologne."[297]

A.P.A. member Jack McKenzie, the ex-policeman from Edin-burgh, agreed to help the Dutch police direct traffic in what was the talk of the country. He had no idea that his impromptu phone call to Levine some six months earlier asking for a job was about to catch up with him. "Everybody in Holland wanted to come and see the specta-cle," said McKenzie. "It was just chaos. David Tomblin had about six two-way radios strung around his neck talking to different assistants all around the town. I was in a combat smock, a red beret with a Sten gun on my shoulder, dressed as a paratrooper. And this Dutch policeman said, 'Jack, they don't teach us to work traffic like this.' And I said, 'Give me your orange sleeve.' I had about five streams of traffic coming in and out of Deventer. Suddenly through this maelstrom of traffic, a huge limousine pulled up, and it was Sir Richard, Sheila his wife, and Joe Levine and his wife. And Dickie said, 'Darling, this is Jack, he's here to train our soldiers.' And the window went down, and it's Joe Levine, and he said: 'You're Jack McKenzie? You realise you telephoned me fucking four o'clock in the morning!' And the window went up, and on he went with a big smile on his face."[298]

The eight houses on the car park on either side of the northern ramp were convincingly constructed out of wood with moulded plastic walls and fasciae, all finished with a high degree of detail. "They were sets that were complete inside and out," Stuart Craig explained. "The movie needed that freedom to move from inside to out. You had to shoot everything in strict continuity, because . . . there was no going back once you started to take the roof off."[299]

The damage is clear in later scenes, where the set looks precarious, with holes in the floor. A.P.A. member Stephen Churchett, who never had a line, did play a corpse: "You can see me in closeup, probably for five seconds. The camera cranes up and there's a hole that has been knocked on the floor and I'm lying dead."[300] The realism does make one wonder how dangerous it must have been for both the actors and the crew with their heavy equipment. "It was all carefully choreographed," Jack McKenzie recalls, "but bits that weren't choreographed like the firing from the rubble and collapsing into a pile of bricks was very uncomfortable. We were rather bruised at the end of the day."[301]

The once immaculate houses were systematically pock-marked, holed, and burned with loving care by John Richardson's FX team. "This meant cutting out the wall to the after-destruction phase of it, rebuilding it with dummy lightweight brick work," Richardson explained. "Using either cork or plaster and vermiculite to give a sort of real brick finish. And then inside the house, we put some pretty heavy steel mortar pots that were sandbagged in with fairly heavy black powder charges. We'd blow the charges in a set sequence, which would project the debris out to give the effect of a tank shell."

Two potential disasters almost wrecked the shoot. To create the palls of smoke across the movie battlefield, old car tyres were set alight in cutoff oil drums. Said Richardson, "Somebody—we never did find out—had pushed one up against the wall of one of the houses. One had got very hot through the plasterwork, and it started to smoulder inside the wall cavity. And the heat built up. Suddenly, there was a very loud, whooshing noise. And this flame just flashed literally from the ground floor right up to the top of the house."[302]

Looking on was art director Stuart Craig: "The first anybody knew about an emergency was that there was smoke and flame at the top of the building. Although the fire brigade was called, it was a plywood and plastic set, so once it was on fire, there was no holding it."[303]

John Richardson sensed disaster as gas cylinders on the roof might explode and cover the area in red-hot shards of flying metal. With that, he calmly walked inside. "I immediately ran in and up to the top. And in those days, I could run up three or four storeys."[304]

Meanwhile, Sebastian Abineri frantically waved at the 500 spectators to stand back. "I said, 'Run! There's going to be a big bang!'" Perhaps thinking this was part of the scene, they all stood still, "smiling amiably at me and nodding." Wearing a German uniform, he took cover behind a wall. "I was allowed to behave like a coward in front of the Dutch." He clasped his steel helmet tightly to his head, gritted his teeth, and waited for the inevitable explosion.

Minutes went by and nothing happened. Abineri gingerly poked his head over the wall to see Richardson stagger out of the smoke-filled building with a bulky gas cylinder on his shoulder. He'd already retrieved several of them. "It was actually one of the bravest things I'd ever seen," said Abineri, "because the last few cylinders he rescued literally blistered his hands—they were ready to explode."[305]

"We got the bulk of the equipment out," Richardson recalled. "I can remember getting some fairly painful burns on my hands and face and things. It was a scary moment and demonstrated to everybody that we weren't being overcautious in the first place."[306]

Danger over, it was the job of Stuart Craig and the art department to salvage what they could to continue filming. "It was for the next several days quite difficult to live with the kind of legacy of this prematurely destroyed building. We actually utilised bits of it and rebuilt as far as we were able."

After one near miss, luck was about to run out. The sequence involved a German Tiger tank blasting its way across the street before being counterattacked by the Paras. The German Tiger was a modern Dutch Army Leopard I tank, which had been enhanced by the art department.[307] But since it was a present-day military vehicle, it was driven by Dutch Army national servicemen. Waddy noted that the army, which was largely a conscript force, "were reluctant to allow their troops to be used, particularly in scenes where they would be plainly visible, and this was not on account of their ultra-long hair!"[308] He does not elaborate on the reason, but the unit noticed that some of the conscripts enjoyed copious amounts of alcohol and smoked pot. "They were just stoned, and they looked just like Oddball in *Kelly's Heroes*," recalled Abineri. "The tanks were full of oddballs, and we thought, *stay away from this tank.*"

The planned sequence was highly complex—and dangerous. It involved the tank rumbling down the rubble-strewn street with German-dressed A.P.A. (including Abineri) using it as cover for the advance. Dave Tomblin delivered concise instructions: "Right, we want the tank to go forward with the German A.P.A. Then we want the British A.P.A. to come out."

With cameras rolling, he called out, "Okay, action!"[309]

Richardson, standing next to the camera, saw the disaster unfold. "It's firmly imprinted in my brain that the tank had to come out of a narrow little gap between two houses and turn to the right," he recalled. "The tank can't see diddly squat. So, he turned a little bit too early and caught the corner of the building. This is made of wood, plaster, and tubular scaffolding. Unfortunately, as soon as he started, it pulled the whole front of the building out. So, it was starting to collapse."[310]

Seeing the action veer away from the plan, "Peter MacDonald grabbed his camera and shot from the shoulder as the tank was plunging through it," Jack McKenzie recalled. "It was a great example of presence of mind."

"When you're looking through the camera, you're in another world," MacDonald recalled, "so I didn't feel the shit going on either side. All I could see in my frame was I got this wonderful tank smashing through buildings with men running in front of it. Then you looked up. You knew then you're in deep shit—it had all gone wrong."[311]

Inside the building was Richardson's FX team manning the smoke-making fishtail burners. "Everybody's yelling and screaming for the tank to stop because they see what's happened. The most important thing was to turn the burners off and get the guys out."[312] One of those was Jan Robert Leerinkson, ex-army, having served with the Dutch 43 Tank battalion. From his vantage point on the first floor, he could see that the Leopard I was careering out of control. "As the building collapsed, I rescued the gas bottles and saved myself by jumping out of the window."[313]

As the tank continued on its path of destruction through the wooden- and plastic-walled set, it revealed the movie fakery. Said Abineri, "It was all dressed on the inside with grandfather clocks, paintings and mirrors, and dressing tables, etc. It was completely wrecked by this tank. David Tomblin went, 'Fucking hell.'"[314]

MacDonald recalled, "Dickie wasn't at all happy and started blaming everyone, including David Tomblin. But because I knew what I had got, I said to Dickie, it was fucking great!"[315]

Jack McKenzie was adamant about where the blame lay. "The Dutch tank crew got through crates of Grolsch beer. Then they climbed into the tank and drove it through the set. These guys were pissed as rats."[316]

And that was a wrap for the day, as the art department assessed how to make good the damage. The rampaging tank became the talk of the town as the unit, including Abineri, descended on their favourite local watering hole. According to Abineri, "We were in the Pelikaan bar. David Tomblin came in and said, 'I'm gonna get pissed tonight, lads. I want you to make sure I get home once I stop drinking.' So, we waited until he got absolutely paralytic. And then we loaded him into a cab back to his hotel. And he got up the next day. Absolutely fine, on time, fresh as a daisy, but he needed that downtime after that had happened."[317]

The shot, despite revealing the set was fake, remains one of the most impressive in the movie.

For weeks during the bridge filming, the "weather cover" were scenes involving the desperately wounded crowded in various cellars. The A.P.A.'s digs at the Old Folks' Home had a usable subterranean space that doubled for Captain Mackay's command across the road from Frost. It's here that Hopkins, after he has made his mad dash to avoid the snipers, briefs Lieutenant Cornish, played by Keith Drinkel, about their precarious position. The actors play their officer characters with pitch-perfect understatement, it being vital that commanders do not show fear, as it undermines morale. Cornish states he's *"a bit surprised to find Bittrich's Panzer troops here."* Frost turns to look at an imposing prisoner, a German officer, smoking a cigarette. Hopkins is superb; his face registers the obvious shock, but he checks himself, before replying, *"Yes, well, surely you didn't believe all that nonsense they told us about the enemy being made up of—what was it—old men, children?"* It is another of those subtle and effective moments that places you slap-bang in the ferocious stress of battle.

Later, on a set constructed inside one of the specially built houses, Frost, now wounded, crawls over to his dying comrade and friend,

Major Carlyle. Frost asks why he always carries an umbrella, and then follows with a line that beautifully, and economically, captures their friendship, as Frost had always refrained from asking the reason because *"I know you were so anxious that I should, and I wouldn't give you the satisfaction."* Carlyle, his face shot to pieces, murmurs, *"Bad memory. Always forgot the password. I knew no Jerry would ever carry one. I had to prove I was an Englishman."*

Good recalls Hopkins' reaction as they prepared to shoot the scene. "I'd spent about four or five hours in make-up to get half my face shot away. What they were doing to me was horrible enough. I don't mean that in realistic terms, but emotionally, blocking my eye and all sorts of things, that there was time enough to think. When he saw me, he was really very shocked, and the scene worked for that reason."[318]

It's a moving and unsentimental death scene that perfectly captures not just their friendship, but also the stoical attitude of professional soldiers. Goldman's script was often maligned in some quarters, but this moment again illustrates his skill with just a few lines that beautifully served the performances. The shallow camera focus, with just Frost sharp and Carlyle's bloody face blurred, on the one hand lessens the gruesome make-up, but allows the dying officer to fade away with dignity. This is echoed in Goldman's script direction: *"They both close their eyes now; the only difference is that CARLYLE is not going to open his again."*

With smoke drifting from the smashed buildings, the remnants of Frost's command sit huddled despondently in the street ringed by Germans with machine guns primed at their hips. The immaculately dressed Maximilian Schell as Bittrich offers some chocolate to a brooding Anthony Hopkins as Frost, his face covered in dust. Peter MacDonald found it poignant. "I loved the scene with Hopkins and all the men when the battle is lost and they just lie outside the house. Especially Tony's expression with that kind of faraway look: the despair of having fought and lost all your friends and colleagues. It doesn't matter how brave you've been—you've actually lost. To me, it was one of the best scenes in the film."[319]

Towards the end of June, with Arnhem suitably flattened and the last remnants of Frost's men marched off into captivity, Deventer got its bridge back. Peter Dukelow's construction teams had to clear up the mess and remove all signs of war and destruction. Luckily, they managed to meet the deadline and avoid a hefty penalty. Meanwhile, the unit moved on to other locations for the rest of the British Airborne story.

The Germans' speedy counterattack at Arnhem prevented the majority of the British Airborne from reinforcing Colonel Frost on the bridge. Over a few days the division was forced into a wide defensive pocket amid the leafy suburb of Oosterbeek. Here, small sections of paratroopers dug fox holes and valiantly defended the 1,000-yard-wide perimeter.

The film omits most of this, and instead uses the HQ at the Hartenstein Hotel to stand in for this brutal battle. Just a few hours before the British arrived, the hotel had played host to the German commander Model (Walter Kohut). In the film, he greets news of a mass parachute drop with incredulity, as there is nothing of value—except for, he decides, him. This irony, the hotel housing warring leaders just hours apart, was actually a small tweak of artistic licence. The general had been ensconced at the Tafelberg Hotel, barely 300 yards away.

Thanks to another example of serendipity, the film company found a burnt-out shell of a country house, Langoed Het School, Voorst, amid 20 acres of grounds nearby to Deventer. The town council had reclaimed the structure after it had been gutted in a fire started by squatters, and local rumours had the City Fathers planning to transform it into a crematorium. Bearing "a passing resemblance"[320] to the Hartenstein, according to Waddy, the art department transformed it with a plaster balustrade to the fascia and fully restored the entrance hall and the main dining room, complete with faux oak panelling.

When Sean Connery's Urquhart finally returns to his HQ after his adventures in Arnhem, he is exasperated to find that *"there is no good news"* about their predicament. The most maddening factor is the lack of supplies; while they are being dropped correctly onto their landing zones, these zones have been overrun by the Germans. And, maddeningly, the RAF is under strict orders to ignore all messages from the ground.

This situation is restaged in the film with frantic Paras making fires and feverishly waving at the supply planes. While a formation of four Dakotas flew over in the distance, high crane rigs nearer the cameras dropped panniers hanging from small parachutes. According to the script, all the supply panniers landed too far away, except one.

This situation leads to a memorable sequence in which a lone badly hit Dakota crashes behind a clump of trees. Implemented by the daredevil pilot John "Jeff" Hawke, the crash is a great example of a movie cheat. To pull it off required split-second timing by the FX crew and absolute precision by the pilot. Hawke was required to take the Dakota, with smoke streaming from a wing, as low as he could after passing the top of a tree. At that moment, John Richardson was to let loose an immense fireball. "It was a big bang, but a cosmetic bang. It was a 50-gallon drum full of fuel buried underground. Few sticks of dynamite in the bottom. Wait until the plane's gone behind the trees, and then let the bang off. The plane's doing on about 200 miles an hour. It's well gone by the time the bang went off."[321] The size and scale of it would mask the reality of the plane banking away to safety. In the used take, it is just possible to see the wing tip poke out of the explosion, as the plane makes good its escape.

Despondent, the Paras hope for *"better luck tomorrow,"* and then someone notices a single pannier floating down to earth. In 1944 it was Sergeant Lawrence Goldthorpe, a glider pilot who, according to Ryan, "had risked his life to retrieve a resupply pannier—only to discover that it contained, not food or ammunition, but red berets."[322] A similar moment had been staged in *Theirs Is the Glory*, although it had omitted the pannier opening and spilling the useless cargo. Goldman's sequence is suspense filmmaking at its best.

Seeing the solitary pannier drop in no-man's land, one soldier, Private "Ginger" Marsh, hands his gun to a comrade and makes a dash for it. He was played by John Salthouse, perhaps best known at the time as the morose Tony in Mike Leigh's seminal TV classic *Abigail's Party* (1977) on British television, and later in the long-running 1980s ITV police series, *The Bill*. For his casting in *Bridge*, Salthouse may have been chosen for his nifty footwork. In the late 1960s, under the name John Lewis, he had played for Crystal Palace Football Club, before his career was curtailed following a severe knee injury. As Ginger bolts across the field, his A.P.A. mates (including James Wardroper, David Auker and Stephen Moore) shout out encouragement. Jack McKenzie recalled he and a few other A.P.A. members were brought back later to Twickenham Studios to record various ad libs for the scene, like: *"Those bleeding snipers will get him."*

Ginger picks it up and almost succeeds in getting it back to the lines until a sniper's bullet finds him. The pathos as his mates finally realise what he died for—a container of berets—is well handled. Perhaps it is melodramatic, but had Goldman let Ginger make it back (the real Sergeant Goldthorpe survived), the impact would have been blunted.

🐝   🐝   🐝

In another sequence shot in front of the battered movie Hartenstein at dusk, judging by the length of the elongated low rays of sunlight, members of the A.P.A. lie around in a ramshackle assortment of wounds and bruises, many sporting tattered bandages encrusted with dried rust-brown Kensington Gore fake blood. A lone voice echoed through a megaphone. It was Dickie: "Okay, boys, now you're all exhausted. And the Germans are going to come across the bridge, and as they come over Jeffrey's going to start playing the flute, and you're gonna start singing one by one 'Abide with Me' . . ."[323]

The setting was the morning after First Airborne had successfully extracted itself across the Rhine. Left behind are the seriously wounded and the medics who volunteered to look after them. A bloodied and dejected Paul Copley (as Frost's batman who had managed to escape from the bridge), was one of those sitting around. Another bridge escapee was the padre, played by Edward Seckerson, who had returned after some months for just this scene. "Dickie wanted the padre to be there in that final sequence administering the Last Rites, and the closeup I have is my head down, and I'm closing a soldier's eyes," said Seckerson. "It was a mute shot, and Dickie was actually talking me through it, which was very hard to remain serious because he was saying things like: 'Edward dear, look up now. See the Germans.' I thought: *just give me the instruction before the shot!*"[324]

With a few extras dressed as German soldiers poised to walk across a little wooden bridge behind the hotel that marked no-man's land, Abineri recalled that one take of this soulful scene didn't quite go to Dickie's plan, as he called out directions through his megaphone. "'Okay boys, ready. Action.' So, the Germans come across the bridge. Jeffrey starts playing the flute, and Norman Gregory said, 'We're not going to surrender to that bunch of wankers, are we?' 'Cut! Who said that?' We all kept shtum. We didn't want to drop Norman in it. But I think it was Norman's last tribute to the airborne."[325]

Seckerson was disappointed that the final cut eliminated the close-ups of soldiers looking up towards the Germans: "That final sequence depended upon subliminally people perhaps remembering faces they'd seen before. I wished he'd kept the camera on me long enough for me to lift my head and be in full-face shot. But he obviously decided to cut it."[326]

> *Abide with me; fast falls the eventide;*
> *The darkness deepens; Lord with me abide.*
> *When other helpers fail and comforts flee,*
> *Help of the helpless, O abide with me.*

Considered a prayer for God to stay with the speaker throughout life and in death, the hymn "Abide with Me" has been a staple of Christian services, particularly funerals, for over 140 years. Scottish

Anglican Henry Francis Lyte, while in the final stages of tuberculosis, recalled the murmured words of a dying friend he had sat with decades earlier: "Abide with me." Before death finally took him, Lyte penned the hymn that would be first sung at his funeral.

Goldman takes his cue for the end scene from a real instance during the battle. Padre G. A. Pare was tending a roomful of wounded in one of the shattered aid stations in Oosterbeek, which was shaking to the shelling outside. Looking around the shattered, bloodied faces, the padre "felt inspired to fight the noise outside with God's peace inside."[327] Despite the ear-splitting barrage just yards away, the men sang and hummed softly:

> *When other helpers fail and comforts flee,*
> *Help of the helpless, O abide with me.*[328]

"I think it's the most poignant scene of the film," said Peter MacDonald. "You recognise very few faces now because the faces you knew were all dead. It was just the kind of hopelessness of war. A lot of men have died as always in war, so unnecessarily." Filmed almost at the end of the shoot in September, it was given added poignancy by the A.P.A. who had toiled for six months to recreate the tragedy of Arnhem. "Over the period of the film, they were trained as soldiers," said MacDonald. "They were marched to work and back again [and] understood what they were portraying. So that was a kind of very touching, very tear-jerking scene."[329]

The scene not only closes the film but marks the A.P.A.'s last appearance as the dogged British Airborne. The mournful singing of the bowed but not cowered defeated soldiers continues to move their contemporary counterparts. "That's the Paras' favourite film," Abineri was told by one. "He says, 'When we've got a few beers and we want to watch a movie. It's either that, or *Zulu*. And we have a few beers and say, great, it's all gonna kick off now, boys.'"[330] One of Jack McKenzie's relatives joined the modern Parachute Regiment. "My nephew and his mates meet for a few beers and watch the film. And when they get to the 'Abide with Me' scene, they all weep buckets."[331]

13
"KLM Job"
The A.P.A. Part 2

"I loved my Lee Enfield .303," recalled Sebastian Abineri. "I thought it was a wonderful weapon. It was just so easy to fire." By now the A.P.A. were well and truly blooded, and just like soldiers, they had strong opinions about the tools of their trade. "I got to the stage that I could get a round a second off with a Lee Enfield, which I think's pretty good," Abineri added. The bolt-action rifle had been the standard issue for the British army in both world wars. "Instead of using the thumb and forefinger to work the bolt, you used to flatten the palm, knock it back up, push the round into the breach and pull the trigger with your middle finger as opposed to your index. And that's very good for laying down fire in a general direction."[332]

Tim Morand was given a Bren gun with its distinctive curved magazine, considered a light machine gun despite weighing 25 pounds (11.3 kilograms). "They said it was always short, stocky guys who are Bren gunners," said Morand. "I was the only one who could actually run with a Bren: fall with it, kick its legs open, and fire it. It was the most amazing weapon. It's just unbelievably lethal, either single shot or the lot—just hair-raising."[333]

The German and American weapons were considered more problematic. "The Mausers (Karabiner 98 kurz) would jam. You couldn't feed the round into the breech properly," recalled Abineri, who played Brits, Yanks, and Germans. He noted Colonel Waddy was also critical of the U.S. Army standard rifle, the semi-automatic M1 Garand, which would automatically eject its spent cartridge clip. "He used to say that would give away your position,"[334] said Abineri. While not so noticeable in *Bridge*, the terrific battle scenes in the later *Band of Brothers* TV series show the flying clips—their zinging sound and glinting metal make them very noticeable.

The sheer number of fireable weapons deployed for the film was a constant worry for the production. "I think there were about 4.7 million blanks fired," said Roy Button, whose job as third assistant director included issuing the weapons and making sure they were returned. "We had two armoury trucks checking weapons in, weapons out. Now you couldn't issue that amount of weapons legally, but it was then."

There were also serious security concerns, which made those armoury trucks a potential target for terrorists. After the war, during which the former Dutch colonies in Indonesia had been overrun by Japan, many had wrestled back their independence. Some 12,500 South Moluccans had been transported and settled in Dutch temporary camps, including the infamous former Nazi transit camp of Westerbork in the north of the Netherlands. By the early 1970s, resentment had grown amongst the second generation that the promised independent state, Republik Maluku Selatan (RMS), was a forlorn dream. Feeling betrayed by the Dutch government, some took radical direct action.

On 2 December 1975, seven South Moluccans seized a train with about 50 passengers on board in Wijster, 40 miles north of Deventer. The tense hijack lasted for 12 days and resulted in three hostages being killed. In Amsterdam a group of seven stormed the Indonesian Consulate and took several hostages. A tense few weeks followed until the hostage takers surrendered after being given vague promises that the authorities would discuss their grievance. The hostage takers were later convicted and given seven-year sentences. "They were paranoid about the arms trucks being hijacked because there's enough in there to arm an entire regiment," said Roy Button.[335]

It had been impressed on the A.P.A. how important it was to keep hold of their issued weapon at all times. Abineri recalled the dreaded euphemism that struck terror through the thespians turned soldiers. "A 'KLM job' was the unforgivable crime of losing your weapon—you were on the airplane home," said Abineri, KLM being the Dutch national carrier operating out of Schiphol Airport. "Absolutely no question, it was the biggest sanction that they could employ," added Abineri. "We were having such a wonderful time that the thought of going home was like dying or going to hell."[336]

Tim Morand, during the many hours of waiting in the sun, would make sure "you'd fall asleep with your rifle sling tied to your belt."[337]

The A.P.A. could get a KLM job in other ways, but no one fell afoul of the number-one requirement. This was not the case with some of the hundreds of Dutch extras who would be drafted in periodically. Once the weapons had been issued, it was down to ex-Marine A.P.A. member Jack McKenzie to supervise: "I was keeping my eyes on kit, making sure people didn't have pocketfuls of blanks, that sort of stuff. Once I found a Bren gun and a can of ammunition outside a public lavatory; judging by the screams of joy inside the lavatory, the call of nature was a bit more exotic than the norm. Then I found a Thompson submachine gun hanging from a tree in the forest. He'd gone to pick bluebells."[338]

Roy Button stressed the vast majority were a professional bunch: "Some of them were Dutch, and some English, some were German. You get a contingency of extras that love doing it. Others who enjoy the casualness. Then there are the high-end people who don't really need the money—usually find they last about two or three days. And then you find a core of people who are doing it for the fun and the money. So, you get great finds—wonderful characters. One bloke was with us on week two and stayed all the way to the end. He was so good."[339]

As in war, the most grinding sap of enthusiasm for all was boredom—the long, hot days spent waiting around thanks to the snail-like process of epic filmmaking. "We were literally cannon fodder," Edward Seckerson recalled. "We'd be a part of all the big action sequences, sometimes in the foreground, sometimes way away from the camera. Most days we were called, we were sitting out there chatting with each other. It was very hot. If we weren't actually shooting, we would just take our gear off and wear a T-shirt for the whole day. Also enjoying the fabulous catering that the big movies lay on. It was like 80-odd degrees every day, and somehow, they'd get cream cakes at tea time to the location. There was never any need to eat in the evening because there were three meals a day, and the food was extremely good."[340]

It was former Desert Rat Jack Dearlove's job to keep an eye on the A.P.A., some of whom became quite creative in passing the long wait. Abineri and a few mates found some ideal cover amid the battlefield. "We'd get under this camouflage net covered in leaves," said Abineri. "And dear Jack Dearlove would pass, saying, 'Where those fuckers gone?' He'd walk right next to us, and we'd be under this camouflage net having a kip. Then one day, we woke up and there were tanks parked all around us. We never did that again. We could have been squashed!"[341]

The music impresario and cricket fanatic David English passed his passion on to the unit. "I said to Richard Attenborough, 'Look, Dickie, while you're setting up scenes, we'll have little cricket matches between the scenes.' 'That's a good idea,' he said. 'Keep them all happy.' So, I got all these great actors like Lord Olivier, Connery, Redford, Hackman, Bogarde, O'Neal, and Maximilian Schell. I got them all playing, and we actually had a big game on this burnt-out bomb site for the film. I said we'll call us lot the A.P.A. 11. And we took on the world's greatest film stars, and Olivier loved it, an off break bowler. Dirk Bogarde was a leg break bowler. Anthony Hopkins thought the whole thing was a hoot. And so, whenever the cameras stopped—they all really got into the cricket."

David English would expand his passion into setting up a highly successful sporting charity. "I started the Bunbury Festival in 1987. I wanted to give youngsters the best chance to fulfil their ambitions to play for England. The four regions of South and West London, East North and Midlands play each other in a round-robin situation. And then at the end of the week we get the best 11, and then they go to Lords, and we play the MCC schools."[342] English estimates over £17 million has been raised for charity; 131 Buns have gone on to play for England plus more than 1,000 Buns into First Class cricket.

Soccer, Britain's other national game, was equally popular during the shoot. An A.P.A. football team was quickly formed, all with the blessing of Dickie, a huge fan and a board member of Chelsea FC. One day, filming concluded just after lunch to allow a crucial match to be played against the technicians, although some underhand tactics were deployed to even the odds. Abineri took his position in the goalmouth, ready for kick-off. "There was a blinding flash as I was surrounded by soot and dust," he recalled. Once the ear-piercing ringing had faded, he saw the spectators, including Dickie, "... falling about with laughter. It dawned on me that the special effects boys . . . had booby-trapped my goal line with a very special explosive mix. I played the rest of the game with a blackened face and covered in soot." Despite ex-pro David English's energetic attacks, the A.P.A. were trounced to a 5–2 defeat. Abineri manfully took the blame for letting in so many goals, saying, "Our defence had been penetrated much too often, and I'd been flying around the goalmouth like a cat in a washing machine."[343] His magnanimous teammates assured him it wasn't his fault. The game was considered a great success, and "all became good mates." Fired up, Abineri approached the Deventer Go Ahead Eagles for a charity match, with Sean Connery as their striker, but the professionals balked at playing amateur "cloggers." Local fire teams and hospital staff were more game and gave the "Max Factors" a run for their money.

Having trained to be convincing soldiers, the A.P.A. demonstrated their real value by creating convincing "business"—background action. Usually assistant directors arrange background, but thanks to their training, the A.P.A. were trusted to do it themselves. Tim Morand recalls working with Dave Auker as a Para for some convincing hand-to-hand fighting around the bridge. "We learnt stage fighting at drama school, and so I knew how to fall. I said, 'Dave, I'm the German, and I'm about to throttle you before I get an attack of fear,' because I thought it would be very interesting to show a moment of cowardice. So, I said, 'While I'm about to run away you shoot me in the back, and then I'll do the slow crawl.' So, we worked it out with our cameraman Peter McDonald. So, there was I crawling along—I didn't hear 'cut.' I lifted my head and there was Peter's camera. And I burst out laughing, and it came up in the rushes the following evening."[344]

As they worked out their action, the pair discussed how to hide their faces from the camera. While the *raison d'être* for any actor is to be in the limelight, the opposite was true for all these keen young performers. So, when Dickie wanted an A.P.A. member to say a line in closeup, it too was classed as the dreaded KLM job. "Some people would suddenly be told that they were going back at the end of the week, because that time was up," Seckerson recalled. "It was like, 'Oh, so and so's got the KLM this week.'"[345]

It would usually fall to assistant director Steve Lanning to pick out an actor to speak a line. "There were the ones who were avoiding the KLM job, and those who couldn't wait to get one," said Lanning, who was amused at the lengths many would go to if summoned to appear close to the camera. "They would say, 'Morning, Captain,' with their arm over their face or 'Over there, sir,' with their back turned. What was funny was how some of them managed to last all six months without being seen, and then sent home."[346]

Perhaps the brightest of the limelight accorded the A.P.A. went to Tim Morand, who had an entire sequence revolve around him. Urquhart, Captain Cleminson, and another officer were surrounded by German troops and forced to hide in the attic of the Derksen family at the Zwarteweg 14, in Arnhem. They were trapped for more than 12 hours during the crucial early stages of the battle. During the see-saw

Simon Lewis

fighting amid the streets of Arnhem, a small detachment liberated the officers. In the film, the huge gun muzzle of a Tiger tank aiming directly at their window is used for dramatic jeopardy.

For the rescue, Dickie and Peter MacDonald planned an elaborate sequence shot using a zoom and lateral tracks. Morand recalled, "Just before the take, Dave Tomblin said, 'Tim, get behind that fucking tree, there's a *Gurman* there, cut his throat, and then kill [stuntman] Doug Robinson, and run straight into the camera.' I was doing Audie Murphy acting."[347] With Morand leading, the Paras would pour out of the trees and gun down the Germans—all in a single shot. As the survivors retreat, Sean Connery appears, much to the consternation of Morand's corporal character, who declares: *"It's the bleedin' general!"* Incidentally, onto his red beret is pinned the badge of the 2nd Battalion, South Staffordshire Regiment. This was a glider-born formation that formed part of Hicks' First Air Landing Brigade. It is a little detail, but no doubt Colonel Waddy's idea to imply that not just the Paras fought at Arnhem.

Playing one of the doomed Germans was Jack McKenzie: "When the general comes out of the house, I clocked my head on the edge of the curb. I just did a tumble. First thing, despite all the other senior actors around, Dickie came over and asked, 'You alright, darling?' He was that sort of person." The actor noted the director's natural warmth and respect for every single person on the production. "It wasn't like 'I'm the director.' It was: 'Morning, darling, how are you?' It was that sort of relationship. It made it very friendly, and it brought us all together as a great team. We were his boys."[348]

Dickie's son, Michael, concurred: "When you walk onto one of Dad's sets, the sense of unity was quite extraordinary. Everybody was pitching in the same direction. For example, he would do something which we do in the theatre, which is on the first day of rehearsal, the first day of shooting, he gathered the whole unit together, and he'd explain why he wanted to make the movie. It wouldn't be intellectual; it would be personal, and everybody bound around that. And so, any-

176

Lieutenant-General 'Boy' Browning

Staff Sergeant Eddie Dohun

Lieutenant-Colonel 'Joe' Vandeleur

Major-General Robert Urquhart

Lieutenant-General Brian Horrocks

Colonel Bobby Stout

Joseph E. Levine presents

A BRIDGE TOO FAR

starring (in alphabetical order)

Dirk Bogarde
James Caan
Michael Caine
Sean Connery
Edward Fox
Elliott Gould
Gene Hackman
Anthony Hopkins
Hardy Kruger
Laurence Olivier
Ryan O'Neal
Robert Redford
Maximilian Schell
Liv Ullmann

From the book by
Cornelius Ryan
Screenplay by
William Goldman
Produced by
Joseph E. Levine
and
Richard P. Levine
Directed by
Richard Attenborough

PG PARENTAL GUIDANCE SUGGESTED · United Artists
A Transamerica Company

Major-General Stanislaw Sosabowski

Lieutenant-Colonel John Frost

General Karl Ludwig

Dr. Spaander

Brigadier-General James M. Gavin

Major Julian Cook

Lieutenant-General Wilhelm Bittrich

Kate ter Horst

77/28

A BRIDGE TOO FAR

"The Fourteen," as they appear on the one-sheet movie poster for *A Bridge Too Far*.

Above: Director Richard Attenborough and Producer Joseph E. Levine begin their epic collaboration. (Everett Collection) Below: Dickie (seated center) talks to production designer Terry Marsh at far left. Camera assistant John Campbell stands above Dickie. Camera operator Peter MacDonald is at right, pointing. Clapper/loader Steve Barron sits next to Dickie. (Steve Barron Collection)

Above and below: Fifteen-year-old Erik van 't Wout's reaction is genuine. Dickie didn't warn the actor before the shot, so the appearance of the Spitfire, piloted by Neil Williams, "scared the hell out of me," van 't Wout recalled. (Kenny Barley Collection)

Above: The liberation of Eindhoven recreated. Right: Tomblin, Unsworth, and Dickie overlook the celebration from a boom. (Both photos, Reineke Kramer Collection) Below: Filming Michael Caine in closeup in Eindhoven. (Voskuil Collection)

Above: James Caan and Nicholas Campbell wait for their scene in the boiling summer sun. (Robert Jan Leerink Collection) Left: Caan's unusual obsession with lassoing is on full display as crew members do their best to ignore him. (Everett Collection)

Above: Connery, Hackman, Bogarde, and O'Neal relax during set prep. (Everett Collection) Left: "There's a lot of money on that lawn," said Dickie. (Joe Gibson Collection) Below: John Waddy in green shirt chats with Oosterbeek battle survivor and local historian Jan Voskuil. Both men would be instrumental in the historical accuracy of the production. (Voskuil Collection)

Above: Pre-production of the Arnhem Road Bridge sequence begins with creation of a scale model, from which structures beside the bridge will be built. (John Richardson Collection) Right: Good and Hopkins receive instruction from Dickie as Frost's battalion advances towards the bridge. (Voskuil Collection) Below: John Richardson preps and then tests the flamethrower that will ignite ammo on the bridge. (John Richardson Collection)

Above: Joseph E. Levine makes an appearance during the bridge sequence shoot. (John Richardson Collection) Left: Cameras roll for the Gräbner attack. (John Richardson Collection) Bottom: Bodies are stacked high at the production's home base in Deventer. (Gelderland Archives)

Above: Production of the bridge battle sequence progresses. (Voskuil Collection) Right: Hopkins takes a rooftop view; A.P.A. member Mark York holds the PIAT. (Everett Collection) Below: Movie John Frost shares a moment with the real hero and namesake of the John Frost Bridge. (John Richardson Collection)

Above: The "surrender" scene, which had to be altered when Frost balked at the script. Right: Maximilian Schell as General Bittrich. Below: Bittrich offers chocolate to Frost in one of the film's most effective moments. (All photos Everett Collection)

Above: Stuntman Alf Joint (left) clowns with assistant location coordinator Joe Gibson. (Joe Gibson Collection) Right: The ter Horst home is recreated and expanded from the original and shows graves of British Airborne. (Gelderland Archives) Below: Laurence Olivier and David Tomblin chat on the ter Horst set before shooting what would become the final scene in the picture. (Voskuil Collection)

Above: Krüger and Olivier negotiate in the town hall in Deventer. (Gelderland Archives) Left: Movie General Urquhart meets with the real Urquhart. (Photo copyright Gerth van Roden) Below: Connery sits for a haircut setside as he chats with Dickie. (Reineke Kramer Collection)

Above: An impressive amount of armour is on display for the XXX Corps advance. (Everett Collection) Right: Pyrotechnics in the breakout battle. Below right: T-6s portraying Typhoons swoop in for the kill. (Both photos John Richardson Collection) Bottom: An intense Michael Caine as Vandeleur considers the job before him. (Everett Collection)

Above: A nervous Dickie and DP Unsworth (right) await the parachute drop. Left: The drop goes off mostly successfully. (Both photos, John Richardson Collection) Below left: General Gavin confers with his screen counterpart, Ryan O'Neal. (Everett Collection) Bottom: Eleven C-47 Dakotas are collected at the former Nazi airfield, Fliegerhorst Deelen, for the loading and takeoff sequence. Ironically, Deelen is located just over the hill from Arnhem. (GKB Collection)

Top: Shooting the arrival of Major Cook's rafts. (Robert Jan Leerink Collection) Above and right: Dickie directs the difficult river crossing with Redford and crew. (John Richardson Collection) Below: The $2 million star relaxes with Levine during a break in production. (Voskuil Collection)

Above: Members of the A.P.A. look for work after the rigorous *Bridge* shoot.

body who threatened to get in his way ran the risk of being murdered by somebody else in the unit."[349]

Some of the A.P.A. would be given a line to say. David English was singled out to play an orderly in Kate ter Horst's house. In the script he and another orderly carry in a severely wounded man into *"a room. It's just awful,"* where Laurence Olivier as Doctor Spaander is trying to operate. To emphasise the carnage, the orderly, after *"looking down at his feet,"* says, *"Amazing—look—my boots are full of blood."*

According to Steve Lanning, "Throughout the six months, David was doing his, My *boots* are FULL of blood! *My* boots ARE full of BLOOD, and it became the standard joke. At some point, he was even called 'boots.' But when he came to do the scene, we ended up not having Laurence Olivier there. So, we gave his lines to the wardrobe driver."[350]

English disputed this and has a photograph of himself with the great thespian knight. Regardless of his performance, it was one of many small lines and moments that never made the final cut—although, English did have a line included, even if his back is turned. As Frost enters the crowded cellar full of wounded, English says, *"Mr. Cornish is straight through there."*

Sebastian Abineri played all the warring soldiers at some point, first glimpsed in the Dakota with the Parachick and then later in a brief closeup during the bridge battle. As Frost prepares to do his 'run,' he calls out to Sergeant Treadwell and would be credited as such. Jack McKenzie also donned all the uniforms. "I was shot dead on the beach at Nijmegen. And I think I was shot dead somewhere else too by Tim Morand. So, I'm always free for other work."[351]

Despite a brief moment playing a corpse, Stephen Churchett's "claim to fame was one day when they bought ice creams out on set. And Sean Connery said, 'Would you hold this?' So, I'm gonna call my autobiography, *I Held Sean Connery's Ice Cream!*"[352]

Morand, following his starring role with Connery, went to great lengths to stay hidden from the camera. "I used to go into make-up and put on moustaches and disguises. There's a scene with Sean Connery, and I'm very discreetly in profile with all the other people smoking. Then in the ter Horst house, I'm covered in blood. Laurence Olivier comes over, and I just close my eyes and die. I sort of planted myself all over the place away from the camera."

For one scene Morand found a live prop. The film shows Frost and his men, having dropped unopposed, hoofing past Kate ter Horst's house towards Arnhem bridge. Their progress is delayed by the euphoria of the locals who think the war is over. "I was the only one amongst the extras that had a little girl on my shoulders. I heard later, because I had a girlfriend there, that girl became a big celebrity because of that one scene. She got to that level."[353] The pretty blonde girl, dressed in a grey dress and clutching a Dutch flag, is clearly visible during a long tracking shot as Carlyle and Frost discuss the apparent *"smashing success"* of the operation so far. Edward Seckerson, who is seen eating an apple behind Frost, also recalls the scene as they marched weighed down with kit. "That was very emotional because these were real locals. Some of them were old enough to remember thinking they were being liberated. But they got very involved in the scene. I remember Dickie saying very unkindly: 'Could someone get rid of that woman who's emoting in front of the camera?' She was a local and was getting really hysterical."[354]

Christopher Good also found the reaction of the Dutch extras in the scene deeply moving. "We were told it was quite a sensitive thing for the Dutch. And I remember the general sense of everybody being terribly happy, and people giving us things like oranges. But there were some people who'd had a terrible time. You saw the pain on their faces."[355]

Despite their blink-and-miss-'em appearances, all the A.P.A. were happy to be cogs in an enormous enterprise. "I was delighted to be part of that vast circus," Jack McKenzie said. "I've never been involved in something so exciting in my life. And I think everyone felt the same way, just to be part of that great incredible spectacle was a joy.

It's something that stays with you for the rest of your life. You learn lessons from it about getting on with people. It was like being in the Forces when people were called up. They have to get on with college boys and brickies, labourers all in the same barrack room; and we were the same."[356]

The A.P.A.'s barracks rooms in the orphanage featured a high ceiling that kept the air cool, even on the hottest days and nights. Seckerson remembers calling his mother in London who was struggling with the extreme heat that summer. "She was saying how she just couldn't sleep because the temperature was not dropping below 80 or 90 degrees at night."

But up to 50 young and energetic men barracked could become unsettling for other reasons. "I heard horror stories," said Seckerson. "I mean, we were a very civilised room, but there were some dreadful stories about people coming home pissed and peeing on beds. There were all kinds of awful pranks played on people or just noise disturbance coming in the middle of the night."[357]

Jack McKenzie noted that while they all rubbed along together, every man was a product of the inherit British class system. "The aesthetic types formed their own little kind of elite squad. But all of us blokes with broken noses and rotten teeth and the funny accents, the Scottish Glaswegian, cockney, Welsh. We were the rebels, and the elite kind kept to themselves. It was very funny—very class distinctive."

The "rebels," which included Sebastian Abineri, David English. and David Auker, made a beeline for a little bar called The Pelikaan. It was a popular watering spot and often marked on the call sheet maps as a reference point for filming locations around Deventer. "I remember Myles Reithermann, who played the truck driver taking the boats to Nijmegen amid shot and shell. He was so drunk his head was on the bar and he couldn't lift his head off it. He was full of Grolsch and Geneva."[358]

"We were real celebrities in the town," Seckerson recalled. "Nothing this exciting had ever happened there. When you go into the bars,

Simon Lewis

we'd request the songs. It was the time of Queen's "Bohemian Rhapsody." We all had our own favourites or requests that we put in. And the social side of it was extraordinary."

Amorous adventures were high on the list of activities for the A.P.A. Seckerson was one of three who went fishing in a different pond. "The idea of all these soldiers with short haircuts, was very tempting for the local gay elements. There was a little gay club in Deventer which was only open three nights a week and run by volunteers. That's how small the town was. We had far more success than any of the heterosexuals." Some mornings at breakfast, Seckerson would see a disgruntled Ben Cross, later the star of *Chariots of Fire* (1981). "He'd say, 'How do you do it? I'm having a miserable time. I can't find any Dutch crumpet.' And I would say, 'The world is our oyster, Ben.' He and I bonded quite well."[359]

One of the rebels, David English, maintained, "We did okay there. All the birds in Deventer were wonderful. It's almost like being a pop star. We used to finish off drinking and go off dancing and cavorting around the town. It was wonderful—like a working holiday."[360]

Fellow rebel Abineri concurred: "We had a wonderful time. Impeccably turned-out girls arrived, as if by magic, from all over Northern Holland with condoms stuffed in their handbags in their pragmatic Dutch liberal fashion. A lot of them 'bent over backwards' to help us have a wonderful time in the bars and clubs to the strains of ABBA—*"Can you hear the drums, Fernando?"*[361]

To smooth an impromptu romantic liaison, there was an unofficial hide-hole at the Old Folks' Home. "There was a honeymoon suite, which was basically a room, which Ben kept the key," Seckerson recalled. "And if you wanted to shack up with someone for the night, he would organise it. I remember spending the night there with a young man. It was just what went on—it was just extraordinary."

On Saturday, 29 May, the top British band The Rolling Stones played their only Dutch gig of their European tour that year. Many of the A.P.A. took a bus to see them at The Hague. Seckerson recalled,

180

"We went as a group, and Ben made the most enormous joint you have ever seen in your life. It was so big—it had a handle! So, this was passed around our group at The Rolling Stones concert. In Holland, hash was so easy to come by. It was a legal drug, and we had the money to buy it.

"I only remember one night when I was the worse for wear. We came back to the honeymoon suite and they handed around the joint. And I suddenly felt really peculiar; I was white as a sheet and on the verge of passing out. Ben took me in hand, and said, 'Quick, we need some coffee.' It's funny how in groups some people find their role, don't they? And Ben was very much one of those."[362]

Jack McKenzie recalled that one of their number "was a bit of a union leader. I won't mention his name. He demanded we get more money and all that sort of stuff, and the money was pretty good for 1976. Then, after he got crabs off his uniform, he insisted we should all be examined by a doctor. The Dutch doctor was delighted. He made a fortune. I know for a fact there's only one way you get crabs; you *don't* get it from dirty uniforms! Anyway, we dutifully queued up and pulled our shirts out and showed them our armpits, our crotches. Then the other thing was, it's so hot. So, he said we need salt tablets. There's enough salt in a cabbage! I knew we didn't need any at all as I'd been in the service."

Overall, members of the A.P.A. found the six-month stint hard work but highly enjoyable. Said McKenzie, "We all queued up for meals and a good chat and a laugh, and guys played football, and we met regularly in the Pelikaan and had a few beers, went home, up at five in the morning again and back into this wonderful world of film."[363]

Each morning, it would be down to Jack Dearlove to chivvy the walking wounded with sore heads and get them into action and ready for the cameras. "He was the sergeant major," Steve Lanning recalled of Dearlove. "He'd come up and say to them: 'You didn't come home last night,' and 'you gotta watch that one,' etc. So, some of them hated it. But a lot became friends."[364]

Seckerson noted that the miscreants or malingerers got short shrift from the Second AD. "Steve Lanning was very funny. Part of his job was to identify people for certain positions. And he knew the actors who were the troublesome ones—and the ones that were mouthy. There was many a time when he said to the make-up department, when they were giving out dressings and wounds, 'Can we have a mouth wound for this one over here, please?'"

During the final retreat scene, where the remnants of the British Airborne stagger through the pouring rain, a handful of the A.P.A. decided they didn't like getting wet. "There were a few in the group who became very lazy and would always want to be on the sidelines. We all had to be involved in this night shoot with Sean Connery. The rain kind of stopped at a certain point in the forest. It was pissing down in the foreground, but in the background, it wasn't raining. So, some of our number decided the best place to be was in the dry at the back! There was a wonderful moment where Steve Lanning set the actor up to collapse as it was all choreographed. And this guy decided that he would fall in the dry bit, but then another of his comrades picked him up and carried him through the rain. So, his little plan to stay dry was completely foiled. I liked Steve a lot. There was another assistant director, Roy Button—was just a lovely, gentle soul. Steve was more like David Tomblin. They were the muscle, really. They had to be."[365]

Overall, Steve Lanning had nothing but praise for the A.P.A. "We had the cream of young actors. There wasn't a film I didn't go on from then on, where there wasn't one of the A.P.A. on." [366]

The best compliments came from the experts themselves. "Americans had even teeth and got well fed during the war. They looked terrific," Jack McKenzie said, "but the Brits had broken teeth. All broken noses, and we fitted that mould. The compliment came from John Waddy's wife, Anne. We were all relaxing between the shots. And she said, 'You know they look just like my John's soldiers.' And General Frost said the same thing."[367]

Sebastian Abineri related that, "Frost said, 'I never would have believed it—you're just like my men. When you've got nothing to do, you sit around drinking tea, smoking, sleeping on your packs or playing football or whatever. I can't believe we got a bunch of actors to do this. Mind you, we did form the SAS from the Artists' Rifles.' And Bill, the armourer, said to us, 'In your case, more like Piss Artist Rifles.'"[368]

Despite all the hijinks, for some the echoes of the past were never far away. One day, Jack McKenzie travelled to the Airborne cemetery in Oosterbeek. He wanted to find his uncle who had died after landing via a glider in the King's Own Scottish Borderers Regiment. Sebastian Abineri asked to come along too. When they arrived off the train in the rebuilt city of Arnhem, he felt the place had "a different atmosphere, which seems to hang over it like a darker pall . . . There seems to be a darkness about the place which had stained the atmosphere." On a bus to the cemetery, the driver asked if they were English. "If you are, you do not pay," he said. Both men felt "humbled that the behaviour of my fellow countrymen had such an effect on the next generation of the Dutch in Arnhem."[369]

Arriving at the cemetery where more than 1,750 Allied soldiers are buried, the pair noted the ages of many of the fallen. "Some descriptions were very moving." McKenzie recalled the words of one, *"Sad to have only known you for such a short while.* I think he was 16-and-a-half or something like that." The graves were tended by an old veteran who would whistle "It's a Long Way to Tipperary."

They also met a regular visitor to the place, none other than Colonel Waddy, who was carefully examining the records. He explained that during the initial jump into Arnhem, he had counted every man out of their Dakota, but when they all reassembled on the drop zone, one young officer had disappeared during the drop. "I've never found out what happened to him, which meant I couldn't tell his parents."[370] Even more than 30 years later, he had continued to be the lost young man's CO.

Leaving Waddy alone, McKenzie and Abineri wandered back into the cemetery and met an elderly Dutch couple who had sheltered almost 500 Paras right under the German noses. Despite the privations and threat of a firing squad, they and scores of their countrymen helped the soldiers to escape to Allied lines.[371]

Weeks later, at the end of filming, Tim Morand, along with his new Dutch girlfriend, also made a pilgrimage to the cemetery. Despite several organised bus trips laid on by the production, he hadn't felt ready to go until then. "I looked at one gravestone, so and so, aged 17, and there were hundreds. And my whole stomach welled up. It's the only time in my life where I cried uncontrollably for the Universe. It just overwhelmed me totally."[372]

14

"Start the Purple"
Batt, Bombs, and Bruises Part 1

On a warm, balmy August day, 10 Sherman tanks sit idling on a narrow roadway. Their throaty Detroit Diesel engines, supplemented by the more benign Land Rover additions, all rev, growl, and splutter amid bursts of dirty smoke. Lined up behind them are scores of khaki-painted vehicles, each stuffed with a mixture of A.P.A. and Dutch extras, dressed as British infantry. At the far end of the smoke-shrouded military column dressed in authentic Allied markings are some of the "enemy." To bolster the number of Charlie Mann's armoured fist, a few German vehicles have been deployed to beef up the numbers. But at the front were the Shermans, and they were ready for action.

The breakout of XXX Corps was staged in a wide plain covered with heather and ringed by trees, blooming with greenery and flowers at the height of summer at Amersfoort, some 30 miles west of Deventer. It was parkland that had also played host to the Dutch military as a tank range and in a bygone age saw the colourful manoeuvres of horsemen. Nearby sat the Dutch cavalry museum. One of the idling Shermans had graced its front gates before being recruited by the tank wrangler, Major John Larminie.

On this summer day, at various vantage points from a dugout to a crane, multiple camera teams ready for the command to "turn over." All are waiting for special effects supervisor John Richardson to be happy. He has laid miles of cables criss-crossed through the heather towards hundreds of explosives primed to rip the landscape apart. This will simulate the creeping barrage that British artillery laid down before the attack on 17 September 1944. On another day, a battery of 12-pounders, still in service with the Dutch Army, will be dressed in British livery and filmed firing blanks. But today is the devastating barrage on the German front line.

When all is ready, one voice will crackle from a megaphone and let loose the "dogs of war." It belongs to Bert Batt, who "had the loudest voice as an AD; people shook when he shouted."[373] Considered the equal of Dave Tomblin, Batt marshalled the newly formed second unit. "We were always going to need a second unit," explained Steve Lanning. "It wasn't something that was needed upfront, but they ended up very busy. It had as big a crew as a main unit. Their assistant director was big time—Bert Batt (along with second assistant directors Andy Armstrong and Chris Carreras). They were an A-team."[374]

Batt learned his craft at the smaller end of the British film industry, marshalling the anarchic talents of the "Carry On" team and the other successful cottage industry, the Hammer horrors. At Bray studios, he became an indispensable part of the team on these tightly budgeted movies, which often starred Christopher Lee and Peter Cushing.

Peter MacDonald was a close friend and recalled Batt as an easy-going, relaxed character off the set. "He was definitely a one-off. Bert loved playing a guitar—not that well—but he'd sit for hours, just being happy and contented in himself. He wasn't like several quite big-time ADs that were really angry people and who thought they were often better than the director they were working with."[375]

Batt had a hidden talent, having penned one of the best Hammer productions, *Frankenstein Must Be Destroyed* (1969). It was his first and only screenplay, but it seems without his efficient AD's hat on, he made a most human mistake. Arriving at the home of producer Anthony Nelson Keys, he realised he'd left his hundred-page *Frankenstein* script on a fast-disappearing bus. Piling into a car, they gave chase through London traffic. "Each corner they rounded; they prayed the bus would come into sight. If only they could overtake it, Bert could leap from the car and reboard at the next stop . . . The hard work of four months was eventually retrieved at the bus depot at the end of the run."[376]

Batt and cameraman Peter MacDonald planned to direct some of Batt's later scripts, which he would produce, but came up against industry prejudice. "I thought he was a very good writer," said Mac-Donald. "But it never really worked out because you'd go to a meeting and they'd say, 'That assistant director fellah wrote this script? Oh, no!' It really upset me. I think Bert was quite a realist and was just happy playing his guitar."[377]

The '60s found Batt's AD skills recognised through work on higher-budgeted films, including several in South Africa. The most famous of these was the Levine-produced *Zulu*, directed by Cy Endfield. As some of the *Bridge* crew found when they went to South Africa to make *Zulu Dawn* in 1978, apartheid created an iron curtain between the races. "We could only work with the Zulus," recalled Bert Batt. "We could not in any way befriend them. We couldn't offer them cigarettes, put an arm around a shoulder, sit and chat with them through an interpreter. You feel ashamed of yourself for what you had to shut your eyes and ears to."

A great example of Batt's quality as a First AD was his inspired but simple idea to swell 250 Zulu extras to something like the historical 4,000 that attacked the mission station at Rorke's Drift. The script called for Zulus to first appear on the hillside, their vast number instilling trepidation in the handful of British defenders. "I saw all these shields lying on the floor," Batt recalled. "I had the idea of putting them on batons. I got them all rigged up on a Saturday afternoon, after we'd finished shooting, with my two assistants. What we did was put the shields on the batons, all at different angles and heights. Then we banged a *knobkerrie* to the back to break up the outline. We got it all up there and saw how it worked. I got Cy and Stanley [Baker] to come down on Sunday and have a look at it. Cy said, 'Jesus Christ, that's terrific!'"[378] The result on film is truly majestic and awe-inspiring.

Just prior to *Bridge*, Batt had worked with Caine and Connery on John Huston's splendid Victorian adventure tale, *The Man Who Would Be King* in Morocco. In his autobiography, *An Open Book*, Huston devoted a lengthy passage extolling the virtues of a great AD. He then named just two from all his 38 films. One was the American, Tommy Shaw, whom he'd worked with several times, and the other, working with just once, was Bert Batt. "Whatever is good about *The Man Who Would Be King*, Bert Batt had something to do with it," stated Huston. "Bert's ideas were always well thought out, and usually they were good ideas. If you didn't go for what he proposed, he didn't turn petulant, but addressed himself to the next problem. He would sometimes be up two days and three nights running, arranging something complicated like a whole troop movement; not only was he a powerhouse of energy, but he was resourceful to an amazing degree."[379]

For his book about the making of *Zulu*, film historian Sheldon Hall asked Bert Batt whether he was proud of the film and his own contribution. His answer, which could equally stand for *Bridge*, is a splendid example of his self-effacing professional modesty: "It was a great film to be associated with. I'm glad that I worked on it but not proud of it. I did the job I was paid to do and there's nothing to be proud in that . . . We were a unit of professionals with all the tools to do the job."[380] Following *Zulu*, Batt was a popular choice for complex, action-heavy subjects. Managing the war films *The Dirty Dozen* (1967) and *Cross of Iron* (1977) added to his experience and expertise, both of which would be called upon for *Bridge*.

"He was determined his stuff was gonna be as good as the first unit," recalled MacDonald. "Once Bert Batt realised that he wasn't getting far trying to explain to some of his team exactly what it was all about, he would just say. 'Okay, let's go—action.' But all the extras loved him and would be doing their bit. I really had a lot of time for both he and David Tomblin. You couldn't have had two better Firsts anywhere in the world."[381]

"At precisely 2:15 p.m., with a thunderous roar, some 350 guns opened fire." So began Cornelius Ryan's dramatic opening of Operation Market Garden. "The hurricane of fire, ranging five miles in depth and concentrated over a one-mile front, caused the earth to shake beneath the tanks of the Irish Guards as they lumbered up to the start line."[382] Goldman's screenplay distilled this as: *WHAM—the woods erupt as batteries of camouflaged artillery guns open fire.* And it was effects supervisor John Richardson's job to turn these words into eye-punching cinema.

The breakout sequence would be a career high. "It was probably the biggest single explosion shot that I've ever laid out. We had something like 30 or 40 explosions all lined up, each one dug into the ground with between 3 to 5 pounds of dynamite with added peat, cork, and all manner of other things thrown in. It amounted to 100 tonnes of materials. We had probably 20 miles of electrical flex laid out to fire all the charges, which took us three days to lay for the one shot."[383]

But before he could start, there had been a hurdle to overcome. The plain, despite being a firing range, was also a conservation area. "At almost the eleventh hour, the commandant of the army range withdrew permission, saying the cement dust would kill the heather! Luckily, my interpreter's father worked in the Dutch government at The Hague, and so I asked him to make an approach on our behalf. Fortunately, they overruled the unhappy commandant at 10 p.m. the night before we were due to film."[384]

To shoot the scene—in one take—would require multiple cameras placed by the second unit. The head cameraman was a close friend of Geoffrey Unsworth and understood he needed to match the main unit's photographic style of diffusion. Harry Waxman, a rather relaxed and gentle soul, was an industry veteran, with his most well-known work the "Citizen Kane of Horror movies,"[385] *The Wicker Man* (1974). Waxman was already experienced with epic action sequences, as he photographed Yakima Canutt's second-unit battles for *Khartoum* (1966) in 70 mm.

Overlooking the narrow road over which the British tanks would advance for the breakout was a wood where German artillery lurked. The contrast range between the dark wood and the bright heather-strewn plain presented a photographic challenge to Waxman. "When I went in there, I thought we were just never going to get anything," said Waxman. "It had to be a bit low-keyed, so eventually, instead of using prime lenses, I stayed with the long end of the zoom and it was just right."[386]

Sebastian Abineri portrayed one of those clad in Wehrmacht field grey manning the hidden artillery. Abineri said, "The third assistant said, 'Now look, you two, it's fucking dangerous. There are explosives all over the place. So, whatever you do—do not move. The shit's gonna fly everywhere. Just stay in your trench.'" Abineri added, "So, it started—action!"[387]

Richardson said, "It took us about 35 seconds to fire it all. It came from about a third of a mile away. This barrage was coming right up to us. You saw this tremendous wall of explosions, debris, and dust. Probably 50 tonnes of cement dust, peat, caulk, you name it, all gone up in the air."[388]

Abineri's shared his perspective: "They were massive explosives coming towards us. It was getting really close with pebbles rattling on your helmet. I completely lost my nerve. I thought, *I'm getting out of here.* And I ran. Which is just what you're not supposed to do."[389]

Richardson said, "When it finally reached us, it literally turned to night in one second. And we were completely covered in this dust and debris. Liz, my girlfriend, was standing next to me laughing her head off as we could not even see one another. It literally went that dark. It just blotted everything out for 10–15 minutes or more."[390]

Abineri said, "The thought of being under real artillery fire is just horrendous. I don't know how they stood it—ground your courage to the sticking place, and bloody well stay where you're supposed to stay—and they did it."[391]

"Cut!" Bert Batt's voice boomed across the heather, which was now covered with grey cement powder. Any concern about the fragile foliage was assuaged later with "one shower of rain and the dust all disappeared."[392]

🦋　　　🦋　　　🦋

With the barrage in the can, the second unit set to work on the tentative advance of the Irish Guards tanks. With the Shermans leading, the column of Charlie Mann's various half-tracks and Bren gun carriers stuffed with most of the A.P.A. in British khaki would shuffle along the narrow roadway.

Assistant director Roy Button recalled the immense challenge of just getting all these elderly vehicles into place. "I might have a column of 30 vehicles on 15 low loaders. Some of these things moved a little and some moved a lot, and some didn't move at all. You've only got to do take two, and then something's overheating because it's that old. Also, having tanks on proper roads tends to suck up the tarmac, especially when you turn them left or right to go back. You're left with an extremely damaged road, and a very unhappy council."[393]

Watching from the sidelines was the original commander, John Ormsby Evelyn (J.O.E.) Vandeleur, the powerfully built six-footer, former commander of the elite Irish Guards, present during these long, dusty, and dirty days of filming. Richardson wondered if his movie barrage would pass muster to a veteran of the actual attack. "You've just sent shivers up my spine,' Vandeleur replied, "because I was back there."[394]

Michael Caine portrayed Vandeleur and noted that when doing his National Service tour in Korea, Caine had "tried to get out of everything." Vandeleur, by contrast, had come from an Irish family of professional soldiers for 400 years and "tried to get into everything."[395] Ryan described him as "the kind of devil-may-care elegance of the Guards' officer," who wore a multicoloured camouflaged parachutist's jacket over his combat garb, topped off with "a flamboyant emerald-green scarf." Caine duly arrived from the wardrobe department dressed with a similar scarf, much to the general's displeasure. Despite it being the colour associated with Ireland, and mentioned by Ryan's book, Vandeleur insisted he disliked the colour green. Caine decided not to argue with a man who had led his tanks into the teeth of German firepower.

Aside from the green scarf, Vandeleur approved of Michael Caine's performance but made a small suggestion when asked what he actually said to launch the great attack. Ryan described a 19-year-old Lieutenant, Keith Heathcote, standing in the turret of the lead tank of No. 3 Squadron, shouting into his microphone: "Driver, advance!"[396] Goldman faithfully copied this in his script, but added, *"Not the most awe-inspiring order of all time."*

The old brigadier informed Caine that he had simply said, "Well, get a move on, then."[397] While not exactly Shakespearean, it was what the man said. On film Caine plays the line, *"Get moving, get moving,"* suitably low key and restrained. A.P.A. Sean Mathias got his KLM as the Irish Guards lieutenant with that less than inspirational line, *"Driver, advance!"*

The file shows the Germans crawling out of their shallow dugouts and redeploying their artillery. A single barrel swings into camera closeup and fires. The convoy is covered in smoke and explosions as the British armour takes a pounding. The A.P.A. were directed to jump out of their vehicles and find cover to give suppressing fire. Movie make-believe was hairy that day: Richardson had placed discreet markers on the ground to indicate where there were hot landmines. They were easy to miss in the chaos.

Tim Morand was one of those who jumped for cover. "We had to clock where the markers were, and before the take, they took them away and there were little mounds of earth dotted around the place. On 'action,' I came off the lorry, and I was behind Jimmy Wardroper."[398]

Abineri said, "Jimmy stood on an explosive. And it blew him up into the air, and he landed on his back. His uniform was on fire, but to do him credit, he stayed completely still."[399]

"I saw him literally jump on it and he did a somersault in the air," said Morand of Wardroper. "His British Army surge was completely black and singed."[400]

With the attack stalling, Vandeleur needed air support to suppress the German artillery. He called over the radio: *"Start the purple."* With this order, coloured smoke shells were fired to create a visible target for the RAF Typhoon fighter bombers. For the film, four Harvard T-6 Texan two-seater training planes were given a makeover and pressed into service to drop 'bombs' made from fire extinguishers. These flew in from the film's airfield base at Deelen. Once again, Richardson needed to simulate the devastating explosions on the small wood that was hiding the Germans. On "action," all went off without a hitch.

"I set explosions at points of impact and placed markers for the pilots to show exactly where they should aim for. These talented guys dropped their bombs bang on target, and it was one of the best sequences that I've ever witnessed. But do you know what? Not one bloody camera caught it! Every single camera had a long lens fitted, obviously looking to capture the dummy bombs dropping, but the second-unit cameraman didn't have a wide shot planned, and so it was all wasted. I was flabbergasted at rushes the next day and pulled Richard Attenborough to one side to firstly express my frustration, but also to beg and plead with him to allow us to do it again. He thankfully agreed, and it is in the film."

Dickie's unhesitating grant of his request was a mark of his deep respect for Richardson's work. "I already worked on *Young Winston*," said Richardson. "He's a great director to work for. He can communicate well with you what he wants for the scenes, so that you're given time to prepare things." He acknowledged Dickie was "terrific" with the actors, but "whilst I'd never criticise Richard, I sometimes needed to battle to get his attention away from the actors to have him watch the tests I'd lined up and get his all-important approval."

John Richardson was a chip off the old block. His father Cliff had been a pioneer in effects work, having started in the fledging industry way back in 1916. John, born in 1946, lived in the family home that often served as test tube for cinematic experiments. "Giant rubber frogs appeared in the garden, every bit as big as me," said John Richardson of his father's handiwork. "A snow machine filling the lawn with white stuff in the middle of summer; and once a huge explosion in the conservatory at the rear of the house, which blew out windows and made a real mess of Dad's hand. He'd been mixing chemicals in a pestle and mortar. Mum was hysterical, a condition she achieved with relative ease it must be said, and that ensured it never happened again."[401]

In his teens, John assisted his father in Spain for the spectacular train wreck for *Lawrence of Arabia* in 1962. By 1968, he was an effects man in his own right. For *Battle of Britain*, he got to destroy a real aircraft hangar earmarked for demolition at RAF Duxford. Having been bomb-proofed for the war, the hangar required tonnes of high explosives to reduce it to rubble. On Ken Russell's *The Devils* (1971), Richardson blew up the huge constructed walls of Loudon, exquisitely designed by Derek Jarman. It was take two that made it into the film, after director Russell regretted his rash decision to fire the blast himself. The mistimed ignition forced the embarrassed *enfant terrible* to hand control over to the expert.

Richardson would be closely associated with the Bond films and later the Harry Potter movies. Just 30 at the time of *Bridge*, John Richardson had already become one of the finest effects men in the business, heading a team of 25, both British and Dutch. "We were making our own mini war, basically," Richardson said, listing his dirty ingredients to create the hell of battle. "We burnt 10,000 old motor car tires to make black smoke, along with 10 tonnes of liquid propane gas. For the explosions, we blew up in excess of 200 tonnes of cement type powder, a tonne of high explosive, and probably 20 tonnes of low explosives and pyrotechnics. Plus, hundreds of bales of caulk and peat to make them look so real. Getting everything to the right places, let alone using them, made it a colossal challenge."

Richardson was not just required to do the big stuff. Following the British Airborne landings, the operation quickly unraveled. General

Urquhart was cut off from his command and forced to run through the sprawling back streets of Arnhem. One of his companions was wounded, and they took temporary shelter in a house only to see a German appear at the window. Urquhart fired his sidearm and shot the German dead. The film presents this almost exactly, with Sean Connery shooting the hapless soldier. But how to "kill" the German?

In the digital age, a shot like this would require the actor to merely perform being hit and then crumple to the ground. The glass shattering and the head shot would be a comparatively easy CGI job. Not so in 1976. "It was a fairly tricky one," said Richardson, "because you needed to see the glass break, and a blood hit on the man's forehead right between the eyes. We positioned a piece of Plexiglas outside the window at a 45-degree angle. The soldier, played by a stuntman outside, was standing behind both pieces of glass. We then had to get an angle on the outside so that we could fire a blood hit from a compressed air gun into the middle of his forehead. Timing it was the trickiest thing. Even at slow motion on video it seems to hold up okay."

Before Urquhart takes his shot on the bull's-eye, he narrowly avoids a hit of his own. Earlier, he is shown in conversation with Brigadier Lathbury about the worsening situation as they are pinned down by heavy German fire. As they talk, the camera tracks along with them and suggests, perhaps subliminally, that the dialogue will continue. Just then, a mortar hits a jeep and throws it high into the air. It is barely feet from one of the world's most expensive superstars. "He was very close to it," said Richardson. "We built a jeep with a cannon in the back of it, which held a tiny black powder charge of three ounces. It is as much as you get in a household firework. The cannon had a sort of steel piston in it with the black powder charge and a telegraph pole. Then we put an effects explosion underneath the jeep and fired the two together, and the explosion went off. The telegraph pole went down, and the jeep went up and it flipped over. Sean was probably no more than 30 or 40 feet away from it, and he was absolutely fine."[402]

Peter MacDonald was experienced enough to treat the spectacular effects with respect and was mindful of potential danger. "To move all that shit up in the air, you need something huge to make it go," said MacDonald. "You could never tell if it's going to grab hold of one piece of metal and send it through someone. At the end of every shot, you always have a little check to make sure everyone's okay. In 26 weeks of nonstop action, we got away with hardly any injury—though there were a couple of accidents off the set."[403]

While the film would be a career high, it would also be tinged with tragedy for the effects man, John Richardson. Previously, he, along with many of the *Bridge* crew, had worked on the horror classic, *The Omen*, directed by Richard Donner. For his small team, Richardson employed Liz Moore, "a very talented sculptress and a very vivacious person" to create the "dogs of hell" sculptures. A few years earlier, she had modelled the Star Child that appears at the end of Kubrick's *2001* and the nude female milk dispensers at the Korova Milk Bar in *A Clockwork Orange* (1971). Moore also made the robot suit for C3PO and the stormtroopers' helmets for *Star Wars*, which was also shooting that summer. She and Richardson became close during *The Omen* production. "Our friendship developed into a relationship and we fell head over heels in love." Despite his parents "disgust," he left his wife to be with Liz and she joined him in Holland for *Bridge*, and "we lived together throughout the summer, and it was blissful."

Thursday, 12 August, Richardson had spent the day rigging explosions on Sherman tanks for the XXX Corps breakout. That evening, he and Liz joined a group of friends for dinner, "but aware we had an early call the next morning, we left just before midnight," recalled Richardson. "At 1 a.m. Friday, 13 August, we were involved in a head-on car crash, with each car said to be travelling at 80 mph. Everything was a blank until I woke up in hospital, my face was shattered, my nose broken, my jaw smashed—the steering wheel went through my mouth. My knee was broken, ribs and other bones, too. I have hazy memories of a male nurse speaking to me and I asked about Liz, but although he didn't answer, the look in his eyes told me she was dead.

I was distraught. The guy driving the other car was killed on impact. I was given four hours to live by the medics." Richardson spent 10 days in hospital, while they "put my face back together. My jaw was wired shut, so I lived on fluids." Despite both his injuries and his grief, he ignored Dickie's offer to rest and continued to the end of the shoot.

Over the years, conspiracy theories have appeared inspired by the diabolical storyline of *The Omen*. These have been fuelled by the various accidents that befell the cast and crew since the film's release in 1976. Liz Moore had left a four-year-old son, Danny, and her death at just 32 has garnered a fair degree of prurient speculation, not to be repeated here. Perhaps these rumours grew from the fact that the accident happened about 30 miles north of Deventer on the road to the Dutch town of Ommen. Richardson has been understandably upset by these puerile ideas. His view: "Was the film cursed? No, I really do not believe it was; there were some strange incidents, but at the end of the day you have to put it down to bad luck."[404]

15
"Roll the Fuckers!!!"
The Famous Fourteen Part 2

For almost six months, Amsterdam's Schiphol Airport was graced with glamour. It became a regular sight for awed tourists by the baggage carousel rubbing shoulders with big marquee names that lived in the nether land of Hollywood. Schiphol also proved a popular vantage point for international paparazzi keen to get an exclusive snap of a star with a hitherto unknown attractive companion. So, the sight of a slight, 70-year-old man with thin grey hair, rimless glasses, and dressed in a shabby suit that was fashionable in the 1940s, his shoes pockmarked with mud, was unlikely to draw much attention. This particular old man, who made his way through the throng of people dressed in garish 1970s colours with flared trousers and kaftans, would wince, not at the sights, but at his own ailments that had been steadily advancing for some years. Passing through customs, he would have used the few words of Dutch that he'd learnt practicing with a tape recorder. As he walked out to the throng of waiting people, he would have seen a taxi driver holding up a card: Lord Olivier.

Laurence Olivier was born to a nontheatrical family, the son of a clergyman. "The ritualistic has always pleased me," he said later. Despite suffering from stage fright, his talent was obvious from an early age. He had the equal protean talent of his American contemporary, Orson Welles. Olivier set the British theatre alight along with fellow heavyweights Ralph Richardson and John Gielgud and soon became an actor-manager in the tradition of Charles Kean and Sir Henry Irving. In the '40s, he and Richardson built up the prestige of the Old Vic. Later, he embraced the caustic works of post-war, angry-young-men iconoclasts like John Osborne by staging *The Entertainer.* He was made a Sir in 1947 and a Lord in 1970 as recognition of his theatrical pre-eminence. For a decade and despite his health problems, his inspired leadership fostered many future stars, such as Derek Jacobi, Maggie Smith, and Anthony Hopkins. Although he nurtured new talent, it was noted, "Olivier's one great fault was a paranoid jealousy of anyone who he thought was a rival."[405]

While the theatre was his lifeblood, Olivier's few forays into cinema have been memorable. Arriving in Hollywood in the late '30s, he starred in *Wuthering Heights* (1939) and Hitchcock's *Rebecca* (1940), before the war brought him back to England to fight. He joined the Fleet Air Arm, where his fellow servicemen treated his stardom with typical British phlegmatic disinterest when they all trooped to the cinema to see *Rebecca*. At the end, no one said a word about his performance, except for one who asked, "Did you have to wear that moustache?"[406] If he had any airs and graces, they were kicked out of him that day. After a flag-waving role as Lord Nelson in Churchill's favourite film, *That Hamilton Woman* (1941) with his wife Vivien Leigh, Olivier stepped behind the cameras with as audacious a directorial debut as Welles' *Citizen Kane* (1941).

Dedicated to the British Airborne forces, Olivier's *Henry V* (1944) is one of the greatest adaptations of Shakespeare, in which he also starred. Two further Shakespeare films, *Hamlet* (1948) and *Richard III* (1955), cemented Olivier's reputation as a first-class filmmaker. But the lure of theatre meant cinema would remain a land less well trod.

His later film roles were often as patricians: *Spartacus* (1960), *Khartoum, Battle of Britain*, and *Oh! What A Lovely War*, each singularly nuanced with a gravitas and sense of command. But it is his 1972 film *Sleuth* that hints at Olivier's underlying charm and magnetism. Despite recovering from serious illness, he gives a *tour de force* in a two-header with Michael Caine. It is a mark of his generosity and intelligence as an actor that he allows Caine to deliver some of his best work, and the pair are an absolute joy to watch. In Goldman-penned *Marathon Man*, his portrayal of Nazi war criminal/evil dentist who tortures Dustin Hoffman is utterly chilling and a fascinating contrast to the benign country doctor, Doctor Spaander, whom he was cast to play for *Bridge*.

Arriving on set, he was welcomed like a king. The A.P.A. and crew stood "open-mouthed. His fascination as far as the watcher is concerned is sheer magic," Dickie commented. The director strode over and gave his mentor one of his bear hugs. Then Olivier twisted and pulled at his crumpled suit. "One believes *I* fit into *it*,"[407] he said proudly. Lifting his mud-stained shoes, he explained he'd used them in the garden and hoped the English mud wouldn't present any continuity issues. The great actor, unlike any of his colleagues, had sought out his costume some weeks before and worn it continuously. Describing it as "working from the outside in," he, like Welles, relied on make-up and appearance to find the way into a role. "I have to have a pillow up my jumper, a false nose or a moustache or wig . . . I cannot come on looking like me and be someone else."[408]

He had just arrived from England during a break in making a TV version at Granada of *Cat on a Hot Tin Roof*, starring the then-husband-and-wife team of Natalie Wood and Robert Wagner. That production would require him back for a few months before resuming *Bridge* in September. All depended on his health, which was precarious. While his marriage to actress Joan Plowright brought him stability after he had divorced Vivien Leigh in 1960, his burgeoning family meant he needed to work to pay their school fees.

Olivier was aware of the aura around him but wore it lightly. Visiting the set, one young American actor had inadvertently sat in a high canvas chair. "I was sitting around the campfire, as it were, having a conversation with my fellow actors," recalled John Morton. "And suddenly the actor in front of me said, 'You're sitting in Olivier's chair.'

And so, I jumped up just in time to turn to him. I apologised profuse-ly because it's something you don't do. He said, 'Don't be ridiculous. Please, just sit down.' And I said, 'Lord Olivier, it is really a pleasure to meet you.' He said, 'Oh, no, don't be ridiculous. Call me Larry.' He was lovely, very humble; just a great guy."[409]

It was late June, and the production had moved to the sleepy vil-lage of Bronkhorst, just south of Zutphen, where an impressive set had been constructed of the Oosterbeek church and rectory. It's here, as the battle rages, that the ageing local Doctor Spaander makes a visit with a difficult request.

🐝   🐝   🐝

She became known as the "Angel of Arnhem," but it was a title Kate ter Horst never liked. In September 1944, she was a 38-year-old mother of five. Her husband, Jan, was a lawyer in the prosperous suburb of Oosterbeek. She, along with thousands of her countrymen, experienced great joy to see the British Airborne troops file past them on that fateful Sunday. She caught the excitement in her diary: "Crazy with joy. We walked through the garden and climbed on the roof so that we can see more and understand more of what is happening. We can hardly believe it. Will it really be true? Is this the long-awaited end of our grief that now falls from the sky? Does this mean freedom?"[410]

The film's recreation was caught on Super-8 home movie by the mayor of the Bronkhorst district, Steven Buddingh.[411] He captures a shirtless AD waving the A.P.A. forward. Some of them walk arm in arm with attractive Dutch ladies, all with perfect 1940s coiffures. At one point, Hopkins is cued and strides forward with a suitable Colonel Frost swagger. As they pass the impressive set of the rectory (much grander than the original), we see the happy ter Horsts. At the centre is the tall, blonde, willowy figure of one of the world cinema's leading lights, Liv Ullmann, described by Jane Hershey as "an earth mother, a better earth than ours."[412] Ironically, Ullmann's Nordic looks made her a dead ringer for the Dutch lady, more so than the half-Dutch bru-nette, Audrey Hepburn, who had originally been sought for the role.

Born in Japan to Norwegian parents in 1937, Ullmann avoided the ravages of Nazi occupation as her family spent the war years in North America. As an actress, she will always be celebrated for her close professional and personal association with the Swedish film master, Ingmar Bergman. She had joined his ensemble company in 1966 and appeared in some of the director's most revered films, with *Persona* (1965) as one of the greatest of all time. Playing opposite a regular co-star, Max von Sydow, the pair starred in Jan Troell's six-hour historical saga, *The Immigrants/New World* in 1971–72. This story of old-world emigration and forging a new life in nineteenth-century rural America proved a commercial and critical success and brought Ullmann to the attention of Hollywood. She starred in two more historical dramas, *Pope Joan* (1972) and *The Abdication* about the seventeenth-century Swedish queen, Kristina, which was photographed by Unsworth and MacDonald. It was the ill-fated musical *Lost Horizon* (1973) that effectively killed her international career. She continued to make intense and intimate films with Bergman, including *Hour of the Wolf* (1968), *Cries and Whispers* (1972), *Scenes from a Marriage* (1973), and *The Serpent's Egg* (1977). She has declined to describe herself as a character actor, but by drawing from her own emotions and experiences, she remains "Liv" in all her performances. Perhaps the qualities she exudes most are an intense compassion and complete honesty.

Although she was not the first choice to play the Dutch housewife, her striking similarity and accent (at least to an English ear) made her an ideal choice to play the Angel of Arnhem. Ullman expressed honour at portraying the onetime housewife turned heroine: ". . . a fantastic person: serene, brave, real . . . I can never be her. I'm portraying something she did, using my face and body . . . though actually I hear we are very much alike . . . I must show a whole human being, and it's very difficult—but I also find it very interesting because I have to rethink everything I've done before in films."[413] She noted the huge *Bridge* crew of over 100 contrasted with Bergman's tiny unit of rarely over 15. When pressed on her reasons for appearing in an epic, she replied simply, "To work with the greatest living actor in the world."[414]

Only a few hours past the triumphant march of the Red Devils, ter Horst came face-to-face with the reality of war. Amid a cloud of dust, she saw a green jeep pull up outside her house. ". . . And this was a jeep, a new thing to us. The English doctor got out in his battle dress and said, 'Well, I'm probably going to have some wounded and would it be possible to have them here?'" This was Medical Officer Warrack, and her acquiescence would change her life forever as the first trickle of wounded men stepped into her beautiful home.

The film staged this with Warrack, renamed Weaver (Richard Kane), explaining to Kate and the audience the precarious position of the division and the need for a temporary dressing station. Spaander (a fictional creation) warns, *"I fear it may be more than that."* Johnstone's *Report* team covered this scene in detail, and he noticed Dickie's very precise direction of the World's Greatest Actor. At one point, regarding a line to Kate ter Horst, *"Is your husband not yet returned?"* Dickie was at pains to stress that her spouse is fighting with the resistance, and so there is a subtle edge to the words. Olivier replied he was aware of this situation and wondered, "Didn't I make that clear?"[415] When rehearsing with ter Horst's children, Olivier, who played the scenes in English for the benefit of Colonel Weaver, wondered what would be a Dutch form of bye-bye for a child. *"Glenchie,"* came the helpful reply from a local woman. This tiny detail was included in the scene and is a good example of the organic process of filmmaking, a constant stream of tweaks and improvements, whether from cast, crew, or even a bystander.

The Super-8 film shows the lighting technique for the scene, which involved huge muslin frames suspended from the set to overhang the actors, diffuse the light, and allow even illumination. The heat and glare behind the scenes are very apparent with crew members baring red and ruddy skin. Olivier seems to be quite relaxed in the intense heat despite his medical issues, but as his filming block continues, a growing fatigue becomes visible. One room in the house, first seen as three wounded A.P.A. soldiers walk in and soil the rug with a squirt of

Kensington Gore, is later turned into a charnel house filled with gruesomely dressed wounded. Here, Olivier's Spaander tries his medical best with limited resources. The actor sometimes struggled to hold the prop scalpel. Steve Lanning recalls Olivier had to go home before his work was complete, leading to some sleight of hand. "We literally used the wardrobe driver, who looked just like him, to double Larry. But he had a hump, we could only do from one side, and we used him to do an over-the-shoulder shot of Olivier."[416]

With her five children in the cellar below, Kate ter Horst recounted the pitiful scene of her home cum hospital. "I walk through the rooms . . . everywhere injured, the dining room, the study and garden room, the transverse corridor, even under the stairs and in the toilet, they are. There is no corner left. Oh, if only I could be a hostess. If only I could give them a hospitable bed and at least fresh water . . .

"At the same time, a hurricane of explosions bursts out over us. Shake the walls. I hear crackling, the house across the street is ablaze . . . Phosphorus, flashes through my head.

"The injured lie back, without a complaint, helpless. Now leave them alone? But I have to go downstairs: five children are longing for me right now, trusting that I will be unharmed to protect them.

"In the evening, I come to the back door to get some fresh air and see the dead for the first time. They lie forward, the shaggy hair over the muddy faces, like forgotten rags."[417]

Andrew "Andy" Milbourne, the veteran without his hands, was one of those who lay in ter Horst's battered house. "This lady, blonde, fair, and to me, in my stupor at that particular time through loss of blood . . . an angel," recalled Milbourne. "And something I'll never forget, the reading of the 23rd Psalm. Whenever I hear it to this day it's very difficult to hold the tears back. And I think of the lads and the courage of these Dutch people. God, what they went through in order to try and save us."[418]

Ter Horst reprised her angelic role for *Theirs Is the Glory*. Tall, incongruously elegant, she walks through the throng of wounded. "My friends," she says, "all I can do for you is to read a few lines from a Psalm I just read to my own children." She pauses, and with the aid of a flashlight, speaks with a beautiful gentle voice, *"He that dwellest in a secret place of the Most High, shall abide under the shadow of the Almighty. Thou shalt not be afraid for the terror by night, nor for the arrow that flies by day, nor for the pestilence that walketh in darkness, nor for the Destiny destruction, that waste is at noonday . . ."*[419] Whilst she reads the words of the 91st Psalm, which could have been written for men in war, we see a montage of the wounded men's faces lit with Rembrandtesque chiaroscuro as they listen enraptured. It is easy to appreciate the peace and comfort this Dutch housewife brought to so many in pain and anguish. In *Bridge*, Ullmann beautifully recaptures this, *"incredibly serene throughout these days,"* in Goldman's words. *"She moves along silently, and if she was afraid, it didn't show."*

Kate ter Horst and her husband were appointed Honorary Members of the Most Excellent Order of the British Empire for their extraordinary bravery and humanity. Peter MacDonald met her when she visited the set. "God, you realised she could have probably won the war on her own," said MacDonald. "This lady was fearless."[420] Tragically, Kate ter Horst was killed near her home at age 85 when a motorist lost control and hit her.

The battle for Arnhem, despite its ferocity, saw one of the few glints of chivalry in the war. With his staff completely overwhelmed, Medical Officer Graeme Warrack received permission from Urquhart to seek a short ceasefire. The medic recalls his commander's emphatic order to ensure there was no suggestion of any "surrender." Warrack, who visited Arnhem for the annual reunion in September 1976, dropped by the film set but was peeved that not only was he renamed, no one had contacted him. Months earlier, his crucial meeting with the German commander Walter Harzer had already been restaged for the camera. Warrack recalled the German was "affable" and deeply regretted both countries were at war before agreeing to a daily two-hour truce to bring out the wounded. Over 2,000 men would be taken to German hospitals, including Andrew Milbourne.

Iain Johnstone was keen to interview at least one German participant for his documentary. The film company had extended an invitation for various figures to come to Holland, but all were informed their safety could not be guaranteed. Instead, Johnstone met up with Harzer at his home in Stuttgart, where the walls were stuffed with war memorabilia. Having been a student in Britain before the war, Harzer remained "mystified" that the Western Allies had not joined with Germany to fight Russia. He admitted the Eastern Front was brutal but told his men that when fighting the Tommies, they must do so with honour. Johnstone was at pains not to present Harzer as some kind of angel of mercy, but pointed out that when he was captured, General Gavin, who had faced him at Nijmegen, went to great lengths to keep Harzer out of the clutches of the Russians for his chivalry at Arnhem.

When actor Hardy Krüger arrived for his costume fitting, he was presented not with one in Wehrmacht grey but jet-black of the dreaded Waffen-SS. More than anyone on the film, he had good reason to feel loathing. In 1945, aged 16, he along with most of his schoolfellows was drafted into the *Volkssturm*, made up of boys and old men, in an effort to hold back the Allies. When the bridge at Remagen fell to American forces, the Germans, now forced to fight for their homeland, were split in two. Krüger, as part of the *Volkssturm*, was sent to hold the south flank with the fanatical Waffen-SS to stiffen their wavering resolve. Krüger, with the typical reticence of a veteran, admitted to not having "pleasant" memories of those men clad in black. He agreed to work on the film to help educate the German youth about the war. "They have no guilt complex and rightly so . . . I think this [film] is a good thing to do because it gives those younger people in Germany firsthand information of the horrors and dangers of such a time."[421]

Krüger was cast as the fictional General Ludwig, Goldman's amalgamation of Harzer and another general, the commander of *SS-Kampf-*

gruppe "Frundsberg" Heinz Harmel, who served under General Bittrich and fought with distinction against both the British and Americans during Market Garden. The similar names and exploits prompted the writer to simplify. Krüger was cast, in part, due to his uncanny likeness to Harzer: blonde and blue-eyed. Donning the loathed black uniform, he worked hard to create a human portrayal. "I've always tried to stay as close to the truth as possible," explained Krüger, "even if I have to play someone extremely dangerous, as this character is."[422] As soon as "cut" was yelled, he shed his costume. "All the German actors were charming," Steve Lanning commented. "They were survivors, but Hardy Krüger just glowed. He was a star."[423]

Krüger had shot to fame playing von Werra, the only German POW to escape British custody in *The One That Got Away* (1957). Krüger portrayed von Werra with a devil-may-care insouciance bordering on arrogance but overlaid with enormous charm and charisma. These were qualities he would bring to all his roles. He played a toy model designer who, against the odds, repairs the crashed plane in Robert Aldrich's classic *Flight of the Phoenix* (1965). He played another officer, this time an eighteenth-century Prussian, in Kubrick's *Barry Lyndon*, again bringing the Krüger charm and intelligence as he easily sees through O'Neal's flimsy disguise as a deserter. Both actors recall the painstaking efforts taken to photograph the interiors just with candlelight, which gave the film its extraordinary lustre.

Filmed in the oak-panelled former town hall in Deventer, Warrack's truce scene was watched by eager members of the A.P.A., keen to see great actors at work. Olivier's Dr. Spaander asks General Ludwig for a ceasefire and then adds, *"Afterwards you can kill us all you want to."* Iain Johnstone noted a splendid look Olivier gave to his erstwhile German enemies at the end of the first take, "a magical half smile, part cynical, part obsequiousness."[424] Wondering if he would repeat that look, Johnstone noticed that Olivier did it right on cue for the successive eight takes.

In the scene, Ludwig reminds the visitors that the Germans are winning and can see no need for a ceasefire. Krüger accepted that his part was small and recognised the problem of working in an epic: "In a film like this, it's not very easy for all the actors because the film is a mosaic of characters, and not being given a lot of time to explore a character, you have to be very, very precise."

Ludwig's commander, Obergruppenführer Wilhelm Bittrich, who was played by Maximilian Schell, beckons him over and overrides his subordinate. Medical Officer Weaver asks Spaander to thank him. *"I just did,"* Spaander replies. Bittrich, who does not speak English, nods his acknowledgment.

Schell was a gifted actor with a steely, intense intelligence, and he is mesmerising as the ruthless, yet civilised, general. "I think Bittrich is seen in the film as a sympathetic character," Schell commented. "Of course, a soldier in the war is never quite sympathetic because his whole purpose is to kill. And certainly, the Germans were probably the best at killing. But Bittrich is an army soldier, and he does his duty, and he's fighting and trying to do his best . . ."[425]

Although often cast in German roles, Schell was Swiss and saw little of the war except for a few combat planes flying over his Zurich family home, with one bullet-ridden Allied plane crash-landing near-by. Post-war, he gravitated to Germany and soon became a leading figure, along with his sister Maria, on both stage and film. He made his screen debut in the German anti-war film *Children, Mothers, and a General* (1955), in which he played a disillusioned deserter who underlined "the insanity of continuing to fight a war that is lost."[426] The same year, he played opposite Wolfgang Preiss in *The Plot to Assassinate Hitler*. Beckoned to Hollywood, he portrayed another German officer opposite Marlon Brando in *The Young Lions* (1958).

His powerhouse performance as the defence attorney for Nazi judges in *Judgment at Nuremberg*, first as a live TV production (1959) and then a movie (1961) directed by Stanley Kramer, remains a career high. It was said the actor prepared by reading the entire 40-volume court transcripts. His dedication earned him an Academy Award as the Best Actor of 1962. In Robert Shaw's *The Man in the Glass Booth* (1975), Schell played the dual roles of a Nazi officer and a Jewish Holocaust survivor. It was a challenge he couldn't resist. "It's just that once in a long while a role comes along that I simply can't turn down."[427]

Schell considered himself foremost a director, his films including *The Castle* (1968), based on the book by Franz Kafka about a man trapped in a bureaucratic nightmare, and *Erste Liebe* (First Love) (1970), another adaptation, this time of Ivan Turgenev, nominated for the Academy Award for Best Foreign Language Film. His next film, *The Pedestrian* (1974), about a German tycoon's Nazi past, garnered another nomination and proved an enormous success nationally.

Apart from playing Bittrich, he would be in constant demand for Nazi-themed roles, including *Counterpoint* (1968), *The Odessa File* (1974), *Cross of Iron*, and *Julia* (1977), for which he was once more tipped for an Oscar for his supporting role, but would miss out.

In *Bridge*, Ludwig oversees the defence of Nijmegen bridge, and is keen to blow it up (against Bittrich's orders) before the Allies can seize it. While the spectacular attack sequence wouldn't be shot until September, Krüger filmed his last scenes two months before on a wooden pillbox mock-up overlooking the bridge. One scene involved the first full closure of the immense Waalbrug, which was one of Holland's major traffic arteries.

Just before dawn on Sunday, 6 June, scenic painters had applied grey paint to the modern road markings to ready the bridge for just one hour. Meanwhile, Colonel Waddy had been charged with bringing 400 extras, all dressed as Germans, with the unit's entire fleet of German vehicles dressed with suitable twig-and-branch camouflage, along with eight Dutch Army AMX SP guns, all the way from Deventer to starting positions near the bridge for dawn. This plan required the extras to dress in their costumes at around midnight.

The brief scene depicted the Germans, having taken Arnhem bridge, streaming south to stop the advancing XXX Corps. In all, three takes were required with Dickie's unit framing Krüger in foreground on the wooden bunker, and another crew stationed on and around the bridge. The extras marched in a continuous loop around a traffic circuit at either end. Many double-taking motorists were astounded to see the imposing phalanx of Hitler's legions sprung back to life.

While the later scenes of the British Shermans crossing the bridge would not be shot until October, Ludwig's reaction shots were filmed on 6 June. Krüger had to imagine Ludwig's dismay as the dynamite charge under the bridge fails to blow. His aide exclaims (in German), "Who can stop them now?" Ludwig, realising his mission has now failed, says simply, *"No one."*

Nijmegen was the penultimate bridge target just a few miles short of Arnhem. Yet, it had been the destruction of a bridge many miles to the south that caused the fatal 12-hour delay to Market's link up with Garden.

The Son bridge, just north of Eindhoven, was the target of the 2nd Battalion of the 506 Parachute Infantry Regiment of the U.S. 101st Airborne. While the regiment's Easy Company, of *Band of Brothers* fame, advanced on Nuenen, other detachments drove hard off the landing zone and headed for the crossing over the Wilhelmina Canal.[428] Pinned down by German 88-mm flak guns, the Americans were unable to grab the bridge before it was demolished. The film stages this with some licence but with a great deal of drama—and a touch of comedy.

Goldman introduces an American, the antithesis of the British umbrella-wielding Major Carlyle, with suitable gusto.

COLONEL BOBBY STOUT of THE AMERICAN 101ST in CLOSEUP. This is one colorful guy. Short, he always wore a large helmet and constantly smoked big cigars, chomping on them. Sometimes, what with the size of the helmet and the size of the cigars, you couldn't get a clear look at his face. He was in his middle to late 30s, and was given, in moments of tension, to a skilled use of the vulgate.

A group of GIs tentatively appear out of the bushes alongside a road. They move forward, first at a trot, towards what looks like an intact bridge. Getting closer, the pace increases. Barging through the throng of the A.P.A. is the burly figure of Colonel Stout, a thick cigar jammed between his teeth.

"Elliott Gould was light relief," recalled Peter MacDonald, who thought the actor was very similar to his character, Colonel Stout. "He was portraying a guy who was gonna make it work—chomping a cigar and just being great. You find when people are scared, whether or not they want to, they try to put humour into a situation. He came off that way as an actor; he was really just fun. Elliott was, and is still, quite a character."[429]

Arriving in mid-August, Gould was the penultimate of the 14 stars to report for duty in Holland. He worked just a week and, more by design of scheduling, would shoot all his scenes in script continuity.

He started at a run.

And right now we're in a moment of considerable tension as we see STOUT leading his men in a wild charge across open terrain toward the highway bridge at Son . . .

Ahead stood a recreation of the Son bridge built over the narrow neck of a lake in the Bussloo Recreation park. It was constructed by Peter Dukelow with some ingenuity. "The bridge didn't actually exist. We couldn't afford to build one," explained John Richardson. "So, we built just the start of the bridge, in perspective, so it was a fairly short lump. It was shot from Elliott Gould's perspective."

Concerns over the fish in the river required a series of small charges being fired under the water to create ripples to frighten them away. Then, with cameras rolling, a series of simulated shells burst along the river before hitting the bridge. "We fired the lot in a sequence with bridge pylons being blown up from underwater, and then the bridge going up after it. We had some separate explosive charges that were blowing boards and debris up in the air."[430]

Stuart Craig recalled Richardson's precise instruction to Gould and the A.P.A. to go no farther than a designated line, "because beyond that point—it's dangerous. And John was absolutely as good as his word," said Craig. "I mean, the final piece of debris landed a yard in front of Elliott Gould's feet."[431]

"I was pretty close to that, and it was a little frightening." Gould recalled, "I mean, we really blew that bridge! And I was saying to our cameraman, Geoffrey Unsworth, 'What if it doesn't work?' And he said, 'Well, we'll have to do it again.'"

In the film, with a cascade of water drumming onto his helmet, Gould turns to camera and mutters, *"Sheeeat!"* In 1977 this author, as an 11-year-old seeing it with his father, found this extremely funny!

Gould, born in 1938, was one of a breed of fresh if unconventional-looking faces that appeared in Hollywood at the height of the late 1960s counterculture. He burst forth from the comedy-drama *Bob & Carol & Ted & Alice* (1969) and garnered a nomination for the Academy Award for Best Supporting Actor. It was his role alongside Donald Sutherland in Robert Altman's Korean War-set black comedy *M*A*S*H* (1970) that rode the anti-Vietnam zeitgeist. He became one of the director's favourite collaborators with leading roles in *The Long Goodbye* (1973) and *California Split* (1974).

Colonel Stout is the quintessential American cliché: a hard-nosed hustler, no nonsense, with an upbeat, can-do attitude. "Perhaps it was Bill Goldman's desire to write a character that was representing a certain kind of American,"[432] Gould commented. Stout is based loosely on the 506th Regiment's commander, Robert F. Sink, who would be depicted in *Band of Brothers* by ex-Marine and movie military adviser Dale Dye. The cultural differences in the English-speaking world are nicely emphasised by Goldman's script line after Stout tells a subordinate to *"hustle up some Bailey stuff"* from those British *"shmucks"* but *"make sure to say please."*

With the bridge blown and the entire Garden plan in disarray, the "Bailey stuff" is hustled up the choked Devil's Highway. These prefabricated truss bridges were standard kit in all Allied divisions and used extensively across the globe. Requiring no special equipment, the compact wood and steel elements could be carried in trucks and then manhandled into place. Getting the trucks up the Devil's Highway, which was not only clogged with vehicles but under enemy fire, is not staged for the film, but the later sequence bringing up the boats shows the immense challenge. Fortunately, thanks to John Palmer's close relationship with NATO, the film company secured the loan of a Bailey, albeit on the military's terms. Producers agreed that a detachment of a Dutch RNA Engineer Squadron and instructors from their engineers' school, plus elements of the BAOR (British Army of the Rhine), would deploy as an exercise under military orders. Filmmakers, for once, would not be calling the shots but would have to work around the army. Despite a 50-guilder bribe, few of the soldiers agreed to chop their long hair short to '40s style, so most of the grunt work was done by their officers, NCOs, and the suitably shorn A.P.A.

While Colonel Waddy felt the fictional Colonel Stout "over-supervised" the bridge building, the actor relished the several days and nights it took to film. "Watching Elliot and his men build the bridge at night was really fantastic, and we almost did it as well," MacDonald recalled. "We had the experts with us, so we had to do some sort of continuity to build up what we were doing."[433]

"As they built it, we filmed it," recalled Craig, "but as always in movies, they got too late in the afternoon on the last day and said, 'Sorry guys, we're going.' And the movie company's saying, 'We're not finished!' They had a different agenda, and they needed to go, and they went."

Ready or not, the bridge's max-load weight had been reduced to allow a faster construction, but this meant the film's real Shermans had to sit and watch from the land as only their plastic replicas could pass. To kick start the drive, Gould's Colonel Stout races along the structure before hitting his mark in closeup. His next line caused some trouble with the British censors in 1977.

While sex and violence continued to be problematic, all the battle action in *Bridge* passed without a murmur. But what Americans call "cussing," then and now, remains a sticking point for those that protect our collective sensibilities.

Goldman described Stout as having a *"skilled use of the vulgate,"* and this is demonstrated during the montage of 12 hours of bridge building as the colonel berates the engineers: *"—let's haul a little ass!"* Finally, when he hits his mark in closeup: *"He looks like one beat son of a bitch and for a moment he just stands there. Then, the loudest we have ever heard him: 'ROLL THE FUCKERS!!!'"* During the UK 1977 release, the last word was re-dubbed as *"ROLL IT FELLAHS!"* The original offending word has now been restored for the home video versions.[434] As the fleet of plastic Shermans trundle past him over the bridge he had sweated 12 hours to build, Stout checks his watch and realises, *"They're 36 hours behind schedule . . ."* The momentary euphoria is undercut with foreboding of the unfolding disaster up ahead at Arnhem.

Before he accepted the role, Gould admitted to knowing almost nothing of the battle, yet over the years his pride in the movie has grown. He and his son, Samuel, have fond memories of that hot summer in Holland. "I have pictures of him looking at the bridge, holding his teddy bear, as it blows up. Afterwards I went to London and bought a watch and had it inscribed to my son: *There is no bridge too far. Love. Dad.* I didn't fully appreciate the picture until recently when I've studied it and find it to be extremely authentic. I'm very privileged and proud to have been a part of *A Bridge Too Far*. When BAFTA gave their Lifetime Achievement Award to Lord Attenborough, I was asked to come over and represent *Bridge* in the presentation, and then as I walked on stage, they played John Addison's theme. It was just marvellous. I felt like I was walking on air."[435]

"The one thing you dreaded seeing on a call sheet was—*EXTERIOR/NIGHT*—oh God!" recalled Peter MacDonald. "Night work is always a pain." Apart from the Bailey bridge sequence, the two other major night scenes were the Poles abortive crossing of the Rhine and First Airborne's final retreat, both filmed around a loop of the Ijssel

River. "The difficulty for any cameramen is to make it night," said Mac-Donald, "because an audience still has to see it. Geoff Unsworth really got night work to perfection. So, you could see just enough because it was mostly back lit, so everything was silhouette and shadows." To light these often-expansive locations, Unsworth deployed four or five 100-foot cranes upon which stood an arc light, "which is a very soft, beautiful slightly blue light that will give you back light as if it was the moon," MacDonald explained. "When we did Hackman's Poles crossing, and they got discovered with flares going off, you can really burn out the negative from being almost night to broad daylight."

To further enhance the atmosphere, Unsworth used his favourite prop, as MacDonald explained: "You can light vast areas by having a smoking atmosphere, and if you back light that, it will just give you acres of light. But you're always hoping the wind is going in the right direction, as it does what it wants to, not what you want it to!"[436]

Filming Urquhart's retreat across the Rhine posed many challenges as the action needed to appear under the cloak of darkness yet be visible. It took three very damp nights along the Ijssel River bend to complete. The script called for John Richardson's team to paint the horizon with fire. "We had smoke from fires and flares burning over the brow of the hill, and guns that fired charges of aluminium powder over the horizon making distant flashes suggesting artillery."[437]

Much of the success of Urquhart's withdrawal from the Ooster-beek cauldron was owed to the timely intervention of the elements—a deluge of rain that masked footsteps and forced the Germans under cover. Thanks to the endless dry summer of '76, rain-making machines and the local fire brigade were recruited to spray 500 extras, the A.P.A., and Sean Connery with water until all were suitably sodden. All appreciated being revived by hot food and liberal tots of spirits.

"The key to a good rain scene, night or day, is how the DP lights it," John Richardson explained of his collaboration with Unsworth. "If you get a three-quarter back light, it shows up a treat. Working together is a major key to that. We get a wood fire burning and add things to create smoke colours to the overall atmospheric that would fill the entire screen area. What we were striving for all the time was reality." [438]

One of those shivering in the streams of rain was A.P.A. member Edward Seckerson playing one of the exhausted Red Devils. "It was awe-inspiring because just the scale of it. There were probably about 10 cameras. And I remember Sean Mathias carried me into one of the boats. Nobody told us what to do, so we created our own little bit of business. I decided that he was a big bloke; he could carry me into the boat because I was exhausted." [439]

As the battered remnants of British First Airborne find sanctuary across the Rhine, the film shows the recriminations before the coda. Here, the eternal victims of all wars, the civilians, are forced to leave their shattered sanctuary and seek an uncertain future.

By September, the once beautifully recreated Oosterbeek church and rectory were a total mess. The FX team had blown huge, blackened holes out of both facades. While the papier mâché headstones stood in the pockmarked churchyard, next door the once-pristine rectory lawn was covered in piles of earth laid in neat rows. Marked by a helmet hanging from a rifle, these mounds represented some of the 64 dead men who had sought sanctuary in the ter Horst house. After the war, the family returned to their battered home and rebuilt it. The garden remained a shrine to those fallen men.

The battered set was also used for the film's poignant coda as Kate, her children, and Doctor Spaander load their meagre possessions and depart Oosterbeek. Shooting this sequence marked the return after some months of a cast member many feared they would never see again. "We had been warned Olivier was extremely ill," said Peter MacDonald, who had worked with the actor several times. "I just adored him. He had an awful time in hospital, and he came back on the last week. He sensed how worried we were. He came and shook my hand, squeezed it as if to say, *I'm fucking back!* He almost crushed my bones. Before he left us, he couldn't even hold the scalpel—it was just dropping out of his hand. And then he said, 'Cricket lunchtime, dear boy?' and I had tears in my eyes."

Despite his fragile health, Olivier, as the elderly doctor, was required to pull a cart with Liv Ullmann and the children walking alongside. One of the last shots involved the camera tracking ahead of them and then gradually speeding up, thus letting the actors get smaller in the frame. "So, we started tracking, and he kept the exact distance from camera," recalled MacDonald. "But when I started to accelerate—he kept up with us. And by now the grips are pulling the camera so fast that Larry and Liv are running with this cart. Afterwards, all he said was, 'Pete, it's very hard.' I said, 'But you weren't supposed to keep up, Larry; we were supposed to let you retreat into the distance.' He said, 'Well, no one told me that.' So, I said we'll go again when you get your breath back. He was just so professional and determined to make it work. He was one of the greatest experiences of my life."

Once he got his breath back, the scene was completed to everyone's satisfaction. "The shot with Liv and Larry with a little cart—just survival and hope for the future. I thought that was very touching and poignant." To sum up the film, Olivier commented, "I think it's rather beautiful in its majestically ghastly way. I've no doubt that a lot of people will find faults in the translation . . . no doubt it will be the subject of after-meal argument for some time."[440]

16

"You Just Fall Off"
Batt, Bombs, and Bruises Part 2

Imagine you are standing 100 feet high on a parapet over a viaduct. You have no support or harness. It is a crisp autumn day, and there is a chill to the breeze that ruffles your hair. Despite the precarious position, you are steady and relaxed. You wiggle your toes to keep the blood flowing to quell the instinctive grip of vertigo as you maintain your balance. In a few moments, you will go against every fibre of self-preservation—and jump.

"I thought there's something wrong with me." Vic Armstrong is one of cinema's most renowned stuntmen. "I get really nervous before a job. I was talking to some footballers, and they said, 'Oh no, we're like that before a game—vomiting before we go out.' I used to think it was just me. But beforehand, I'm literally vomiting too."[441] In 1981 Armstrong prepared for a precarious stunt for the second sequel to *The Omen*. "My high fall on *Final Conflict* was like 100 feet onto an airbag. The night before, you think about everything that can go wrong," Armstrong said. "You're going to step off the edge, and you'll fall 60 miles an hour into an airbag, and your cranium will come within just three feet of making impact with the Earth at a pretty frightening speed. These are the moments when you realise just how risky your line of work actually is."[442]

"You're standing at the top, having prepped it for a few hours beforehand. This, that or the other could go wrong. Yeah, it makes you nervous. But when you actually start doing the job, everything goes calm, and you're collected and controlled."[443]

With cameras rolling, he jumped . . .

🐝　　　🐝　　　🐝

Back in May 1976, Armstrong's friend and mentor, the six-foot, forty-eight-year-old Alf Joint, adjusted his tight-fitting German uniform, which stretched over a wetsuit for added protection for his 190-pound body. Poised to play a sniper who gets shot and plummets to the ground, he was standing on the roof of the tallest house set around Deventer bridge. Behind him on the rooftop crouched a handful of the A.P.A., including Sebastian Abineri.

On the ground was another A.P.A. member, Tim Morand, drafted in to hold the inflatable air bed to break Joint's fall. "We all had a rope to stop it from turning over. Just before the action, Dickie shouted up to Alf: 'Now, I don't want any acting as if you've been shot—you just fall off.'"[444]

Alf Joint was the most experienced stunt man on the film, and along with Vic Armstrong coordinated all precarious action skits. Almost every day on the six-month shoot, the call sheet listed the stunt team required for a variety of potentially dangerous work. Like Vic Armstrong, Joint too ran the gamut of emotions as he peered down at the ground. He would have calculated every eventuality. His job that day was almost run-of-the-mill for this world-class high diver who had once represented England in the Olympics. His impressive physique made him an ideal double for Sean Connery as James Bond, although the tables were turned on *Goldfinger* (1964) when he played Capungo, the would-be assassin who is bested by 007 by being electrocuted in a bathtub, prompting the quip, "Shocking, positively shocking." Doubling for Richard Burton in *Where Eagles Dare* (1968), Joint took part in the fight scene atop a cable car and performed the perilous jump from one to the other.

For a generation, without his face ever being seen, he epitomised the romantic macho man. He was the mysterious "Milk Tray Man" in the famous 1970s British television adverts. Dressed in black and carrying the prized chocolates, he launched himself off a cliff into the sea "all because a lady loves Milk Tray," he recalled. The stunt involved a then-record 163-foot drop. On take two, he broke his back, but after a brief hospital spell, returned to work.

"Alf knew every trick in the book," said Malcolm Treen, who worked with Joint towards the end of his long career on the popular 1990s ITV series, *London's Burning*. "He knew every camera angle a director should use and how to arrange mayhem and murder at the drop of a hat with economy and safety. He was a good man and for someone in his line of work, a slightly shy and humble person. I feel privileged to have known him because he was the fount of all knowledge about stunts."[445]

Unfortunately, on that day in 1976 one element made Joint a novice. Traditionally, a huge stack of cardboard boxes broke high falls. Simple and effective, the trick had served him well for many years. "It's not the falling that hurts you, as we say—it's the stopping," Armstrong explained. "You can jump 2,000 feet as long as you take a long time to slow down and stop. But you can fall 30 feet, and if you stop in a foot, then it's an awful lot of damage to your body. So, box rigs are literally that, a 2x2-foot cardboard box. You put softer boxes in and you crack them a little bit, and then put a sheet over the top. So, as you hit, the box crumbles and slides so it dissipates the impact. There's lots of tricks and things to it."

But one must move with the times, and the inflatable airbag served as cutting-edge technology, with quicker deployment than hundreds of boxes. "They'd just been invented in America, and that was a prototype," said Armstrong. "But the principle of an airbag is—you hit it and displace the air out of vents on the side, and bomp—you land."[446]

With the cameras rolling, David Tomblin called, "Action!"

Alf Joint jumped . . .

"I was behind him," recalled Sebastian Abineri, "And I saw him go. I thought he hadn't fallen right. Then I just heard that awful sigh."[447]

"It was horrifying," recalled Tim Morand, who was holding a rope to steady the airbag. "Instead of throwing himself slightly out, where he would've landed in the middle of the cushion, he fell and hit the edge of that big inflatable thing. And none of us could hold it down, and the whole thing went. I saw his face, and he was totally still as if he had died."[448]

"Unfortunately, if you land on the end of it," Armstrong said, "it's like a tube of toothpaste, all the air rushes up the other end. On those early ones, you had to hit in the centre. He (Joint) literally scraped down the side of the wall and hit the very edge of it, but it cushioned his fall a little bit, as obviously he would have been killed."

Vic Armstrong believed it was Dickie's last-minute direction not to do a spectacular fall, which would have placed him in the centre, that may have blindsided Joint. "Dickie Attenborough said to just flop over the edge," Armstrong said. "Alf clearly wasn't planning on doing that type of fall. If he'd used the old-fashioned box rig, he'd have been okay because it's the same wherever you hit it."[449]

Actor Christopher Good went to visit Alf Joint in hospital and recalled he was in good spirits despite his body shattered into pieces: a collapsed lung, chipped shoulder blade and hip, plus a broken rib. As the call sheets testify, Joint was soon back at work, although letting the younger men do the tricky stuff. Good recalls the stunt men were a tough lot: "I just thought these guys are completely off their heads. They were stunt crazy, and Vic Armstrong said, 'Do you know what the stunt guys want? They live for danger.'"[450]

Despite the momentary bravado, Armstrong insists, "Our job is to eliminate as much danger as we can, but you can't eliminate all, though. It's a fine line we walk."[451] Without that care and attention, he would not have been named as the world's most prolific stuntman in the *Guinness World Records*. "When I started, there were probably 40 people doing it, and now there are 400. It's still a 'lovely business,' but it's very competitive. I was very lucky that I met some of the people who formed the business. I came in at the cusp of the new wave."

Armstrong had entered the industry as an accomplished horse-man. "My dad was a racehorse trainer, and all I ever wanted to do was race steeplechasers. When I was 14, I started to race, but I was quite big and had to starve myself to get to 160 lbs, so I only ever stayed as an amateur jockey."[452] He'd ridden and stunted a fall in the cavalry charge in *Young Winston*, and his last stunt would be on horseback as Indiana Jones races the German tank in the third film of the series. For-tuitously, Armstrong bore more than a passing likeness to two mega stars—Harrison Ford and Ryan O'Neal—which made him a useful stand in. His early jobs included abseiling into Ken Adam's enormous set for *You Only Live Twice* (1967) and battling the worst the Atlantic Ocean could throw for the storm sequence in *Ryan's Daughter* (1970). "We wouldn't go to work unless it was a threatened Force 10 coming in, and then we'd sit in our trailers at the top of the clifftops waiting for the waves."[453] He met his future wife, Wendy Leech, on the set of *Superman*. She was doubling for Margot Kidder, and she had to do an 80-foot backwards fall into cardboard boxes, "which is really tough to do."[454] Following the three Spielberg-directed Indiana Jones films, which he considered his favourites to work on, Armstrong moved be-hind the camera in 1984 to direct second-unit action.

But he acknowledged *Bridge* as his career turning point, and it was thanks to Alf Joint. Dickie fretted that Britain's leading stuntmen were all in middle age (as was Joint too). Instead, the director wanted people who could be seamlessly intercut with the youngsters of the A.P.A. Joint suggested Armstrong. "With that, Attenborough almost did a backflip. 'I love Vic. That's exactly the type of person I want.' Of course, he remembered me from *Young Winston*," said Armstrong. "Alf called my house in a panic. 'You've gotta do this film or I'm in big trouble. The only reason I got the job is because of you.'"[455]

The core party of six led by Joint and Armstrong included Dougie Robinson, "tough with steel-grey hair and a solid physique," and Paul Weston, "a tall, dark, and good-humoured guy"[456] who later doubled for Christopher Reeve in *Superman* and for Roger Moore in his 007 outings. The last two were Paul's brother Bill along with Yorkshireman Roy Alon, "a complete madman," Armstrong recalled. "We asked him to fall out of this car at 25 mph. He just pitched himself out on his head, bounced and rolled down the road, got up and said, 'Was that all right, Chuck? Do you want to go again?'—'Stick him on the list,' I said."[457]

The complex scenes often required legions of stuntmen. "It was only a 26-quid flight then from England," recalled Steve Lanning, "but the core band of Alf Joint and Vic Armstrong were out for the whole shoot, and we supplemented them when needed." Each stuntman was paid a princely £500 per week, with a flat £50 for each individual stunt, regardless of how precarious. Lanning recalls the casting session for local Dutch stuntmen. "We had a couple of days of testing—some of the funniest things you've ever seen. Hilarious watching people do an eight-foot fall onto a mat and not doing it properly. And then doing car skids and having them roll the car. We ended up with using two or three. One of them, Henry Weissenman, became the leading special effects person in Holland. He had a cleft palate, and was about five-foot-four, so you couldn't use him for anything. But he was the lead. We had quite a big stunt team, which most films didn't do."[458]

One of the many things Armstrong learnt from his mentor Alf Joint was the importance of rehearsal. For the film, the stunt team had the use of an empty car park and ample time to prepare. It was an opportunity to experiment with new ideas, not all successful. One day, they plotted out Gräbner's charge, with cone markers on the ground to represent obstacles. "In this car park I slipped arse over tit," recalled Armstrong. "I saw these ball bearings, no bigger than grains of sand. They were actually unexpanded polystyrene, but hard as granite. So, I had this idea we'd use them for car spins, because a German Kübelwagen had to come down the bridge and slide sideways.

"We did a rehearsal and threw handfuls of this stuff on the ground. Mark Boyle was driving, and Paul Weston was hanging on the side. The Kübelwagen roared towards us and did an amazing spin, but unfortunately when the ball bearings ran out, it gripped hard on the real road surface, jerked sideways and then flipped upside down with these two guys in it—no roll cage or anything. 'Oh my God, they're dead,' I thought. Mark stayed inside, and Paul got thrown out; unbelievable how it never killed them. We never used the stuff again after that."[459]

Forty-six years later, Armstrong stumbled across the "stuff" again—safely this time. "I was cleaning out a shed the other day, and I found a barrel of them. After the film, I've kept them ever since, probably thinking they might be useful one day."[460]

Rare mishaps aside, the preparation was meticulous. Unlike the show-stopping spectacles in the Bond and Indiana Jones movies, the stunt work is subtly integrated into the action. As Dickie's direction to Alf Joint illustrates, a deliberate approach created as realistic a look as possible. From the first filmed sequence involving James Caan, the stunt team played a key part in any action scene. But whether playing Germans dodging Caan's jeep or performing a multitude of falls and jumps, their work was as important to the film's texture as the A.P.A. Except for Joint's injuries hitting the edge of the airbag and Paul Weston breaking his leg, the work was performed with precision and safety. "Every single incident is planned to the tee. We'd been working on it for weeks with the guys. I drove a flaming tank across a bridge, and then I drove a Kübelwagen that flipped over," Armstrong recalled. "But everything's rehearsed, and it's all shot in segments. It is like building up a tapestry—you just keep adding as you go along in sequence."

The stunt team would alternate between the units. So, when Dickie's main unit was shooting an intimate dialogue sequence, Bert Batt would be deploying the team for action. "The second unit was phenomenal," Steve Lanning recalled. "On *Bridge*, there was a line in the script that said *'the 82nd broke out.'* It was one line in the script, and it was six weeks filming for the second unit: tanks, planes, crowd. With a script you normally do several pages a day. This was one or two lines. Six weeks. Huge unit."[461]

In the script some brief scenes show elements of Gavin's 82nd inching towards Nijmegen bridge against determined German resistance. It seems a great deal of work went into this action. Unfortunately, none of the "breakout" material ended up on the screen. One tiny glimpse exists, though. Batt's unit spent time in a dilapidated part of Deventer, called Noorderbergkwartier, a once picturesque neighbourhood that had fallen on hard times. The city had earmarked it for renovation and so were happy for the film company to do their worst. Narrow streets of old buildings had their facades shattered and pockmarked to look authentically war-torn.

Herb Lightman, esteemed editor of the industry magazine *American Cinematographer*, spent some weeks visiting the set in September. Apart from interviewing Geoffrey Unsworth, Lightman caught up with his old friend Harry Waxman, the second unit's director of photography. Lightman described Waxman as "a very warm and friendly man, whose eyes fairly twinkle with the excitement of it all." Lightman noted the energy and "roadrunner agility" of the 64-year-old as he scurried up a ladder to check the framing of a camera poised behind a shattered window.

In his subsequent article, Lightman described the filming of one scene in detail. "Around the corner at the far end of the street comes a Nazi patrol vehicle. It inches its way down the street, flanked by German foot soldiers with rifles at the ready, cautiously probing. As they draw nearer, the effect is so realistic that a chill runs through me, sparking memories I'd just as soon not recall."

Lightman, who had served as a combat cameraman with the U.S. 167th Signal Photo Company across war-torn Europe, had seen the brutal reality up close. "Our record spoke for itself," he, then a U.S. Army sergeant, wrote of his unit in October 1945. "The 167th had participated in four major battle campaigns, shot footage during a period of 250 consecutive combat days, and had been presented with the Meritorious Service Award."[462]

Standing near to Waxman, Lightman got a ringside seat of the

German-uniformed A.P.A. "They are 10 yards from the main camera when all hell breaks loose. Ambushing Allied soldiers hurl grenades, firing from doorways and second-storey windows. There is a violent eruption of carnage and then all the Nazi soldiers lie 'dead' in the smoking debris.

"'CUT!' Everybody gets up and dusts themselves off. The scene is repeated twice more and then we all troop off to enjoy a very good stand-up location lunch, with soldiers from both sides fraternising freely."[463]

The scene doesn't appear in the screenplay and is listed as "montage" on the call sheet.[464] Montage sequences serve as an effective way to convey a sense of time passing, whether the building of an aeroplane or a romance. A great example of its use in a war film is during the Battle of the Bulge sequence in *Patton*. The blood-and-guts general has ordered up a "weather prayer." In the film, George C. Scott reads it aloud with only the music to accompany his voice, with all sound effects muted. Onscreen is a series of shots of the deadly battle in the snow. It is not only deeply moving but dramatic and helps to convey the immense battle in barely a minute of screen time. It is probable Dickie envisioned a similar sequence playing to music to suggest the final desperate push to take the last bridge before the hallowed prize of Arnhem.

The contents of the montage were a collective effort. Vic Armstrong recalls one of his team had a bright idea: "Paul Weston did some really inventive storyboards of a German patrol coming down an Alpine pass and being ambushed, until we said to him, 'It's great Paul, but Holland's as flat as a pancake; there's no Alps here.' 'Oh bugger,' he said."[465]

What is intriguing about this story is how close it is to the scene Herb Lightman described above. "The Alps thing was quite funny because we had a think tank. Alf and I let the boys in and said give us all your ideas. And Paul came up with this idea of the convoy coming down this curling mountain road. The script gives you a rough outline.

But we come up with ideas and situations and then we break down how it's going to be done. So that's all part of our job."[466]

Other tantalising glimpses of the second unit's hard work are found in Waxman's interview with Lightman, where he described they'd been "quite lucky" to shoot some realistic battle footage. He described a scene of a German Tiger tank ploughing through a building, which sounds very similar to the impromptu near disaster that damaged the bridge set. They had the run of a disused factory complex with roadways between the buildings. Using the same Leopard I tank dressed to look like a Tiger, it "pushed through a brick wall and right out the other end of the factory, and down came the roof," Waxman explained. "We had it planned so that real bricks and burning beams came down on top of the tank. Very exciting stuff."[467]

Armstrong would have been closely involved with all these scenes and recalled the unit's superlative leadership: "Bert Batt was a wonderful AD with a very deep voice. You never stopped learning from people like that. He didn't take any shit from anybody. He was a wonderful guy, just a great leader of men and a superb organiser on a level head, never panicked, and trusted people to do their job. Just one of the best in the business."[468]

While everyone who worked with the second unit recalls Bert Batt, both vividly and fondly, the credits list Sidney Hayers as its director. Hayers, a former film editor, was predominantly a TV director, having worked on series such as *The Persuaders!* (1971–72), *Arthur of the Britons* (1972–73), *The Zoo Gang* (1974) with both Armstrong and Bert Batt, and *The New Avengers* (1976–77). His horror-flavoured features had been notable for his penchant for tension and the macabre, with some lurid titles: *Assault* (1970), *Revenge* (1971), *Deadly Strangers* (1974), and *Diagnosis: Murder* (1974).

It seems while Batt handled the action scenes, Hayers oversaw the more intimate second-unit moments involving actors. One of those was a small but crucial scene involving the discovery of the complete operational plans of Market Garden. This presented a headache for

Waxman as to how to photograph it. Historically, it was never established whether the officer who took the map case to Holland was American or British. Some fevered discussion with Waddy took place about the potential controversy—how to avoid pointing the finger cinematically at one ally or the other. The action involved the portly Dutch actor, Tim Beekman, gingerly approaching a crashed glider, firing some warning shots, then entering and picking his way through a cluster of bodies to find the case of maps.

"The solution was to keep it a low-key thing and to show just the elements—a hand with blood on it, or the back of a head (but not an identifiable helmet)," explained Waxman. The cramped interior was set up on the edge of the Deelen airfield, and Waxman was concerned about how to light it sufficiently: "When I originally saw it, I said that we'd have to take the glider into a studio where we could control everything, but we ended up shooting it on location. It presented really tremendous problems."[469]

The production featured many disparate units filming, including the aerial unit. But sometimes one unit could be formed for a small, ad hoc requirement. One of the assistant directors on the film had badgered Dickie and Dave Tomblin for a chance to shoot something. As he was related to a significant personage connected to the team, he received his opportunity. Sebastian Abineri and another A.P.A. were sectioned off during the bridge filming. "I won't use his correct name because it was a bit embarrassing," said Abineri. "He was dying to direct a sequence. So, Dickie said, 'Okay, we need a couple of pickup shots of guys firing rifles, and then a PIAT.' Dave Tomblin said to us, 'You boys with your rifles, don't you fire at the camera as that's fucking expensive if it gets broken.' So, Davey went off to shoot something else. And this assistant director went, 'I've got a great shot idea. I'm gonna get the PIAT shell going right down the camera lens, but it will not hit the camera because it's gonna bounce off the unbreakable glass in front of the lens.'"

It was Bill Aylmore's job as the armourer to fire. "It went straight through the glass, down the filters into the camera and punched the cameraman with a massive black eye. And the camera is completely shafted, this shell sticking out of it. Dave Tomblin went absolutely nuts. The assistant stayed well away for a long time after that. But Dave forgave him in the end—but only just. It's about the worst thing you can do is break a camera!"[470]

🐝   🐝   🐝

Not only did most of the second unit's work hit the cutting-room floor, so did the atmospheric Noorderbergkwartier. It survives in one scene, which illustrates what an evocative location it was. Laurence Olivier, as Doctor Spaander, is driven through the blasted ruins of Arnhem to discuss a ceasefire with General Bittrich. The havoc on display is highlighted by a series of poignant closeups of the smashed normal lives, while Olivier's performance beautifully and powerfully underscores the scene—his face capturing the look of horror and pain. The sequence plays to the heartfelt strains of John Addison's music and becomes one of the most moving in the film.

🐝   🐝   🐝

Post Script. Forward to 1981 on the *Final Conflict* set . . . Vic Armstrong throws himself off the viaduct. "When you're falling 100 feet," he said, "you're looking straight down and thinking: *This could be it. This could be the end.*"[471]

He landed safely.

17

"Hard Like in Coal Mining"
Directing an Epic

"Directing a film is one of the most brutally difficult occupations imaginable," William Goldman wrote in his bestseller, *Adventures in the Screen Trade.* "It's hard. I don't mean hard, like it was hard for van Gogh to fill a canvas or for Kant to construct a universe. I mean hard, like in coal mining." In particular, he noted the enormous workload on Dickie's shoulders, neatly summed up as "the pressure of failure."[472]

It was Dickie's third film and his biggest. Yet he guided the multi-million-dollar production over six gruelling months during the hottest summer for almost a century. He lived on the second floor of the bijou Keizerskroon Hotel in Deventer. Each day, Dickie arrived on location by his own reckoning "about eight in the morning, and we went on to about six or seven in the evening. Then I went to the daily rushes every night. Then I cut the film, usually for about an hour. After that, I would spend an hour or so in the production office. I usually ate at about 11 and got to bed at 12 or 12:30. Then I was up about 6:30 for the next day's shooting."[473]

Ever since Attenborough signed on in early 1975, the punishing schedule took no prisoners. "Just as I was under pressure," Goldman commented, "so was Sir Richard under pressure. Because he was travelling all over the world—casting, trying to find German actors—back to Holland—he was jet-lagged constantly. It was a horrible amount of work. It was brutal."[474] Luckily, Dickie said he was blessed with restless

230

energy: "People used to say to me, 'Why don't you take a weekend off or go and do something else?' You can't relax. You've got two hours, fifty minutes of film in your head in terms of tempo, the dramatic, dynamic, character development, and relationship. If the concept leaves you, you've had it."[475]

"He did have a great ability to look like a very powerful light," his son, Michael, recalled. "He'd focus on what he was thinking about and forget everything else. If I went to his office, he'd say, 'Darling, close the door.' He'd ring down to his secretary, 'Don't bother me until Mike and I are finished,' and he would give me his full focus. Or he'd tell me, 'Not now, darling. I'll talk to you this evening' or whatever. But he would not want to give less than 100 percent to you."[476]

"The most important thing with a film of such complexity is to be absolutely certain about your research," Dickie explained later. "Never go on the floor uncertain as to the tale that you have to tell with that particular sequence. You had to know the script backwards. I don't think I ever refer to a script on the floor—I know it. The other thing was to be well and strong and rested. It's a question of energy, as all the big directors will tell you. I was talking to Anthony Minghella (*The English Patient* [1996]) recently who said, 'You don't need talent; you just need strength.'"[477]

Dickie's stamina owed a great deal to what Michael called an "infuriating ability to fall asleep whenever he wished. It drove my mother absolutely barking mad," his son recalled. "When they were doing *Whistle Down the Wind* for nothing, he and Bryan Forbes shared a bedroom in some ghastly hotel in Burnley. Bryan used to do a wonderful impression of Dad walking towards the bed chatting away about tomorrow's shooting, and then his head would hit the pillow. And he'd be fast asleep. He could sleep anywhere. He could do it for five or fifty minutes or so. I mean he was ferociously energetic, but he needed to sleep. But he always got it. He didn't know what insomnia meant."[478]

Roy Button was third assistant director: "Attenborough does bring a lot of passion, a lot of commitment to actually making a good movie; he really is story driven. He knows his craft extremely well. He's quite an adept technician as well as a good politician with the actors. Being an actor himself, he understands them very quickly but, being a technician who's made as many films as anybody, also knows what to do. What he's extremely talented at is picking some good people and leaving them alone to do their job because he trusts them. He is clever enough to do that."[479]

Peter MacDonald said: "As a crew, you surround even a bad director with as much strength and knowledge as you can. The DP, the camera operator, continuity girl, and the AD work very closely with the director. We will do what we can to help." Inevitably, during a shoot, a director's idea might not be either practical or desirable, and an experienced eye might see an alternative. "We all had a great relationship with Dickie. I mean, you'd never say anything in front of the stars, but you would speak to Dickie quietly afterwards that 'maybe it'd be better because . . .' but he was always appreciative."[480]

Christopher Good remembers Dickie's softly-softly directing style. "He was very gentle. There wasn't that thing of instructions, wasn't as bold as that, it was much more subtle. He would say, 'When you're talking to Tony (Hopkins), I want you to think about the status. You're a strong guy. What's your relationship?' He would just put these thoughts into your head—he wound me up and let me go. Occasionally, he would direct, particularly if you had to get from point A to point B, the practical things. But within that, there was a kind of fluidity. Because I was lucky enough to be playing with Tony Hopkins, I could see what he was doing and pick up clues as I went along."[481]

A.P.A. section leader Jack McKenzie remembered an endearing vignette of Dickie during the intense filming on the bridge. Despite the pressure of the schedule, the director found time for two young visitors. The wife of one of the crew members had brought their two children to watch. "And Richard stopped what he was doing and took the kids' hands and walked them across the bridge, saying to them, 'Now, we're doing that over there,' etc. It was wonderful."[482]

"Dickie is a great leveller," MacDonald commented. "He's such a nice, very caring, generous man. Sometimes you'd think, *is he really directing this huge film?* Because he's not like one of those Americans I've worked with, shouting and screaming. But Dickie kind of quietly leads and allows people a lot of their own imagination to do their own work but will step in if necessary."[483]

"He wasn't always Mr. Nice Guy," recalled one who knew him best, son Michael. "I mean, I speak as a son who bears a number of verbal scars, so I can tell you he can be bloody frightening. Oh boy, when he wanted to rollick someone, he wouldn't hesitate to pull someone out if he thought they were fucking around." But these moments on set were rare; instead, Dickie used his enormous charm to get what he wanted. His reliance on theatrical pleasantries has become legendary, although their deployment was very simple. "The one thing he always said about calling people 'darling' is that he couldn't bloody remember people's names!" recalled Michael. "I've definitely adopted it too. Because the great thing about 'darling' is that you're saying to the other person, 'You're terribly important to me and I'm terribly fond of you. The fact that I can't remember your name is totally irrelevant.' But I can tell you, the person he idolised most in the world was his mother. She was very effusively middle class and warm. And she called everybody 'daaarling.' But it wasn't a particularly showbizzy thing to him to do."[484]

Edward Seckerson, who got to know Dickie very well over the years, said, "Dickie's a very safe pair of hands as a director. He has moments of inspiration, but his best quality is bringing an actor's eye to bear on something. He's very good with actors, there's no question about it. He puts them at ease. He had another side to him to those that knew him could tell—he was very cunning."[485]

Steve Lanning, who worked with Dickie several times, suggested there was a method to his actions. "Dickie always had time for people—because it paid. He was a crafty old bugger. There was nothing subtle about it. He would come up to you and say, 'The grip, what's his wife's name?' And you'd tell him. And about five minutes later, he would walk past the grip, say, 'Hello Mike, how's Vivian?' If Dickie was doing his English bulldog walk, you would find there's a documentary unit filming at the time. Nothing by accident. We worked with Dickie on *Gandhi*, and it was a really good relationship. But with him, nothing happened by accident."[486]

"That's absolutely accurate," Michael Attenborough, himself a successful theatre director, agreed. "I served for 17 years on the board of RADA. And I watched how he chaired the meetings there. He was a brilliant diplomat and incredibly nice to people, even ones he thought were complete pricks. He made people think that he was fond of everybody. He was an arch politician. In my career, in a much small-er way than Dad, I've run four theatres, including the largest theatre company in the world—the RSC (Royal Shakespeare Company). And boy, you have to get to know people's names, and you have to know if someone's just got a grandchild, or a baby, and make sure you bloody congratulate them. You do these things quite consciously."[487]

Moviemaking, particularly of the scale of *Bridge*, required nothing less than a military-style operation. "Dickie does good films. He loves talking with the actors, but he's not a logistical genius," commented second assistant director Lanning. "*Bridge* was an AD's film. We ADs, we were very close with the effects people and the camera team. It was what was needed." Lanning considered that the key to leadership, which Dickie demonstrated, is very simple. "If you're good, you can delegate. Dave Tomblin had the respect of Dickie. We were allowed to plan, and we were always logistically clever."[488]

Actor John Morton joined towards the end of the shoot. He could immediately see the smooth operation. "That's Attenborough's style. He really built community. I did not see any of the hitches that must have been there. But it was all a very pleasant environment and very much of a big family. And these things all originate from the top. At-tenborough kind of ran it the way he wanted."[489]

Journalist Iain Johnstone spent a great deal of time on set and considered Dickie something of an enigma. "On face value, he tends to be jolly, verbose, intense, anxious to please, and one of the most hard-working film directors I have ever witnessed," said Johnstone. "But beneath that exterior, he is well-nigh unfathomable."[490]

Perhaps at heart was an almost child-like exuberance and driven passion. This was something John Morton found when he first met Dickie for a casting call. "I went out to his house in Richmond. He said, 'I'm really excited about this film. But the film that I really want to make is *Gandhi*. I've agreed to do one more film with Joe Levine, so that I can do it.' I mean, what's he telling this kid this kind of stuff for? But he was just a wonderful man."[491] It would be another five years before Dickie achieved his dream and completed *Gandhi*.

Back in Holland in September 1976, Dickie was asked what sequence troubled him the most. "Oh, the paratroop drop, definitely—it was murder."[492]

18

"A Marvellous Approach"
The Parachute Drops

EXT. AIRFIELD - ENGLAND - DAY

Another airplane starting, considerably more noise. And now another propeller starts. And another and now two more and each time the noise builds and builds.

Twenty-two 1,200-horsepower Pratt & Whitney radial engines emit a deafening sound. The force from the combined yakking propellers is enough to push a grown man backwards. At Deelen Air Base, just north of Arnhem, 11 World War II-vintage Douglas C-47 Dakota twin-engine transport planes stood quivering on the tarmac. With a wingspan of 95 feet (29 metres), a cruise speed of 155 miles (250 km) per hour, and a range of 1,600 miles (2,600 km), these planes had been the mainstay aircraft for Allied forces' logistics during the war. The Americans called them C-47s, the Brits preferred using the name Dakotas.

And as more propellers start, you can almost sense the earth itself trembling and the instant that happens—

On a day in September 1976, with their throttles pushed forwards, the 11 old war birds taxied along the runway, gradually gathering speed before, one after another, lifting off into the air. Each plane had 28 passengers, each one was a serving member of the British Parachute Regiment, that day dressed as their 1944 counterparts. In a few minutes they would fall out of the sky to recreate the Arnhem drop.

EXT. COUNTRY CHURCH – ENGLAND – DAY
The PARISHIONERS emerge and like everyone else stare up in
amazement as the mightiest airborne force in history passes by . . .

Several of the Dakotas that arched through the sky had flown halfway across the globe to this corner of the Netherlands. Dubbed Attenborough's Private Airforce, it was the job of associate producer John Palmer to form and maintain it. He was adept at such assignments, having put together the immense armada of planes to refight the cinematic *Battle of Britain* in 1968. For *Bridge*, Palmer turned to two aerial experts who had helped him before.

The first was a dapper bowler-hatted Scotsman, Hamish Mahaddie, a war hero, memorably described by Leonard Mosley: "With his button-bright eyes, his pink complexion, his unquenchable energy and his constant smile, he resembles a leprechaun dressed in his Sunday best, and when you meet him for the first time you expect him to burst into the theme song from *Finian's Rainbow*."[493] Born in 1911, Mahaddie joined the RAF in 1928 and by the outbreak of war was a highly experienced pilot. In October 1942 he joined the elite Pathfinder group, who flew ahead of the bomber formations and dropped target markers. It was a highly skilled and risky job for which Mahaddie became an expert and was promoted to wing commander. He later received a variety of medals, including the Distinguished Flying Cross (DFC). Various citations praised him for having "consistently attacked heavily defended targets with coolness and determination often in adverse weather . . . powers of leadership of a very high order . . . unflagging enthusiasm [that] has had an inspiring effect on his comrades."[494]

After the war he found a new role locating aircraft for the movies. This started with that most famous of British war movies, *The Dam Busters*. In 1955 Mahaddie put his fingers on several Lancaster bombers that were just being phased out of service with the RAF. The 1960s found him in great demand. He formed the Mosquitos for *633 Squadron* in 1964, followed by aircraft for *Operation Crossbow*. His finest hour for cinema was *Battle of Britain*. Over two-and-half years, he scoured the world for flyable Spitfires and the rarer Hurricanes. His war record opened many doors, and he was instrumental in negotiating with the Spanish Air Force for use of their large fleet of modified German bombers and fighters. This combined armada of vintage war birds allowed the filmmakers to recreate the dramatic days of 1940 with extraordinary fidelity and scale.

Helping him was a colourful character, very different from the dapper Scot. Ex-RAF John "Jeff" Hawke, although much younger than Mahaddie, had become a legend in his lifetime as a very likeable rogue.[495] His nickname derived from the popular science fiction comic strip, *Jeff Hawke*, about a pilot outwitting aliens. He had helped Mahaddie on several projects, including *Battle of Britain*, when he flew his own converted B-25 Mitchell as a camera plane, dubbed the "Psychedelic Monster," having been painted in garish colours for easy identification. In 1965 he found himself outside the law when he was accused of supplying some B-26 bombers, arms, and ammunition to the Portuguese Air Force, which violated the United Nations arms embargo against Portugal over its brutal colonial war in Angola. Hawke was arrested in Florida and stood trial. He defended himself by saying he had been approached by the CIA for a secret operation.[496] He said his code word was "Sparrow"—a play on his surname—but the CIA denied his claim and disowned him. A subsequent inquiry cleared him of any "conspiracy to smuggle." In 1992 Hawke would die in a mysterious air crash, his body discovered two months later in the Adriatic Sea.

Associate producer Palmer engaged these two very different characters to find the required Dakotas. At first, it looked like the Moroccan Air Force could supply the full number—until the deal fell through. The fleet eventually included planes from Finland, Denmark, ex-Portuguese colonies, and Djibouti in the Horn of Africa. Three from the Royal Danish Air Force and four from the Finnish Air Force came with fully trained military crews, all experienced with paratrooper drops. Hawke also sourced four Harvard (T-6) two-seater trainers to be mocked up as Thunderbolts that would simulate bombing German positions during the XXX Corps breakout. Another trainer, the dinky-looking Auster III, was borrowed from Gilze Rijen Aero Club to play Browning's plane for Dirk Bogarde's tetchy scene with Ryan O'Neal *"with typical British understatement."* And that most recognizable of warplanes, a Spitfire F Mk IX, was flown in from England for the reconnaissance flypast scene. Also, a variety of camera planes and helicopters assembled at Deelen, although one made a rough landing and had to be replaced.

On 16 July 1976 the two Dakotas from the Portuguese Air Force arrived at Deelen—the first to reach the production. It would take a month before all 11 were assembled and readied for the film. The job of maintaining these ageing birds fell to Dakota specialist Arthur Heath of F&H Aircraft Ltd., he being the "H" of the business. The two Dakotas from Djibouti required all his expertise to get them up to standard. During the war, the planes would have been painted with green-brown camouflage, ideally suited for flying in Northern Europe. Unfortunately, what might be ideal for war is not so for a movie camera that would struggle to see the planes from some angles. The decision was made to repaint them all in desert yellow-brown to allow much better contrast. The fleet would also need a repaint with interchangeable RAF and U.S. Army Air Corps insignias for the different British and American drops.

Preparations for the Dakotas were painstaking and wide-ranging. While they needed to be airworthy, they also had to meet modern safety standards. An RAF team had used the first Dakota that became available for a series of ever more stringent tests with dummies, and then instructors jumped in live descents. There were some close shaves involving opening canopies brushing the tailplane.

A team of top pilots, which included Hawke, lived in caravans on the airfield during the hot summer. They proved a highly experienced bunch that included Urban Drew, an ex-USAF pilot who, in a P-51 Mustang, had provided aerial cover over Holland during Market Garden, and ex-RAF Roland "Monty" Burton, who in 1953 flying a Canberra won the London–Christchurch (New Zealand) race in under 24 hours. Dutch KLM pilot Ad van Ommen became a national celebrity when he captained the Dutch team on the Euro-wide TV favourite, *It's a Knockout!* in 1974.

Despite their many thousands of hours of flying experience, they all needed RAF instructors to teach them how to fly in a 1944-style tight formation known as a "Vic of Vics" or a nine-ship element. Aircraft arrayed in the form of the letter V fly with the leader upfront, and the rest of the flight *en echelon* to the left and the right. Unfortunately, mechanical problems with the venerable Dakotas often marred the intense training and made it impossible to achieve the "Vic of Vics" safely and practically, and so the "Vics in line astern" was adopted instead. *The Arnhem Report* shows Dickie and Peter MacDonald on location, calmly discussing this issue with an air force officer who assures them: "I think the Victor V will give a marvellous approach."

Confident that they were safe to fly in, Iain Johnstone and his *Report* crew had climbed aboard one of the Dakotas for a practice flight. It was an experience Johnstone never wanted to repeat. Sitting behind the pilot, he saw up close the extraordinary skill required to keep their plane not only flying, but also in formation. The wing tips of the surrounding C-47s were nudging ever closer amid a chorus of colourful language, "which was enough to make the air traffic controllers blush, and certainly introduced me to a new combination of epithets" said Johnstone. At one point, one of the air crew tried to open a jammed window with a shove. Unfortunately, it ripped off its hinges and dropped like a bomb to earth. The ferocious shuddering and rattling of the 35-year-old war birds took its toll on journalist Johnstone, who looped a ceiling harness around his fist and held on tightly. Seeing his fear, the co-pilot offered him some pills as he said, "You look a little white!" As Johnstone swallowed a pill gratefully, the airman added, "Bumpy old things, Dakotas." Praying he wouldn't be sick and would reach the airfield in one piece, Johnstone glanced down at the floor and noticed a large pool of black oil snaking towards him.

Barely concealing his panic, he shouted to the pilot, "We're in trouble." The pilot merely shrugged; of course, there was oil everywhere. He said, "It's a fucking Dakota, isn't it?"

Meanwhile, back in England, Exercise New Market/Gulls Wing was approved by the Ministry of Defence, and 350 officers and men of the 16th Parachute Brigade had their orders. This crack British army unit had just finished a stint with the BAOR in Berlin and were due to fly to the troubled island of Cyprus to join other UN Forces for peace-keeping duties. The brief sojourn of the 16th at the Airborne Museum Aldershot training on its own Dakota must have been an enjoyable diversion. This was necessary as the modern Paras tumbled out of the rear hatch of a Hercules, and it took some practice to jump from the smaller Dakota door. Also, they needed to master the unfamiliar 800-foot drop.

They were then flown over to Holland for accommodation in the RNAF barracks at the Deelen airfield. Several practice jumps followed at Terlet and the Speulderveld/Houtdorperveld near Garderen, with the last one treated as a filmed dress rehearsal for Dickie and his team. Hawke, with Dickie, Unsworth, and chief aerial cameraman Robin Browne, flew back to London with the film so they could view the rushes on the following morning. This practice run enabled them to make last-minute adjustments to the filming arrangements ready for the proper jump the next day.

Browne, "a reticent, almost nervous man" was considered one of the world's specialists in aerial film work and recently had made expensive commercials for Concorde. His mentor had been Johnny Jordan, who supervised the combat footage for *Battle of Britain*. A few years later, the pair were in Mexico filming the fleet of B-25s for *Catch 22* (1970). Jordan, keen to get a great shot from the camera plane, had unclipped his safety harness, leaned out too far, and fell to his death. Powerless to stop him, Browne saw his friend fall, and unsurprisingly, it haunted him for years. Iain Johnstone noticed that despite "being better look-ing in the flesh than any of the stars," there was a sadness that hung over Browne, "[as] if his mind is elsewhere in a more remote and sadder location." It's not hard to imagine that the potential dangers were never far from Browne's thoughts as he planned the *Bridge* drop.

🐝   🐝   🐝

Saturday, 11 September 1976, would be the biggest and most challenging day of the entire production. The Paras would do five jumps for the film, but that day a recreation of the British First Airborne drop would be the biggest. The intention had been to use the original landing zone of the 4th Parachute Brigade at Ginkelese Heide, where up to 50,000 spectators watch the annual memorial drop. Wing Commander Mike Jenkins, RAF, who was responsible for flight safety, highlighted too many issues with using the historically accurate Ginkel Heath location. Luckily, Speulde Heide, a spot some 12 miles north, was found to be ideal, with few modern intrusions nearby. Speulde Heide also would be much easier to police given the expected crowds.

Unfortunately, the balmy weather that had graced the production thus far chose to be contrary, raising two concerns that day. Firstly, it was just too windy. In a wartime situation, a jump would be attempted in a 25-knot wind, but peacetime regulations put a limit of 15 knots. Secondly, a misty haze under thin cloud made for poor visibility for both the aircrews and the 20 assembled cameramen. It would be solely Wing Commander Mike Jenkins' decision based on intel from the RAF meteorological detachment. All eyes were trained on the Met man's seemingly bizarre ritual every 15 minutes of releasing a red balloon, then following its trajectory through a telescope before making calculations with a slide rule. Each time the answer was the knots are still too high.

Waiting on the heath were 500 Dutch extras and the entire A.P.A. dressed as Red Devils. The *Report* shows the taciturn David Tomblin calmly giving directives over the PA system. He instructed that they must hold on to their semi-inflated parachutes, before reminding everybody of the very real danger of so many men falling from the sky: "Be careful they don't land on you because they will hurt you, and certainly hurt themselves." It had already been a long day. While the unit call was 6 a.m., the extras had to assemble five hours before at Twello for costuming before being bused to the location. With the original 7 a.m. drop postponed, the pressure was visible on the one man who was ultimately responsible: Dickie. As he sat down to be interviewed by Iain Johnstone for *The Arnhem Report*, perhaps to kill some time, Attenborough paused and looked up at the hazy skies, "Oh Lord, the light's really going, isn't it, dear me . . ."[497]

Being on a Saturday, the shoot attracted many visitors. "It was unbelievable, like a million people came for the day," remembered Roy Button. "We had a VIP area. Prince Bernhard and his family came. I think they had trouble getting in because no one recognised them. But they got there in the end."[498] One of those who had no trouble getting to watch was superstar Robert Redford, who had recently arrived ready for his filming block. Herb Lightman of *American Cinematographer* noticed the superstar's aura. "Dressed in a slightly scruffy denim jacket and jeans, he looks no different from your average all-American boy next door," wrote Lightman, "but Gail Samuelson almost swoons at the sight of him—a reaction I've noticed to be almost epidemic among young ladies catching an in-the-flesh glimpse of the unassuming Redford." Towards the end of his block, Redford went into the production office and invited all the female secretaries out to dinner. Apparently, they accepted with great enthusiasm!

Gail Samuelson's father ran Samuelson's, the London-based movie equipment hire company, whose largest item of kit was the huge "Sam-Mighty" crane that could rise to 27 feet. But that day it was suitably camouflaged with leafy tree branches and "rears up from the flat Dutch terrain like some preying monster out of a Japanese movie," Lightman commented. In all, 20 camera teams were hidden across the heath. Lightman caught up with his friend, Geoffrey Unsworth, on that very stressful day. "He seems to be hugely enjoying his current assignment," said Lightman, "and when I ask him about the problems of shooting on such a vast canvas, he looks at me as if to say, 'Problems—

what are they?'" He was putting a brave face on what was heading for a no-show day. Nervous eyes continued to glance over at the RAF meteorological detachment. Sometime after four in the afternoon, the Wing Commander nodded. He was happy with the calculations. The order was given to go.

EXT. SKY - DAY

And right now, looking at the steady stream of aircraft, you get the feeling that you would walk from wing to wing, all the way to Holland—except that's not all because now, from another part of the sky comes another stream of planes, and as we watch, slowly, the two come together and form one super chain and still if what we saw at first was startling, well, it's awesome now.

Peter MacDonald, manning one of the many cameras, recalled the mounting tension. "We had spotters a mile or two away. Over the radios they were telling us what was happening: They've taken off—they're five miles away—they're three miles away—they're over the top now."

EXT. SKY ABOVE BRITISH AIRBORNE DROP ZONE - DAY

A sky full of Dakotas.

In the far, far blue distance, a teeny white dot.

Now a second dot. Still far away.

Five dots now. Little bigger, little closer. But still no more than just that; dots.

Now twenty dots.

Now twenty more.

Now we realize those aren't dots, those are parachutes opening and before we know it, we're into one of the giant shots of this or any film, the drop.

Once over the target, a batch of 20 men known as "sticks" would stand up in the shaking Dakotas and, holding their static lines connected to an overhead rail, shuffle towards the port side door. Next to it were two lights: red for standby; when green flashed, each man stepped up to the door and, with a pat from his commander, jumped.

Once in the ether, the static line became taut and automatically pulled the chute. Each man controlled the angle of descent by tugging right or left on his harness straps. While they were all suitably costumed, veterans would have noted the lack of cumbersome 1944 equipment—kitbags, weapons, etc.—that each man would have been dropped with. This was not allowed for safety reasons with the modern PX parachute.

Aerial cameraman Robin Browne had installed cameras on several Dakotas: in the astrodome (the hemispherical transparent dome in the cabin roof), under the belly, on the port wing, and in the cockpit. A camera helicopter was supplemented by a small twin-engine Piper PA-23 Aztec that could fly deftly above and behind the formations. One cameraman donned a costume and jumped from a plane with a Bell and Howell Eyemo camera attached to his helmet. This footage is used effectively in the final film.

Journalist Lightman and the other observers were politely asked to dart under the camouflage: "I watch spellbound as, at some predetermined signal, they begin spewing hundreds of paratroopers into the sky. The chutes billow open and the men, with pendulum-like movement, come floating lazily down out of the blue. They look beautiful and I forget for the moment that their real-life counterparts in the actual assault came floating lazily down into Death."

Watching the men fall from the sky, Dickie cited this sequence as his most nerve-wracking. "When these poor chaps jumped there was nothing I could do about it. If a gust happened to catch them, or their chute got tangled in the tail of a plane or if they hit another guy or landed in a tree—too bad. They were just professional soldiers. They didn't get any extra pay."[499]

With cameras scattered across the heath and the air, every possible angle was covered. Once the drop was on, Dickie could contribute little as a director. "You couldn't storyboard," he said. "You didn't know what the wind would do, etc. So, you had to have cameramen who to all intents and purposes had the expertise and the knowledge of documentary film: A guy who was prepared to put a camera on his shoulder and catch what he could as it happened."[500]

Peter Macdonald pushed his zoom to its maximum magnification. "We doubled up our 10-to-1 zoom lens. What we'd worked out is, as you see the first parachute drop out, you wait 40 seconds before you start tilting down. I had my grip, Frank Batt, counting seconds. I'm screaming at him: No, you must have got it wrong! This is a disaster because I'm seeing all these guys in my foreground, and they've all gone by the time I pan down. Eventually, he got to about 35, and I lost my nerve. I started tilting down and zooming out. And sure enough, our theory was right that you caught up with the ones which dropped earlier."[501]

Assistant director Steve Lanning recalled the horror of witnessing a potential fatality. "Peter Mac was following a parachute down and he sees there's something dangerous going on. And while he was filming, he told me to get an ambulance."[502]

MacDonald: "One parachute had taken the wind out of the other one underneath it, and he suddenly went treble its speed. And this guy hit the deck at about 25–30 feet in front of us with the most awful scream."[503]

Lanning: "The parachutist didn't die, but he was injured. Who knows what happened, other than you knew for that 10 seconds there was something going on that you couldn't control."[504]

MacDonald: "We really thought he's dead. We made sure no one touched him because the worst thing for anyone with a back injury is to touch them. So, I just sat and tried to comfort him because he was very scared."[505]

Roy Button: "The ambulance trundles over. And the officer comes. We said, 'He's hurt!' This officer looks straight at me, and says, 'That's what he's paid for. Don't worry, we'll give him an injection.' They gave an injection right through his smock. He was out like a light, and they carted him off on a stretcher."[506]

MacDonald: "They took him away, and we all felt very depressed.

And it was about three or four months later before he made a total recovery . . . Having one injury was bad, but not fatal was very lucky and also showed the skill of these guys who jumped out of a plane that they'd never jumped out before."[507] Apart from that accident, there were four other major parachuting casualties, ranging from sprains to broken bones, all fully recovered after spells in hospital. One 18-year-old faced an 85-day detention following a court martial after he refused the order to jump at the last moment.

Christopher Good, as the eccentric Major Carlyle, was the only named actor on the call sheet that day. He was required to do a mini stunt—a parachute landing. A step ladder had been arranged, and as the real Red Devils were making their descent, "this stunt guy said, 'You're going to jump into view with your parachute,'" said Good. "That was the only time Attenborough put the fear of God into me saying we can't do this twice. You heard the planes. It was so odd to be looking down [from the ladder] thinking, *I don't know how I'm going to do it!* It was so rich, but not just what I was doing, but just the whole panoply of action with the planes flying overhead."

Although Good did not see it, he too heard the thud of the injured parachutist: "I remember the sound—that scream. There was so much going on. I just thought, *I wonder if that's going to be a thing?*" He didn't have much time to think about it before his own jump was cued. "I remember jumping onto the moor—just shocked. But I know it was cut. They only got me on the ground."[508]

Safely done with the ladder, Good recited a line detailing soldiers to rally to certain points: *"B company over there, A company to me."* In the film, Hopkins' Frost is also on the landing zone blowing his horn. This part of the scene had been shot much earlier in June, with just the landed troopers in the background.

As the jumpers arrived, it was time for the A.P.A. and the extras to manhandle their parachutes, pretending they had just landed. Jack McKenzie recalled the A.P.A.'s mother hen Jack Dearlove calling out: "All right, lads, act like you're acting!"[509] Tim Morand recalled the enormous silk chutes were difficult to control, and not just due to the wind. "The parachutes were catching the wind, and we were sort of tobogganing across the heather. And then hiding under our parachutes and smoking a few joints. We were high as kites. It was one hell of a day!"[510]

Colonel Waddy, watching with a keen soldier's eye, considered that the men were running too fast towards the RVs marked by different coloured smoke: "Initially, the men were sprinting past the cameras despite being told that they must act as if they were carrying a 90-pound load but, as the long, hot day wore on, their dash and enthusiasm were suitably reduced."[511]

The mile or so wide location meant some of the extras felt they were forgotten. The 500 Dutch extras were organised into 15-strong sections, each commanded by an A.P.A. member. Over the vast heath, the long day and the blazing heat almost led to a mutiny. Edward Seckerson, who had enjoyed an easy time, said, "I did fuck all in that sequence. I was sitting around most of the day watching it happen. It was quite a spectacle." As the last of the men had landed, and the scene completed, some of the far-flung units trundled back. "A lot of our guys were marshalling Dutch extras miles away from the camera and catering didn't reach them. So, it was hot, they were pissed off. Their gripe was taken up by the equity rep, and he said to Dave Tomblin, 'Sorry, we are not marshalling Dutch extras. That's not what we're here for,' and it was very tense."

Word got back to Dickie, who came up with a quick way to defuse the situation. Said Seckerson, "When we got back to the accommodation that day, and this was a very good example of Dickie's guile, or whatever you want to call it, there was a big crate of alcoholic beverages, and a note saying: *A.P.A., thank you for all your hard work today, Dickie.* Which was a bribe. He was a diplomat."[512]

One corner of the DZ doubled up for the Polish drop that took place a few days later (they also sported British uniforms). By the time Sosabowski's men landed and attempted to link with First Airborne, the area had been overrun with Germans. Some 25 A.P.A., including Sebastian Abineri, donned Wehrmacht costumes and took pot shots at the descending real-life Red Devils. At first, they were transfixed by the awesome sight above them, "each one giving birth to around 15 little baby Paras with their static lines like umbilical cords," said Abineri. "We watched anxiously, praying there was no malfunction."

Colonel Waddy, thinking they were not behaving like aggressive Germans, shouted: "Don't stand there staring at them! Fire! Fire! Fire!"

The sharp crackle of small arms fire hyped up the real soldiers descending to earth. "We opened up on them and they weren't expecting to be fired at," said Abineri, who noticed "one bloke . . . floating down around 20 yards from me. He stared at me anxiously whilst I carefully took aim with my Mauser rifle and pulled the trigger. As I fired, he gave a little involuntary movement, as if expecting to be hit. And I thought, hang on a minute, we could be on a sticky end of a counter-attack here."

The Paras took one look at his grey German uniform, and one said, "Let's 'ave him and round the day off properly!" Later, Abineri described to Colonel Waddy what happened: "Nothing. The only thing I did was a hot turd, which ran down my trouser leg and into my jack-boot." The colonel then "laughed uproariously . . . It appealed to his warped ex-SAS sense of humour."[513]

To head off trouble, Abineri offered to pick up the parachutes of the attackers and put them in the jeeps. "I said, 'Come to Deventer tonight, and have a few beers with us.' So, the whole battalion turned up, 300 of them, and crammed themselves into the Pelikaan." Propping up the bar was the tough old veteran Andrew Milbourne, who had lost both hands in the battle and was serving as an advisor. Abineri recalled, "He kept buying us beers, and he asked if we'd been in any fights yet? I said, 'No.' He said, 'Ah, you have to have a few fights.' I said, 'Hang on a minute, Andrew, we're a little bit outnumbered here.' And he said, 'Outnumbered?! We're fucking used to that! I'll tell you what, all us old lads, we'll come on your side.'" The 21-year-old balked at the odds. "I climbed out the window and went home!"[514]

Something of the rambunctiousness of the Paras can be glimpsed in *The Arnhem Report*. Robert Redford, sporting a Red Devil's beret, is interviewed by Johnstone, but something catches his eye. He beckons over a rough-and-ready Para, sporting a black eye, to sit beside him before the camera. The star enquires if he got that from the jump. The Para admits, "I got into a bit of an argument." Redford tries to get to the bottom of the tale. It appears the previous night the Para had been in a spat in the bar, and the bad blood had continued during the drop. "So really the most dangerous part of the wars is in the bars afterwards," Redford concluded.

After all the hours of tense waiting, the drop scene was over very quickly with "cut!" echoing across the heather. To Johnstone, Dickie looked visibly relieved, "not speaking, barely moving, but his eyes filled with tears." As the Paras packed up, the crew drew breath and discussed with "glee the excellence of their shots," Johnstone wrote.[515] Dickie stepped over to Dave Tomblin and gave him a hug.

That evening, the movie "generals" had a powwow. Although the drop had gone well, the hazy light conditions meant the camera team felt the photographic quality had been compromised. Dickie agreed but would have to ask Levine for another day. The producer was in a hospital in New York amid an enforced six-week convalescence for a leg injury. Goldman was with him and recalled Dickie calling from Holland. He wanted Levine's permission to spend another $75,000 for a reshoot. "And Levine said, 'What's the weather prediction for tomorrow?' And Attenborough said, 'It's grey, more of the same.' And Levine screamed at him, 'You limey bastard, you no good . . .' But he gave him the day."[516]

Proof of the trust Levine had with Dickie is evident from a Telex he sent early in the production, while dogged with health problems, "Thank God for you, I feel safe with our film safe in your hands. Notwithstanding, I would give one of my legs to be with you."[517]

Goldman maintains only the footage from that extra day was used in the film. It seems unlikely the editor Anthony Gibbs would not use footage from all the shoots. There was some material, though, that would end up on the cutting-room floor. When watching back the hours of rushes, Dickie and his team plus the invited A.P.A., including Sebastian Abineri, watched a beautiful shot following a group of parachutists all the way to the ground. Unfortunately, on that particular angle, the camera tilted down to find—a cricket match! "It captured them all on film keeping wicket, smacking the ball into the boundary. Upon seeing the descending Paras, they pulled stumps and ran to their weapons and opened fire. They were so engrossed in the game they hadn't heard the command, 'action!' Dickie said, 'We'll have to cut that bit . . . can't have the Germans playing cricket in the middle of the battle!'"[518] It was one of David English's impromptu cricket matches, which had become a popular pastime for the A.P.A. between takes.

While the U.S. 101st Airborne is depicted only post jump, Gavin's U.S. 82nd was captured over two drops in one day. These were done by a supply-drop section of the Royal Corps of Transport and 50 Belgian Para Commando. The scene is most notable for Ryan O'Neal as Gavin appearing to land via a parachute—another complex and dangerous moment to achieve.

Stuntman Vic Armstrong doubled the star dangling high off the ground. He was attached to a large ring held aloft by a tall crane. "I designed a rig that holds all the shroud lines up on little L-shaped brackets," recalled John Richardson. "This was held up by wires that all went to one release hook in the middle. So, when the release hook went, all the shroud lines dropped together. They had probably a 10- or 15-foot drop while the shroud actually filled up—then just floated down. The beauty of it when released at 80 feet was you knew where it would land, and it wasn't going to come down at 90 miles an hour."[519]

"I remember hanging there waiting for the planes to come over, watching the loops on my shroud lines gradually popping off in the wind," recalled Armstrong. "When I did drop, the wind was so strong

I was immediately blown backwards out of shot and hit the ground hard. The next morning, I could hardly lift my head off the pillow because all the muscles on my neck were strained from the heavy American helmet I was wearing, but it probably saved me from cracking my head. Funnily enough, I got awarded an Oscar a few years later for adapting a parachute landing simulator called a Fan Descender, used to control stunt falls."[520]

Ryan O'Neal, who bore a remarkable resemblance to Armstrong, was strapped in for some closeup shots. Plainly enjoying himself dangling from the rig, he had some pictures taken of himself and distributed to the press. The production's publicity department was none too happy about these unauthorised images.

The last component of the film's winged cast was the 12 glider replicas built in a Deventer factory. They were first deployed peppered across the landscape during the drops. Six were three-dimensional, and the others were simple flat cut outs for the far distance. This was a minor inaccuracy as gliders were landed only after the pathfinders had secured the DZ. It is a shame that the film makes no attempt to show one skidding across the landscape, but the logistics were too difficult. *The Longest Day* had staged such a scene for the seizing of Pegasus Bridge the night before the invasion, with the darkness helping to hide the use of a miniature. In the broad daylight of Market Garden, such a technique may not have passed muster in 1976. The last of the airborne troops to be depicted landing, the Screaming Eagles of the U.S. 101st, are shown milling around a broken stack of gliders, which at least suggests their contribution to the battle.

Art director Alan Tomkins recalled, "We were asked to prepare the Horsa gliders in their crashed state before they were to be shot in parked formations, prior to being towed along the runway for the boarding scenes. This is the somewhat crazy side of filmmaking!" As none had survived the war, the Horsa replicas had been designed by Tony Remington using scant drawings kept by the Imperial War Museum in London. Some cost-cutting had opened up the space between the plywood ribs and wing formers, the designer knowing that they were to be landlocked penguins. "On damp mornings, the 88-foot wingspan had a droop each end!" Tomkins recalled. "So, a long 'H' iron girder was inserted into the top of each glider to keep the wings straight. It gave us real respect for the construction of the original flying plywood monsters, only 7 feet shorter than a C-47 (Dakota) wingspan."[521]

Jack McKenzie recalled that despite being land birds, the wind could stir them to move: "The gliders were so accurately built. They had to bolt them down because it kept lifting off the tarmac. I think they would have flipped."[522]

Thanks to some clever movie magic, the film suggests that some not only take off, but fly. A modern two-seat LET L-13 Blanik glider belonging to the London Gliding Club was brought over and mocked up as a Horsa. Piloted by aviator Henri Labouchère and with a camera looking forward, it was dragged by one of the Portuguese Dakotas as a tug plane. Photographed from several angles and intercut with the coils of rope unfurling, the craft conveys a convincing sense of an immense glider armada. The sharped-eyed aviation expert will note that the Blanik in the film was towed with only one cable, unlike the Horsa's two. "Tony Remington, who designed them, put his money where his mouth was," recalled Stuart Craig, "and he sat in there [the Blanik] with a joystick in his hand. They were pretty good replicas to the point where they actually were doing 60–70 miles an hour down the runway, they actually started to lift. This was a hair-raising, alarming moment. He very nearly left the ground not to return. Fortunately, nobody was killed, but they might have been."

By September 1976 the pace of production was little short of insane. In between the upcoming Waal crossing and the various drops, another major sequence consumed three days of filming—the capture of the Grave bridge, later to be cut. The coordination and organisation fell to Eric Rattray and the assistant directors, led by David Tomblin and Steve Lanning.

"We were working 24 hours a day," said Lanning. "You would do a parachute sequence on, let's say, a Monday, Wednesday, and Friday, starting two o'clock in the morning. The next day's filming started at seven o'clock, perhaps something that didn't have big stuff on a Tuesday or Thursday. My wife came over to see the parachuting stuff. I saw her twice in bed over two weeks. It was funny when it came to doing our timesheets. The production supervisor, Eric Rattray—a lovely guy—would say, 'I didn't know how to pay you! There isn't any time you weren't working.' I said, 'We leave it to you to be fair.' You couldn't have shot that film on an 8–10-hour day. But it was logistically exciting."[523]

19

"Hail Mary, Full of Grace"
Four Sundays in Nijmegen

Over four Sundays, one of the principal highways in Holland paused 1976 and returned to 1944. In a major coup, the film company negotiated with the Nijmegen authorities for the exclusive use of the Waalbrug for one hour each day. This involved not just the very busy highway but also the freight traffic on the river Waal.

Nijmegen is one of the oldest cities in the Netherlands. The low ridge of the Hunnerberg district of the city dominates the southern bend of the Waal River. Eventually, this moraine would be crowned by Nijmegen's largest and oldest church, the Grote of Sint-Stevenskerk, known locally as Steven's Church. This promontory, coupled with Nijmegen's central placement in the country, made the city important both economically and militarily.

In the seventeenth century, during the Dutch Revolt against their Spanish masters, Nijmegen formed part of the hotly contested border of the fledgling Republic of the United Provinces. This small Protestant state would continue to fight for its survival against Spain and then France for over 100 years. Nijmegen would endure multiple sieges, as the political map of Europe was constantly redrawn. Following the Dutch-assisted victory at Waterloo in 1815, relative peace on the continent gradually brought stability and prosperity to the region.

In 1875 a railway bridge was built across the Waal. With the increase of motor traffic following the Great War, the Zeldenrust ferry

255

was no longer sufficient for the needs of the new century. An ambitious road bridge, designed by architect G. Schoorl and purported to be the largest on the continent, began construction in 1931.

Described as a two-hinged arch bridge, the base stretches for 604 metres (1,982 feet), with a width of 26 metres (87 feet), and towers to 65 metres (213 feet), and the arching steel structure spans to 244 metres (801 feet). On 16 June 1936, Queen Wilhelmina of the Netherlands, in the presence of 200,000 people, opened the Waalbrug. Sadly, this impressive structure would soon be cursed with destruction.

Early in the film, Goldman's script attempts to ratchet up the tension as General Gavin (Ryan O'Neal) discusses the forthcoming attack with Captain Arie "Harry" Bestebreurtje (Peter Faber), his Dutch liaison officer. To drum home the almost suicidal mission for the U.S. 82nd Airborne Division, Bestebreurtje relates how in 1940, German paratroopers attempted to take the bridge *and got slaughtered.*" It appears this is pure Goldman and has nothing to do with Cornelius Ryan—or fact.

The Germans lightning invasion of Holland in May 1940 involved taking the country's many bridges. A small Waffen-SS armoured recce battalion rolled past Dutch forces at top speed to Nijmegen and seized both the Waalbrug and the railroad span. But the Germans had arrived too late, as both bridges had been blown by the Dutch 20 minutes earlier. While the Dutch defenders fought the Waffen-SS battalion, there is no evidence to suggest this was much more than a brief firefight. The German capture of Nijmegen served as their first victory in their invasion of the Netherlands. As the country shook to the stamp of the jackboot and occupation, the Germans repaired and reopened both bridges in 1943. On 22 February 1944, American planes heavily bombed Nijmegen, causing substantial damage to the city centre and killing over 800 Dutch civilians. The Allies maintained it was a mistake as their intended target was the nearby German city of Kleve.

The bridges would once again become targets in September 1944, as their capture would allow XXX Corps to make the last dash to Arnhem bridge. But first, Gavin's 82nd Airborne would eschew its wings and learn to paddle, as an attempt was made to cross the 150-metre-wide Waal under merciless enemy fire.

At 15:15 hours on Wednesday, 20 September 1944, Major Julian Cook and his 3rd Battalion of the 504 Regiment led 260 men across the Waal in what has been described as one of the most courageous acts of the entire war. In modern war there must be few opportunities to watch brutal action safely but close by. Lieutenant Colonel J.O.E. Vandeleur joined other senior commanders, including Horrocks and Browning, at the PEGM factory overlooking the Waal and would give Cornelius Ryan a vivid description of the ensuing action as Americans in 26 boats attempted to cross the river. "It was a horrible, horrible sight. Boats were literally blown out of the water. Huge geysers shot up as shells hit and small-arms fire from the northern bank made the river look like a seething cauldron."[524]

Captain Moffatt Burriss was in the thick of it. "My particular boat, I was sitting on the back wrung along with an engineer. I saw his wrist turn red, and he looked at me and said, 'Captain, take the rudder, I've been hit.' Just as I reached for the rudder, he caught a 20-mm high explosive, and it blew his head off. I caught some of the shrapnel in my side and was covered with his brains and blood. He fell over, and I dumped him overboard. Approximately half of us made it across the river. And then we had to charge 900 yards across a flat pasture up to a dike that had a road on top of it. And lined up behind it were machine guns—we had to charge straight into a continuous band of machine gun fire, men dropping on your right and on the left, but nobody hesitated."[525]

The filmmakers wanted to restage this extraordinary action as authentically as possible. Post-war reconstruction precluded use of the original site of the attack, but as luck would have it (again), a suitable area lay on the other side of the bridge, occupied by a small tight-knit community living on houseboats. It was Reineke Kramer's job as Dickie's Dutch assistant to negotiate. "They were kind of hippies and were protesting enormously because we wanted to remove them. I had to go down there to negotiate with them: Please, we pay you to move your boat for a certain amount of time. And then they did that at the end."[526] Once cleared, Terry Marsh's art department could dig the various slit trenches and slug them with sandbags and suitable camouflage.

It was a very early start on Sunday, 12 September 1976. Bleary-eyed crew members, some grumbling that the early call had curtailed their Saturday night bacchanalia, gathered at dawn for a bacon sandwich from Phil Hobbs' catering vans. It was a tough weekend as the previous day had been the epic parachute drop. This Sunday would prove equally nerve-wracking. H-Hour was 7:45 a.m., when traffic on both the bridge and the river would cease for just 60 minutes. The first closure back in June had involved a relatively simple sequence of German troops marching past. This day would be in a class of its own.

John Richardson and his effects team had arrived first to rig the hundreds of explosions. "We'd had a four o'clock call, got out there, and laid the charges. We'd get one take."[527] While many charges were planted in the sandy bank of the German position, most would be floated along with the flotilla to be detonated on command. Several boats were crewed by costumed dummies sitting upon a literal powder keg.

The American soldiers had used Goatley boats in their 1944 crossing of the Waal. Named after Fred Goatley of Saunders-Roe Ltd., more than 1,000 boats were deployed during the war. Weighing around 150 kilograms (330 pounds), the canvas craft could be assembled in two minutes and carry up to 10. Art director Alan Tomkins had been sent to research them at the Royal Marines Museum in Southsea and said of Goatley boats, "They looked, it must be said, very flimsy." In all, 16 were constructed "to exacting standards"[528] by Mike Turk Film Services based in Richmond, who would also be responsible for their use on the Waal.

One person had the latest start time—just 15 minutes before kick-off. This was the megabucks talent in the handsome form of Robert Redford, cast as Major Cook, the last major actor to join the shoot, his service to comprise three weeks. Redford's schedule would be punctuated with these short but vital Sunday shoots in Nijmegen.

Dickie was feeling the pressure that day. With barely minutes to go before action, his top star had not appeared. Eventually Redford, sporting Malibu-bleached hair, arrived, blaming his driver for getting lost. "Dickie was not happy," Peter MacDonald recalled, "and said, 'I'm not going to talk to him.' I said, 'You're the director, you have to!'"[529]

Redford took his position in the boat. There being no make-up person nearby, he looked for the best mirror he could find. Perched behind MacDonald and his large Panavision camera was documentary cameraman Martin Bell's 16-mm camera. Redford peered into it and ruffled up his hair. Dickie was incensed, and exclaimed, "Redford's supposed to be a butch soldier, and you show him checking his make-up. Now piss off!"[530] Dickie then jumped into his speedboat and returned to the bank. Bell's shot made it into the opening montage sequence of Iain Johnstone's *The Arnhem Report*.

The usually even-tempered Dickie by now felt the months of immense responsibility piling up, coupled with an average of six hours of sleep a night. "It was a strain," he said later. "I think I got a little edgy at times, a bit irritable with the people I was closest to, especially at the end of the day. I don't think I knew just how exhausted I really was until the end of shooting."[531]

Redford, with his hair now under control, wanted one last word with Dickie. Peter MacDonald, poised with his camera focused on the star, became the *de facto* director on the spot and explained that Dickie was far away on the viewing platform. "He [Redford] said, 'I want to ask about my motivation.' I said, 'Well, that's easy, Robert—it's survival.'"[532]

With everything set to go, it was hoped there wouldn't be a repeat of the rehearsal a few days earlier. Assistant director Roy Button recalled that "no one had considered, because none of us was seafaring folk, that the tide was quite strong." Despite each boat being manned by stuntmen using paddles and rifle butts, the tide pulled them "like two miles over there," said Button, pointing.[533] The problem was solved by installing hidden inboard motors that maintained the illusion while ensuring the boats went in the right direction. If strong stuntmen couldn't steer their craft to the target, the mind boggles at the sheer grit and determination of the original boys of the 504th who made the crossing under shot and shell.

As H-hour approached, the pressure mounted. "We were shooting a 360-degree set," MacDonald recalls, "we had seven or eight cameras on the far shore, several on the shore we were leaving. And two or three cameras travelling in the boats. We had the river closed, there was no question—we had to go."

David Tomblin's voice echoed through the Tannoys, "Action!" They were off. "You're a bit apprehensive," recalled Macdonald. "The river flows very fast—there's a long way down to the next stop, which was probably near the Alps!" The various seaborne cameramen, including MacDonald and his 20-year-old assistant, had dressed as American paratroopers. "I had Steve Barron with me as my focus puller. I wanted someone young along in case we went into the water."[534]

Redford was glad not to have many lines to say as he too paddled across. His character Julian Cook was a devout Catholic and during the assault muttered, "Hail Mary, full of grace." He said it helped to maintain an even tempo for rowing. It was the commander's very personal method of quelling his fears as he strove to lead from the front. Redford noted how the chants and yells of attacking Indians on the American plains were less a war cry and instead simply them "expelling fear, their own nerves."[535] Of all the action scenes involving Dickie's 14 stars, the Waal River crossing proved the riskiest. "What he had to do was physically cross that river," Dickie said of Redford. "Believe me, I died a million deaths."[536]

While Dickie watched, control fell to John Richardson, who

would fire the hundreds of special effects. His top priority was safety but also to make it look as spectacular as possible. "I placed one member of my crew in [each of] six small boats, all with a dynamite charge on a predetermined length of string with a cork float. The idea being the float was big enough for them to see (and avoid) but the camera wouldn't pick them up. I cued my guys on the radio to let them know it was all clear and each charge sent up 150-foot columns of water into the air."[537]

The decision about when to explode the simulated shell fire rested with Peter MacDonald, who, whilst framing his multimillion-dollar star in the foreground, waited for the boats with dummy soldiers to appear in shot behind. But he had a problem: "As the boats left the shore, they all changed position. All I could see were canvas boats, some trailing explosions, and some with dummies in which we were going to blow up." [538]

MacDonald stayed in open radio contact with Richardson, who was poised with the firing trigger. Keeping his star nicely framed, MacDonald said, "I thought, *Now, is that a dummy boat in front of me?* I had to be brave, so I closed my eyes and said, 'Let number one go.' Luckily, it was a boat that wasn't that close to us but gave us the effect. I think nine or ten explosions went off, eight in shot about 15–20 feet behind." Drenched by the spray, Redford flinched. "You look fucking great, get on with it!" yelled MacDonald.

"Because of the strata and the rock formations under the river, the ground was shaking every time a charge went off," Richardson recalled. "We had probably, in one or two minutes, a hundred charges going off. And the ground was constantly shaking, and watching it was like being at war."[539]

Playing a young padre was American actor John Morton. "It was really like being in combat because [of] the explosions, the noise and the confusion, plus the very strong flow of the current. The danger was if you fell out of the boat prematurely and an explosion in the water happened, you would have lost an eardrum. So that was pretty hairy."

The plan had been for each boat to aim for a designated position on the shore, which had been marked with a numbered stake during the rehearsals. "But trying to get the boats in line, even when the stakes were there, was just impossible," Morton recalled, "and then the stakes were removed. Every part of the shoreline looked the same. So, none of that worked."[540]

Once across, the soldiers jumped out of the boats and fired their rifles. Cameraman Peter MacDonald wanted to capture Cook leading his men forward into the maelstrom. He radioed Richardson to ensure there was enough movie carnage to spare—12 charges. "Your adrenaline is pumping so high. As we landed, I'm screaming abuse like some sergeant at Robert, 'Don't be a pussy—Run! Run! Run!' And it got him really psyched up. I radioed to Johnny to let everything go! So, with the stunt guys running through explosions flying up in front, Robert's got to follow them. And he did."[541]

As Redford started running, he had an advantage over the others like John Morton. "All of us were wearing the GI boots, which got waterlogged. It's like wearing cement. And as you land, you were clunking in the sand. But Redford's boots were canvas, so even if they were waterlogged, he could jump out and pass all of us and run like Mercury. That was the advantage of stardom!"

After one take, one of the attacking A.P.A., Tony Forrest, offered to swap with John Morton's padre uniform so Morton could join the fray. "Hey, John, you got to experience this as a GI." Morton and the other soldiers were told to take notice of the hidden explosions in the sand, covered with Fuller's Earth. "I stormed the beach as an A.P.A., and I immediately saw that's an explosion right in front of me. So, I rolled over to my side, just in time, as this thing exploded. I'm amazed that people weren't hurt because of the fog of war. These squibs could have been life threatening, or at least you could lose your eyes."[542]

In the sequence John Ratzenberger, cast as an *"old-looking lieutenant,"* had to throw a hand grenade into a German machine gun nest, followed with a suitable pithy line. Before he achieved instant fame as Cliff in the '80s TV comedy series *Cheers* and lasting fame as the voice of *Toy Story*'s Hamm, he was renowned for his improv skills with a well-known comic company called Sal's Meat Market with Ray Hassett. "And the line was something like 'take that you dirty Krauts,' or something typical," Morton recalled of his friend. "And Ratzenberger went to Attenborough and said, 'Hey, can I play with the line a little bit?' Attenborough said, 'Sure.' So, when they shoot the scene, he pulls the pin out of his with his teeth. And as he's heaving the hand grenade over to the pillbox, he said, 'Scrambled eggs.' And I think that was a print. It's vintage Ratzenberger."

During another of the action scenes, Morton was watching by the camera, as "one extra, right in the middle of a take, went completely out of character. He just kind of turned around and started walking back as everybody else was going towards the bridge. This guy went rogue and he ruined the shot! Dickie and Dave Tomblin were absolutely furious."

While the movie crossing may have been a pale shadow of the original, it still proved hard toil. "I just laid back totally exhausted," recalled MacDonald. "Suddenly a shadow came over the top of me. It was like a scene from a *Tom and Jerry* film. The face was totally black—just the eyes and teeth showing. It was Robert Redford—and he was angry. He'd run into the first explosion, which was made of soot and sand. He said, 'I've never in my fucking life experienced anything like that.' And I said, 'I agree with you. It was fantastic and was so real. And everyone knows it's you! Because you are there in the big foreground.'" This didn't seem to placate the blackened star, and MacDonald was disappointed by his response. "I said, 'What upsets me is, I've always wanted to work with you, ever since *El Cid* when you galloped out of the castle, even though you were dead, everyone followed you.' He said, '*El Cid*? (of course, it was Chuck Heston) Yeah, that was one of my better films!' He could see the funny side of it. We were still both laughing when Dickie came across in this high-powered motorboat. He was very pleased, and said, 'I think another take, poppet, to see more action.'" But with their hour ending, the river traffic was itching to get going. "Those skippers were giving us the finger. And Dickie said, 'I guess you're right, poppet; yes, it may be a bit dangerous.' 'It's not a bit dangerous,' I said. 'It's very dangerous!'"[543]

Camera assistant Steve Barron recalls what happened next as the most hair-raising experience of his life. "At one end of the river there were three giant cargo boats coming in, and two on the other side, and we were in the middle. So, Dickie says, 'Okay, Bobby [Redford], come into our boat.' They start the engine, but there was a back flow on the propeller and it wasn't going anywhere. We started hearing the horns on these massive boats. I thought we were going to cop it.

"Norton 'Nifty' Knatchbull, the location manager, who was zooming around in his little cruiser boat, came and grabbed hold of the side of ours. Revving up his engine, we were turning rather than going forward. Then I looked up at these boats coming. They were like a seven-storey building—enormous things. And they came on not going right or left but sandwiched in the middle. And just as Nifty revved and got past, one of the outside boats turned and missed us by a matter of feet, but the wake nearly flipped our boat. Everyone was hanging on for dear life. But we made it back to shore. Everyone was in such shock! Because it was so close that nobody said a word. That was the river crossing, one of the scariest moments I had."[544]

The following Sunday, 19 September, was designated for another crack at the sequence, mainly "to shoot wide angles with the bridge as a background."[545] That day's production progress report stated that over 14,000 feet of film was exposed, running nearly 150 minutes from 10 camera setups covering three scenes. The day's work was estimated to have captured just 30 seconds of screen time.[546]

The final touches for the Waal crossing scene were completed in a water tank, specially built by Peter Dukelow, situated at Welsum near Deventer. With a wide, painted cyclorama and holding just a few feet of water, it would be used for closeups. One of those involved John Morton as the padre paddling for his life. "I look absolutely terrified. I mean, there's no acting there. Although it was in a bathtub with explosions going off all around. But right next to me off camera was a burly electrician making the thing go up and down."[547]

To create the water explosions, John Richardson used industrial steel piping welded to the concrete base about six inches beneath the waterline. "I sat these on car tyres and hung the explosive charge in the middle," said Richardson. "It had the desired effect of firing water into the air, but because it was only just below the surface, you could be really close to it and not be hurt by any shock waves. Necessity is indeed the mother of invention."[548]

At dawn on Sunday, 26 September, the painters were out early erasing modern traffic markings on the bridge for the last part of the crossing sequence, the taking of the Waalbrug itself. An army of extras plus 18 members of the A.P.A. had to report at 4 a.m. for their respective costumes. Eight stuntmen including Alf Joint and Vic Armstrong, dressed as Germans, strapped themselves high up to the girders of the bridge to play snipers. The art department oversaw the placement of a large wooden *"cradle (with explosives)"* under the bridge. Major Laramie readied his nine Shermans just out of sight at one end of the span. All waited for the one-hour window at 7.45 a.m. when the Waalbrug shut to traffic.

The scenes involved Redford as Cook leading his men to take the Waalbrug. Then having shot down the German snipers posted in the girders, he would wave XXX Corps' Shermans across while *"standing directly above the explosives, only of course, he doesn't know it."* Colonel John Waddy objected to this sequence on two points. One, it gave Cook an almost James Bond role as an action hero. Also, it downplayed the role of the British 2nd Armoured Battalion, Grenadier Guards. In history, their Sherman tanks, with Sergeant P. T. Robinson in the lead, had stormed across the Waalbrug. They then pushed 1,500 yards into the city before meeting with the Americans at dusk. Dickie's problem was this was the money shot for his top box-office draw: Redford had to be seen actually doing something—and heroically, to boot!

This tension between Hollywood and history led to a public tussle witnessed by British journalist John Sandilands of the *Observer*. Waddy, "wearing his old jumping smock and a flat tweed cap at the nose-hugging Sandhurst angle," engaged in a heated discussion with "lanky" co-producer Richard Levine. Waddy "pointed out sternly" that the bridge taking was "notably a British operation." Levine Junior attempted to placate the Colonel, saying, "The facts, *Jahn*, would be more difficult and expensive."

The colonel, as the peak of his hat "took on more of an aggressive tilt," explained that while the Americans did take the nearby railway bridge and outflank the Germans, they were too far back to take the Waalbrug in the manner the script proposed. "Doing it this way means an awful lot at the box office, *Jahn*," pleaded Richard Levine. Waddy was "now sufficiently incensed to produce the actual 'harrumph' of scandalised senior military men." His counterattack was a low blow against the combined efforts of the production to respect the facts. He reminded the young American of a Hollywood war film that had become "a laughingstock" to wartime British audiences (and the subject of an official complaint from London to Washington).

It was the 1945 Warner Bros. film *Objective Burma*, which suggested that a tiny crack unit of GIs defeated the Japanese, where the so-called "Forgotten" British Fourteenth Army battled for years against an implacable enemy. "It purported to show how an American [*sic*] actor conquered Burma single-handed." After a pause, the colonel "lobbed his final grenade: His name was Errol Flynn." Levine could see how seriously the colonel regarded the issue and used all his diplomatic skills to sooth the waters. Putting his arms around the veteran, Richard assured him, "Dickie wouldn't do it if it wasn't right."[549]

Historian Pieter Jutte points out: "Cook was made a greater hero in the movie; they could not give Redford a position in the rear of the attacking paratroopers. His subordinate, Captain Moffatt Burriss, declared that Cook never fired his weapon when they hit the shore of the Waal river."[550] Cook in the film is a composite character, drawing particularly on Burriss' exploits. It was Burriss who led the vanguard up the concrete steps towards the upper part of the bridge. "Actually, at that time, Major Cook was somewhere else," Burris maintained. "I was the one that actually charged up the steps with a handful of men."[551]

One wonders if this was why the film company did not make much effort to invite Cook over to Holland. Upon finally seeing the film, Cook was dismayed to have been given such a prominent action role. Over the question of who actually took the bridge, he maintained, "My men got there first—at 7:15 that day."[552] Eventually a compromise was reached, but for now the scene as written would go ahead.

The filmed sequence comprised many setups, with every change of a camera position a lengthy and cumbersome operation. Shooting a complex action sequence in one-hour blocks is a tall order—a tribute to Peter MacDonald and his crew. "I had multi-cameras, and we were leapfrogging each other," said MacDonald. "So, you'd have two or three cameras on the bridge, and you would send people ahead of you with equipment. But you yourself were doing the shot. It was like a relay race."[553]

John Morton recalls how Redford carefully clocked each camera angle. "Redford was so professional. When we rehearsed, he walked it and made a note of where each camera was hidden at various points doing his run. For the take, he knew exactly where he was supposed to look as he passed the camera."[554]

MacDonald: "I've done this a few times, and the actors also get into it, because they know the pressure is on. Dickie, a couple of times, would say: 'I don't know. Maybe if we . . .' I used to get angry with Dickie sometimes. I said, 'We've got another half hour left, we got to do this.' There wasn't time for Dickie to waffle." Dickie often delegated much of the action to MacDonald and Tomblin, "but he was always very appreciative of whatever you did for him."[555]

❦   ❦   ❦

In *Adventures in the Screen Trade*, Goldman describes 3 October, the production's final Sunday as "The Million Dollar Hour." It was the last time the Waalbrug could be closed, and even more significantly, their expensive star would be at the end of his contract. If, Goldman explained, this day's shoot wasn't completed, the producers would need to renegotiate another closure. The kicker for Levine and his team was the entire shoot was planned to finish on the following Wednesday. If Redford was still required, his contract kicked into "overage." While this was also true for the vast army of technicians, this one American alone would cost $125,000 per day. One man was at the centre of all this pressure: Dickie Attenborough.

The screenwriter, who had enjoyed a ringside seat by the director, described the scene as Alf Joint and his stuntmen dressed as Germans, roped themselves securely to the high girders of the bridge. Giving the thumbs up, Alf signalled that he and his crew were ready. "You can see the confidence flowing into Attenborough," said Goldman. Then several assistants trotted up to check that the boss was happy with the placement of the props, tanks, and 'corpses.' To each question, reported Goldman, "He's snapping back the answers crisp and fast," including that "the corpses must keep their eyes shut at all times." Now satisfied, he issued the order to start the smoke pots. At that moment, one final question from an assistant: "What about the jeeps in the orchard, sir?" Goldman watched Dickie. "For a moment his eyes glazed over, and he had to be thinking that suddenly the world had gone mad or was the world sane and the mistake his? Had he forgotten . . . forgotten something vital?" The mental checklist was visible on the director's face as he racked his brain. The omission could lead to the dreaded "overage." After an agonising pause, "he smiles very sweetly to his aide and says, 'We will not require jeeps in the orchard at all. Thank you so much for reminding me.'"[556]

That day's call sheet gives a more sober picture of Goldman's "Million Dollar Hour." Only part of two scenes were scheduled for the bridge that day. These were pickup shots of scenes not quite completed the previous Sunday. David Tomblin, in compiling the call sheet, was confident they would be speedily achieved, as he scheduled the unit to reassemble in the Bemmel orchard nearby for 9 a.m.[557]

It was this scene that the ill-timed enquiry of jeeps referred to. A few days before, they had shot Cook's "George Washington" speech, and this Sunday would involve the last part as the Bedford trucks belatedly arrive with the boats. Redford was joined by John Ratzenberger and John Morton, plus the diminished cadre of A.P.A. with the jeeps correctly placed, followed by the action of the soldiers constructing the boats and carrying them up to the lip of the dike, which completed the day's work.

Camera assistant Steve Barron, now recovered from his river ordeal, recalled having an embarrassing moment as he and Robert Redford waited for "action." The two of them were placed at some distance from the crew, probably for a telephoto lens. The 20-year-old had enjoyed not one but two romantic liaisons (with a slight crossover) during the shoot. He was stunned to learn that heartbroken sobs had reached the ears of a Hollywood superstar. "I was sitting on the grass filling out the clapperboard, and I heard this voice, 'Hey, Steve?' It was Robert Redford! I was quite shocked, as how would he know my name? I looked up at him in the sunlight. He said, 'You know, it's none of my business. But I just thought I'd let you know that [name omitted] was sort of crying yesterday.' And I went bright red." The girl in question was an employee of their shared hotel and had inadvertently found out Steve was "entertaining" someone else in his room. "I felt so terrible. I was young—and that's my only excuse. It was a bad thing to do. Robert said, 'I just thought I'd tell you. You do what you like. None of my business.' So, he just was very aware of everything. But he was amazing, coming from God—Robert Redford—to me."[558]

With the Waalbrug successfully captured and the overage avoided, there was time to shoot the "Cook compromise." To make it clear that the capture of Nijmegen was truly the work of both allies, Dickie agreed to create a scene showing British Guards' Shermans fighting in the streets of Nijmegen. The unit's flexibility to achieve this small but important historical detail impressed Colonel Waddy—a picturesque square overlooking the Waalbrug was rented at dawn for just two hours. The art department brought in tonnes of rubble, created false fronts of ruined houses, and littered the area with broken trucks, guns, and bodies. One hundred extras dressed as British and German troops plus four Sherman tanks battled through the smoke and chaos. At one point, Waddy noticed that a sleepy resident appeared on his balcony to investigate the noise. Looking down, he could see two gory German "corpses" slumped over a machine gun. With a look of surprise, he retreated inside, slammed his door, and yanked down the blinds.

Reverberations of the "Cook compromise" were still echoing the following year at the film's press show. Dickie was on the back foot having to justify that the actions on both the railway and Waalbrug spans had been amalgamated. He also pointed out that the shot of Cook waving the tanks across, although filmed, was later cut. How information about this scene fell into the hands of the press is unknown. Dickie complained that "advance press criticism of the Redford episode was unfair, especially as the picture was not even finished at the time and when no one had seen the completed film."[559] There would be more reverberations to come.

In warfare, knowing your opponent's strengths and weaknesses ultimately matters more than who is the strongest. The question posed around the final sequences to be filmed: Was Market Garden an avoidable disaster? During planning stages of the operation, a lowly major in British Intelligence, Brian Urquhart (no relation to the general), had pieced together disparate reports of a sizeable German presence around Arnhem. He later told Ryan that he was "quite frankly horrified by Market Garden because its weakness seemed to be the assumption that the Germans would put up no effective resistance."[560]

Goldman lifts almost all Urquhart's interview quotes from Ryan's book and fashions three very effective scenes. The only change to the material was his name. To avoid the audience's confusing the man with the First Airborne commander, the major became Fuller and was played with great subtlety by the Irish actor Frank Grimes.

Born in 1947, Grimes had made his name in Dublin's famous Abbey Theatre that had played host to Orson Welles, Dan O'Herlihy, and Micheál Mac Liammóir amongst many others. It was here in 1967, aged just 20, he received rave reviews for the stage adaptation of Brendan Behan's hard-hitting autobiography *Borstal Boy*. When the production moved to Broadway, he was nominated for a Tony Award for Best Actor. A move to London followed, where Grimes played the lead in director Lindsay Anderson's production of the David Storey play, *The Farm*. Grimes' experience well positioned him for the role of cautious Major Fuller.

Fuller first collars Browning outside the Moor Park HQ. Initially, his commander is tolerant and polite as he listens to the nervy junior officer, who says, *"I just want to be sure our airborne carpet consists of live troops, not dead ones."* Browning gives him the okay to order another *"low-level reconnaissance."* In the nicely judged scene, Browning is almost fatherly as he assures Fuller, who frets at his own doubts about the plan: *"If I were you, I wouldn't get too worried by what people say."* And in a marvellous piece of Goldman characterisation, adds: *"You see, you're just somewhat brighter than the rest of us. That tends to make us somewhat nervous—"* Grimes recalls that for some reason, "Bogarde did not want to say the line, but Dickie insisted."

The next scene, an interior, is a splendid example of Dickie as a great director of performance. Fuller fumbles with the photos taken from a Spitfire recon over the Dutch countryside and is trying to load them onto a slide projector. He is nervous and flustered. Browning, in contrast, sits ramrod still, sipping tea. Browning seems to know Fuller is onto something, but absolutely cannot show it. A horizontal stab of light from the projector, extenuated by the anamorphic Panavision lens, punctuates the tension. As the slightly blurred images of the half-hidden German tanks appear on the screen, it is the moment Browning has dreaded. Bogarde very subtly shows Browning registering the shock and the potential repercussions. Stepping up to the screen to inspect the grainy images, he bats away, if half-heartedly, Fuller's plaintive cries. The scene climaxes with Browning losing his temper. *"Are you really asking us to cancel the biggest drop since D-Day because of five photographs?"*

The dilemma (almost verbatim from Ryan) that this scene presents is: who is right? With so much at stake, could Browning have challenged his boss, Montgomery, to cancel the operation based on just five photographs? Without the luxury of hindsight, there seems to be little doubt that Browning had to disregard this evidence. Equally, Fuller, perhaps afflicted by being *"somewhat brighter than the rest of us,"* was compelled to push his sincere belief, based on evidence, that the Germans were there in force. The film, perhaps with Bogarde's nuanced performance, suggests that Browning did accept Urquhart's evidence but, like so many subordinate commanders before and since, must carry out his orders, regardless of the cost. Herein lies the tragedy of war—and Operation Market Garden.

Goldman's written scene ended with a rather facile line of Browning justifying himself: *"No one here is evil; all we're trying to do is end the war. Why do you want to spoil the party?"* By filming, the line had been improved to: *"Sixteen consecutive drops have been cancelled in the past few months for one reason or another. And this time the party's on and no one is going to stop it."* It's much more businesslike and to the point, devoid of philosophical musings that Browning, with just days to go until the attack, is unlikely to have indulged in.

The final Fuller scene finds him alone in the leafy grounds of Huize De Voorst, which doubled for the Airborne HQ at Moor Park. It is dusk as Grimes plays the shuddering nervous breakdown that Fuller appears to be suffering. Dickie's stalwart brother-in-law, Gerald Sim, makes a small but effective cameo as an Army doctor called Sims.

Sim nicely balances the pastoral care of a medical man with the more strident demands of the military, where one man's mental health is of little concern. Fuller's plea *"not to be left behind"* is brushed with a cold and evasive, *"Out of my hands, laddie."* As they disappear into the dusk shadows, we hear Fuller echoing Browning's irony-soaked words, *"I didn't want to miss the party."*

Forty-five years later, Grimes' memory of his time on the film was hazy. "I was only on that epic for three days. The last evening, I accompanied Bogarde to watch the rushes of Redford unloading the boats from lorries (filmed the previous Sunday). There was such a lot of shouting from Dickie off camera directing Redford to exhort his troops that Dirk slowly turned to me and slowly raised an eyebrow."[561]

With a return to Twickenham Studios for some final pickup shots, *A Bridge Too Far* was in the can. Unlike its subject, the schedule had lost just one day over more than four months. John Sandilands for the *Observer* caught up with Dickie in the last few days of production. "I am completely whacked," explained the director, who much preferred to be working than at leisure. "I have, I suppose, an excess of energy, but I have had to pace myself very carefully to get to the end of this picture. I can't believe that we're right on schedule and under budget. But principally, I'm tired."[562] Finally arriving home in London, Sir Richard Attenborough took to his bed and slept four days straight, waking only for meals.

With his $26 million production now wrapped, Joe E. Levine was on course to make a 15 June 1977 premiere.

20

"Oh, All Right for Me, Darling, That Is Perfect"
Post-Production

While Dickie recovered from his gruelling six months' exertions, the sum total of all that work was being painstakingly assessed. Approximately 400,000 feet of film had been exposed, with around 300,000 printed up as rushes or dailies for editing (74/55 hours respectively)—not excessive considering the scale of the production. A similar-sized epic, *Waterloo*, made in 1969, exposed about 350,000 feet, while Stanley Kubrick's *The Shining* (1980) consumed over 1.5 million.

Every day during production, the camera negative was flown to Technicolor's lab near London for processing and creation of a positive print, known as rushes or dailies, which would be shipped back to Deventer. There, in a makeshift cutting room, assistants laboriously synced up the soundtrack using the clapperboard as marker. Then in a little cinema in the factory at Olafstraat, Dickie and his team viewed the rushes and made notes for editor Antony Gibbs to begin piecing it all together.

Gibbs had earned a reputation for innovative and daring work with the British New Wave of the 1960s. He had served as apprentice to leading editors Ralph Kemplen and Alan Osbiston in the mid-1950s at a time of uncertainty driven by dwindling box office and the new threat of TV. Gibbs, like Peter MacDonald, got his foot in the door on various drama series being produced for ITV, Britain's first commercial channel. But it was the seismic social changes following the country's retreat from Empire and exacerbated by the humiliation of Suez that ushered in less deferential, angry voices. Coupled with the exciting developments in French cinema with the *Nouvelle Vague*, filmmakers like Karel Reisz and Lindsay Anderson brought forth an exciting, if brief, movement in British cinema.

Another leading light was Tony Richardson. Despite making several so-called, "kitchen sink" dramas, such as *A Taste of Honey* (1961), he soon let loose his natural romantic dynamism and took an eighteenth-century literary classic and gave it a modern twist with verve and spirit. *Tom Jones* (1963) was a sensation, both commercially and critically. Its editing by Antony Gibbs lifted what could have been a staid period piece into a contemporary satire, while retaining its milieu. Not all appreciated Richardson's innovative approach as executed by Gibbs. Writing in 2006, Charles Taylor commented: "Richardson's style changed abruptly with 1963's *Tom Jones*. He employed a commercialized version of French New Wave techniques, and the film was hugely popular, winning the Academy Award for Best Picture. But the jump-cutting, the straight-to-camera digressions and the generally antic tone were wildly inappropriate for an adaptation of an 18th-century novel, and the movie has by now dated to the point of being a curio."[563]

Gibbs would work with Richardson on *The Loved One* (1965) and display similar creativity for Richard Lester on *The Knack . . . and How to Get It* (1965), which cemented his reputation as a dynamic and innovative cutter. Gibbs has been cited as one of the inspirational figures behind America's New Wave of the late 1960s. Dede Allen, who was considered one of Hollywood's greatest editors, said of Gibbs: "There was a definite evolution in filmic style, and it came from England. The "angry young men" films that Tony Gibbs cut, *The Loneliness of the Long-Distance Runner* (1962), had a more direct influence on me than anything. I loved the way those pictures were cut. It was incorporated into pictures cut in New York like *Bonnie and Clyde*."[564] Dede Allen's seminal work on Arthur Penn's gangster classic is recognised as inaugurating arguably the most exciting decade of American cinema. If *Tom Jones* was instrumental in bringing unprecedented Hollywood investment into the British industry, one film at the fag end of the decade called "time."

Performance (1970), starring Mick Jagger and James Fox, related a kaleidoscopic trip set in a single West London house. Directed by Nick Roeg and Donald Cammel, the juxtaposition of imagery is extraordinarily daring even half a century later. Gibbs' editorial approach is about as experimental and creative as any commercially released movie of the time—and a world away from *Bridge*.

Moving to California in the early '70s, Gibbs integrated into the Hollywood machine and tempered his virtuosity. He formed a lasting creative partnership with Norman Jewison for the musical *Fiddler on the Roof* (1972). Despite several BAFTA nominations, Gibbs never received recognition by the Academy. He liked to describe himself as "an actor's editor" and laid great emphasis on prioritising snatches of performance: "Bits that maybe other directors and editors ... [would consider] ... the wrong size of shot ... you can never look at any of my movies and say, 'Yes, well, he's cut this in the classical manner, and it's graceful, and we're moving to the right size of shot,' because I don't do that, I'm looking for the acting all the time."[565]

Gibbs moved back to England in preparation for *Bridge* and the task of assembling footage through the long filming months as per the script. It's probable his "editor's cut" would have run to over three-and-a-half hours. Eventually, when Dickie returned, a consensus was reached about how to shape the final cut. The immovable issues to be grappled with: 1) achieving a final running time below three hours, and 2) seeing that none of the (expensive) famous fourteen were eliminated. At the same time, the pace and rhythm needed to be maintained and the story had to flow coherently.

At first sight, the work of Antony Gibbs on *Bridge* is in the classical manner, which reflects the way it was filmed. Camera operator Peter MacDonald, who framed most of the shots, makes full use of the wide Panavision image. Many scenes play in medium long shot where you see characters grouped. This ensures the audience is mindful of the spatial relationship between actors. Gibbs' cutting style reflects this with only judicious use of closeups for emphasis. An example is the early scene in the signal room where Steele and Cole discuss potential problems with the radios. Goldman adds a human touch with Steele asking the whereabouts of his biscuits. The action plays in one wide shot. This neutrality reflects the apparent mundanity. Only at the very end, where Steele pops a biscuit into his mouth, do we cut to a closeup, as he says, *"If anyone rocks the boat, it won't be me."* More recent filmmakers would be tempted to intercut closeups in the misguided assumption that close shots make a scene more dramatic. Understanding how to underscore drama is the key to great editing.

The art to action-scene cutting is to never confuse the audience, while still maintaining the excitement and tension. More recent films employ rapid and frenetic editing, which often draws attention to itself. Gibbs, in contrast, always maintains screen direction, reflecting the rigorous adherence of the camera team. Simply put, if a character aims and fires looking screen left to right, the target must travel right to left. Breaking this rule is known as "crossing the line." Take almost any random movie scene or TV chat show, and you will notice how people will always face each other when intercut. Cutting to a front-on shot that re-establishes the spatial arrangement is a useful way of re-aligning the "line." The numerous action scenes, despite their apparent chaos, are all cut to these classic precepts.

It is remarkable how closely the visuals in the finished film resemble the writing in the screenplay. While many scenes have tiny deletions or line changes, very few have been deleted entirely. Much of the second-unit work showing elements of the U.S. 82nd pushing through to the Waalbrug had been cut from the film, and an entire earlier sequence showing the U.S. 101st taking the Grave bridge almost unopposed was also lost. In narrative terms, the importance of its capture is effectively and simply sold by the radio operator (played by

Ray Jewers), who exclaims ecstatically to Colonel Stout that they have taken it *"completely intact."* Although the action showed unqualified success, it was nullified by the destruction of the Son bridge. Another deletion is a series of Greek chorus-like scenes of two logistics officers, one American and one British, who discuss some of the mounting issues for the forthcoming operation. It's easy to see why these dropped away—such cuts would result after some horse trading as Dickie and Gibbs strove to get the final cut to 176 minutes.

Sadly, none of these outtakes have ever resurfaced—with one exception. In 1978 the BBC began transmitting one of the great drama series of the '70s. *Secret Army* told the story of Belgian Resistance fighters sending shot-down RAF fliers along escape routes back to safety. Over three seasons, it would recruit many faces from *Bridge*, including Christopher Good, Paul Copley, Jack McKenzie, and Sebastian Abineri. Arnhem was featured in one episode of the final season. Director Andrew Morgan didn't want to use stock footage and chanced his arm by writing a sob-story letter to Dickie. He explained that this episode was his "first ever job as a freelance and asked if he'd be prepared to give me some off cuts that he hadn't wanted for the film. [Dickie] was very sweet and said, 'Go and see my editor at Pinewood,' and I went down and chose some fantastic footage.' I was charged £100 for charity!"[566] The episode, called "Bridgehead," includes the only ever seen deleted footage from *Bridge*.

The final cut of *A Bridge Too Far* does, however, have one major addition not in the shooting script. The problem of how to contextualise a historical film has always been a headache for filmmakers. While some audience members may know their history, most do not. The makers of *Battle of Britain* and *The Longest Day* were confident these seismic events of the recent past needed no introduction, and duly launched unadorned into their respective stories. Perhaps mindful of the American audience, it was felt *Bridge* needed an introduction. Rather than use a male voice-of-God delivering a history lecture, we instead hear a female voice, later revealed to be a victim of war. What follows is one of the most moving openings of any war film.

A square image with grainy archival film of shell bursts opens in the centre of the wide Panavision frame. It is followed by a shot of three bombers, each dropping a load of bombs. The picture freezes and a woman's voice continues: *"It's hard to remember now, but Europe was like this in 1944."* The film resumes, and the dark blobs of high explosive continue their fall until they carve up the ground in a series of immense blasts.

A beautifully taut, fact-laden summary follows: *"The Second World War was in its fifth year and still going Hitler's way. German troops controlled most of Europe. D-Day changed all that."* Although the Russian advance from the east had turned the tide against Hitler, the woman, later revealed to be to Kate ter Horst, played by Liv Ullmann, is living under the yoke of occupation. She is an ordinary housewife—one of us—and articulates the military strategy in layman's terms. Over a series of fast-cut newsreel footage, she describes the supply problem that was hampering the Allied advance and the personality clash between Montgomery and Patton. *"Each wanted to beat the other to Berlin."* She then details the *"new and spectacular plan given the code name Market Garden."* As the grainy image of the allied supreme commander, General Eisenhower, freezes and zooms into his face, this masterpiece of exposition ends with the sentiment that will prevail throughout the film, *"The plan, like so many plans in so many wars before it, was meant to end the fighting by Christmas and bring the boys back home."* At this point, the music which has been slowly building reaches a crescendo with the immensely catchy "A Bridge Too Far March."

"I think "The March," which is the most conspicuous piece of music in the film, is probably overused," said Edward Seckerson, former member of the A.P.A. and now a leading classical music critic and broadcaster on BBC Radio 3. He is one of many who are ambivalent about the film's music. "It was a catchy tune, but to me, it slightly trivialised the whole thing, and became a bit more of a standard movie. When there was no music, and most of the battle sequences had no music in them at all, it was much more effective. But I admire John Addison hugely."[567]

"Jock" Addison's score would be the most personal of his lengthy career as a film composer. Born in Surrey in 1920, he displayed a musical gift from an early age. After attending the Royal College of Music in London, he intended to make "serious" music and would later score a ballet, *Carte Blanche*. War service interrupted his studies. He joined the newly formed 23rd Hussars, a tank regiment driving Shermans, which formed part of the 11th Armoured Division. He landed in Normandy just after D-Day and his regiment quickly became embroiled in the vicious fighting around Caen where Montgomery's British and Canadian troops struggled to capture the ancient capital of Normandy against stiff German resistance.

During the fighting, Addison was wounded when a German shell hit his Sherman. Addison managed to save one of his comrades but was forced to look on hopelessly as his driver and wireless operator were consumed by flames. He rejoined his regiment in September and operated on the flank of XXX Corps during its drive towards Arnhem.

During his military service he befriended Roy Boulting, one half of a sibling partnership that would become a leading player in the post-war British film industry. Upon demobilization, he continued his studies at the RCM while doing brief film stints for the Boulting brothers. An early assignment was a jazz orchestration for *The Guinea Pig* (1948), which featured a fledgling Dickie performance. Boulting, who had faith in his friend's ability, asked him to score *Seven Days to Noon* (1950). "This was a daring gesture on his part because I'd never written a film score before. I had not been especially interested in the cinema, but as soon as I started writing for films, I became fascinated by it."

His talent was soon recognised, and he became a much sought-after film composer in the indigenous film industry: including *The Man Between* (1953), *Reach for the Sky* (1956), and *I Was Monty's Double*

(1958). In 1966 Alfred Hitchcock turned to Addison with short notice to score *Torn Curtain*, after he and his longtime collaborator, Bernard Herrmann, fell out in acrimonious circumstances. Addison thrived on the often-short deadlines producers imposed. "The time limitations do at least get the adrenalin going," said Addison, "and in fact in my concert music, I've always enjoyed commissions rather than just sitting down and writing something for myself, so that I've always responded to having stimulation of that kind. But obviously, the more time you get, the better; and you might be amazed to hear that I actually had three months to write the score of *Tom Jones*."

Like Antony Gibbs, his creative partnership with Tony Richardson would be the hallmark of his career. The light and breezy score Addison created for their 1964 Oscar winner (Addison received the Best Music Oscar) was in contrast to the ironic and moody *The Charge of the Light Brigade* (1968). Addison produced a score that adds atmospheric depth to the biting satire of monstrous ego and incompetence that threw 600 men down the Valley of Death. His music helped to counteract the seemingly glacial characters caught in pre-Raphaelite hues. He would be Oscar nominated for the superb Olivier/Caine two-hander *Sleuth* and again for *Bridge*.

It was in early 1977, while recording the score for Richardson's *Joseph Andrews*, that Addison was approached to score *Bridge*, although Dickie "had some doubts as to whether he needed any music," said Addison, "because it had such a powerful effect on everybody who had seen it. He felt that conventional film music might diminish the documentary quality of the film." Addison suggested he be allowed to view the current cut of the film, and said afterward, "When I saw it in New York, I was enormously moved by the picture that I could not speak. But I did think that a contribution could be made by music."[568] Watching the film brought back vivid memories of the vulnerability he felt while driving his tank across the "bog-lined roads in Holland with no way of avoiding the anti-tank guns . . . I think some of my feelings affected the score."[569]

He and Dickie got to work in earnest. "I spent several days just running the picture on my own, making notes, and then we got down to the 'spotting,' which is the process of deciding exactly where to put the music," said Addison. "I knew that Dickie did not want music during the battle scenes, and that I should be concerned more with the characters in the film, using music very sparingly."[570]

When Dickie returned to England for "looping" the myriad of voices that needed to be re-recorded, Addison set to work at the MGM studios in Hollywood: "I did some research into military music. But in the end, I decided not to use regimental marches, but create all the music myself." Despite the short time scale, Addison was delayed by having to wait for a dupe of the film, a black-and-white 35-mm slash print copied from Gibbs' cutting copy at Twickenham studios. "More-over, alterations were still being made to the picture," said Addison. "So, I started thinking of themes while waiting for my dupe. When I'd done all the work I could do, the film still hadn't arrived, so I went skiing for three days." Eventually, the print arrived, and he was able to start "work in earnest." He said, "When you finally get down to com-posing the score, certain things happen which you're not completely in control of: the inspiration that comes from the subconscious. I believe that what I wrote was affected by my battle experiences and my strong emotional reaction to the film."[571]

In March 1977, barely two weeks before recording was due to begin, Dickie and Levine travelled to Addison's Los Angeles home, where Dickie said they "listened to him playing the score on his piano for the first time, [and] we were both on the verge of tears. He had, indeed, written some truly wonderful music."[572] The composer was re-lieved: "It would have been worrisome if there'd been any big problems at that late stage," said Addison. "Fortunately, Dickie was very pleased with what I'd done, and I think there were only three things in our discussions that involved changes, luckily. There was time to rewrite before the recording session."[573]

Addison composed just shy of 40 minutes of music. For the sound, he used a small military band rather than an orchestra with 60–70 players—then the standard for film scores. The score was recorded over two weeks in April 1977 at the Music Centre in Wembley, and CTS Senior Engineer John Richards ensured that the "sessions ran smoothly with a focused energy and respectful rapport between Addison, the musicians, and the engineer."

In 2020 Chris Malone produced a reissue of the soundtrack. Sifting through the eight rolls of two-inch 24-track Dolby-A encoded tapes in the MGM vaults, he noted that the rejected takes, "were slightly more strident and expressive than the versions that wound up in the film, indicating the filmmakers were after a more low-key score."[574]

"The job of a film composer is often far more complex than I think most people, and even in many cases most filmmakers, realize," said Jon Burlingame, a leading film music expert and regular contributor to *Daily Variety*. Burlingame has written several books and teaches the history of film music at the University of Southern California. A confessed fan of Addison, he considers the score for *Bridge* as one of the composer's best. Music for *A Bridge Too Far* comprises three main themes, from which Addison derives variations. The first is the main theme: "It symbolizes the spirit of the land forces," Burlingame explained, "a spirited lively march played at various tempos throughout the picture, sometimes slow, sometimes stately, sometimes very obviously martial heard at moments of triumph, such as the completion of the Bailey bridge."

The second is the "March of the Paratroopers," which we hear during Frost's seemingly triumphant advance as the soldiers are welcomed by the Dutch people. It is a suitably stirring anthem, very upbeat and optimistic. As the operation lurches towards disaster, Addison adapts the tone using his signature woodwind instruments to create a sense of foreboding.

The final theme is the mournful "Dutch Rhapsody." "This symbolizes what Attenborough later called the tragic stoicism of the

Dutch people," Burlingame explained. "It's one of Addison's most heart-breaking melodies, often voiced by woodwinds and strings. It's heard to best advantage late in the picture for scenes of the devastated Arnhem, particularly the death of the teenage boy that we've come to know."[575] While the catchy title theme often steals the attention, this deeply moving dirge is the heart of the score, acting as a powerful counterpoint to the jaunty air of the march.

Ever since that first tearful screening with Dickie, Addison had an immediate affinity with the project. "Sometimes the work is what you want with all your being and this, for me, is one of those," he said. "If I can't write something wonderful for this film, then I should give up." Dickie, who had known Addison for 30 years, believed the music was deeply imbued by the composer's harrowing wartime experience as a tank officer. "The music is, in one sense, his requiem for those who fought beside him," said Dickie.[576]

In turn, Addison believed the film encapsulated Dickie's sensibility and attitude to war. "One of the final images left on the screen is of a small child marching along proudly with his toy rifle over his shoulder—to the sounds of the once cheerful march," said Addison. "This, perhaps, is Richard Attenborough's last comment."[577]

During that summer of '76 in a nondescript warehouse in California, a group of young men and women were attempting to marry cutting-edge computers with 80-year-old film technology. Under the company name Industrial Light and Magic, their efforts on a sci-fi film set in a "galaxy far, far away" would change popular cinema forever and propel special effects from the backroom into a multimillion-dollar industry.

"Special effects is really a first-aid department,"[578] said Wally Veevers, commenting on the relatively low regard (and underinvestment) in which his craft was held until the late 1970s. With a career stretching back 40 years to the landmark *Thing to Come* (1936) and Vincent Korda's *Thief of Bagdad* (1941), Veevers along with a small select group of other FX specialists spent decades honing technology little changed since the dawn of cinema. The main techniques were matte paintings and the versatile, if complex, travelling matte process that involved shooting actors against a blue background into which another image could be placed. Using an optical printer, essentially a projector aimed at a camera, matte work was an exhaustive process requiring precision, skill, and inordinate patience.

Veevers and his contemporaries had perfected endless variations and combinations of these techniques. For almost five years in the mid-'60s, they had been pushed to their limit by Stanley Kubrick on *2001*, which, despite the extraordinary technical leap forward, did not spark a taste for visual-effect films. Veevers, a master of the optical printer, continued to apply subtle enhancements to many films. For *Battle of Britain*, which spectacularly used real aircraft, he multiplied some of the aerial shots to create an armada of warring planes. For other shots, he simply glued stills of aircraft to several sheets of glass. Through stop motion, synchronised Selsyn motors operated from a central controller moved each layer on its own prescribed axis, a technique that lent a realistic feeling of depth and perspective. The layers were then superimposed over location footage in what were known as "Wally's 'sausage factory' shots." To enhance the realism, he added some camera movement. This technique was used for several aerial shots in *Bridge* showing the Horsa gliders being towed behind Dakotas.

Clutching storyboards, Veevers went on location for the parachute jump. He ensured that ground cameras would take suitable long shots of Dakotas in formation. They would be multiplied and combined with the only British location-filmed scenes to show the immensity of Market Garden: a street scene filmed at Francis Street, Reading, at an unidentifiable church, and in Holland at the Burgers E.N.R, a derelict old bicycle factory in Deventer that doubled as Horrocks' command post. Then a monochrome painting was created that blacked out the foreground. From this were derived "male" and "female" mattes that, via an optical printer, allowed the Dakotas to be added into the clear sky.

285

For the mass takeoff scene filmed at Deelen, artist Doug Ferris did some matte paintings in the top part of the frame of the waiting Dakotas and gliders. These are virtually undetectable unless you pause it on home video. They beautifully demonstrate why this most venerable of cinematic tricks is still used even in the modern digital realm.[579] Another almost undetectable painting by Ferris, consisting of the top end of Nijmegen bridge, appears in the long shot of Cook berating the slowness of XXX Corps to advance. Some A.P.A. members are seen "brewing up" tea while just the bridge span is visible in the background. It emphasises they are just on the outskirts of Nijmegen.[580]

Following *Bridge*, Veevers would lend his expertise to the team of effects masters who would "make you believe a man could fly" for *Superman*. This film, coupled with the enormous success of *Star Wars*, helped push film optical effects to their zenith over the next decade.

Once the final cut had been approved, a team of sound editors led by Les Wiggins and Peter Horrocks spent many busy weeks "laying" the sound effects. This involved re-recording hundreds of different guns firing, explosions, vehicles moving, cries and shouts, etc. Eventually, Gerry Humphreys and his dubbing team at Twickenham studios would carefully balance these thousands of individual sounds. Becoming head of the sound department in 1969, Humphreys would garner more than 250 film and TV credits and receive nominations for five BAFTAs, winning twice, for *Bridge* and for *Cry Freedom* (1987).

This acknowledgment of Humphreys' work with Dickie underscored a close and highly creative partnership. "If I could only dub for one person ever, it would be Dickie Attenborough," Humphreys explained after his retirement in 1995. "He is fantastic. He gives you time, total freedom, and guidance ... He might not always accept your ideas—it would be terrible to think that he did always accept them— but he will listen and give an objective view of why on this occasion."

Humphreys noted Dickie's canny people management skills to get the best out of everybody. He recalled one incident when they were working past 10 at night after weeks of similar hours. "I was used to that and so I thought, *why am I tired?* I am never tired at the end of dubs," said Humphreys. "It is meat and drink." Having finished work on a reel (around 10 minutes), they wound it back to the beginning and sat through it as one run without stopping and starting. When it was finished and the lights went on, "Dickie was sitting behind me, and I said, 'All right for you?'" recalled Humphreys. "'Oh, all right for me darling, that is perfect for me. If it is all right for you, it is all right for me.' So now you think, *Oy yoy yoy*. Because there is a slight imperfection that only you have heard because you know you didn't do your hand movement just the way you wanted something, and you would take that secret to your grave if you never said. No one else even knows it is there. It is only you that has got it and if it goes through, it certainly ain't going to spoil the soundtrack. But now he throws the responsibility back onto you. So, I say, 'I think I would just like to go again.' That then became the norm. So, you get someone who cares and has got the ideas but will also listen; they are up there on a pedestal."[581]

Few people in 1977 heard Humphreys' soundtrack at its optimal best. During the 1950s and '60s, many epics and musicals were mixed into multi-track stereo for playback in select urban roadshow venues. Often using high-definition 70-mm prints, these presentations are still fondly remembered decades later. It was pure showmanship. But after a series of expensive failures in the late 1960s, the roadshow concept withered. Although *Bridge* was mixed into stereo, it would have been heard in only a handful of city cinemas playing the expensive magnetic-stripped, 6-track 70-mm or 4-track 35-mm prints. The vast majority of venues played standard mono sound 35 mm. It was this technology, barely advanced since 1930, that Dolby Labs would enhance to change movie audio forever with its famous stereo process.[582]

With just a few weeks to go before the film opened, Dickie engaged in a spot of subterfuge. The trap was laid in Antony Gibbs' cutting room at Twickenham. While Gibbs busied himself on his

287

green-painted, wrought-iron Moviola editing machine, next to him was a tall, lithe man dressed in a white coat. Eamonn Andrews was one of the most recognised faces on UK TV in the 1970s. He hosted the top-rated ITV show, *This Is Your Life*, a weekly cavalcade of celebrities, both great and small, who would be reunited with old friends and family, sometimes long lost—a simple but heart-warming format for a more innocent age.

Speaking in his familiar lilting, mid-Atlantic drawl, Andrews explained where he was, and that in a few moments "Sir Richard Attenborough, who's just made the film about that wartime airborne assault, is going to help us meet a legendary hero of that battle . . . I'm temporarily assistant to the real editor, Tony Gibbs here, who has also given us permission to insert an extra special scene into what's going to be watched on the Moviola. Our man hasn't got the faintest idea what's gonna come up there."

After turning his back and pretending to reel some film, Dickie appeared with General Frost, who seemed completely unperturbed by the gathered TV crew. Gibbs switched on the Moviola and up comes the Gräbner attack on the bridge. Just as the German half-track erupts in flames, Andrews appears: "General, just a moment. I know you couldn't possibly expect to see me here. We have met once before. But I want to meet you again tonight for a very special reason. Just turn around and look behind you." Back in the cutting room, Frost turns to see Andrews with the famous thick red book in his hands. "Major General John Frost, MC, DSO and Bar, hero of Arnhem and many battles besides, tonight, THIS IS YOUR LIFE." The general, just caught in an ambush, maintains a calm, bemused expression.

As members of his family, many former comrades, and even a one-time German adversary and now friend, appear on parade, Frost allows only a flicker of emotion, but his reticence cannot hide his genuine pleasure. Dickie gives a warm tribute, followed by a video message from Anthony Hopkins regaling his favourite running story. One touching moment has Frost's 24-year-old daughter, Caroline, a "beautiful youngster who's grown up to be a fashionable model," admit she did not know of her father's exploits. "I didn't really appreciate the full extent until I was about 17 or so. But you really have done a lot for all of us. And I think it's tremendous, and you're not bad as a dad either."

The show ends with the reunion of a special old comrade whom Frost last saw amid the ruins around Arnhem bridge. "But for 33 years," Andrews explained, "you've never given up the search to find him, even taking out newspaper advertisements, asking for information. Well, John, we found him for you. And he's here, ex-Private Denis Wicks."[583] Played by Paul Copley in the film, Wicks was his batman. Although divided by rank and class, theirs was a close relationship bound by respect and comradeship.

As the TV credits rolled, Dickie, who used all his cunning and guile to get the show made, must have hoped he would have the veterans of Arnhem on his side. But even before the premiere, there was an unmistakable sound of heavy artillery trained squarely on *A Bridge Too Far*.

21

"But What Do You Think?"
Release and Reception

As Joe E. Levine had promised two years before, *A Bridge Too Far* opened on 15 June 1977 in 448 North American cinemas. Princess Anne attended its Washington premiere to keep up the British end. Within two weeks, it had grossed over $5 million.[584] Citing its educational value, United Artists chairman Arthur B. Krim had secured the all-important "PG" rating to maximise audiences, surmounting two issues facing Motion Picture Association of America's (MPAA) rating appeals board: they felt that some of the war scenes were "too gory," and were adamant that Elliott Gould's raw line, *"Roll the fuckers!"* warranted an automatic "R" rating, which Krim argued would have "inhibited children's attendance."

Epics had long been an easy target for critics, and few took more potshots at *Bridge* than Roger Ebert in the *Chicago Sun Times*. Ebert condemned "such an exercise in wretched excess, such a mindless series of routine scenes, such a boringly violent indulgence in all the blood and guts and moans they could find, that by the end we're prepared to speculate that maybe Levine went two or even three bridges too far." He found little to celebrate except for Fox's Horrocks, who had "I was going to say 'best,' but make that 'only good' scene." Despite its stars and expense, Ebert stated, "It's the longest B-grade war movie ever made."[585]

Praise came from Cary Arnold in the *Washington Post* for what he found an "unusually conscientious and impressive war epic . . . When it falls short, it does so without insulting your intelligence or losing your respect." While noting "Levine's gambit," with its roster of expensive stars, Arnold considered Robert Redford "has paid better dividends on the screen than one might have expected." Arnold was less impressed with Ryan O'Neal and Liv Ullmann, who "are the only downright unsatisfactory performers," but he praised Anthony Hopkins, "whose customary neurotic creepiness has totally vanished in the role of Frost." Arnold reserved his highest praise for Edward Fox's turn as Horrocks: "This is the kind of rousing, delightful performance that seems to jump off the screen without jumping out of character . . . you feel ready to follow this particular man to the ends of the earth." While applauding *Bridge* as "an unqualified pictorial achievement," Arnold felt its episodes "don't quite add up to a movie with a unified, powerful vision . . . One may feel limitations on the dramatic side."[586]

Charles Champlin of the *Los Angeles Times* found *A Bridge Too Far* a worthy endeavour: "It is spectacular in the size and range of its effects, earnestly well-acted by a starry and able cast, well-paced and swift despite its length, and marked by an evident attempt to give the balanced truth of a tragic episode from history."[587]

While most applauded the physicality of the production, its running time and "bigness" were considered its fundamental flaws. Vincent Canby of *The New York Times* summed it up: "The movie is massive, shapeless, often unexpectedly moving, confusing, sad, vivid and very, very long."[588]

William Goldman was not prepared for the tenure of some reviews. "I've never been involved in a project where authenticity was more sought after and achieved," said Goldman. "And in the end, as far as many American critics were concerned, that may have proved our undoing. We were too real to be real . . ."[589]

For the European premiere, Levine wanted the city that had hosted his mammoth production—Deventer. The only suitable venue was the tired old cinema on the Brink called the Luxor. Opened in 1918, it could seat barely 250 people. The council wanted to refurbish it—and Joe Levine to pay for it. Having sunk literally millions of dollars into the city, the producer felt the request aped his film title—and declined. But determined to honour the country that had not only borne Montgomery's 90 percent success, but also welcomed his own massive enterprise, Levine chose Amsterdam instead.

On 23 June 1977, the film premiered at Amsterdam's City Theatre in the presence of Queen Juliana, Prince Bernhard, and the Royal Family. A Royal Charity Performance followed the next day at London's Leicester Square Theatre in the presence of HRH, the Duchess of Kent and Earl Mountbatten of Burma. During its run in the capital, it played at the then-biggest screen venue on the continent, Odeon Marble Arch, which boasted an immense 75-foot Dimension-150 screen. Martyn Butler served on the projection team that handled the only 70-mm print of the film in the UK. "When you spend years handling 35 mm, when you get a 70-mm print, it feels like you are trying to lace up wallpaper," said Butler. "We gave it the full roadshow treatment. We even chose a track from the original soundtrack recording to use as an overture (play-in music), tabs open to masking set for the black and white sequence. When the film cuts to colour—hit masking to awesome! We got the opportunity to make *ABTF* shine."[590]

The British critics were more favourable, but almost all echoed their American cousins with whines about the length—and those $9 million faces. "By the end of this extravagant film," wrote John Pym in the *Monthly Film Bulletin*, "we have a fair idea of the who-did-what logistics of a costly military operation. The root problem, however, is that the top-heavy complement of stars never allows for any focus of attention."[591]

But a vociferous section of the press had focused their attention on one of those faces, with a public storm in a teacup resulting. Patrick Gibbs of the *Daily Telegraph* lit the fuse by suggesting if General Browning were alive, "what is shown of him appears to be actionable."

Gibbs said of Bogarde's portrayal: "This general is not one I would have trusted to run a cocktail party."[592] The following day in the *Times*, the outspoken General Sir John Hackett, who had commanded an airborne brigade at Arnhem, was incensed by the portrayal of a man he knew well. "It is untruthful," stated Hackett, "because it shows a superficial, heartless, shallow person who is uncaring—even almost flippant—about the fate of brave men committed to his charge and displays, instead of strength of character, a petulant obstinacy born of weakness. He was not like that at all and could not have commanded such widespread loyalty if he had been."[593]

For the next two weeks, the *Times* Letters column was ablaze with the debate. Another veteran, Colonel Frederick Gough, who had assumed command at Arnhem bridge after Frost was wounded, weighed in with the familiar brickbat for historical movies. He questioned why the filmmakers had "assumed a right to trample on people's feelings and to play ducks and drakes with historical facts in order to dish up an extravaganza fit for the American massed cinema market."[594] It was a powder keg that had been laid even before the film had been conceived.

General "Boy" Browning never escaped some culpability for Arnhem. Retired three-star Dutch Major General Mart de Kruif, who commanded over 40,000 troops in Afghanistan, issued a scathing opinion of Browning: "He was not only ultimately responsible for the planning (wrong landing terrains, structural underestimation of the enemy, denial of intelligence indicating the presence of German units around Arnhem), but also tried to pass on the failure of the operation to Sosabowski. In short: (unfortunately) failing leadership."[595]

After Browning's death in 1965, his family became staunch defenders of his reputation. His wife, the famous novelist Daphne Du Maurier, knowing the power of words, displayed particular sensitivity. Cornelius Ryan's UK researcher had been given short shrift when he approached the famous writer asking to see her husband's wartime papers. She maintained that not only didn't she have any, but her husband had spoken little about the battle, except for a deep regret for the loss of life.

Upon the book's publication, she approved of her husband as described by Ryan having "the appearance of a restless hawk."[596] But she was apprehensive about the forthcoming film version, a mistrust born out of some Hollywood adaptations of her own works. Writing to Dickie, she asked to see a copy of the script, a request he readily granted, assuring her that due respect would be paid to all real-life characters.

In the spring of 1976, she received the draft screenplay and immediately took issue with the presentation of her "Moper" as a "dandy who shrank from dirty work," but more damning, she felt he was made "the fall guy of the whole Arnhem disaster . . . came out of it with no credit at all."[597] She highlighted several issues, including the veracity of the aerial reconnaissance photographs scene. But it was the most famous line that formed the title of both book and film that raised her hackles. She insisted that as it was spoken before the operation, that a scene should be created showing Browning airing his misgivings to Montgomery. Dickie, now busy amid filming, promised to address her concerns.

Dirk Bogarde prepared for his role blissfully unaware of the ticking time bomb. Interviewed on set by Iain Johnstone, the actor admitted he didn't look like Browning. With a condescending air, Bogarde said that as this was merely a "movie," he was not required to get himself into "the man's intelligence." Having seen Browning from afar during the war, he considered him popular with his men, and "very, very English. He might have been called effete by the Americans."[598] This word, which the actor doubted the Yankees would understand, meant a certain sense of style. The actor wore a perfect replica of Browning's specially designed uniform, perhaps the very epitome of the word.

Du Maurier considered her late husband "an elegant and fastidious man." In a private letter she vented her unhappiness at Bogarde's casting as she feared he would depict her husband as "effete and mincing," adding, "I saw him in *The Servant*, and he was a homo in that. Whatever Moper was, he certainly wasn't a homo!"[599] While there is no evidence she expressed these thoughts publicly, the insinuation would percolate through much of the reaction to Bogarde's casting.

Since becoming a pin-up star, Bogarde had been circumspect about his private life and only later admitted he had been in a long-term relationship with his manager, Tony Forwood. Yet, as du Maurier's letter showed, it was an open secret. His appearance in Basil Dearden's *Victim* (1960) was acclaimed for its daring, partly by putting his career and reputation as a romantic lead on the line. The story of a married man whose secret gay life proves a tempting target for blackmail helped to highlight what was increasingly seen as an unacceptable persecution in British society.

One of Bogarde's biographers has suggested that "war films, no matter how well-intentioned, have the basic problem of having to revel in what they are supposedly criticising. Any accusation of 'femininity,' as the furore around Bogarde's portrayal demonstrates, is inevitable; seen as a threat to the masculine myth of militarism."[600]

Du Maurier, who refused to see "that bloody film," tried to persuade Lord Mountbatten to boycott the London premiere. Browning, or "Boy" to his friends, had been well liked by the Royals, even holding various prestigious positions in the Royal Household. Mountbatten, who had been unofficially portrayed by the equally "effete" Noël Coward in *In Which We Serve* (1942), refused her request as it was a charity event. Upon seeing the film, he could find "nothing really detrimental to Boy . . . nobody could think Boy's magnificent reputation tarnished."[601]

Mountbatten was almost a lone voice in the British establishment that continued a fevered series of letters to the *Times*. Intelligence Officer Brian Urquhart, portrayed as Fuller, joined Du Maurier in objecting to the reconnaissance photos scene, which he felt misrepresented his disquiet about the operation. In his defence, Goldman lifted almost verbatim Urquhart's own words in Ryan's book. Interestingly, those who had advised on the film, Waddy, Frost, and Roy Urquhart, chose to keep their opinions private, although the last mentioned had aired his misgivings about one scene to Iain Johnstone. This was the penultimate confrontation moment between Urquhart and Browning after the failure of First Airborne, an exchange "which couldn't have been less real," said General Urquhart. "And I can't imagine either of us using the words and expressions in the script."[602] It was this moment that most rankled the film's detractors.

The scene had been filmed during Bogarde's first day on the movie, and he wasn't in the best of moods. He smarted that Sean Connery was being paid more. "With so many layers of barely concealed animosity," said Diana Hawkins (later Dickie's co-producer), "the atmosphere on set that morning was decidedly edgy and . . . would take Dickie a very long day to shoot . . . smoothing the ruffled feathers of his tetchy stars in verdant Apeldoorn."[603] This perfectly mirrored the drama depicted.

One aspect of these scenes that no one seemed to pick up on is Browning's entry. Urquhart, who has declined the offer of a bed, props himself against the mantelpiece. Connery conveys an animal restlessness and simmering, barely suppressed anger. As Browning enters, the two exchange cold pleasantries as Browning makes immediately for his desk. What is most apparent is the lack of that most British form of etiquette—the handshake. This would have been *de rigueur* between upper-class Brits and, more importantly, friends. Considering the talent in that room, and the comparative time for rehearsals, it seems inconceivable that omitting a handshake was not a deliberate choice.

Unfortunately, it makes Browning appear, to use Bogarde's own words, a bit of a "prick." Prior to filming, Dickie had written to Bogarde with some character notes. He felt it was vital the actor conveyed that for all the general's "urbane sophistication," he cared for his men: "It will result in a man," wrote Dickie, "not only of considerable stature, but, indeed, of real flesh and blood."[604]

While no discussion of Browning's culpability seems to have taken place on the set that day, the film shows tension and thinly veiled recriminations between the characters of Browning and Urquhart. Both being thoroughly British, they elected not to say what they really felt and instead maintain a veneer of politeness. It hadn't impressed Philip French writing in the *Observer*, who found Bogarde's performance, "Twitchily neurotic . . . at his most uningratiating."[605]

The voluminous criticism stunned the actor as he relaxed in Clermont, his French property. He wrote a stinging letter to Dickie accusing him of "treachery." The nub of his anger was that Bogarde feared earning the ire of the establishment would scupper his chances of a knighthood. "You have absolutely ruined any possible recognition that I might receive nationally," wrote Bogarde to Dickie. "And I shall not forgive you for that."[606] In an attempt to assuage the critics and the friendship, Dickie told *The Sunday Times*: "In my opinion he gives a quite superb performance and if the end result, in terms of interpretation, is to some unsatisfactory, then the blame accrues to me and not to Mr. Bogarde."[607] For a while, despite being occasional neighbours, their friendship was severely dented. Regardless, Dickie continued to lobby for Bogarde's coveted knighthood, which he duly received in 1992. He died aged 78 in 1999.

And what about that line that formed the title which Du Maurier took issue with? In the script draft she read in March 1976, it had Browning explaining:

> *"I've just been on to Monty, he's terribly proud and pleased." UR-QUHART (blinks) "Pleased?" BROWNING "Of course. He feels Market Garden was 90 percent successful." URQUHART only shakes his head. BROWNING'S good face breaks into a reassuring smile. BROWNING "We just tried to go a bridge too far."*

This does imply that the thought just popped into the general's head. Dickie clearly heeded her desire to change it, and Goldman's final script draft clarifies that it was spoken before the operation. He interjects Urquhart between Browning's last two lines with him pressing: *"But what do you think?"* Browning's answer not only suggests he had previously aired his misgivings, not just to his commander, but also to his subordinate, Urquhart: *"As you know, I always thought we went a bridge too far."*

While it is doubtful Browning would have admitted to a fatally flawed plan before sending his friend into battle, the film suggests Browning harboured these doubts and had voiced them before the operation. In strict narrative terms, placing this line at the beginning would have made Browning's actions highly reprehensible.

But was this most famous of phrases that has passed into everyday speech actually said at all?

History is replete with famous phrases that have become legend. The historian Sir Antony Beevor leafed through the evidence for his 2019 book, *Arnhem*. He argued that Browning, having been given command of three airborne divisions, "was unlikely to oppose" Montgomery and his proposed use of these formations in upcoming operations and had "strenuously supported Comet, which included Arnhem." For his title, Ryan took the quote directly from General Roy Urquhart's memoir, *Arnhem*, published in 1957. It purports to have been said at the final planning meeting before the operation, which, according to Beevor, Urquhart did not attend. Furthermore, nor did Browning, and therefore it "is highly improbable"[608] the phrase was ever uttered. But back in 1977, during the angry to-ing and fro-ing, no one questioned that it had been said, not least Mrs. Browning herself.

"It was a depressing movie," William Goldman admitted. "You had to want to see it. Because this particular story was bleak and sad. You want it to find an audience, and when it doesn't, that's very sad."

The summer of 1977 was one of the industry's most competitive with 14 movies jostling for attention. *Bridge* was the most expensive followed by William Friedkin's *The Sorcerer* ($23 million), *Exorcist II: The Heretic* ($14 million), and a certain *Star Wars* ($11 million). Released by a nervous 20th Century Fox in May, George Lucas' space adventure took the North American box office by storm, eventually raking in over a half-billion dollars. Ecstatic word-of-mouth spread like wildfire and by the time *Bridge* opened in mid-June, *Star Wars* had grown into a phenomenon, in every sense a galaxy away from a "depressing" war movie. Meanwhile, *Variety* expressed concern at *Bridge*'s modest returns considering that the "length will hold down the take."[609] But with a tally of $10.3 million after nineteen days, it was holding its own, leaving *The Sorcerer* and *Exorcist II* far down the field in the flop zone.[610]

Unsurprisingly, the film fared better in Europe, partly helped by a six-month *Star Wars* hiatus. It broke house records at London's Leicester Square Theatre ($42,524) and the Odeon Marble Arch, where it ran in 70 mm ($30,318), and after four months on general release had made an impressive $750,000 in the UK. The Rank circuit reported that it was their second most popular film that year, piped to the post by 007's return in *The Spy Who Loved Me*, and held the fifth place of all UK exhibitors. In Paris it was considered to have the largest initial haul of the summer; it broke house records in Dublin, while in Thailand, it was the top foreign picture during the Christmas period.

But *Bridge* needed an exceptional haul to cover not only its negative cost, but the cinema prints (a three-hour 35-mm print cost approximately $2,500, and nearly 500 were ordered for North America alone) and advertising on top. By the '70s, it was the marketing budget that often exceeded the cost of a production, some times more than double. Chasing the distracted recreational dollar, pound, etc., required a big investment—a single prime-time 30-second TV commercial spot could cost a cool $250,000. This would have been United Artists' outlay.

By the end of its release in 1978, UA announced the film's total haul in global rentals (the amount the studio received) was $25.1 million, almost equal to the film's production budget but well short of the spend to release it. But it should be remembered that the studio was liable only for the $12 million they paid Levine for the distribution rights, plus the prints and advertising. Whatever the short fall, UA's company accounts would have been soothed by their unqualified hits that year, notably the $39 million accrued by *The Spy Who Loved Me*.

What about the man at the centre of the labyrinthine finances? According to William Goldman, the veteran producer was already in profit by "presales" before the film even opened. In a testy exchange with a journalist that it had underperformed, Levine was bullish: " 'What do you mean *A Bridge Too Far* was a flop? That (expletive deleted) film made $21 million!' He stops and stares, then he pokes the reporter with his walking stick. 'Write that down!' "[611]

Levine had held out for a massive $15 million for the film's U.S. television premiere. But after CBS balked at that figure and a readjusted $10 million, NBC drove a hard bargain for a meagre $4 million. Slugged with numerous adverts, it was screened over two nights in July 1979, but with little audience enthusiasm (the first part ranked eightieth for the year in viewing figures, with the second dropping to below a hundred). But over the pond, the UK TV premiere on ITV in September 1982, drew an impressive 12.2 million viewers, and ranked thirteenth for the week.

A re-release in 1980, plus international TV sales and eventual home video releases, would certainly have pushed the film comfortably into the black. Hitchcock once compared studio finances as akin to the mysteries of a restaurant kitchen: you never know what goes on! Dickie and Levine's relationship would sour over the question of the director's promised 10 percent profit share. The latter was cagey about the exact negative cost of $26 million, and suggested it was higher thus raising the profit bar. But what this squabble does suggest is that *A Bridge Too Far* did indeed make it into the black.

While the 1978 50th Academy Awards completely ignored the film, BAFTA saw fit to praise its immense contribution to the British Film Industry. *Bridge* earned a Best Supporting Actor award for Edward Fox; a Best Cinematography award for Geoffrey Unsworth; Best Soundtrack for Peter Horrocks, Gerry Humphreys, Simon Kaye, Robin O'Donoghue, and Les Wiggins; and the Anthony Asquith Award for John Addison's Best Original Film Music. *Bridge* received BAFTA nominations for Best Film, Direction (Attenborough), Production Design (Terence Marsh), and Editing (Antony Gibbs). Finally, the *Evening Standard British Film Awards* gave its blessing for Best Film.

William Goldman was immensely proud of the film and considered it his most positive collaborative endeavour. It was born out of one's man determination to keep a promise to a dying friend. Against the odds—the gamble had paid off. "Mr. Levine was retired. He wanted to come back. For whatever reason, he decided to come back with *A Bridge Too Far*. He spent his own money, there was no studio money behind it . . . And he was rich, but he wasn't that rich. If the movie had been a disaster, he would have been fine."

Epilogue

"It's amazing how it still resonates with people," Edward Seckerson, former A.P.A. and now a leading classical music critic, mused about *A Bridge Too Far*. Although his name is buried in the long end credits, he notes the film's aura as people discover it anew on TV. "It keeps coming back to haunt us."[612]

"It was the most wonderful experience I've had in my life," said A.P.A. member Sebastian Abineri of those six months in the heat wave of 1976. "So much so that my wife said, 'Can you stop talking about it, please, and turn it into a book.'"[613] His highly entertaining memoir, *The Boys from the Bridge*, was published in 2017 and is thoroughly recommended.

Stuart Craig, who would graduate to become one of the industry's leading production designers, noted he was part of a select band: "It was a unique experience. What was remarkable—for years after, you would bump into carpenters, plasterers, construction guys, and the people collecting the jeeps, and so on. And they would remember that one film and say, 'Wasn't that great? Do you remember when ...?'"

"If you just go back on the unit list," assistant director Roy Button suggested, "all the people on that are now talented Oscar-winning experts. Look at Stuart Craig—charming man. He's won three Oscars. You've got John Richardson. He's done the Bonds since then. His crew comprised five of the major special effects supervisors on the floor today. Others have become very famous in their own right—Peter Mac-Donald, for instance."[614]

While Dickie led from the front, MacDonald believed due credit for keeping the vast movie production going belonged to the back-room team. "There was a huge respect from the crew to the way the film was run by Eric Rattray and the production office," said MacDonald. "There was never a time when we didn't get what we needed to shoot. He's like a kind headmaster in a small school, doesn't look like a dynamic person. He's the unsung hero that ran that show. It was the experience of a lifetime filming wise, you know."

Stuart Craig wanted to credit the production's generous and patient hosts: "The movie was so ambitious, and it only got made because the Dutch were so supportive. They were amazingly cooperative and went to enormous lengths to facilitate this film. I think it was because they recognise the integrity of the director, the writer, the producers, and the whole sort of motive driving the film."

Almost no other war epic has such a definable mark of its director as *A Bridge Too Far*. "I think there's a pornography in the film," Dickie admitted. "It's a pornography of violence, the obscenity of violence, the obscenity of man's inhumanity to man, and the waste of human beings. That's what we're making a *cri de cœur* about."[615]

On 26 November 1980, Dickie's dream became a reality as filming began in India for *Gandhi*. He was reunited with some of his *Bridge* crew, notably associate producer Terence Clegg and the AD heft of David Tomblin and Steve Lanning. Famously, they herded a crowd of 300,000 for the funeral scene in New Delhi—the largest assemblage of extras in film history according to *Guinness World Records*.[616] To play the Mahatma, Dickie's son Michael suggested a young stage actor, Ben Kingsley. This inspired choice ranks as one of the most electric screen debuts ever. After six months of production at a cost of $20 million, the film opened to rave reviews and swept the board at the 1983 Oscars, winning Best Picture, Director, and Actor, plus five others.

Gandhi is a triumph and has stood the test of time. Perhaps if it has one flaw, it, like *Young Winston*, shows few negatives about the character. While Gandhi was a truly extraordinary man, one wishes his flaws (which he, like all of us, possessed) had been explored like the other great biopics, *Lawrence of Arabia* and *Patton*. But it's a testament to Kingsley's performance that he hints at the ego and vanity that must have lurked somewhere beneath the surface.

There was one prominent figure who could not bask in the film's success. "Despite his avowals, Joe Levine never shared my passion for *Gandhi*," Dickie said later. "The very qualities I so admired in the Mahatma—self-deprecation, renunciation of worldly goods, passive resistance—all ran counter to what made my maverick mogul tick."[617]

In early 1980 the pair had been on course to make the film—it would have been their third collaboration. Following *Bridge*, Levine was set to make *Magic*, written by William Goldman and to be helmed by Norman Jewison. After Jewison dropped out, Levine persuaded Dickie to step in—again dangling the *Gandhi* carrot. Casting Anthony Hopkins as a ventriloquist who goes mad, *Magic* proved to be a little movie gem—tight and tense. Dickie netted $150,000 profit share of the two films, but Levine held onto this and tried to leverage a brutal deal for which Dickie would have to forego his director's fee for *Gandhi*. Dickie walked but eventually secured the money from Indian and British sources.

Levine would make one more film, the 1981 skin flick *Tattoo*, before finally retiring. He passed away, aged 81, in 1987. He was, to quote one of his own penned press releases "a colossus, towering above lesser moguls of filmdom." His biographer A.T. McKenna neatly summed up this unique larger-than-life movie figure: "Joe was certainly not the nicest man in show business . . . He was a tough and shrewd businessman who could be fantastically generous or gratuitously brutal in his business dealings. He was more of a rascal than an ogre. A scoundrel showman, capricious and contradictory."[618]

Following *Bridge*, many of the crew moved on to *Superman*, which stills stands as the gold standard for a comic-book adaptation. Poignantly, the film opens with a sombre dedication to its cinematographer, Geoffrey Unsworth, who in 1978 had died of a heart attack in France while shooting Roman Polanski's *Tess*. His friend Peter MacDonald (who was working on another film) offered to break the news to Unsworth's wife, Maggie, a renowned script continuity crew member. "So, I drove straight to Beaconsfield at 10:30 at night," MacDonald remembered. "As Maggie opened the door, she thought something had happened to me or my family. And I'm trying to sit her down, and then the kids, in their very early teens, came down. In a way, it's like a comedy really as I can't get it out, because she's consoling me. It was the worst experience of my life. I'd worked with Geoffrey for 25 years. Not only was he my boss, he was very much like a father figure, too."[619]

In recognition of Unsworth's enormous standing in the industry, many leading figures helped out Maggie and her children, including Liza Minnelli giving $10,000, Gene Hackman $5,000, and David Lean, who paid off the mortgage on the family home. But MacDonald was bemused by Sean Connery, who was keen to know if his cheque had arrived—all 50 pounds!

Bestowed an OBE by the Queen, David Tomblin also received the Outstanding British Contribution to Cinema Award in 2003 as recognition of the universal high regard in which he was held. During the 1980s and '90s, he was the favourite AD for George Lucas' and Steven Spielberg's UK shoots. When seeking a U.S. Green Card, said Tomblin, "I had to write down every film that I had ever been on. I got to 478 and then decided that was probably enough to convince them that I had a reasonable amount of experience."[620] He passed away after a short illness at age 74 in 2005.

Dickie continued in the vein of *Gandhi* with *Cry Freedom* (1987) about the murder of South African activist Steve Biko and the crusade of a journalist who battled to tell the story. It was an impressive epic film with a standout performance by Denzel Washington. Another pet project, *Chaplin* (1992), although penned by Goldman, was ultimately unsatisfying in attempting to squeeze a very full life into a few hours, not helped by studio interference. A final collaboration with Anthony Hopkins in *Shadowlands* (1993), however, told an intimate and immensely moving doomed love story about the bookish university don and famed writer, C. S. Lewis. Dickie yearned to film the life of Thomas Paine, the Age of Enlightenment philosopher and writer of *The Rights of Man*. With an estimated budget of over $100 million, it would be an unrealised dream.

As recognition of his unique place in British cultural life, Dickie was made a life peer, as Baron Attenborough of Richmond upon Thames in 1993. He and his equally feted younger brother, David, were highly respected figureheads of a variety of institutions. During a TV interview with both, David was asked why so many organisations were keen for a bite of his brother's crowded diary. "Well, I suppose they feel that half a Dick is better than no Dick at all," he replied.

Dickie's blackest day was almost certainly 26 December 2004. His daughter Jane and granddaughter Lucy were killed in Khao Lak in Thailand along with 160,000 others in the deadly tsunami that consumed much of the South East Asia coastline. "I looked at my parents and thought, they really don't deserve this," recalled Michael Attenborough. "These are people who've given their lives so generously to others. This scale of tragedy just felt so unjust and unfair. And it took a while for him to be able to talk about Jane at all."

After a fall at his office at Beaver Lodge in 2008, he struggled to recover and joined his wife Sheila in a nursing home. "He fell down a flight of stairs about six years before he died," said Michael Attenborough. "When he finally came out of his coma, it obliterated all the lovely parts of his personality. All his generosity, warmth and sensuality, humour and all that—gone. And what was left was anger. He was like swinging his fists at the world. He was in a wheelchair; he could barely string a sentence together. He was angry, bitter and very depressed." It was a sad coda for a life well lived. Michael added, "He was my hero, and footsteps that are quite hard to follow, not as an artist particularly, because we were both directors. Actually, it was as a man. I was much more daunted by him as a human figure. I wondered whether I could ever follow in those footsteps. But he was an extraordinary example."

On 24 August 2014 Sir Richard Attenborough died, aged 90. His memorial at Westminster Abbey, which Michael organised, attracted 2,000 people—not just industry figures, but the general public too. As they filed out of the Nave, "across the street there were some road workers," said Michael. "They had one of those big electric signs that says one way or diversion, etc., and it just said: *Rest in peace, Sir Richard.* And I thought, *oh my god*, I've got Judi Dench and Michael Caine following me out, and even road workers are paying tribute. Ben Kingsley said something absolutely wonderful about Dad. And it's so true. He said he democratised every space he walked into. And what he meant was, he had no sense of status. He might be at a Royal Garden Party, and he'd stand there talking to the man with the tray of champagne. He was that kind of guy. There was no sense of him being the kind of distant celebrity. He was very much a man on the streets; a friend really is a friend."[621]

Author's Conclusion

Few would disagree with William Goldman that *A Bridge Too Far* is "a depressing movie" and a long one—to reach the end of its 176 minutes is an emotionally arduous journey. But it is also an honest one. As while it leaves the audience on a downer, it is a sober reminder that the "good guys" don't always win.

To echo General Sherman's phrase that "war is hell,"[622] onscreen it has too often been glamourised and trivialised. What is laudable about *Bridge* is its sincere attempt to show the terrible cost of combat, but inevitably, by showing deeds of courage against the odds, it also illuminates the glory of war that is the very stuff of regimental and national pride. Ex-combat cameraman Herb Lightman, while watching the parachute drop scene, commented, "There were occasional images of beauty like this flashing through the horror of it all."[623] It is the inherent contradiction in this ghastly beauty that the film captures perfectly while walking the thin red line between good taste and revulsion. For all its horrors, wars bring out not only the worst, but certainly the best in humanity, and it is perhaps this that keeps bringing audiences back to experience simulated warfare onscreen.

Bridge therefore should be applauded for its courage in presenting unpalatable truths about combat. It also is a valiant and honest attempt to retell a huge historical event. Goldman and Attenborough deserve immense credit for endeavouring to make it as authentic as possible within the unforgiving commercial realities of Hollywood. Richard Attenborough strove to create something more akin to a symphony than a documentary. While some bemoan that at times it veers from the historical record, Dickie's job was to fashion a living drama with peaks and troughs of emotion from Goldman's script; this required telescoping, adapting, and even ignoring some of the facts.

Many war films suffer from repetitious action scenes that are essentially similar. Peruse almost any fictional action flick, James Bond in particular, and you will immediately notice how scriptwriters fashion completely different fighting scenes, changing locations, weapons, obstacles, etc. You can see that Goldman tried to do the same with the XXX Corps breakout, Gräbner's dash across Arnhem bridge, and the Waal crossing—all very different and memorable. The subsequent street fighting becomes quite ubiquitous, and this may have been another reason for cutting so much of the second unit's battle footage.

While the epic struggle around Oosterbeek is short-changed, with the action around the Hartenstein Hotel standing in for it all, to make space for more would have required cutting somewhere else. The only sequence that could have been deleted and not hurt the story is the Dohun hospital section. There is some merit in that charge—it is an expensive star cameo—but if anything, it is the American involvement that could have justified expanding. Overall, I consider that Dickie and Goldman succeeded in a fine balancing act for all five nationalities.

"If you remade that film, it would take a third of the time, and a third of the money—and it would be more impressive, because you can do much more with CGI," said Roy Button, who rose from Third AD to head of Warner Bros. UK. "The thing is, while the very latest CG work can make it look really impressive, in the end it flows over you. You're not in awe of what you're looking at. But if you go back to *Bridge*, that was all real, guys!"

It's easy to imagine how the film would look if made today: gravity-defying camera moves, Krakatoa-size explosions, hyper-realistic bullet hits. Advantages might include a realistically devastated Arnhem, glider landings, the huge scale of XXX Corps lumbering up that single road, etc. But to this middle-aged author, CGI too often emphasises its plastic reality without the charming fakery of old-style analogue back-projection, et al. It's certainly an age thing, as Roy Button believes of younger modern audiences, "They don't believe what they're seeing is real. They all think it's done in the computer, anyway. You can't put a caption up saying this is real. Unless you know it was all 100 percent real, you're not in awe of it."[624] It is no accident that some contemporary filmmakers with clout, notably Christopher Nolan, insist on doing as much for real as possible, rather than resort to CGI (although his resistance to computers meant his anaemic and spartan-looking 2017 feature *Dunkirk* failed to show the chaos of more than a half-million men clinging to the beaches).[625]

I believe *A Bridge Too Far* has passed the test of time with flying colours. Its classical-style photography and gimmick-free editing has allowed it to escape the datedness of many '70s movies. The script, I contend, does a superb job of telling a huge, complex story, boasting Goldman's pithy, memorable dialogue. All of it trips effortlessly from a uniformly excellent cast, whether star or walk-on. Each is flawless and underscores Dickie's equal attention to every character, big or small. As time has dulled the lustre of some of the stars, what you are left with is a host of believable and often charismatic performances. Without doubt, the A.P.A. are the heart of the film; they help to flesh out the background with consummate authenticity, which raises the film to the highest level.

The film is inevitably compared unfavourably with *Theirs Is the Glory* and dismissed as a Sunday matinée movie. To me, there is no battle to fight. The former is a powerful work with the poignancy of the real heroes depicting their exploits with typical British reserve and understatement. Sadly, it will remain a little-seen museum piece for most audiences. *A Bridge Too Far* in colour, widescreen, and stereo sound, will remain, for good or ill, the primary *aide-mémoire* of Montgomery's great gamble with the Dutch people—Operation Market Garden.

Acknowledgments

Writing a book such as this is a collaborative effort, and I owe a debt of gratitude to the following for their unstinting support and assistance: Michael Attenborough CBE; David English CBE; Reineke Kramer; Jan Robert Leerinkson; Peter MacDonald and Madelyn Most; Jack McKenzie; John Richardson and Edward Seckerson. So many more have contributed generously in countless ways, both big and small: Sebastian Abineri (*The Boys from the Bridge*); Vic Armstrong; Kenny Barley; Colin M. Barron; Steve Barron; Liz Beacon; Geesje Bruinewoud; Anthony Burke; Jon Burlingame; Martyn Butler; Roy Button OBE; Sir Michael Caine; Terence Clegg; John Coldstream; Peter Cook; Allan Esler-Smith and David Truesdale (*Theirs Is the Glory—Arnhem, Hurst and Conflict on Film*); Sir Edward Fox; Christopher Good; Joe Gibson; Peter Grimes; Rob Green (*After the Battle* Magazine); Sheldon Hall (*Zulu: With Some Guts Behind It*); Brian Hannan; Richard Heffer; Jane Hershey; Patrick Jalhay (Facebook.com/eenbrugtever); Iain Johnstone (*The Arnhem Report*); Pieter Jutte; Harry Koning; Major General (Rt) Mart de Kruif; Steve Lanning; Charles Malouf Samaha; Doug McCabe; A.T. McKenna; Tim Morand and Nicola Lane; John Morton; Coert Munk; Christopher Neame; Joris Nieuwint (*The Battlefield Explorer*); Gareth Owen; Andy Priestner (*The Complete Secret Army*); Victoria Ryan Bida; Michael Shapiro; Robert Sellers; Max Seymour; Vicky Standing; Lisa Tomblin; *Andere Tijden;*

Erik van 't Wout; Robert Voskuil; Heather Wankowska (International Auster Club); Ann Willmore (dumaurier.org); Pete Wilton; Dave Worral (*Cinema Retro*). Also, British Entertainment History Project; BFI archives; Richard Attenborough Papers, The Keep, University of Sussex Library; Rense Havinga, Curator at Vrijheidsmuseum (Freedom Museum), Groesbeek; Historisch Centrum Overijssel, Deventer. Special mention to historians and podcasters, Robbie McGuire and Matthew Moss at *Fighting on Film* for permission to use their podcast with members of A.P.A. Great effort has been expended in tracking down copyright of quotations; please contact publisher with any enquiries.

Huge thanks to my agent Lee Sobel. Ultimate praise and hats off to Mary Rothhaar at GoodKnight Books for her splendid support to get this book published and also the judicious editing by Robert Matzen and his sterling work on assembling the choice images to accompany the text.

Closer to home, thanks to my darling wife, Claire, and stepson, Sam, plus a menagerie of four-legged darlings: Lulu, Peggy, Wilma, Monty, and Max. Their collective love and support is beyond measure.

Appendix A
Cast and Crew

Cast (in appearance order):

Siem Vroom..Underground Leader
Marlies van Alcmaer...Underground Leader's Wife
Erik van 't Wout ....Underground Leader's Son
Wolfgang Preiss...Field Marshal Gerd von Rundstedt
Hans von Borsody .... Gen. Blumentritt
Josephine Peeper..Cafe Waitress
Dirk Bogarde..Lt. Gen. Browning
Paul Maxwell...Maj. Gen. Maxwell Taylor
Sean Connery...Maj. Gen. Urquhart
Ryan O'Neal...Brig. Gen. Gavin
Gene Hackman .... Maj. Gen. Sosabowski
Walter Kohut..Field Marshal Model
Peter Faber .... Capt. 'Harry' Bestebreurtje
Hartmut Becker...German Sentry
Frank Grimes ....Maj. Fuller
Jeremy Kemp.. R.A.F. Briefing Officer
Donald Pickering .... Lt. Col. Mackenzie
Donald Douglas .... Brig. Lathbury
Peter Settelen..Lt. Cole
Stephen Moore..Maj. Steele
Edward Fox .... Lt. Gen. Horrocks
Michael Caine ....Lt. Col. J.O.E. Vandeleur
Michael Byrne .... Lt. Col. Giles Vandeleur
Anthony Hopkins... Lt. Col. Frost
Paul Copley .... Pvt. Wicks
Nicholas Campbell .... Capt. Glass
James Caan..SSgt. Dohun
Gerald Sim .... Col. Sims
Harry Ditson .... U.S. Private
Erik Chitty ....Organist

Simon Lewis

Brian Hawksley .... Vicar
Colin Farrell ....Cpl. Hancock
Christopher Good .... Maj. Carlyle
Norman Gregory...Pvt. Morgan
Alun Armstrong .... Cpl. Davies
Anthony Milner ....Pvt. Dodds
Barry McCarthy..Pvt. Clark
Lex van Delden .... Sgt. Matthias
Maximilian Schell .... Lt. Gen. Bittrich
Michael Wolf....................................... Field Marshal Model's Aide
Hardy Krüger .... Maj. Gen. Ludwig
Sean Mathias... Irish Guards Lieutenant
Tim Beekman... German Private
Edward Seckerson ....British Padre
Liv Ullmann ....Kate ter Horst
Tom van Beek...Jan ter Horst
Bertus Botterman ....Dutch Villager
Henny Alma ....Dutch Villager
Elliott Gould .... Col. Stout
Ray Jewers .... U.S. Radio Operator
Frank Jarvis... Col. Frost's Aide
Geoffrey Hinsliff ....British Wireless Operator
Keith Drinkel .... Lt. Cornish
Mary Smithuysen ....Old Dutch Lady
Hans Croiset ....Old Dutch Lady's Son
Fred Williams..Capt. Gräbner
John Peel... German Lieutenant
John Judd.. Sgt. Clegg
Ben Cross ....Trooper Binns
Hilary Minster..British Medical Officer
David English... Pvt. Andrews
Ben Howard .... Sgt. Towns
Michael Graham Cox..Capt. Cleminson
Johan te Slaa, Georgette Reyevski .... Elderly Dutch Couple
Pieter Groenier, Adrienne Kleiweg...........................Young Dutch Couple
Denholm Elliott...R.A.F. Met. Officer
Peter Gordon... U.S. Sergeant
Arthur Hill...U.S. Medical Colonel
Garrick Hagon .... Lieutenant Rafferty
Brian Gwaspari...U.S. Engineer
Stephen Rayment...Grenadier Guards Lieutenant
Timothy Morand ....British Corporal
James Wardroper ....Pvt. Gibbs
Neil Kennedy.. Col. Barker
John Salthouse... Pvt. "Ginger" Marsh
Jonathan Hackett...Glider Pilot
Stanley Lebor ....Regimental Sergeant Major
Jack Galloway..Pvt. Vincent

Milton Cadman...Pvt. Long
David Auker...'Taffy' Brace
Laurence Olivier...Doctor Spaander
Richard Kane...Col. Weaver
Toby Salaman...Pvt. Stephenson
Michael Bangerter..British Staff Colonel
Philip Raymond ....Grenadier Guards Colonel
Myles Reithermann..Boat Truck Driver
Robert Redford...Maj. Cook
Anthony Pullen Shaw ....U.S. Captain
John Morton..U.S. Padre
John Ratzenberger..U.S. Lieutenant
Patrick Ryecart ....German Lieutenant
Dick Rienstra ....Capt. Krafft
Ian Liston...Sgt. Whitney
Paul Rattee ....Pvt. Gordon
Mark Sheridan ....Sgt. Tomblin
George Innes...Sgt. Macdonald
John Stride ....Grenadier Guards Major
Niall Padden.....................................British Medical Orderly
Michael Graves.....................................British Medical Orderly
Simon Chandler ....Pvt. Simmonds
Anthony Robb ....German Officer
Edward Kalinski...Pvt. Archer
Shaun Curry...Cpl. Robbins
Sebastian Abineri ....Sgt. Treadwell
Chris Williams ....Cpl. Merrick
Andrew Branch ....Flute Player
Anthony Garner ....British Staff Major
Feliks Arons...Dutch Priest
John Careless... British Paratrooper
Stuart Blake, Roy Boyd, Stephen Churchett, Jon Croft, Patrick Dickson, Gerard
Franken, Adrian Gibbs, Jason Gregory, Stewart Guidotti, Patrick Hannaway, Brian
Haughton, Anthony Howden, David Killick, Dan Long, Gerald Martin, Edward
McDermott, Tony McHale, Jack McKenzie, Francis Mughan, Richard Ommanney,
Peter Quince, Robin Scobey, Farrell Sheridan, James Snell, Michael Stock, David
Stockton, Paul Vaughan-Teague, Jason White, Robert Wisepart, Mark York ....
....Assorted Soldiers

Crew

Director ....Richard Attenborough
Producer ....Joseph E. Levine
Co-producer ....Richard P. Levine
Screenwriter...................William Goldman (based on the book by Cornelius Ryan)
Associate Producer ....Michael Stanley-Evans
Production Supervisor .... Eric Rattray
Associate Producer ....John Palmer

Production Manager..Terence Clegg
Location Manager.. Norton Knatchbull
Production Manager, Second Unit ....Dickie Bamber
Unit Manager...Grania O' Shannon
Second Unit Director ....Sidney Hayers
First Assistant Director .... David Tomblin
Assistant Directors .... Steve Lanning, Roy Button, Geoffrey Ryan, Peter Waller
First Assistant Director, Second Unit...Bert Batt
Assistant Directors, Second Unit...........................Andy Armstrong, Chris Carreras
Director of Cinematography ....Geoffrey Unsworth
Camera Operator .... Peter MacDonald
Clapper Loader .... Steve Barron
Camera Assistant...John Campbell
Camera Grip ....Frank Batt
Second Unit Camera Operator.. Ken Coles
Aerial Photography ....Robin Browne
Parachute Cameramen ....John Partington-Smith, Dave Waterman
Second Aerial Camera Operator ....John Cardiff
Lighting Cameraman, Second Unit ....Harry Waxman
Camera Operators, Second Unit .... Wally Byatt, Louis H. Lavelly
Focus Pullers, Second Unit..David Lenham, Chris Pinnock
Chief Rigger... Nobby Clarke
Gaffer, Second-Unit .... Roy Larner
Electrical Supervisor..Jack Conroy
Still Photographers...Bob Penn, Frank Connor
Lighting Technicians..........................Danny Eccleston, John Fenner, Geoff Glover
Production Designer..Terence Marsh
Art Directors .... Stuart Craig, Roy Stannard, Alan Tomkins
Sketch Artist .... Michael White
Construction Manager ....Peter Dukelow
Production Buyer...John Lanzer
Set Dresser ....Peter Howitt
Property Master...Jack Towns
Plasterers .... Ken Barley, Michael Guyett
Drapesman ....Chris Seddon
Costume Designer..Anthony Mendleson
Wardrobe Master...John Hilling
Wardrobe Mistress ....Margaret Lewin
Chief Hairdresser .... Ronnie Cogan
Make-up Supervisor... Tom Smith
Make-up Artists.. Ernest Gasser, Nick Maley
Special Effects Supervisor ....John Richardson
Special Effects Technicians........Ron Cartwright, John Evans, George Gibbs, David
        Harris, Marc Ratcliffe, Jan Robert Leerinkson, Ian Wingrove
Military Vehicle Coordinator ....Charles Mann
Marine Coordinator .... Michael Turk
Armourer.. Bill Aylmore
Stunt Arrangers .... Vic Armstrong, Alf Joint

Stunts	Roy Alon, Joe Amsler, Dickey Beer, Marc Boyle, George Lane Cooper, Jim Dowdall, Joe Dunne, Stuart Fell, Nick Hobbs, Gregory Hodal, Billy Horrigan, George Leech, Rick Lester, Doug Robinson, Tony Smart, Alan Stuart, Rocky Taylor, Chris Webb, Henry Weissenman, Bill Weston, Paul Weston, Jason White
Stunt Driver	Valentino Musetti
Sound Recordist	Simon Kaye
Dubbing Mixers	Gerry Humphreys, Robin O'Donoghue
Sound Boom Operator	David Stephenson,
Film Editor	Antony Gibbs
Assistant Editors	Chris Blunden, Brian Mann, Bryan Oates
Sound Editors	Les Wiggins, Peter Horrocks
Music Composer	John Addison
Music Engineers	Eric Tomlinson, John Richards
Optical Effects	Wally Veevers,
Matte Artist	Doug Ferris
Title Design	Joe Caroff
Continuity	Connie Willis
Casting	Miriam Brickman
Production Consultant	Gabriel Katzka
Director's Assistant	Reineke Kramer-Pirk
Production Accountant	Arthur Tarry
Dutch Liaison	Cornelius van Eijk
Production Assistants	Sheila Collins, Annette Chaplin, Judy Humphreys, Loretta Ordewer, Dena Vincent
Production Runner	Matthew Binns
Producer's Secretary	Judi Bunn
Publicity	Gordon Arnell, Lois Smith, Jane Hershey
Meteorological Advisor	Peter Davies
Military Advisor	Colonel J. L. Waddy, O.B.E.
Chief Technical Advisor	Kathryn Morgan Ryan
Military Consultants	Major General J.D. Frost C.B. D.S.O. M.C., General James M. Gavin U.S.A., Colonel Frank A. Gregg U.S.A., Lieutenant General Sir Brian Horrocks K.C.B. K.B.E. D.S.O. M.C., Major General R.E. Urquhart C.B. D.S.O., Brigadier J.O.E. Vandeleur D.S.O., Jan Voskuil

Filmed in Panavision Colour by Technicolor.
176-minutes distribution by United Artists, 1977.

Appendix B
The Hardware

Vehicles

American scenes: Twenty Jeeps (repainted for British scenes when required), 6 Jeep trailers, an Airborne trailer, 2 Para cart/trailers, 3 Jeeps (expendable), a Dodge Command car, 3 Dodge weapon carriers, Dodge Ambulance, 2 GMC 6x6s, Chevrolet U/2-tonner, Dodge Recovery Vehicle, Diamond T wrecker, Clark airfield tractor, Plymouth Sedan staff car, and 2 Harley Davidson motorcycles.

British Scenes: Five Bren Gun carriers, T16 carrier, 7 International half-tracks, White Scout car, 2 Humber armoured cars, Daimler armoured car, 4 Daimler Scout cars, 2 Scammell heavy recovery vehicles, Ford WOT 6 3-tonner, Bedford QL Trooper, 2 Bedford QL GS Trucks, Bedford QL (expendable), Bedford MWD Infantry Truck, Morris 15cwt CS 8, Austin K2 Civil Defence Vehicle, 2 Austin K2 ambulances, Bedford OYC Bowser, Dodge D15 water tanker, Chevrolet C 8 A/1C5, Humber heavy utility, Bedford OY NAAFI tea-van body, Humber staff car, 3 BSA M20 motorcycles, 2 Royal, Enfield 350 m/c, Matchless m/c, and one Welbike (Brockhouse) m/c. **Artillery and armour:** A Battery of 25-pdrs, 3 6-pdr anti-tank guns, 2 Bofors AA guns, 8 M4 Sherman tanks, an M4 Sherman Dozer, 5 Replica Sherman tanks, and several tank hulks—ex ranges.

German Scenes: Horsch staff car, 2 Mercedes staff cars, Citroën staff car, 2 *Schwimmwagens*, 4 *Kübelwagens*, 5 *Volkswagen/ Kübelwagen* replicas, a *Kettenkraftrad*, 3 BMW motorcycle combinations, Zundapp m/c combination, BMW solo m/c, 2 Zundapp m/cs, Krauss-Maffei half-track, Demag half-track, Hanomag replica, Hanomag (expendable), Hotchkiss Brandt/Marder 2, 2 replica 6-wheel armoured cars, 2 replica 4-wheel armoured cars, Bus-

sing-NAG 5-tonne truck, German Ford 3-tonne truck, Auto Union personnel carrier, Opel Blitz 1-tonne ambulance. **Artillery and armour:** PAK
35 anti-tank gun, PAK 50 anti-tank gun, 2 80-mm field-guns, 3 80-mm
guns (replica), Nebelwerfer rocket-launcher, 4 Leopard tanks modified to
Panther IVs, 4 AMX self-propelled guns—modified to look German. To
supplement the vehicles listed in the German retreat scenes, a number of old
buses, trucks, carts, etc, were obtained from collectors in Holland.

Small Arms

10 x .45 Revolvers, 20 x .38 Revolvers (British Officers), 10 x .45 Auto Pis-
tols (American Officers), 6 x 9-mm Mauser Pistols (German Officers), 10 x
9-mm P 58 Pistols, 200 x .303 Enfield Rifles (UK Infantry), 100 x .30 M1
Carbines (U.S. Paras), 200 x 7.9-mm Mauser Rifles (German Infantry), 100
x 9-mm Sten Guns (UK Paras), 60 x 9-mm Thompson or Grease Guns (U.S.
Paras), 40 x 9-mm Schmeiser Sub M/ch guns (German troops), 4 x .303
Vickers LMG (British), 6 x .30 Browning LMG (U.S.), 6 x .303 Bren LMG
(British), 10 x 7.9-mm M.G. 54/42 LMG (German), 2 x .5 Browning M/ch
Guns (British/U.S.), 4 x 1" Signal Pistols, 2 x 1½" Signal Pistols, 1 x Flame-
thrower (British), 2 x 3" Mortars with bombs and primary shells (British), 2 x
50-mm Mortars (German), 4 x PIATs (British), 2 x Bazookas (U.S.).

Aeroplanes

All collected for the film at the Royal Netherlands Air Force base at Deel-
en. Eleven C-47 Dakotas. One Spitfire F.IX (MH434) G-ASJV. Four Har-
vards (T-6) disguised as Thunderbolts and Focke Wulfs. One Auster III,
PH-NGK, trainer (Gilze Rijen Aero Club). Six full-size Horsa (non-flying)
gliders. A two-seat Blanik glider from the London Gliding Club to simulate
drag takeoffs.

Sources: Colonel John Waddy and Colin M. Barron, *Battles on Screen*, Extremis Publishing Ltd, 2017.

Endnotes

Preface
1   Lewis, Simon. *Waterloo: Making an Epic.* Bear Manor Media. 2021.

Introduction: Market Garden 1944
2   Sometimes overlooked, several infantry regiments formed part of First Airborne, and they fought and died as valiantly as the more glamourous Paras. In North Africa the Paras would often get covered in dust from the local red soil, their appearance together with their fighting spirit led the Germans to dub them *Die Rote Teufel.*
3   Ryan, Cornelius. *A Bridge Too Far.* Simon & Schuster. 1974
4   Maj. Gen. Mart de Kruif to author.

1. *Theirs Is the Glory*
5   Based on Penny's interview at https://historyproject.org.uk/interview/c-m-cyril-pennington-richards
6   https://historyproject.org.uk/interview/c-m-cyril-pennington-richards
7   Truesdale, David and Esler-Smith, Allan. *Theirs Is The Glory. Arnhem, Hurst and Conflict on Film.* Helion and Company. September 2016.
8   Quoted in Truesdale, Esler-Smith.
9   Esler-Smith, Allan. *Theirs Is The Glory—65th Anniversary of the Filming of the Movie, Mini story number 106.* Published by Friends of the Airborne Museum Oosterbeek. November 2010.

2. Ryan's Final Battle
10   Ryan, Cornelius and Ryan, Kathryn. *A Private Battle.* Simon & Schuster. 1979.
11   Kelley, Frank and Ryan, Cornelius. *Star-Spangled Mikado.* New York: R.M. McBride. 1947.
12   Shapiro, Michael. *The Reporter Whom Time Forgot.* Columbia Journalism Review May/June 2010. https://archives.cjr.org/second_read/the_reporter_who_time_forgot.php?page=2
13   McCabe, Doug. Introduction Carlton books release of *The Longest Day.* 2014.
14   Letter from Ryan to Maj. Gen. R.K. Belchem, dated 18 June 1969. Ryan Papers. Ohio University.
15   Ryan Bida, Victoria to author. 2021. All subsequent quotes from this source.
16   Ryan. *A Private Battle.*
17   Shapiro.
18   Ryan. *A Bridge Too Far.*
19   Shapiro.
20   Kramer, Reineke to author. 2021.

3. "Forget That B Picture of Yours": Levine and Attenborough
21   Johnstone, Iain. *The Arnhem Report.* Star. 1977.
22   O'Neil, Paul, "Super Salesman of Supercolossals." *Life.* 27 July 1962.
23   Dunn, Peter. "The Last Movie Mogul," *The Sunday Times.* 5 February 1978.
24   Talese, Gay. "Joe E. Levine Unchained." *Esquire.* January 1961.
25   Parsons, Louella. "How to Get into The Movie$." *LA Herald Examiner*, Pictorial Living, 20 September 1959.
26   *Newsweek.*, 22 February 1960.

27 Hamill, Katherine. "The Supercolossal–Well, Pretty Good–World of J. Levine." *Fortune*. March 1964. Some sources suggest it made a profit.

28 Levine, Joseph. E. *A Bridge Too Far: Notes from A Filmmaker*. J. E. Levine Presents. 1977.

29 Attenborough, Richard. 55th Academy Awards ceremony. 11 April 1983.

30 According to his son, Michael, he preferred to be called Dick by his family and close friends.

31 Johnstone.

32 Attenborough, M.

33 Hawkins, Diana and Attenborough, Richard. *Entirely Up to You, Darling*. Arrow. 2009.

34 Johnstone.

35 Hawkins, Attenborough.

36 Attenborough, M.

37 Johnstone.

38 Johnstone.

39 Rosenthal, Donna. "Self-Made Mogul Hangs On: Joseph E. Levine, 82, Is Still Wheeling and Dealing." *Los Angeles Times*. 5 July 1987.

40 Levine.

41 Bach, Steven. *Final Cut, Dreams and Disaster in the Making of Heaven's Gate*. Faber and Faber.1985. Bach would oversee *Heaven's Gate* (1980), which went so wildly over budget and flop so badly, it sunk the studio. It was eventually bought by MGM.

42 "UA To Release 'Bridge.'" *Hollywood Reporter*. 18 May 1976.

43 Goldman, William. *Adventures in the Screen Trade*. Warner Books. 1983.

44 Levine.

45 Higgins, John. "Richard Attenborough's Quest for an Indian Grail." *The Times*. 24 July 1975.

46 *A Bridge Too Far: Richard Attenborough—A Director Remembers*. DVD extra. 2004.

47 Attenborough, Richard. *In Search of Gandhi*. The Bodley Head, Ltd. 1982.

48 Levine.

49 Johnstone.

50 Higgins.

4. "But *Which* Story?": Goldman and the Raid

51 Goldman, William. *A Bridge Too Far*. DVD Commentary. 2004. All his quotes,

unless otherwise noted, are from this source.

52 Goldman. *Adventures*.

53 Hasselbring, A. D. Pepperdine University. *Swimming Upstream in Hollywood: William Goldman in His Own Words*. Americana: An Institute for American Studies and Creative Writing. 2020.

54 Goldman. *Adventures*.

55 His elder brother, James, wrote *The Lion in Winter* play and film.

56 Squire, Jason E. (ed.). *The Movie Business Book*. 1st Edition. Simon & Schuster. 1983.

57 The film was retitled *Charly* (1968).

58 Goldman. *Adventures*.

59 Goldman.

60 Goldman. *Adventures*.

61 Attenborough. *In Search*.

62 Goldman.

63 Goldman. *Adventures*.

64 *A Director Remembers*.

65 Goldman. *Adventures*.

66 Matzen, Robert. *Dutch Girl: Audrey Hepburn and World War II*. GoodKnight Books. 2020.

67 Goldman. *Adventures*.

5. "It's All a Question of Bridges": Preparations

68 Clegg, Terence to author.

69 Lanning.

70 Clegg.

71 Lanning.

72 1976 archive material shown on *Andere Tijden—A Bridge Too Far*. TV documentary. 2004.

73 Johnstone.

74 Tomkins, Alan. *Stars and Wars: The Film Memories and Photographs of Alan Tomkins*. The History Press. 2015.

75 Craig, Stuart, *A Bridge Too Far*. DVD commentary. 2004. All his quotes are from this source.

76 Tomkins.

77 *Andere Tijden*.

78 Waddy, Col. (Rt) John. "The Making of A Bridge Too Far." *After The Battle-Special Issue*. Plaistow Press. 1986.

79 *Andere Tijden*.

80 Mosley, Leonard. *Battle of Britain: The Making of a Film*. Macmillan. 1969.

81 Clegg.

82 Waddy.

83 Morton, John. https://www.starwars.

com/news/shake-hands-with-the-money-remembering-david-tomblin-first-assistant-director

84 Lanning.
85 Button.
86 MacDonald, Peter to author.
87 Lanning.
88 MacDonald.
89 Barron, Steve to author.
90 MacDonald.
91 Barron.
92 MacDonald.
93 The star, Elizabeth Taylor, became very ill, not helped by the bad weather, and the production was shut down. The film eventually began again on newly constructed sets in Rome. The rest of the shoot was beset by problems pushing the budget to almost $36 million.
94 The aerial unit decamped to the South of France to complete the scenes.
95 Button.
96 Lanning.
97 *Andere Tijden.*
98 Craig.

6. "The Party's On": Filming Begins
99 https://collectieoverijssel.nl/ (475 BB08423 Band of Kabel Omroep Deventer)
100 Erik van 't Wout to author, 2021.
101 *Andere Tijden.*
102 Lanning.
103 Ryan. *Bridge.*
104 Lightman, Herb. *American Cinematographer.* April 1977.
105 van 't Wout.
106 Lightman.
107 Letter from Richard Attenborough to Kate ter Horst, 16 June 1976. Reineke Kramer-Pirk Collection.
108 Tomkins, Alan. "A Bridge Too Far: Heroes from the Sky." *History vs. Hollywood,* series 1, ep 5. 2001.
109 Filmed 26 May 1976. Kerksteeg, Deventer.
110 Sellers, Robert. "A Stunt Too Far? The Vic Armstrong Story Part V." *Cine Retro* 7.
111 Lanning.
112 Hershey, Jane. "Adventures of an Amateur Publicist." *American Film.* April 1977.
113 Lanning.
114 Button, Roy to author.
115 Filmed 25 August 1976 in The Brink and Polstraat, Deventer.
116 Lanning.
117 MacDonald.

7. "You Wouldn't Really Have Killed Me, Would You?": James Caan
118 Husband, Stuart. "Sheer Caan." *The Guardian.* 22 Aug 1999.
119 Husband.
120 Morell, John. "Caan Man." *Orange Coast Magazine.* November 1981.
121 Husband.
122 He and fellow *Godfather* actors, Al Pacino and Robert Duvall, lost to Joel Grey for *Cabaret* (1972).
123 Morell.
124 Barron.
125 Craig.
126 MacDonald.
127 Craig.
128 https://m.imdb.com/name/nm0001001/trivia
129 Barron.
130 MacDonald.
131 Barron.
132 MacDonald.
133 Barron.
134 MacDonald.
135 Barron.
136 MacDonald.
137 On another project, an interviewee who worked with Dickie some years later related that the director did reveal the name to him: it was an American, but it was not Caan, Gould, Hackman, or Redford.

8. "There's a Lot of Money on That Lawn": The Famous Fourteen Part 1
138 Pickard, Roy. "Attenborough's Battles." *Photoplay.* July 1977.
139 Johnstone.
140 Goldman. *Adventures.*
141 "Eye View: Gambling Again on Arnhem." *Women's Wear Daily.* 1 September 1976.
142 Button.
143 Hershey.
144 Johnstone.
145 MacDonald.
146 Johnstone.
147 Pickard.
148 Hershey.
149 Johnstone.
150 Hershey.
151 Clegg.
152 Hershey.

153   Kramer.

154   Johnstone.

155   Hershey.

156   Coldstream, John. *Dirk Bogarde: The Authorised Biography*. Weidenfeld & Nicolson. New Ed edition. (2011).

157   Johnstone.

158   *Dirk Bogarde—Above The Title. A Conversation with Russell Harty*. YTV. 1986.

159   Johnstone.

160   Button.

161   Johnstone.

162   Goldman, William. *Story of a Bridge Too Far*. Coronet Books. 1977.

163   "Gene Hackman: Least Likely to Succeed." *Deseret News*. Unknown date.

164   Johnstone.

165   *Inside the Actors Studio*,.S8.2. Broadcast. 14 Oct 2001.

166   Meryman, Richard. "Gene Hackman, Dustin Hoffman, and Robert Duvall: Three Friends who Went from Rags to Riches." *Vanity Fair*. March 2004.

167   Johnstone.

168   Her husband, the impresario Michael Todd had died in a plane crash in 1958. She made an uncredited appearance as a favour to Michael Todd Jnr. The non-nasal version, Holiday in Spain was restored for home video. It is a charming, if undemanding, travelogue.

169   Johnstone.

170   Coldstream.

171   The ITV show premiered its 10,000th episode in February 2020 and celebrated the 60th anniversary later that year.

172   Pickard.

173   Johnstone.

174   These included *Men in Battle* (1956-57), which featured Montgomery and U.S. Generals Gavin and Maxwell Taylor. The author has a vivid memory of watching one of these programs in the mid-1970s as a ten-year-old.

175   http://www.bfi.org.uk/features/attenborough/bridgefar.html

176   Goldman. *Story*.

177   Filmed 17 August 1976, Prince Kazerne Vlasakkers, Amersfoort.

178   https://www.countrylife.co.uk/out-and-about/theatre-film-music/edward-fox-on-acting-162049

179   Caine, Michael. *The Elephant to Hollywood*. Hodder & Stoughton. 2010.

180   Elliot Norton Reviews. Michael Caine. WGBH Boston. 1972.

181   Filmed 9 August 1976. The silo, built in 1962, is situated at Zuiderzeestraat in Deventer and is now magnificently converted into an office complex.

9. "We've Got to Get This Right, Boys!": The A.P.A. Part 1

182   English, David to author.

183   *A Director Remembers*.

184   Seckerson, Edward to author.

185   Abineri, Sebastian. Brickman plays herself in the casting session scene at the end of Anderson's *O Lucky Man!* (1973).

186   McKenzie, Jack. *Fighting On Film: Attenborough's Private Army on A Bridge Too Far*. 10 September 2021. The Armourer's Bench. https://www.youtube.com/watch?v=-j3AuKaG5_e0

187   Morand, Tim. *Fighting On Film: Attenborough's Private Army on A Bridge Too Far*. 10 September 2021. The Armourer's Bench. https://www.youtube.com/watch?v=-j3AuKaG5_e0

188   English.

189   Abineri. *Fighting*.

190   Good, Christopher to author.

191   Seckerson.

192   Abineri, Sebastian. *The Boys from the Bridge*. The Book Guild Ltd. 2017.

193   Abineri. *Fighting*.

194   McKenzie. *Fighting*.

195   Abineri. *Boys*.

196   Seckerson.

197   Abineri, *Boys*.

198   Seckerson.

199   Abineri. *Fighting*.

200   Waddy.

201   Abineri, *Boys*.

202   Seckerson.

203   Abineri. *Fighting*.

204   McKenzie, Jack to author.

205   Morand. *Fighting*.

206   Good.

207   Morand. *Fighting*.

208   Seckerson.

209   McKenzie. *Fighting*.

210   McKenzie.

211   *A Director Remembers*.

212   Waddy.

213   Churchett, Stephen. https://www.anderetijden.nl/aflevering/456/Een-Brug-te-Ver

10. "You Get the Prize...": Deventer Bridge Part 1

214 *Andere Tijden.*
215 McKenzie.
216 Seckerson.
217 https://www.pegasusarchive.org/arnhem/tatham_warter.htm
218 Good.
219 Abineri. *Boys.*
220 Good.
221 Abineri. *Boys.*
222 Good.
223 Abineri, Sebastian to author.
224 https://www.theage.com.au/entertainment/old-hand-returns-with-new-tricks-20071108-ge68wb.html
225 Ryan. *Bridge.*
226 Richardson.
227 Lightman.
228 Richardson.
229 Lightman.
230 Johnstone.
231 Lightman.
232 For the bridge burning, the unit returned months later on the night of 26 August.
233 Richardson.
234 MacDonald.
235 Good.
236 MacDonald.
237 Lanning.
238 Johnstone.
239 McKenzie.
240 MacDonald.
241 Richardson.
242 Hawkins, Attenborough. The camera held 100 feet of film, just over a minute.
243 MacDonald.
244 Johnstone.
245 MacDonald.
246 Good.
247 Johnstone.
248 Waddy.
249 Johnstone.
250 Diana Potts. *This Is Your Life—Johnny Frost.* (S17E24). ITV. 06 April 1977.
251 Jimmy Sharp. *This Is Your Life.*
252 Rudolph Witzig. *This Is Your Life.*
253 *Battle of Arnhem Archived.* 29 September 2006 at the Wayback Machine.
254 Abineri. *Fighting.*
255 *Heroes from the Sky.*
256 Telex from Joseph E. Levine to Richard Attenborough, circa April/May 1976.
257 Attenborough. *In Search.*

11. "There's More Power in Stillness": Anthony Hopkins

258 Anthony Hopkins addressing an AA meeting around 2000. https://youtu.be/34iZt4B_DU0
259 Hopkins, Anthony interviewed by Brian Linehan for *City Lights* TV show. 1978.
260 Hopkins. AA.
261 Hopkins, Anthony interviewed by Bobbie Wygant, 1977. Bobbie Wygant Archive.
262 Falk, Quentin. *Anthony Hopkins: The Biography* (4th ed.). Virgin Books. 2004.
263 He would reprise the role in BBC series *The Edwardians* in 1972.
264 Linehan.
265 Wygant.
266 Linehan.
267 English.
268 *Andere Tijden.*
269 Seckerson.
270 Linehan.
271 Seckerson.
272 Good.
273 MacDonald.
274 Linehan.

12. "Is He Nuts? Run!": Deventer Bridge Part 2

275 Filmed 16 June 1976.
276 Ryan. *Bridge.*
277 Modern historians consider this a later Victorian invention. But in the 1940s, the phrase was part of the Waterloo mythology and would have been well known to soldiers like Mackay.
278 *Heroes from the Sky.*
279 Johnstone.
280 Waddy.
281 *A Director Remembers.*
282 Wygant.
283 *A Director Remembers.*
284 Wygant.
285 *Heroes from the Sky.*
286 *A Director Remembers.*
287 Abineri. *Boys.*
288 MacDonald.
289 Abineri. *Boys.*
290 Ryan. *Bridge.*
291 Man was made to mourn: A Dirge/Many and sharp the num'rous ills/Inwoven with our frame!/More pointed still we make

ourselves/Regret, remorse, and shame!/And man, whose heav'n-erected face/The smiles of love adorn, −/Man's inhumanity to man/ Makes countless thousands mourn! Robert Burns, 1784.

292 Johnstone.
293 https://www.chroniclelive.co.uk/ news/north-east-news/tribute-fusili- er-who-overcame-war-1449448
294 Ryan. *Bridge.*
295 Johnstone.
296 Hershey.
297 Craig.
298 McKenzie. *Fighting.*
299 Craig.
300 *Andere Tijden.*
301 McKenzie.
302 Richardson.
303 Craig.
304 Richardson.
305 Abineri. *Boys.*
306 Richardson.
307 Experts suggest it resembles more of panther. But it was referred to as a tiger for the production.
308 Waddy.
309 Abineri. *Fighting.*
310 Richardson.
311 MacDonald.
312 Richardson.
313 Leerinkson, Jan Robert to author.
314 Abineri. *Fighting.*
315 MacDonald.
316 McKenzie.
317 Abineri. *Fighting.*
318 Good.
319 MacDonald.
320 Waddy.
321 Richardson.
322 Ryan. *Bridge.*
323 Abineri. *Fighting.* The Para flutist was playing the third movement from the Bran- denburg Concerto #6 (BWV1051), written by Johann Sebastian Bach.
324 Seckerson.
325 Abineri. *Fighting.*
326 Seckerson.
327 Ryan. *Bridge.*
328 *Abide With Me* (1847). Words by Henry Francis Lyte.
329 MacDonald.
330 McKenzie. *Fighting.*
331 McKenzie. *Fighting.*

13. "KLM Job": The A.P.A. Part 2
332 Abineri. *Fighting.*
333 Morand. *Fighting.*
334 Abineri. *Fighting.*
335 Button.
336 Abineri. *Fighting.*
337 Morand. *Fighting.*
338 McKenzie. *Fighting.*
339 Button.
340 Seckerson.
341 Abineri. *Fighting.*
342 English.
343 Abineri. *Boys.*
344 Morand. *Fighting.*
345 Seckerson.
346 Lanning.
347 Morand. *Fighting.*
348 McKenzie. *Fighting.*
349 Attenborough, M.
350 Lanning.
351 McKenzie. *Fighting.*
352 *Andere Tijden.*
353 Morand. *Fighting.*
354 Seckerson.
355 Good.
356 McKenzie.
357 Seckerson.
358 McKenzie.
359 Seckerson.
360 English.
361 Abineri. *Boys.*
362 Seckerson.
363 McKenzie.
364 Lanning.
365 Seckerson.
366 Lanning.
367 McKenzie,.*Fighting.*
368 Abineri. *Fighting.*
369 Abineri, *Boys.*
370 McKenzie.
371 The later *Band of Brothers* TV series depicted this with the titular heroes of the U.S. 101 Airborne's Easy Company playing a major part in the operation.
372 Morand. *Fighting.*

14. "Start the Purple": Batt, Bombs, and Bruises Part 1
373 Thompson, Jennifer, assistant editor on *Zulu.* Hall, Sheldon. *Zulu: With Some Guts Behind It, The Making of the Epic Movie.* Tomahawk Press, Revised Edition. 2005.
374 Lanning.
375 MacDonald.

376   Neame, Christopher. *Rungs on a Ladder: Hammer Films Seen Through a Soft Gauze.* Scarecrow Press. 2003.

377   MacDonald.

378   Hall. *Zulu.*

379   Huston, John. *An Open Book.* Da Capo Press. 1994.

380   Hall. *Zulu.*

381   MacDonald.

382   Ryan. *Bridge.*

383   Richardson.

384   Richardson, John. *Making Movie Magic: A Lifetime Creating Special Effects for James Bond, Harry Potter, Superman & More.* The History Press. 2019.

385   *Cinefantastique.* 1977.

386   Lightman.

387   Abineri. *Fighting.*

388   Richardson.

389   Abineri. *Fighting.*

390   Richardson.

391   Abineri. *Fighting.*

392   Richardson. *Movie Magic.*

393   Button.

394   Richardson. *Movie Magic.*

395   Goldman. *Story.*

396   Ryan. *Bridge.*

397   Goldman. *Story.*

398   Morand. *Fighting.*

399   Abineri. *Fighting.*

400   Morand. *Fighting.*

401   Richardson. *Movie Magic.*

402   Richardson.

403   MacDonald.

404   Richardson. *Movie Magic.*

15. "Roll the Fuckers!!!": The Famous Fourteen Part 2

405   Robert Stephens, an actor at the National Theatre. Quoted in Lewis, Roger, "In the Shadow of a Giant—Laurence Olivier. *The Sunday Times.* 12 November 1995.

406   Hutchinson.

407   Johnstone.

408   Holden, Anthony. *Olivier.* Weidenfeld and Nicolson. 1988.

409   Morton, John to author.

410   http://www.battle-of-arnhem.com/kate-ter-horst-the-angel-of-arnhem

411   Op set van 'A bridge too far' in Bronkhorst, 1976. https://www.youtube.com/watch?v=wtR-5wN9nuc

412   Hershey.

413   Goldman. *Story.*

414   Hershey.

415   Johnstone.

416   Lanning.

417   http://www.battle-of-arnhem.com/kate-ter-horst-the-angel-of-arnhem/

418   Johnstone.

419   *Theirs Is the Glory.* Gaumont British. 1946.

420   MacDonald.

421   Johnstone.

422   Goldman. *Story.*

423   Lanning.

424   Johnstone.

425   Goldman. *Story.*

426   Reimer, Robert C. and Carol J. *The A to Z of German Cinema.* Rowman and Littlefield. 2008.

427   Ebert, Roger. Interview with Maximilian Schell. 17 August 1975.

428   Depicted in *Band of Brothers*, Episode 4: "Replacements." 2001.

429   MacDonald.

430   Richardson.

431   Craig.

432   Sellers, Robert. "Call Sheet: A Bridge Too Far." *Film Review.* July 2004.

433   MacDonald.

434   All current home video versions also include James Caan saying "fucking" when threatening the doctor. Without viewing a 1977 UK print, is it not possible to know if this was on that soundtrack. It is probable this was dubbed with something less offensive to the British censor.

435   Sellers.

436   MacDonald.

437   Richardson.

438   Richardson.

439   Seckerson.

440   Goldman. *Story.*

16. "You Just Fall Off": Batt, Bombs, and Bruises Part 2

441   Armstrong, Vic to author.

442   https://www.vanityfair.com/hollywood/2011/09/stunt-icon-vic-armstrong-won-t-fall-down-a-flight-of-stairs-for-

443   Armstrong.

444   Morand. *Fighting.*

445   https://jamesbond007.se/eng/memoriam/stuntmannen_alf_joint_1927-2005

446   Armstrong.

447   Abineri. *Fighting.*

448   Morand. *Fighting.*

449 Armstrong.
450 Good.
451 https://www.vanityfair.com/hollywood/2011/09/stunt-icon-vic-armstrong-won-t-fall-down-a-flight-of-stairs-for-
452 https://www.vice.com/en/article/wd7a34/vic-armstrong-stunt-man-indiana-jones
453 Armstrong.
454 https://www.vanityfair.com/hollywood/2011/09/stunt-icon-vic-armstrong-won-t-fall-down-a-flight-of-stairs-for-
455 Armstrong, Vic, and Sellers, Robert. *The True Adventures of the World's Greatest Stuntman.* Titan Books,.2011.
456 Abineri. *Boys.*
457 Armstrong, Sellers.
458 Lanning.
459 Armstrong, Sellers.
460 Armstrong.
461 Lanning.
462 https://ascmag.com/articles/cameras-in-shooting-war
463 Lightman.
464 Second-unit call sheet no. 26. 1 September 1976.
465 Armstrong, Sellers.
466 Armstrong.
467 Lightman.
468 Armstrong.
469 Lightman.
470 Abineri. *Fighting.*
471 https://www.vanityfair.com/hollywood/2011/09/stunt-icon-vic-armstrong-won-t-fall-down-a-flight-of-stairs-for-

17. "Hard Like in Coal Mining": Directing an Epic
472 Goldman. *Adventures.*
473 Pickard.
474 *Heroes from the Sky.*
475 Pickard.
476 Attenborough, M.
477 Sellers. "Call Sheet."
478 Attenborough, M.
479 Button.
480 MacDonald.
481 Good.
482 McKenzie. *Fighting.*
483 MacDonald.
484 Attenborough, M.
485 Seckerson.
486 Lanning.
487 Attenborough, M.

488 Lanning.
489 Morton.
490 Johnstone.
491 Morton.
492 Pickard.

18. "A Marvellous Approach": The Parachute Drops
493 Mosley.
494 https://www.bombercommandmuseum.ca/chronicles/hamish-mahaddie-a-horsethief-for-the-pathfinders/
495 https://www.key.aero/forum/historic-aviation/30971-jeff-hawke
496 This is taken from a news story in *The Daily Telegraph.* http://www.users.waitrose.com/~g8jan/html%20files/wattisham%202.html
497 Johnstone.
498 Button.
499 Pickard.
500 *A Director Remembers.*
501 MacDonald.
502 Lanning.
503 MacDonald.
504 Lanning.
505 MacDonald.
506 Button.
507 MacDonald.
508 Good.
509 McKenzie. *Fighting.*
510 Morand. *Fighting.*
511 Waddy.
512 Seckerson.
513 Abineri. *Boys.*
514 Abineri. *Fighting.*
515 Johnstone.
516 *Heroes from the Sky.*
517 Telex from Joseph E. Levine to Richard Attenborough, April 1976.
518 Abineri. *Boys.*
519 Richarson.
520 Armstrong.
521 Tomkins.
522 McKenzie.
523 Lanning.

19. "Hail Mary, Full of Grace": Four Sundays in Nijmegen
524 Ryan. *Bridge.*
525 *Heroes from the Sky.*
526 Kramer.
527 Richardson.
528 Tomkins.

529 MacDonald.
530 Johnstone.
531 Pickard.
532 MacDonald.
533 Button.
534 MacDonald.
535 Johnstone.
536 Pickard.
537 Richardson. *Movie Magic*.
538 MacDonald.
539 Richardson.
540 Morton.
541 MacDonald.
542 This sequence was filmed over several days. John Morton's memories have been conflated for the purposes of narrative.
543 MacDonald.
544 Barron.
545 Notes of meeting held on 1 September 1976 at Nijmegen Police Headquarters.
546 Daily progress report no. 117. 19 September 1976.
547 Morton.
548 Richardson. *Movie Magic*.
549 Sandilands, John. *Observer*. 27 March 1977.
550 Jutte, Pieter to author.
551 *Heroes from the Sky*.
552 Johnstone.
553 MacDonald.
554 Morton.
555 MacDonald.
556 Goldman. *Story*.
557 Call Sheet 130. 031076.
558 Barron.
559 Waddy.
560 Ryan. *Bridge*.
561 Grimes, Peter to author.
562 Sandilands.

20. "Oh, All Right for Me, Darling, That Is Perfect": Post Production

563 Taylor, Charles. "Richardson's Lively Disaster: Waugh's The Loved One." *The New York Observer*. 30 July 2006.
564 LoBrutto, Vincent. *Selected Takes: Film Editors on Editing*. ABC-CLIO. 1991.
565 Perkins, Roy and Stollery, Martin. *British Film Editors: The Heart of the Movie*. BFI Publishing. 2004.
566 Priestner, Andy. *The Complete Secret Army*. Classic TV Press. 2008.
567 Seckerson.
568 Crosthwaite, G., Martyn interview with John Addison. *Music Gazette*. August 1978.
569 Crosthwaite, G., Martyn interview with John Addison. *Music Gazette*. October 1978.
570 Crosthwaite. August 1978.
571 Crosthwaite. October 1978.
572 Attenborough, Richard. Original LP liner notes for *A Bridge Too Far*. 1977.
573 Crosthwaite. September 1978.
574 Malone, Chris. Liner notes for 2022 CD re-release of *A Bridge Too Far* soundtrack.
575 Burlingame, Jon. Bridge commentary.
576 Attenborough, Richard. LP liner notes.
577 Ashton, Richard. Liner notes for 1998 CD release of *A Bridge Too Far* soundtrack.
578 Pirie, D. *Anatomy of the Movies*. Macmillan. 1984.
579 The cityscape behind the Barnums' first apartment in *The Greatest Showman* (2017). Old-school matte painter Leigh Took meticulously hand-painted the backgrounds on large canvas for *The Electrical Life of Louis Wain* (2021).
580 Filmed 01 October 1976 at Elburgerweg, Dronten, near Amsterdam.
581 https://historyproject.org.uk/interview/gerry-humphreys
582 Dolby Stereo encoded a matrixed four-track stereo signal on the optical track which only required a suitable decoder and additional speakers. The genius was these 35-mm Dolby SVA prints were completely backwards compatible, so they could be run on any projector in the world, albeit reproducing in mono. While *A Star Is Born* (1976) had been the first Dolby Stereo release, it was *Star Wars* that would popularise the format, and ensure its rapid adoption over the next two decades before morphing into the digital realm.
583 *This Is Your Life—Johnny Frost*. (S17E24). ITV. Transmitted 06 April 1977.

21. "But What Do You Think?": Release and Reception

584 *Hollywood Reporter*. 23 June 1977
585 Ebert, Roger. "A Bridge Too Far." *Chicago Sun-Times*. 17 June 1977.
586 Arnold, Cary. "A Bridge Too Far: War Epic at the Head of Its Class." *Washington Post*. 16 June 1977.
587 Champlin, Charles. "World War II

Writ Large in 'Bridge Too Far.'" *Los Angeles Times*. 12 June 1977

588   Canby, Vincent. "Film: It's a Long War In 'Bridge Too Far.'" *The New York Times*. 16 June 1977.

589   Goldman. *Adventures*.

590   Butler, Martyn to author.

591   Pym, John. "A Bridge Too Far." *Monthly Film Bulletin*. July 1977.

592   *Daily Telegraph*. 24 June 1977.

593   *The Times*. 25 June 1977.

594   *The Times*. 25 June 1977.

595   Maj. Gen. Mart de Kruif to author.

596   Ryan. *Bridge*.

597   Forster, Margaret. *Daphne Du Maurier*. Chatto and Windus. 1994.

598   Johnstone.

599   Oriel Malet (ed.). *Letters from Menabilly: Portrait of a Friendship*. Weidenfeld & Nicolson. 1993.

600   Huckvale, David. *Dirk Bogarde: Matinee Idol, Art House Star*. McFarland & Co Inc. 2020.

601   Quoted in Coldstream.

602   Johnstone.

603   Hawkins, Attenborough.

604   Coldstream.

605   French, Philip. *Observer*, 26 June 1977.

606   Coldstream.

607   *The Sunday Times*. 30 October 1977.

608   Beevor, Antony. *Arnhem*. Penguin. 2019.

609   Hannan, Brian. 'A Bridge Too Far at the Box Office, Film Focus on A Bridge Too Far." *Cinema Retro* no.56,.May 2023.

610   The former made $7 million worldwide, while the latter's $30 million was considered a poor return on the original which broke box-office records in 1974.

611   Baltake, Joe. "Fun? Flops? Levine Has 'Em." *Detroit Free Press*, 23 November 1978.

Epilogue

612   Seckerson.

613   Abineri. *Boys*.

614   Button.

615   Wygant.

616   It was filmed on the thirty-third anniversary of the funeral on 31 January 1981.

617   Attenborough, Hawkins.

618   McKenna, A.T., *Showman of the Screen: Joseph E. Levine and His Revolutions in Film Promotion* (Screen Classics). University

Press of Kentucky. 2016.

619   MacDonald.

620   *Six Into One: The Prisoner File*. (1984) Channel Four TV.

621   Attenborough, M.

Author's Conclusion

622   As is often the case, the exact sources of famous phrases are difficult to pin down. During a speech in 1880, General William T. Sherman is reported to have said, "Some of you young men think that war is all glamour and glory, but let me tell you, boys, it is all hell!" Regardless of the detail, his sentiment is clear.

623   Lightman.

624   Button.

625   The 1958 version and the famous sequence take in *Atonement* (2007), by contrast, both succeeded in showing the epic chaos of this 1940 battle.

Bibliography

A Bridge Too Far: Heroes from the Sky. History vs. Hollywood, series 1, Ep 5. 2001.

A Bridge Too Far: Richard Attenborough—A Director Remembers. DVD extra. 2004.

Abineri, Sebastian. *The Boys from the Bridge.* The Book Guild Ltd. 2017.

Armstrong, Vic and Sellers, Robert. *The True Adventures of the World's Greatest Stuntman.* Titan Books. 2011.

Arnold, Cary. "The Final Decision Will Be Mine." *The Washington Post.* 15 June 1977.

Arnold, Cary. "A Bridge Too Far: War Epic at the Head of Its Class." *The Washington Post.* 16 June 1977.

Ashton, Richard. Liner notes for 1998 CD release of *A Bridge Too Far* soundtrack.

Attenborough, Richard. Original LP liner notes for *A Bridge Too Far.* 1977.

Attenborough, Richard. *In Search of Gandhi.* The Bodley Head Ltd. 1982.

Bach, Steven. *Final Cut, Dreams and Disaster in the Making of Heaven's Gate.* Faber And Faber. 1985.

Badsey, Stephen. *Arnhem 1944.* Campaign Series, 44. Osprey Publishing. 1993.

Baltake, Joe. "Fun? Flops? Levine Has 'Em." *Detroit Free Press.* 23 November 1978.

Barron, Colin M. *Battles on Screen.* Extremis Publishing Ltd. 2017.

Barron, Steve to author. 2021.

Battle of Arnhem Archived. 29 September 2006 at the Wayback Machine.

Box Office. 31 May 1976.

"Bridge to NBC." *Variety.* 20 July 1977

Butler, Martyn to author.

Button, Roy to author.

Caine, Michael. *The Elephant to Hollywood.* Hodder & Stoughton. 2010.

Canby, Vincent. Film: "It's a Long War In Bridge Too Far." *The New York Times.* 16 June 1977.

Champlin, Charles. "World War II Writ Large in Bridge Too Far." *Los Angeles Times.* 12 June 1977.

Coldstream, John. *Dirk Bogarde: The Authorised Biography.* Weidenfeld & Nicolson, New Ed edition. 2011.

Craig, Stuart. *A Bridge Too Far.* DVD commentary. 2004.

Crosthwaite, G., Martyn interview with John Addison. *Music Gazette.* August/October 1978.

Daily Variety. 17 Jan 1977.

Daily Variety. 13 May 1977.

Dirk Bogarde—Above The Title. A Conversation with Russell Harty. YTV. 1986.

Dunn, Peter. "The Last Movie Mogul." *The Sunday Times.* 5 February 1978.

Ebert, Roger. A Bridge Too Far. *Chicago Sun-Times.* 17 June 1977.

Elliot Norton Reviews. Michael Caine. WGBH Boston. 1972.

Esler-Smith, Allan. *Theirs Is the Glory—65th Anniversary of the Filming of the Movie, Mini story number 106.* Published by Friends of the Airborne Museum Oosterbeek. November 2010.

Falk, Quentin. *Anthony Hopkins: The Biography* (4th ed.). Virgin Books. 2004.

Fighting On Film: Attenborough's Private Army on A Bridge Too Far. 10 September 2021. The Armourer's Bench, Episode 41. https://www.youtube.com/watch?v=j3AuKaG5_e0

Ford, Ken. *Operation Market-Garden 1944 (2) The British Airborne Missions.* Osprey Campaign 301. 2016.

Forster, Margaret. *Daphne Du Maurier.* Chatto and Windus. 1994.

Fowlie, Eddie and Torne, Richard. *David Lean's Dedicated Maniac Memoirs of a Film Specialist.* Austin & Macauley Publishers Ltd. 10 Dec. 2010.

Goldman, William. *A Bridge Too Far* screenplay. 1976.

Goldman, William. *Adventures in the Screen Trade*. Warner Books. 1983.

Goldman, William. *Story of a Bridge Too Far*. Coronet Books. 1977.

Good, Christopher to author. 2022.

Grimes, Peter to author. 2021.

Hall, Sheldon. *Zulu: With Some Guts Behind It. The Making of the Epic Movie*. Tomahawk Press, Revised Edition. 2005.

Hamill, Katherine. "The Supercolossal—Well, Pretty Good—World of Joe Levine." *Fortune*. March 1964.

Hannan, Brian. "A Bridge Too Far at the Box Office." Film Focus on *A Bridge Too Far. Cinema Retro* no. 56. May 2023.

Hasselbring, A. D. Pepperdine University. *Swimming Upstream in Hollywood: William Goldman in His Own Words*. Americana: An Institute for American Studies and Creative Writing. 2020.

Hawkins, Diana and Attenborough, Richard. *Entirely Up to You, Darling*. Arrow. 2009.

Hershey, Jane. "Adventures of an Amateur Publicist." *American Film*. April 1977.

Higgins, John. "Richard Attenborough's Quest for an Indian Grail." *The Times*. 24 July. 1975.

Holden, Anthony. *Olivier*. Weidenfeld and Nicolson. 1988.

Hollywood Reporter. 22 Sep 1975.

Hollywood Reporter. 18 May 1976.

Hollywood Reporter. 8 Jun 1977.

Hollywood Reporter. 23 Jun 1977.

Hopkins, Anthony addressing an AA meeting around 2000. https://youtu.be/34iZt4B_DU0

Hopkins, Anthony interviewed by Bobbie Wygant. 1977. Bobbie Wygant Archive.

Hopkins, Anthony interviewed by Brian Linehan for *City Lights* TV show. 1978.

http://nzpetesmatteshot.blogspot.com/

http://www.bfi.org.uk/features/attenborough/bridgefar.html

https://ascmag.com/articles/cameras-in-shooting-war

https://en.wikipedia.org/wiki 1976_British_Isles_heat_wave

https://historyproject.org.uk/interview/c-m-cyril-pennington-richards

https://historyproject.org.uk/interview/c-m-cyril-pennington-richards

https://historyproject.org.uk/interview/gerry-humphreys

https://jamesbond007.se/eng/memoriam/stuntmannen_alf_joint_1927-2005

https://weaponsandwarfare.com/2015/09/09/nijmegen-bridge-1940/

https://weaponsandwarfare.com/2015/09/09/nijmegen-bridge-1940/

https://www.anderetijden.nl/aflevering/456/Een-Brug-te-Ver

https://www.bombercommandmuseum.ca/chronicles/hamish-mahaddie-a-horsethief-for-the-pathfinders/

https://www.bombercommandmuseum.ca/chronicles/hamish-mahaddie-a-horsethief-for-the-pathfinders/

https://www.countrylife.co.uk/out-and-about/theatre-film-music/edward-fox-on-acting-162049

https://www.key.aero/forum/historic-aviation/30971-jeff-hawke

https://www.key.aero/forum/historic-aviation/30971-jeff-hawke

https://www.paradata.org.uk/people/andrew-r-milbourne

https://www.paradata.org.uk/people/john-waddy

https://www.pegasusarchive.org/arnhem/tatham_warter.htm

https://www.starwars.com/news/shake-hands-with-the-money-remembering-david-tomblin-first-assistant-director

https://www.theage.com.au/entertainment/old-hand-returns-with-new-tricks-20071108-ge68wb.html

https://www.vanityfair.com/hollywood/2011/09/stunt-icon-vic-armstrong-won-t-fall-down-a-flight-of-stairs-for-

https://www.vice.com/en/article/wd7a34/vic-armstrong-stunt-man-indiana-jones

Huckvale, David. *Dirk Bogarde: Matinee Idol, Art House Star.* McFarland & Co., Inc. 2020.

Husband, Stuart. "Sheer Caan." *The Guardian.* 22 August 1999.

Huston, John. *An Open Book.* Da Capo Press. 1994.

Hutchinson, Tom. *Battle of Britain* souvenir brochure. Sackville Publishing. 1969.

Irish Times, The. 11 April 1981.

James Caan on John Wayne. *filmSCHOOLarchive.* https://www.youtube.com/watch?v=dD1cdRFQy2o

Simon Lewis

Johnstone, Iain. *The Arnhem Report*. Star Books. 1977.

Jutte, Pieter to author. 2021.

Kramer, Reineke to author. 2021.

Lanning, Steve to author. 2021.

Lebo, Harlan. *The Godfather Legacy*. Fireside, 98. 2005.

Levine, Joe E. *A Bridge Too Far: Notes From A Filmmaker*. Joseph E. Levine Presents. 1977.

Lewis, Roger. "In the Shadow of a Giant—Laurence Olivier." *The Sunday Times*. 12 November 1995.

Lewis, Simon. "A Blockbuster Too Far? Film Focus on A Bridge Too Far." *Cinema Retro* no. 56. May 2023.

Lewis, Simon. *Waterloo—Making An Epic*. Bear Manor Media. 2021.

Life. 02 June. 1947.

Lightman, Herb. *American Cinematographer*. April 1977.

LoBrutto, Vincent. *Selected Takes: Film Editors on Editing*. ABC-CLIO. 1991.

MacDonald, Peter to author. 2021.

Malone, Chris. Liner notes for 2022 CD re-release of *A Bridge Too Far* soundtrack.

Matzen, Robert. *Dutch Girl: Audrey Hepburn and World War II*. GoodKnight Books. 2020.

McCabe, Doug. Introduction to 2014 edition, *The Longest Day*. Carlton Books. 2014.

McKenna, A.T. *Joseph E. Levine: Showmanship. Reputation and Industrial Practice 1945 -1977*. PhD Thesis submitted to the University of Nottingham, School of American & Canadian Studies. March 2008.

McKenna, A.T. *Showman of the Screen: Joseph E. Levine and His Revolutions in Film Promotion*. Screen Classics. University Press of Kentucky. 2016.

Morell, John. "Caan Man." *Orange Coast Magazine*. November 1981.

Morton, John. https://www.starwars.com/news/shake-hands-with-the-money-remembering-david-tomblin-first-assistant-director

Mosley, Leonard. *Battle of Britain: The Making of a Film*. Macmillan. 1969.

Munk, Coert. *ABTF deel 1*. Logboek 4/5. 2021.

Neame, Christopher. *Rungs on a Ladder: Hammer Films Seen Through a Soft Gauze*. Scarecrow Press. 2003.

Newsweek. 22 February 1960.

Newsweek. 16 August 1976.

New York Times, The. 16 June 1977.

Norman, Philip. "Dickie Darling." *The Sunday Times.* 24 January. 1971.

Notes of meeting held on 1 September 1976 at Nijmegen Police Headquarters. Courtesy of Reineke Kramer.

O'Neil, Paul. "Super Salesman of Supercolossals." *Life.* 27 July 1962.

Osgerby, Bill. *Biker: Truth and Myth: How the Original Cowboy of the Road Became the Easy Rider of the Silver Screen.* Globe Pequot. 2005.

Parsons, Louella. "How To Get Into The Movie$." *LA Herald Examiner.* Pictorial Living. 20 September 1959.

Perkins, Roy and Stollery, Martin. *British Film Editors: The Heart of the Movie.* BFI Publishing. 2004.

Pickard, Roy. "Attenborough's Battles." *Photoplay.* July 1977.

Pirie, D. *Anatomy of the Movies.* Macmillan. 1984.

Priestner, Andy. *The Complete Secret Army.* Classic TV Press. 2008.

Richardson, John to author.

Richardson, John. *Making Movie Magic: A Lifetime Creating Special Effects for James Bond, Harry Potter, Superman & More.* The History Press. 2019.

Rosenthal, Donna. "Self-Made Mogul Hangs On: Joseph E. Levine, 82, Is Still Wheeling and Dealing." *Los Angeles Times.* 5 July 1987.

Ross, Albert. https://www.key.aero/forum/historic-aviation/30971-jeff-hawke

Ryan Bida, Victoria to author. 2021.

Ryan, C. Letter to Maj. Gen. R.K. Belchem. June 18. 1969. Ryan Papers. Ohio University.

Ryan, Cornelius. *A Bridge Too Far.* Hamish Hamilton. 1974.

Ryan, Cornelius and Ryan, Kathryn. *A Private Battle.* Simon & Schuster. 1979.

Samuelson Film Service Catalogue 1975.

Sandilands, John. *Observer Magazine.* 27 March 1977.

Second-unit Call Sheet. 44. 240976. Courtesy of Patrick Jalhay.

Sellers, Robert. "A Stunt Too Far? The Vic Armstrong Story Part V." *Cine Retro* 7.

Sellers, Robert. "Call Sheet: A Bridge Too Far." *Film Review.* July. 2004.

Shapiro, Michael. *The Reporter Whom Time Forgot.* Columbia Journalism

Review May/June 2010. https://archives.cjr.org/second_read/the_reporter_who_time_forgot.php?page=2

Squire, Jason E. (ed). *The Movie Business Book.* 1st Editon. Simon & Schuster. 1983.

Talese, Gay. "Joe E. Levine Unchained." *Esquire.* January 1961.

Taylor, Charles. "Richardson's Lively Disaster: Waugh's The Loved One." *The New York Observer.* 30 July 2006.

This Is Your Life—Johnny Frost. (S17 E24). ITV. 6 April 1977.

Tomkins, Alan. *Stars and Wars: The Film Memories and Photographs of Alan Tomkins.* The History Press. 2015.

Truesdale, David and Esler-Smith, Allan. *Theirs Is the Glory. Arnhem. Hurst and Conflict on Film.* Helion and Company. September 2016.

Variety. 13 Oct 1976.

Variety. 3 Jun 1977.

Variety. 8 Jun 1977.

Variety. 22 Jun 1977.

Waddy, Col. (Rt) John. "The Making of A Bridge Too Far." *After The Battle–Special Issue.* Plaistow Press. 1986.

Waddy, John interviewed by Julian Thompson. IWM. 2001-02-06. https://www.iwm.org.uk/collections/item/object/80024597.

Washington Post, The. 1 August 1987.

Zaloga, Stephen J. *Operation Market-Garden 1944 (1) The American Airborne Missions.* Osprey Campaign 270. 2014.

Index

Larminie, Major John 55, 185, 265
Last Battle, The (book) 20
Last Valley, The (1971) 111
Lathbury, Gerald 5, 195
Lawrence of Arabia (1962) 54, 194
Lean, David 30, 31, 47, 51, 54, 305
Leech, Wendy 222
Leerinkson, Jan Robert 162
Leigh, Vivien 199, 200
Levine, Joseph E. 23, 25-27, 30-31, 33-36, 39, 42, 43, 45, 46, 47, 48, 66-67, 68, 92, 95, 134, 136, 142, 250, 273, 282, 290, 300, 301, 304
Levine, Richard P. 47, 266
Levine, Rosalie 33, 68
L-Shaped Room, The (1962) 30
Lévy, Raoul 19
Lightman, Herb 72, 225-226, 227, 243, 245
Lion in Winter, The (1968) 33, 145
Liston, Ian 126
Löcherer, Friedrich Wilhelm. See Williams, Fred
Loneliness of the Long-Distance Runner, The (1962) 275
Long, Dan 120
Long Ships, The (1964) 58
Longest Day, The (book) 18-19, 94
Longest Day, The (1962) 77, 252, 278
Loved One, The (1965) 275

M*A*S*H (1970) 212
MacDonald, Peter 62-63, 64, 65, 70, 73-74, 75, 79, 83, 84-85, 87, 88, 93, 111, 134, 135, 136, 137, 138-139, 148-149, 155-156, 158, 162, 164-165, 169, 174, 176, 186, 187, 188, 195-196, 202, 205, 213, 214-215, 216-217, 232, 233, 244, 246-247, 259, 260, 261, 262, 263-264, 267, 276-277, 303, 305
MacLaine, Shirley 63
Mackay, Eric 152, 163

Magic (1978) 149, 304
Mahaddie, Hamish 237-238
Malone, Chris 284
Man for All Seasons, A (1966) 51
Man in the Glass Booth, The (1975) 209
Man Who Would Be King, The (1975) 92, 188
Mann, Charlie 55, 65, 137, 185, 190
Marathon Man (1976) 39, 200
Marsh, Terry 51, 52, 85, 125, 258, 301
Mary, Queen of Scots (1971) 51
Mathias, Sean 192, 216
Matzen, Robert 43
Maxted, Stanley 12, 13
Maxwell, Paul 5, 104
McCabe, Doug 18
McGoohan, Patrick 60
McHale, Tony 121
McKenzie, Jack 115, 119, 120, 121, 122-123, 125-126, 137, 158-159, 162-163, 167, 169, 172, 176, 177, 178-179, 181, 182, 183, 184, 232, 247, 253, 278
McQueen, Steve 43, 44-45
*Memphis Belle (*1990) 46
Mendleson, Anthony 58
Mike Turk Film Services 258
Milbourne, Andrew 156-157, 158, 204, 206, 249
Milner, Anthony 131
Model, Otto 2
Montgomery, Bernard Law 1, 7, 8
Moore, Liz 190, 196, 197
Moore, Roger 106
Moore, Stephen 167
Morand, Tim 115-116, 121, 122, 170, 172, 175, 176, 177-178, 184, 192-193, 219, 221, 247-248
Morgan, Andrew 278
Morton, John 59, 60, 200-201, 234, 235, 261-262, 263, 264, 267, 269
Mosley, Leonard 54, 237